Han Suyin is the daughter of a Belgian mother and a Chinese father who, a Mandarin and scholar entitled to enter the Imperial Academy, had chosen instead at the age of nineteen to travel on a scholarship to Europe.

She was moved by the poverty and sickness she saw around her to take up medicine. She studied Chinese classics and mathematics while waiting for a place at Yenching University. Then, after completing her pre-medical education, she travelled across Siberia to Europe on a scholarship and continued her studies at the University of Brussels. In 1938 she returned to China, married an ex-Sandhurst Chinese officer, who later became a general in Chiang Kai Shek's army, and practised midwifery in the interior during the Sino-Japanese War. From this experience she wrote her first book, *Destination Chungking*, in 1940. In 1942 she came to London, where her husband had been appointed military attaché. Three years later he returned to active service in China, leaving Han Suyin to complete her medical studies in London. After her husband was killed in 1947, she spent a year as a house surgeon at the Royal Free Hospital before accepting a doctor's post in Hong Kong. There she wrote the Eurasian love story (her own) that brought her international acclaim and success as a writer. The Sunday Times described *A Many-Splendoured Thing* as 'an astounding love story . . . brilliantly topical, but far more than that, for she handles an eternal theme with power, insight and unfailing artistry.'

Since that time she has written numerous books, both novels and non-fiction. Her combined autobiography and history of China in five volumes, has been hailed as an important contribution to international understanding. Bertrand Russell said of the first volume, *The Crippled Tree*, 'during the many hours I spent reading it, I learnt more about China than I did in a whole year spent in that country'.

D1205998

By the same author

China: Autobiography, History

The Crippled Tree
A Mortal Flower
Birdless Summer
Phoenix Harvest

Novels

A Many-Splendoured Thing
Destination Chungking
. . . And the Rain My Drink
The Mountain is Young
Cast But One Shadow and *Winter Love*
Two Loves
The Four Faces

Non-Fiction

China in the Year 2001
Asia Today
Lhasa, The Open City
The Morning Deluge: Mao Tsetung and the Chinese
  Revolution 1893–1953
Wind in the Tower: Mao Tsetung and the Chinese
  Revolution 1949–1975

HAN SUYIN

My House Has Two Doors

China: Autobiography, History, Book 4

**TRIAD
GRAFTON BOOKS**

LONDON GLASGOW
TORONTO SYDNEY AUCKLAND

Triad
Grafton Books
8 Grafton Street, London W1X 3LA

Published by Triad Grafton 1982
Reprinted 1988

Triad Paperbacks Ltd is an imprint of
Chatto, Bodley Head & Jonathan Cape Ltd and
Grafton Books, A Division of the Collins Publishing Group

First published in Great Britain by
Jonathan Cape Ltd 1980

ISBN 0-586-05413-8

My House Has Two Doors was originally
published as one volume under this title.
In Triad Paperbacks it is published in
two volumes: Vol 1 *My House Has Two Doors*
Vol 2 *Phoenix Harvest*

Printed and bound in Great Britain by
Collins, Glasgow

Set in Times

Contents

1949–1965

CHAPTER 1

December 1948 to September 1950

In that month of grizzled distemper I tossed away the marooning clutch of a career in England, despite the anxious admonitory chorus of friends predicting disaster, and by Christmas of 1948 departed with Yungmei for Hong Kong. In my ears still linger their expostulations: 'Crazy to cast a child into all this chaos', 'At least leave Yungmei behind', 'There's a revolution, Hong Kong may fall at any moment'. But I was ensconced in seeming recklessness; so inwardly certain that it was right to go that outwardly I could afford to look hesitant until the last goodbye.

I could not explain that even if I could not live in the New China that the Revolution would bring forth, phoenix reborn and the sound of its beauteous wings filling the air for me, at the same time I could not bear to stay, for to stay in England would be to renounce China. The New China might be my executioner, but still I had to go, at least to stand on the threshold, and be both reckless and prudent, and survive. In Hong Kong I would breathe the dust, smell the shift of air from China; if I did not go I would shrivel, inelastic living mummy; and this not because I was positively unhappy in England – I was not – but precisely because I had lost the faculty of happiness or unhappiness – I wrestled only with a numb mantling which magnified small events into major preoccupations and swallowed all sensation into a coma-like unreality. I longed for the absent forest where the new-born phoenix would sing, and I would hear its wings beat the air.

'I don't want flimsy non-events keeping me awake and that vague pettiness of ease gnawing at my days.' On a viscous grey afternoon of November 1948 I had called on Professor Gordon King. He was Director of the Department of Obstetrics and Gynaecology at the University of Hong Kong. Briefly in London for a visit, he had agreed to see me.

The meeting with Gordon King had been arranged by my friends Francis and Cecilia Pan, whom I had known in Chungking,* and who turned up, in that fateful November of 1948, in London. Manchuria was being won by the Red Armies of Mao Tsetung; and while Chiang Kaishek proclaimed victory just in sight, he was transferring 400 million dollars' worth of gold to Taiwan. Francis Pan was in the Finance Ministry of the Kuomintang government and in London probably on yet another money-raising mission, but I did not inquire and he did not tell me. We had not met since January 1942 when, carrying Yungmei in a big wool blanket, I had flown over the Himalayas to Calcutta and thence proceeded via the Cape and Trinidad and New York to England, because Pao, my first and Chinese husband, had been promoted Military Attaché to the Chinese Embassy in London.†

Unchanging in their friendship, the Pans had tried to find me as soon as they reached London in October 1948; but the Chinese Embassy did not know my whereabouts; I had dropped all connection with them and my at one time numerous diplomatic friends. 'I reflected,' said Cecilia, miming reflection with one lovely hand to her brow, 'then I thought, "Isobel Cripps must know where she is." '

She did not ask me why I had thus vanished; she guessed that I had locked out that part of my life; out of the person I had become since March 1945, when Pao had left London by train, waving his stick at me in farewell, to return to China, and to die in bitterness upon a battlefield not of his own choosing, killed by his own soldiers; realizing at last that his life had been given to a dictator he now despised, Chiang Kaishek. Shivering in the cold morning, I had gone back to the Royal Free Hospital to start my entrance examination, my new life as a medical student, after having been a member of the Diplomatic Corps.

'Things are a bit unsettled at the moment,' said Francis agreeably. Chiang Kaishek's high officials were moving

*See *Birdless Summer*.
†Ibid.

wealth and families to Hong Kong; the Pans had also rented a house there, 'just in case things get a bit out of hand'. Through the next three decades, Francis and Cecilia would live in Hong Kong; Cecilia giving piano lessons and Francis teaching at the University and for a while doing some stockbroking. They would hold, intact, a certain vision of China, even when it became spectral, non-substance. They would not skimp their loyalty or withhold friendship from people such as myself, even when we no longer felt or thought alike. And in their courteous fortitude, they never blamed my headlong explorations, or my discovery of a reality which, in the end, would infuse with validity and hope both the past and the future of China and her people.

'We must wait for the dust to settle,' said Cecilia. We agreed. We sipped tea; theirs was a very luxurious hotel, all felted purple velvet. But we preferred to wait for the dust to settle in Hong Kong rather than in London. Cecilia sprang to action when I told her I wanted to go back. 'I'll ring up Gordon King; he's here now on a visit; if anyone can fix a job for you in Hong Kong, he can.'

I remember the impact of Gordon King's startling blue eyes, shaded by strong eyebrows, his rather disconcerting grin, due to ill-fitting dentures. In those years, Australians were prone to wearing artificial dentures, and Gordon King was Australian. He understood perfectly my need to be near China. 'So many Chinese feel like you . . . they can't do without China, but they're also worried about communism, what it might do to them . . .' I spoke about Yungmei: 'She is Chinese, she must get the feel of her own country.' 'We'll manage to find you a job in Hong Kong,' said Gordon King, clenching his jaw in an encouraging grin.

In those days aeroplanes dawdled; halted at sundown. There was dinner, a stroll, hotel beds and breakfast before the morning takeoff. We spent agreeable nights in Cairo, Karachi, Calcutta, and stepped down in Bangkok, where I was to stay a week, until the next aeroplane to Hong Kong, with John Coast. 'You can't miss Thailand, a most gorgeously civilized country,' John had written. 'Before you immolate yourself in that raging inferno further east, why not have a look at an enchanting country?'

Bangkok then was not today's nightmare of concrete gone amok, of packed raucous streets choking with the exhaust of jammed cars. It was a green and nonchalant huddle of bungalows interspersed with mosaic-dappled temples ringing little bells in the breeze. Banana and palm trees elegantly signalled pathways to entrances, grenadier-bright rows of cannas delineated tranquil mud roads with bullock carts and an occasional car. Rain trees along a magnificent mud avenue flung immense arms between sky and earth, and I have never forgiven the Thais for cutting them down.

Mango and champak trees adorned John's typical Siamese chalet. It was indeed enchanting, except that I had little time for enchantment. But the sun and the warmth worked their wonders; and within three days I had recovered acuity of perception and delight of eye and nose. John and other white men went, clad in pale seersucker, free floating like oil droplets upon water among the golden tranquil Siamese stepping gracefully about them. Here was, apparently, no friction or hostility – John and his friends all commented on it: 'So different from other countries where now they spit at a white man!' Almost, here, they could claim to have become partly melded within what they called 'the soul of Asia', a grandiloquent, subjugating phrase. I went to temples, the flower market, the *klongs*;* John explained South East Asia to me. He had resigned from the Foreign Office to devote himself to Indonesian independence. In November and December of 1948 the Dutch had started a military campaign to retake Indonesia; a return of Western colonial power in military guise in Asia still appeared possible to some Western politicians. It was, however, too late, and John knew it. He was buying guns and flying gold bullion for the Republic of Indonesia and Sukarno, commuting between Manila, Singapore, Djakarta and Bangkok.

In the late afternoon of January 5th, Yungmei and I

---

*Klongs: water canals webbing part of Bangkok.

watched through the aeroplane window our somewhat perilous landing in Hong Kong; for the diminutive airport lay in a narrow gorge between cliffs; the aeroplane circled and then thrust itself at the ground. Hong Kong was golden islands and cobalt water, and the sky was like an opal above the Nine Dragon Hills of Kowloon. 'Why, it's beautiful, beautiful,' I cried. 'Only in the winter,' said the English businessman who sat next to us. 'It's pretty awful in the summer.' He went on to explain that the Peak was wrapped in fog for a good part of the year, that Chinese New Year was hell because of the firecrackers, 'and all the boys and amahs go away', and to tell me that I must 'sign the book' at Government House as soon as possible.

We came down the gangway and there it was. I said to stolid Yungmei, clutching her small travelling case, 'You're home, Yungmei, almost. Look, everyone here looks like you.'

Francis Pan took us by taxi to Church Guest House, where Cecilia had booked (requisitioned is more apt) 'living space' in a Hong Kong awash with the exodus of missionaries and businessmen from China. Church Guest House was a small grey building at mid-level on Hong Kong Island; pitched just below the public park, where giant ferns like weird umbrellas dripped gentle seed upon the loiterers. Church Guest House has disappeared; I can no longer find it in the massive array of dinosaurian skyscrapers, the treeless and gardenless canyons crowded with frantic speeding cars like pursuing felines which is Hong Kong today.

Already in 1949, Hong Kong's metamorphosis into its Manhattan shape had begun; never has a city torn and built itself with such feroocity; nor has it stopped tearing and building throughout these thirty years. Hong Kong is always bulldozers and cranes; always higher buildings, now on precarious ground, since the granite ridges of the hillfolds are built up and room must be made for yet taller constructions. Bays are filled to make building space until the sea itself becomes an extension of abode for Hong Kong's architectural sprawl.

The first week we shared a room with a forever-knitting English missionary, unemphatic about China. 'It had to be, my dear, the people were just too miserable,' she murmured as she poked and clicked. We then moved to the basement to share a room with Ada Chung, her two children and her wolf-hound, Soossee. Ada was Cantonese, a widow, a Christian, energetic and discreet, hardworking and respectable. Soossee took up more space than the other five of us. We arranged ourselves and our luggage around her. She compelled us to become a courteous community.

Hong Kong was a delight; the piercing blue sky; the reflecting, crystal, merry sea we crossed and recrossed by ferry to Kowloon to hear the gurgle and suck of water under the boat and feel the mild, cool wind upon our faces. We went to Cameron Road, where the Pans had their house, on the Kowloon side. I walked the slopes of Victoria Island, up Conduit Road. Poinsettias in pots spread their carmine explosions atop the stone walls which banked old and graceful villas. The ladder streets escalating the slopes, the innumerable tiny shops open day and night, and the food, the food! Everything was bliss of flesh, and Yungmei and I grew fat, almost, in that short respite. I found the Fung Ping Shan library, took a subscription, and started voraciously reading Lu Hsun.* I discovered the Peak, not only as a geographical promontory with a magnificent view of the Bay, but as a token of Hong Kong's ladder hierarchy. Here the great merchant-princes – Jardine Matheson and others – lived in lofty summitry. Most of these *taipans*† were Scots, and the eating of haggis on a certain day of the year was the most solemn of Hong Kong's functions. An invitation to Jardine's was more fraught with social significance than a 'do' at Government House.

---

*Lu Hsun is the Gorky of China. Controversy raged round his role in the Chinese Revolution during the last ten years and became an issue of which Madame Mao (Chiang Ching) and her clique made much use to seize power. See *The Morning Deluge* and *Wind in the Tower*.
†*Taipans:* name given to the merchants of the East India Company in the nineteenth century.

Government House was at mid-level; it had white unobtrusive pillars and looked like a modest wedding cake when seen from the Peak. I signed the visitors' book and was duly asked to lunch.

Alexander Grantham (HE in Hong Kong's parlance) was very tall; his American wife, diminutive, deaf and charming, wore Shirley Temple curls which never altered. I admired her flawless skin; it never changed either. 'I do hope you'll like it here,' said Alex Grantham. Somehow the Granthams and I got on famously; and from then on I was often – at least four times a year – invited to Government House, and even, later, to HE's box at the races.

Alexander Grantham had an eminent gift which he strenuously concealed. He understood history; felt it in his bones. He saw the time in which he lived as I did; in all its impermanence. And so I like to think that his liking for me was part of an extra-sensory, unvoiced recognition. We were both, in our dissimilar ways, pioneers, bridge builders between the old and the new. For him Hong Kong, product of British colonialism and Chinese labour and want, would hold one day a special place in a new scheme of things. And he was right.

The blight of colonialism is that it produces in the colonized, when they accept its order, a willing and eager self-stunting of creative passion. This sensation of a lost identity not only pervaded a good many of the Chinese 'upper class' in Hong Kong, it also infected the British; who laboriously revived, in order to feel non-alien, the habits of their homeland, and ascribed to the weather their curious indolence in the arts. And how the niceties of social distinction, long in abeyance in England, here survived to redeem the hierarchy and make it feel worthy of itself! How much effort went into the minutiae of a decrepit pomp and how violent and enduring the hostility towards those who disturbed the almost Victorian prudishness of Hong Kong society!

In the 1950s, intermarriage between an Englishman (or should I say Scotsman?) and a Chinese girl was regarded

with animadversion, certainly in the business houses; where
it led to swift demotion. The students of Hong Kong
University (English-speaking) were educated to be docile
and subdued, trained not to think, and to avoid offending
'authority' by word or deed. They became doctors and
lawyers, to fit into that wedge of society which their wealth
(most of them came from wealthy families) entitled them to
occupy, and where money made money.

And yet in that year of 1949, all this was already beginning
to change, and the change was due to the change in China;
although at first unperceived in Hong Kong. Today, Hong
Kong is no longer the Hong Kong of meticulous distinction
of race and colour and emolument. It is now an asset for a
promising young Englishman not only to speak Chinese but
to marry a Chinese girl (of good family, of course). Hong
Kong University has become bilingual; its professors (many
of them Chinese) take their students to China on trips, and
come back to make glowing speeches on China, duly
reported in the flourishing 'communist' and non-communist
newspapers of the Colony. Today there are painters and
musicians, sculptors and even writers in Hong Kong; many
of them Chinese, catering, in Chinese, to an ever-growing
appreciative public, but also appreciated by the Westerners
living there. Amiably, the Hong Kong government co-
operates with the People's Republic of China, and rumour
has it that Hong Kong actually has two HEs; the British one
(Scots, of course), still functioning in Government House,
and an occult, unknown Chinese one, who drops occasional
wise hints so that there should not be the slightest
disturbance in Hong Kong's prowess of prosperity, either
now or when the time is ripe for Hong Kong's return to
China, an event which no longer spells dismay.

In February I began my assistantship in Gordon King's
Obstetrics and Gynaecology Department at the Queen Mary
Hospital. Gordon's house surgeon, a nice girl called Sophie
Bard, a white Russian from Shanghai, was leaving to get
married in April, when I would take her place. Meanwhile, I

went every day to the Queen Mary, and on Sophie's day off I occupied her room. To my consternation, the first thing I did was to break her lamp by leaving the windows open, forgetting the sudden gusts from the sea which invaded the hospital rooms.

My salary was around 700 Hong Kong dollars per month; ample for one person, but a little tight because of Yungmei to feed, to clothe, to put to school. Where would Yungmei stay when I was permanently on call, save for one day a week, at the Queen Mary? Once again Cecilia rescued me: she would house Yungmei, who would share a room with Cecilia's daughter, Shirley. But it would become increasingly difficult for the Pans when their own relatives and friends descended upon them from China, all through the summer of 1949, when the great offensives of the Red armies, begun in April, conquered Nanking and Wuhan and Shanghai so swiftly in fantastic campaigns. Yungmei then boarded at school, St Stephen's, and her upkeep took more than half of my stipend. Nevertheless I managed. I trained myself to eat a solid meal but once, in the evening, and five cents' worth of peanuts at lunch.

At first all went well. I worked hard; I was fervent and eager, although here too was hierarchy. The professors were English, the students Chinese. The upper nurses and matrons were English, the amahs and lower staff were Chinese. I had little to say to the other housemen; they were typically 'Hong Kong'; they read only the comics, and only on Sunday. They were very keen to 'get on'; what was happening in China was, for them, unmentionable. They feared 'the Reds' even more than their masters, the British. However, time the devourer has also digested their mediocrity. Since then a good many have changed their views, although in 1949, the fact that I subscribed to the *Takungpao*, the pro-communist daily, led to ostracism by some of my colleagues. But then refugees from China who came here also remained apart from the Hong Kong-born. My friends were the 'China Chinese' like the Pans. 'The Hong Kong-born are not like us,' Cecilia would say. 'Their minds don't work the same way.'

Again this is no longer true, and even then, I would, in the end, make good friends among real Hong Kong women like the almoners, and Ada Chung, and Teresa Kwa. The Hong Kong group was resentful and fearful of being pushed aside by people from Shanghai or 'Shanghai more far', that is, north China. Their colonial training enhanced their dread of rivalry. Already, in a few instances, excellent doctors from 'Shanghai more far' had come to Hong Kong and had been hired in the hospitals. The British colonial service did not have enough British staff, especially in the lower ranks; such recruitment of Asian personnel was also much cheaper. Within six months students from China would be enrolling at Hong Kong University. Within two years some of them would pass examinations and compete for government service with the Hong Kong doctors. Within three years a Chinese university would be set up. Along with the refugees, money poured into Hong Kong and transformed it from a sleepy port into a massive metropolis of wealth.

I was busy. Operations and ward rounds and outpatients' clinic at Saiyinpun Hospital in downtown Hong Kong. But after some weeks of an avalanche of wombs and vaginas, vaginas and wombs, I realized that this was not my vocation. Hysterectomies and more hysterectomies interspersed with ovariotomies were not filling me with enthusiasm. In fact, I craved no more pelvises to dig into, although the obstetrics part, the child's cry as it emerges into life, would always move me. But at the hospital few births were 'normal' cases, except those of the first-class private patients. I began to realize that it takes a special kind of person to like this speciality; and Gordon King was that special person. My talent lay in diagnosis, in smelling out disease; a perception about skin and flesh and what lay within, and this I have kept until now. But I have no deftness of finger and I was slow in operating, and clumsy with a needle. I could detect a faint heart murmur where no one else did; tap a dull tone in a chest when others passed it by; but I could not easily stitch up an ordinary appendectomy; and this awkwardness did not improve with time, although Gordon was extremely patient. And after a while, another assistant, who did not like me, would show me up. 'Forceps . . . cut . . . tie . . .' she would murmur behind her white mask, always a little ahead of my gesture, and she was always right. Who could prevent this upwomanship? She wanted my job. She would get it in the end.

Of course, I also had my small victories; discovering a bleeding uterus, sent in for operation as·fibroids, to be a leukaemia; or an ovarian tumour, diagnosed so even by a great white consultant, to be a pregnancy; but the patient was a widow of seven years' standing, and so deeply Confucian were my colleagues, and even my superiors, that they could not imagine that a Chinese widow would become pregnant . . .

However, in surgery and gynaecology, a talent for cutting and stitching is needed, and this I did not possess. Gordon was in love with his profession and would rear extremely good gynaecologists, such as the small and wonderful Daphne Chun. Daphne's hands were a marvel; tiny and so able, so nimble! She was quite happy operating all day, and I both envied and resented her enthusiasm, the beam upon her face when yet another belly had to be opened . . .

But the main reason why I became unsatisfactory was that I fell in love, into a sargasso churn of emotion, a torrid and absolute passion which, like a Hong Kong typhoon, carried all my resolutions before it and left me racked and changed.

By April, Hong Kong's dazzling winter had turned to spring, and Stanley Smith surfaced. I had met him in Chungking, so he said, though I do not remember how or where; but he had lived in a house belonging to my Third Uncle. We met at tea at the Gloucester Hotel, and he invited me and Yungmei to his beautiful house on Deep Water Bay. There, on my free days, I could swim with Yungmei, and it did the child a great deal of good.

Stanley was Australian; amassing a fortune from iron ore mines in Malaya. Tall, whipcord tough, with a bulging forehead and a thin mouth, he was a gifted wealth-maker, and his big house contained many valuable trophies. In his drawing room, prominent among other antiques, was a startling Chinese painting of a beggar in all his verminous degradation, extending, with a leer of disquiet and insolence upon his face, a twisted hand cupped in front of him. That hand seemed to thrust into the room, to pick and pluck at my very flesh; I hated it, but Stanley revelled in describing how he had acquired it from a painter in Shanghai 'in the good old days' before the Communist armies had swept all away and made it impossible to have any more such bargains. I felt the beggar explained some obscure yearning in him. 'There, but for my wits and my ruthless energy, go I,' Stanley seemed to say as he gazed upon his painting with singular joy. May, his wife, was Chinese, round and pretty, and we spent many happy hours together sunning on Stanley's beach while Yungmei swam and ran and ate enormously. I revelled in her health, as I did in mine.

Stanley warned me: 'People are saying that you are a communist.' I laughed. 'Of course I'm not, but I'm not against the revolution. I'm for it if it does any good for the Chinese people.' I thought my attitude logical; no one else appeared to think so. Only one attitude was allowed, and that was vehement anti-communism, horror at the revolution in China. Anything else classified one as 'communist'. Already the Special Branch in Hong Kong was opening a file on me, entirely based on my emitted opinions. I explained to Stanley my dilemma, which was that of so many Chinese intellectuals. I would wait and see, wait until the dust settled. But inevitably I must go back to China one day. Stanley shook his head and told me I was crazy.

One day in the street I met Kung Peng. She had been my classmate at Yenching University in Peking. And now she had worked for many years under Chou Enlai. I had not seen her since 1941, when on the street in Chungking I had begun to sob because of the massacre by Chiang Kaishek of the

New Fourth Army medical teams.* Now here she was, climbing a ladder street while I pelted down it. 'Kung Peng' I cried, and she lifted her head, and recognized me. She was unchanged, beautiful as ever, in a black dress. I talked first, volubly, telling her why I was there. She listened coldly. 'Where are you staying?' she asked. I told her. 'I'll write to you,' said Kung Peng, and walked on. A little perturbed, I went home, but two days later had a letter giving me her address and asking me to come to see her. I was so politically naïve that only with her address did I realize that she was at Hsinhua, the communist news agency, which had a branch in Hong Kong. Despite the anti-communist stance and the shouting, the government of the Colony allowed not only communist newspapers and organizations but also leading communists into Hong Kong. This was political wisdom and foresight; and it would last urbanely, despite America's pressures on the British government, throughout the next two decades.

Kung Peng and her husband, Chiao Kuanhua, had arrived in Hong Kong the year before with the staff of the Hsinhua news agency. The offices of Hsinhua were small and cramped, in a nondescript building in the populous Wanchai district. I sat with Kung Peng and Chiao, drinking tea; I asked them about returning to China and Kung Peng turned to her husband. '*If* you want to do so, don't put it off for too long,' said Chiao lightly. When I left them, I was discouraged. I was glad that Kung Peng still spoke to me, but I sensed hesitancy; an aloofness, and I understood it well.

Of course, many hundreds of intellectuals were going back; but few had achieved my strange inconsistencies; managing to marry a Blueshirt, a Tai Lee man, a Chiang Kaishek addict, a general in Chiang's armies who had died in the war, on the wrong side. I knew in my bones, not with my brain, that a revolution starts by 'cleaning up', and in the 'cleaning up' process many people get killed or jailed; and I could not see these tough guerrillas who had slogged it for so

*See *Birdless Summer*.

many years, and suffered so much, able to understand and accept easily that I was *not* a spy, not a secret agent. Even before the campaign for 'remoulding intellectuals' had begun, I sensed that each and every intellectual would be thoroughly scrutinized. I could not see Kung Peng, with the best will in the world, able to vouch for me, merely because of my protestations of innocence . . .

In 1938 I had not hesitated to plunge into the maelstrom of war; but then it was different. No one asked me my political inclinations, and at the time I did not have Yungmei. Now I had Yungmei, and if something happened to me, what would happen to Yungmei?

'I'll finish this year in Hong Kong, then I shall see.' So resolved, I went on to live through the spring.

Conduit Road was at mid-level on Victoria Island; lined with those graceful stone houses with deep verandas and high ceilings dating to the early 1920s (alas, all gone today). There, among camelfoot trees and hibiscus, was the house of Dr James Anderson, known as Andy, a successful surgeon. Andy and his wife Sheila were friends of Molly and Terence Millin in London. Terence Millin, himself a famous surgeon and the originator of a new technique for prostate operations, was Irish; Molly and I had met in Regent's Park, where we promenaded our respective children (she had two daughters). We had become excellent friends, and when I left for Hong Kong, Molly wrote to Sheila, and now Sheila asked me to dinner.

So in the late pink and gold afternoon, I climbed the winding path up the sloped garden to their porticoed veranda, and was violently greeted by Tattybogle, the Russian greyhound, and Dainty, the Dalmatian. We sat in the living room, and Sheila and I liked each other immediately. There were some guests, and then in came a man with an auburn shock of hair and a Shan bag, not very tall, but who walked like a Siamese cat, with prehensile feet, and he was introduced to me as Ian Morrison of *The Times* (in those days, the word Times was enough to denote the

London *Times*, but I committed the gross discourtesy of asking which *Times*!).

I remember still with a catch of heart the topaz shimmer of that bright afternoon dissolving so reluctantly into night, the trees with great swathing movements of immobility gathering the night as we went to dinner. It is now thirty years ago; thirty years since I watched Ian come across the room on soft cat feet, and still my foolish heart leaps at the memory, although content that things should be as they are. Does one ever get cured of memory? How does one bury memory irrevocably? For after that, for a short while in time, but for ever for me, each day was to be sunflower splendour, time no more, and here again it rises, unbearable almost.

We talked, and left when Tattybogle, whose private sofa had been usurped by an agile and vociferous woman, started to bark, signalling the time for departure. Sheila would confirm to me that she had nearly trained him thus to get rid tactfully of her guests. For in Hong Kong, as in Malaya, white people tended to cling to each other through the balmy hours of parties, unwilling to return home. Not so the Chinese, who always get up and leave fifteen minutes after the meal is over.

There was a letter from Ian the next day, asking me to dinner on my day off, Wednesday. I hesitated, even went to seek the advice of a friend, Anne Doyle, an American journalist whom I had met in that easy way of meeting people which has always been mine. And so it began.

Words have their nostalgia; their whisper challenges time and death. Words, the wind in motion of living. And that spring and summer words were oasis, marvel and privilege which my ears have not ceased hearing. I then discovered again the birds; the song and the sight of wagtail and laughing thrush, and the chorus of francolin and golden oriole at dawn. We met seldom, but Ian wrote to me, wrote to me, wrote, every day, twice a day, even when we were in the same city, and I grew very distraught for I had not wanted this, I had not wished this disturbance, this frightening potency of trouble. And tenderness. How difficult, how impossible when once it has begun is this strange thing now disfigured with the name of love.

Oh, what is going to happen to me, I cried, watching the moon rock the sea gently in her shining summer arms. It was not until August and four months later that we entered the great country of love and its power, and felt ourselves immortal, transcendent inhabitants of that mirage land where is no time or space. We walked, for a while, in the golden extravagance of a summer which dazzled the sea, and upon us was bestowed the stintless grace of that enormous illusion which moves the world.

And so of course my work began to suffer; delving into pelvises I could not burrow away from the shimmer of each of my body's cells. The heat of summer spread its grey haze upon Hong Kong; but our bedlam season unhinged us and I only remember coolness; the breath of the moon rocking the sea; the troubled stolen minutes spent in silence, between two cases, just outside the hospital gates. And now that all this has been resurrected with words, what shall my busy heart do?

In January 1949 I had written from Hong Kong to my father in Peking. Peking had been liberated by the Red armies that month. In August came his answer. The miraculous Chinese post office, which had functioned throughout the Sino-Japanese war, forwarded mail across battle lines reckoned unpassable and seldom lost a letter, continued to do so. By that August the waters around Hong Kong bristled with ominous grey battleships, American men-of-war and a couple of British ones 'to defend Hong Kong from the Red menace', so the newspapers wrote. Meanwhile Hong Kong made a great deal of money out of China, out of the refugees. These came out with solid gold, in bars, in ingots, in rings, hidden within their body cavities. The colossal inflation in China (more than a twelve-million multiplication in the last five years) had made almost everyone turn to gold, but the entry of gold into the Colony was 'illegal'. Special plain-clothes police stood at all points of arrival; one of them told me how good he was at detecting gold carried by a woman in her vagina. 'It's the way she walks when it is in.' At night the sky was aglow with the beacons of work crews, building and levelling hills for mansions; a fungoid growth of slums crept upon the granite rock and the Secret Societies of Shanghai, complete with their top bosses, moved in. One of these Godfathers, Tu Yusen, was to die of old age on the Island and be buried with such pomp as a great philanthropist in a prime cemetery of Hong Kong.

My father wrote that he had recovered from his illness; that the present government was kind to him and had asked for his co-operation in rebuilding the coalmines. 'I think for the time being you should help your mother and sister; they are now in Chungking with your Third Uncle.' The next week brought a letter from Chungking. It was Tiza's. Twelve pages, fairly incoherent but definitely demanding help.

Tiza had been cheated by her Chinese husband; he had made money as a black marketeer with the Americans, 'yet I had to pay him to get a divorce'. Wherever the Americans went there flourished corruption; miles and miles of barbed wire, cans of all kinds of food, chocolate bars, cheap fountain pens and engine spare parts and nylon stockings and oh, so much clothing, shirts and shoes and jackets, and when they left, they left all the stuff behind and the black marketeers scavenged mightily. Tiza's husband had sold American throwaways and had been arrested by the Communists. Mama and Tiza and Tiza's baby were now in Chungking. 'But we moved out of Third Uncle's house because Mama found it too noisy.' I was to write to her care of the British Consul in Chungking; I was to go to the Hong Kong police and sign an affidavit to guarantee her and Mama residence in Hong Kong; I was to do all this very quickly, before the Communists came, otherwise all would be lost. I was to send money.

The postscript infuriated me. 'Papa was ill when we left, but he's all right now. I think he had some sort of stroke.' I could see Papa lying in bed, saying in his low, spent voice, a little breathless, 'Don't worry, I'll be all right.' And Mama did not worry, of course not, not for him, but thudded about, hauling her luggage and making last minute recommendations to Papa and to the servant, Hsueh Mah. Mama had left Papa and gone with Tiza. It would always be Tiza . . . I wrote back to Tiza that I was in no position to guarantee her stay and that of Mama in Hong Kong; I had visions of both of them, and the baby, trying to live on my small salary; of Mama stirring up trouble (how good she was at it) between me and Tiza . . .

When the letter had gone, anger subsided and compunction arose. Perhaps I should try to get them out. Perhaps I should sign affidavits. Then came Third Uncle's letter, in his beautiful calligraphy. 'Your mother is healthy. However, the food does not suit her.' This meant that they must leave. Szechuan province was still under Chiang Kaishek, who swore that he would win the ultimate victory or commit suicide. And everyone knew he would do neither, but simply run away. Third Uncle of course did not mention the war, although he too must have known that it was only a matter of a few months, a few weeks, before the People's Liberation Army came in, like a great tide, into Szechuan, into all the hinterland. Nothing could stop the Chinese conquest of China.

In early September I asked Gordon for a week's leave, to go to Szechuan and see my family. He said yes immediately. Off I went, and took with me Cherry, my friend from England. Cherry had now arrived in Hong Hong. Although she had called it madness on my part to leave England, she had decided to come and have a look. She had obtained a position at the Queen Mary Hospital, in the Department of Internal Medicine. Being English, she was paid about three times my stipend, and also had the benefit of a flat, which she shared with another English girl, a physiotherapist.

Ian came to see us off at the airport; the milky dawn had dispersed and rough light mottled the sea. 'I must know it is not only the sun and summer in Hong Kong,' I told him. Even then, even in that ecstasy there were other stirrings within me, waiting to be born . . . which one of those many mes would be the forever me? And once that fixed star of self-completion was reached, would my bones at last become resigned?

I have described the journey to Chungking;* arrival; the remembered landscape jolting me, bringing me home; the leaden heat, the dirt, the disintegration of everything, the smells, the beauty of the hills, their sinuous disarray and the fuzziness of their slopes across the heat-bleached sky; the sharp rock of the city like a ship's prow riding between the Yangtze River and the Chialing River, and the immense and terrifying misery, and the hope . . .

Seven straggly hours by bus to reach Chungking; Third Uncle's house up the cliff of Koloshan just outside the city, and there they were in the light of lamps fitfully dotting the night, Third Aunt all smiles, and my cousins, and Third Uncle, loud and happy and trying not to show his joy, and a bustle of teacups and hot towels and talk, amiable, glad shouts, and always avoidance of even the nuance of impending threat. Cherry and I shared a room, a vast ornate Szechuan bed wrapped in a huge silk mosquito net, and also a large blue ceramic pot thoughtfully placed in a corner and regularly emptied, morning and evening, but maintaining in its rotund depths a permanent odour of excreta.

I went to see Tiza that very night, since the British Consul's residence was just down the pebbled road and belonged to the Meifeng Bank; and Third Uncle was on its Board of Directors. Into the English-style drawing room with its over-stuffed settee came Tiza, holding a candle (electricity had stopped functioning) and I could hear in the bedroom beyond Mama hovering, the faint dry rasp of her hands on the bedsheets, her voice whispering, 'Tiza, the baby is waking up . . .' She did not come out to meet me. And because of that rustle of hers, the suffocating, acrid tide of childhood resentment rose between Tiza and myself; Mama

*See *A Many-Splendoured Thing.*

knew so well how to deal me a shadow blow; simply with a cough and a smoothing of the baby's bedclothes.

It was only when Mama died in 1966 that Tiza and I began to like each other. She then took lessons in square dancing, married again and became a charming, humorous person whose company was a delight.

Tiza had fallen in love with an American officer in the US Marines' contingent sent to help Chiang Kaishek. Tiza had wanted to marry, but suddenly had come the order: 'No fraternization'. The officer had been moved and Tiza was pregnant; she had the baby and was proud of it. 'We'll manage,' she said. And now Tiza thought, 'If the Communists come, they will kill me and my baby.'

I went back and lay in the large bed, and Cherry complained of the smell of our toilet. I told her she would get used to it; 'everyone does in Szechuan'.

The next day I went back to the British Consulate. Like three judges upon the sofa sat Tiza and Mama (holding the baby) and the British Consul, frowning heavily. He was a portly, decent man who immediately upbraided me for my heartlessness in *not* sending a guarantee for my mother and sister to live in Hong Kong. I told him that I myself was not secure. 'You are the British Consul, you can get them a guarantee any time you wish. Why don't you do it?' This stopped further argument, and in fact within the next two months he had done what was necessary, and all three would come together to Hong Kong. Later Tiza and Mama went to Italy, and then to America in 1956.

When Tiza and Mama arrived in America, they stayed with my other sister, Marianne, who had married an American and had two children. Marianne's husband died suddenly of a heart attack while having breakfast, in June 1956. Marianne was at first overjoyed when Tiza and Mama came to live with her that year. And of course, pretty soon there was trouble, and again it was because of Mama. Poor Marianne, who hungered for love withheld, from Mama! Poor Marianne, whose childhood had been warped by Mama's indifference to her, the last of the brood! Mama and

Tiza moved into a small house of their own; Marianne was not invited, and then she cracked. 'If I'm crazy, it all started there, right in Mama's lap,' she cried to me one night over the telephone, from Arizona to Singapore. And yet, despite all this, her two children turned out beautiful, sensible and gifted; both made successful marriages and happy lives, unaided, and both look after Marianne, and so do I, but none of us can give her back the love she never had.

The next few days with the family were happy. And of course the Kangs, the Tengs, and other families related to ours by marriage ties and ties of commerce and banking, all held little dinners, and we enjoyed ourselves as if nothing was to change. I walked about Chungking; I wrote to Papa in Peking. Third Uncle quietly let drop that 'Szechuan is talking', meaning that negotiations were going on for the peaceful takeover by the Communists of the province. When this happened, the streets of Chungking would be a stream of red flags and joy. Third Uncle was staying put, and so were the other families. The Kangs, like ourselves, had younger members who had joined the Communist Party.

One afternoon Third Uncle opened Pao's many suitcases of clothes, so many clothes. 'The person is no more, the clothes remain,' he said, and we distributed them to the servants.

I flew back to Hong Kong with Cherry, and the ginger smell of autumn was about. Yungmei was now exactly like her Hong Kong schoolmates, chewing gum and reading comics and wanting to go to the cinema and to swim at Repulse Bay. There was a press of patients, and too little sleep for me; I told Ian about Chungking and about Third Uncle, but not about Tiza and Mama. 'It's fascinating. You must write it down,' he said. 'I will, one day,' I replied. And so I would, when I came to write of the love between me and Ian Morrison.

Of that brief autumn, when time and space were a crystal sphere seemingly suspended for ever in a happy heaven, there was so much to remember, remembrance both pain and fearsome pleasure. Ian's talk about himself and about his father; small driblets of his life kept coming up between long silences while we paced the hills or sat on rocks hot with sun, in the company of lizards. How miserable he had been at Winchester, because he was an Australian. How he and his brothers were frightened of their father, a man of great severity, who believed in discipline and toughening, and thought Ian weak.

Dr George Morrison, the famous Morrison of *The Times*, had revelled in his white man's burden; he was, of necessity, an absolute Victorian, but his son was assailed by doubts about the same burden. George Morrison had paced the Chinese earth as if it was an unkempt property of his, treated all natives with a contempt fortified by his unflinching belief in a Divine Purpose (though he was virulently anti-missionary). His dispatches had earned him great fame. But now times had changed, and Ian knew it, and refused to get intemperately emotional over the Chinese Revolution. When a British gunboat, the *Amethyst*, mistaking 1949 for 1909, tried to sail up the Yangtze right in the middle of the civil war between Mao Tsetung and Chiang Kaishek and had been fired upon by the Red Army (*Fired upon!* Furore in Hong Kong; a stampede of correspondents) Ian went swimming with Yungmei and me and said, quoting Molière, '*Mais que diable allait-il faire dans cette galère?*'

Ian gave me his father's book, *An Australian in China*, describing a journey in 1894: 'Simply . . . 1,500 miles up the Yangtze River, followed by a quiet though extended excursion of another 1,500 miles along the great overland highway into Burma.' 'The Burma Road before it existed,' said Ian. Under the casual modesty there was such arrogant assertion of George Morrison's capacity, as an Australian, for walkabouts! Perhaps that was his way of getting his own back on the English, who must at first have jeered at his accent. Ian also went on walkabouts. Thus in 1948 he had gone to north-west China and covered well over 1,500 miles, meeting the legendary New Zealander, Rewi Alley, in Kansu province, where Rewi ran co-operatives, and trekking with him. They had gone together to the famous Buddhist grottoes of Tun Huang, explored the caves and seen their extraordinary Buddhist frescoes, dating back to the fifth century A.D., and spent an afternoon at the Crescent Moon Lake, near Tun Huang. Nothing ever tarnished the lake's sapphire; round it the sand humped in hillocks, and broke into musical sound when one trod upon it. 'The singing sands . . . *The Times* expected me to report on the civil war in China, but I'm afraid Rewi's conversation entranced me. He really explained to me why the Chinese Revolution was inevitable; and so I came up with something which my newspaper found slightly disappointing.'

Twenty-three years later, in the summer of 1972, I would also go to Tun Huang, on the edge of the Gobi Desert, to see the Buddhist caves. The man who took me round was the great scholar, painter and archaeologist, Professor Tsang. He had spent already more than three decades in Tun Huang, maintaining and restoring the frescoes, and during the first years of the Cultural Revolution in 1966, and until 1968, had had a very hard time preserving them from destruction. 'But Premier Chou Enlai gave orders that all should be preserved.'

After his father's death, Ian had become in his turn correspondent for *The Times*. But he was not made of the same stern stuff as his father. He was in what he called 'a state of permanent confusion'. His not the steel-shine of absolute conviction; for him the world was not simple, divided between the 'Reds' who represented Evil, and Good, which was the Western democracies. He no longer knew, and said so candidly, what role the white man had to play in Asia. 'I doubt that we have any role at all,' he wrote. This befuddlement he bore cheerfully. It was not, however, shared by his Anglo-Saxon colleagues in Hong Kong. A very righteous, rabid hate-the-Reds lot, it was fascinating to hear them argue with the French correspondents who, however averse to communism, were not afraid to argue about its merits in Asia. They did not, like the Americans, feel polluted when producing neat intellectual arguments in its favour – this mental exercise, for them, had nothing to do with the practice of anti-communism. But the Americans had to scream, strenuously, of their hatred and horror of communism in order to function against it, and this made conversation with them rather boring – except with one man, a geographer-journalist, Norton Ginsberg.

'How can we ask the peasants of Asia to be anti-communist when communism is the only hope they have for a decent *human* living?' said Ginsberg.

On October 1st, 1949 the People's Republic of China was proclaimed, and Mao Tsetung stood at the Gate of Heavenly Peace of the Forbidden City in Peking, facing the south, the sun, and said, 'The Chinese people have stood up . . . no one will insult us again.'

And I was happy, as also were some of my Chinese friends (the almoners, some of the lower nurses at the Queen Mary Hospital, but not, of course, the doctors). I procured in a small, obscure street in Wanchai a beautiful picture of San Mao dancing the Yangko. San Mao – Three Hairs – is the Tintin, the Peanuts of China; his creator, Chang Loping, an artist of talent, is still alive in Shanghai, though he suffered very much during the Cultural Revolution when San Mao was suppressed as 'insulting to the Party'. This poster of San Mao, the cherubic little boy dancing the seed-planting, a folk dance which the Communists had adopted and popularized in Yenan, hung above my desk in my room at the hospital. It would later bring me a good deal of trouble.

In October Ian went back to Singapore. 'There are so many material and mechanical difficulties we have to contend with,' he wrote, 'that more than anything else, our love is comical.' Ah, but how we clung to its hilarious, almost farcical untowardness. Now he had been told that news of his liaison had reached his wife. Like all men, he hated scenes; but there had to be one, and he was away for three weeks, telling me, 'I will not let you go by default.' When he returned it took him six days to tell me that his wife had refused a divorce; no surprise to me. How could Ian ever think that he would get a divorce so easily? 'But I want to marry you,' he said simply.

My only concern was *not* to turn this hitch into a tragedy. And my calm impressed Ian. But then he refused to accept what I kept on saying, that there could not really be for us a future together. In his quiet obduracy he was determined to marry me, to take me away from 'that monstrous godlike structure where you spend your days and nights'. That was the hospital.

Yet it was more than the hospital he would have to wrest me from; it was this vision and hope and unreachable within reach monster phoenix stirring just beyond the hills of Kowloon. Perhaps that was precisely why Ian persisted. 'You are so many women – who are you?' ... 'You are not a demanding woman,' he said, merely because I kept silent. 'I am more demanding than any woman you will ever know,' I replied.

The end of November, and he was off again. On a great walk, to test himself; for he was now afraid of his own emotions, and also there was Christmas and that meant going back to Singapore, to become the other Ian, father and husband, round the Christmas tree ... 'There will be parties, and they are a must.'

During the next eleven weeks he wrote not a single word.

'He's dropped you.' That was Cherry.

'He's got a girlfriend in Vietnam.' News through some fellow correspondents, kindly relayed to me.

Christmas, New Year and Chinese New Year.* Now I had a small host of Chinese friends. The Chou sisters (three of them) from Peking, with snatches of children; Ada Chung, Miss Ku and Miss Lu, the hospital almoners; the Pans; European and American friends. The Andersons, and among Ian's colleagues the Liebermans (*New York Times*), who threw a large party for Chinese New Year, at which Hank Lieberman wept over China. He had been in China, had interviewed some of the Communist leaders; had been captured by their logic, their reasonableness and charm.

*The Chinese New Year, or lunar first day of the first month, falls three to five weeks later than January 1st.

'Those people were friends . . . we spoke heart to heart off the record . . . now they've betrayed us . . . They're dishonest and I can't bear dishonesty,' said Hank, sweating profusely. In what way had the 'Reds' been dishonest, I asked. It was the United States which had suddenly been seized with phobia. Hank, an excellent newsman, responded to America's current anti-Red obsession, which was to blossom with Senator Joseph McCarthy.

Among the Chinese newsmen were Eric Chou and Liu Pengju, both of the newspaper *Takungpao*. Liu Pengju came from Szechuan; he was a lineal descendant of Liu Pei, emperor of the Western Han dynasty and hero of that fabulous tale, 'The Three Kingdoms',* known almost by heart by everyone in China (including the Szechuan coolies, who sang of Liu Pei and the great strategist his adviser, Chuke Liang, as they staggered under their inhuman loads up the steps of Chungking).

Liu Pengju had the oblong face, the widow's peak, the long-lobed ears of Liu Pei; and he wrote marvellous Chinese (he was a poet) as well as excellent English. We called each other cousin.

Pengju understood me well. 'Wait until the dust settles – your case *might* be complicated.' He was steeped in Chinese history.

Eric Chou was a heavily built northerner, witty and unctuous. He had openly declared himself for the People's Republic. He played bridge and mahjong ably, pointedly told me that, with my past, I would have 'complicated problems' should I return to China. I could not quite make him out until, in 1959, he absconded and 'went over' to the Americans. Perhaps he had a good reason; he had been suspected of playing a double game and was jailed in China for around eighteen months and then released. Eric did a great deal to discourage me. 'People in China don't know you except as the wife of a Kuomintang general.' So did a Mrs Poong, who held tremendously emotional 'born again'

*A.D. 220–80.

meetings condemning atheist China (I attended one of them, and was not enlightened). 'They are investigating everyone. Every intellectual. Many are being killed.' The Communist cadres, said Mrs Poong, were guerrillas from the villages; they did not understand city people, they did not understand the intelligentsia. Everything they could not understand they killed.

Perhaps I should mention here the campaign conducted at the time in Hong Kong to gather 'Red atrocity stories'. Atrocity stories were concocted in Hong Kong. The great shake-ups, which did lead to some true gruesomeness, would come much later, in 1951–2. 'Any atrocities?' was the standard question that newsmen poised at Lowu, the border station on the railway to China, asked of every refugee and Westerner coming out. And an amiable young American had a famous line, used by every reporter when a refugee denied having suffered 'atrocities'. 'Your information is incorrect. I have got quite different info from my sources in Taiwan. And these people wouldn't lie to me. They know who I am. They trust me. You have been tortured.'

In February, my year with Gordon King was almost up; I did not wish to renew it, and neither did he. By now my reputation as a 'Red' was all too forcibly brought into prominence; and the poster of San Mao, seen by my colleagues, had a great deal to do with it. But there was also the fact that Yungmei was losing weight and her appetite, always capricious, was now very poor. I must find a job which had fixed hours; which enabled me to have her out of boarding school and with me, where I could give her more time and care.

To make my departure more certain, a very tragic accident occurred; I was called one night at four in the morning by a British government gynaecologist who asked me to help him in a delivery. I hurried to the operating room to find an appalling situation. The British doctor was reeling about; it was clear that he was drunk; and the woman was dying, with the baby's head still high up, and the doctor had tried forceps. Within two minutes of my arrival the woman was dead. There was nothing to do. The rumour was spread that it was I who had applied the forceps. It was not true. But then the nurse in attendance did not dare to report a British doctor . . .

Gordon, I think, believed me. By then, he knew how many pinpricks, small sabotages of my work, I had had to endure from some of my 'colleagues'. I got a job in the Department of Pathology, under Professor Hou Paochang; undoubtedly with the help of Gordon King.

This job pleased me. It was from nine to five, and I could now find a room and have Yungmei with me, at least at weekends. I already had friends in the Pathology Department, for with the number of cancer cases in the gynaecology wards, I made frequent trips there. There was Dr Lim from Penang, a gifted young man whose hobby was goldfish and passion was beautiful pathology slides. 'Look,' he would whisper, entranced, allowing me to peer through his microscope at the most fascinating landscape of uterine sarcoma or oat-cell carcinoma of lung, or giant-cell cancer of marrow. These monster cells gone amok were there, iridescent in all their magnificent horror. Lim spent hours and days trying the best of various stains upon them and would shout with happiness when he had discovered a particularly effective dye. He would ring me late at night, to come and see a beautiful slide. 'That was your multiple myeloma woman – look at those cells, A-one, man!' As for Professor Hou Paochang, there was ecstasy upon his face as he plunged his hands into a corpse and palpated an unsuspected cancer: 'Ha . . . I've got the bag!' he would say. Bag was his prudish abbreviation of bugger.

Professor Hou Paochang had come from China, which made understanding of our similar hesitancies, dilemmas, and self-questioning immediate, and our relations excellent. He too was waiting for the dust to settle. Educated by missionaries, he was fiercely nationalist, in love with Chinese culture, and deplored its destruction in Hong Kong. 'A great and necessary earthquake', he called the Revolution, but he did not exhibit his opinions, being prudent. He had escaped the mindlessness of some of the more praised English-educated Hong Kong-born, hovering in the no man's land left to them by colonialism. (However, so many of the Hong Kong-born, within the next twenty years, and because of China, were to get out of that state of coma and assume self-assurance and identification with their Chinese roots.) Hou Paochang had seen so much change in so short a time that he needed a space to reflect in, and that was the Pathology Department of Hong Kong University. We both hated colonial subjection, but we were also products of this subjection, and in this duality became supple, flexible, knowing our quandary not havoc; since behind us were many centuries of dilemmas surmounted, upheavals lived through; and fortunately neither he nor I were guilt-complex ridden, despite our respective Christian upbringings. We accepted ourselves, tolerating well the perpetual discomfort of being never entirely right, never entirely true, but in our imperfect way entire and flawless in our faith to our only religion, China.

Hou Paochang and I talked by hints and indirectnesses and stray sentences and long silences left suspended in air; and the silences were the most fruitful part of our dialogue. In the end the Chinese Revolution would make us whole; the new world coming so painfully into being would bring us to assimilate our own internal contradictions. We shambled after its comet process through the years, but also took our time. 'When I go back I shall go with clean hands and a clean heart,' said Hou Paochang one day. And he did.

After some failed attempts on my part to get a room, Ada Chung invited me to stay with her; she had a small flat in the university compound, where she looked after a students' dormitory. I was gratefully with her for some weeks; and then Sheila Anderson came to see me. 'We have a guest room,' she told me, and for a minute sum here was a superb room, with breakfast, and Yungmei could stay at weekends. Such tolerance, generosity, astounded me. For in Hong Kong this was simply not done. Apartheid flourished and was the normal state of society, and Sheila was kicking in the teeth every white woman in Hong Kong by having me (me, a Eurasian, and a woman openly flaunting a liaison with the *Times* correspondent) in her house! 'My dear, aren't you afraid that . . .' said her friends to her, and Sheila, knowing what they meant, would look at the speaker with faint contempt in her soft brown eyes and reply, 'Oh, but Andy and I do enjoy her conversation so much.'

So here we were, in luxury, and Yungmei with me, at least two days a week; and eating better. Professor Hou set me on a study of liver pathology, as well as my keeping all the records of the Pathology Department, and the stipend was a little more than what I had received before, so I could buy Yungmei and myself some new clothes.

Daily I chopped or sliced livers in the morgue, a quiet and businesslike concrete barn with concrete slabs, and there at times would come a young English homosexual much fascinated by death. He would some years later die in a sailors' brawl in Cyprus; but meanwhile he did very good work among the slum children of Hong Kong. The livers we examined were very often gorged with flukes. 'The Cantonese eat raw prawns and raw fish,' said Professor Hou, who liked only northern Chinese food, well-cooked. Like a stream of swimmers the grey-brown parasites came lizarding down when we opened gall bladders and bile ducts and Hou would wade in joyfully with gloved hands shouting, 'Ha, ha'. He was looking for possible cancerous or pre-cancerous changes due to the flukes, since liver cancer was also very prevalent in the fluke-infested regions of south China.

Professor Hou took me walking with him during the lunch hour up and down the ladder streets of Hong Kong; he hovered round Cat Street, tirelessly going from dim shop to dimmer, peering for old pottery and books and painted scrolls. So much, so much of value and beauty was coming out of China and being sold for almost nothing in Hong Kong . . . Hou bought and bought. One day he found a small beige pot and exclaimed, 'Shang ware! So even archaeological finds are coming out!' Into the backs of shops

redolent with incense, amber and garlic he and I would go;
the owners would materialize in the twilight of an inner
room, we would sip tea in sumptuous and fragile porcelain;
from smooth-running drawers would be extracted rare
paintings; out of fragile silk paper deft hands unpacked
statuettes and snuff bottles. We would sigh with happy
surfeit of eye and heart at the sight of it all. Hou knew the
name and story of every famous Chinese painter and their
works, way back to the seventh century. Haloed with
happiness, and laden, we would go back to the Pathology
Department, and me to chopping livers.

From these jaunts I acquired a love and an understanding
of Chinese painting, a shiver and gooseflesh when I saw a
good piece. Hou communicated to me his passion and a little
of his knowledge. The strength of a brush stroke now came
to me, as did the quiver of jade when shape was coaxed out of
its gathered light. Calligraphy entranced me now, and I
understood why, to strengthen wrist and finger, calligraphers plunged their hands in sand and untiringly, back
and forth, pushed their fingers through the gravelly
substance. Knowing the great hunger within Hou Paochang
for his own country, I was not surprised when, upon his
retirement, he took his family and the treasures he had
accumulated in Hong Kong and went back to China. I met
him there in 1963. He was teaching at the Higher Medical
Institute in Peking. 'God damn it, they're way behind in slide
technique,' he muttered. 'Ah, if only little Lim were here,
he'd show them how to prepare slides properly.'

Hou Paochang was given a very fine old-style house in the
western district of Peking. Alas, in 1966 the Cultural
Revolution started and I did not see Hou again. I heard that
his house had been ransacked by some of the more violent
Red Guards. I heard . . . but through those extraordinary
years from 1966 to 1976, when nothing was really what it
seemed, one heard so many things later proved to be untrue.
I asked to see him, but was not allowed to do so. And then I
realized that the time was not a good one for inquiry. Merely
a letter of mine, addressed to a friend who had begged me to

write to him, had caused his death. I protected many of my friends by ignoring them.

So I burrowed, and waited, and tried to find out without placing in physical danger my friends and my relatives. And it was in 1978 that I was finally able to visit the family of my old friend, Professor Hou Paochang.

I went down the lane in Peking to the same beautiful house in which he had lived in 1963. Mrs Hou was there, and though now eighty-six she was still strong and vibrant, and clasped me in her arms, and told me the whole story. 'At last I can tell you. If you had come a year ago, I would still have been too afraid to tell you anything. Nothing was done to us when the Cultural Revolution began because we were protected by the Prime Minister, Chou Enlai. He tried to protect all the scientists, and he knew there were four eminent pathologists in China, of whom my husband was one.

'But in 1967 Premier Chou was himself being attacked, and it was then that Chiang Ching, that wicked woman, sent a band of the youngsters she controlled to "turn up hidden goods" in my son's wing of our house.'

Like all old-fashioned families, Hou Paochang's three sons, and their wives and children, lived with him in the same large house. His eldest son was a scientist of renown, who had spent many years abroad, in America and England. He was, therefore, an ideal target for attack.

'My husband watched his son's quarters being ransacked, his son hauled away to jail . . . he could not understand why all this was happening. And one day he heard that of the other three pathologists he knew, two had committed suicide. His heart gave way and he died of a heart attack.'

The bulk of Hou Paochang's collection was saved, however, by being donated to Peking's national museum. By order of Chou Enlai the museum was closed, and a good many art objects were thus saved.

Another episode; seemingly pointless, but for me fraught with importance: my meeting with Lao Sheh in Hong Kong in November 1950. It was Hou Paochang who arranged this. He asked me to dinner, and he also asked Ian. The only other guest was a short man with glasses and a quiet, smooth, clever face. It was Lao Sheh, China's greatest modern writer.

Born in 1897 of a poor Manchu family in Peking, Lao Sheh showed talent early; but his poverty forced him to become a teacher. He studied English, and in 1924 he was teaching Chinese at the School of Oriental Studies in London, which was then run by a Mr J. F. Johnston, who had been the tutor of the ex-Emperor of China, Puyi.

Lao Sheh became acquainted with many English writers, including Arthur Waley, whom he helped in his translations. By 1958 Lao Sheh had written more than 150 plays, short stories and novels, including the famous *Rickshaw Boy*, which was a best-seller in the United States when it was translated.

In 1949 Lao Sheh was travelling and lecturing in the United States. It was then that Chou Enlai, in Peking, sent him a message through his friend, the playwright Tsao Yu, asking him to return to China. And Lao Sheh immediately set sail, and he was now in Hong Kong, on his way back to China.

I watched Lao Sheh, entranced. I had read him; his style and wit was of Peking, and he was both funny and tender when he evoked the people of the *hutungs*, the small dust lanes that wind entrail-like through the city. His voice was beautiful, a light tenor, and only a Manchu could handle the Chinese language so elegantly. Such pure Pekinese! Almost I forgot Ian, almost said to Lao Sheh, 'I'll go with you, and all the way I shall listen to your voice, and all my childhood is in the sound of the syllables that cast a spell upon me.' Lao Sheh and Hou Paochang talked of Sung dynasty glazes and the perils of translation from English, and the next day Lao Sheh went back to Peking, by a devious route, via Tokyo.

In Peking he was greatly honoured; and unlike some other writers, who suffered from mental block, he went on being creative and prolific, writing plays, and short stories, and essays, and he was at work on a major novel when he died. I would meet him fairly often, when I went back to China, and he would always say something striking, and definite, which would remain, like a vermilion seal, upon the year of our meeting. 'History goes too fast nowadays; it is hard for a writer to have both the solace of distance and the attention of an audience perpetually distracted by new events.' . . . 'I know the past well, the present not so well, but I am still teachable . . .' Always there was a tinge of irony within his gravest pronouncements. The grace of faint sarcasm was his; and his face remained unperturbed behind its large myopic lenses as he said things which, in Chinese, were perfectly outrageous.

It was from his wife, a talented painter that, at last, and only in 1978, I would hear the story of how Lao Sheh died. 'But had you come to me before today, I would not have told you. I would not have opened my mouth. Now, I can speak.' She knew how much pain his death had caused me; and how I had expressed, in China, my strong indignation at the manner of his death.

'It was August 23rd, 1966, and the Cultural Revolution was on; and Lao Sheh wanted to participate. He was always taking part in all the political campaigns. So he went to the Ministry of Culture as usual. But that day was the day that the devil-woman Chiang Ching had picked for an assault upon the Ministry, and Lao Sheh and about thirty other writers and Ministry officials* were made to kneel while in front of them were burnt all the embroidered robes and accoutrements of the Peking opera; a mountain of such apparel was burnt. And the hooligans who were burning them also beat the kneeling people, among them my husband.'

It was not true, she said, that the Red Guards had made Lao Sheh wear an old Manchu robe and crawl round and round. Neither had his house been ransacked. 'Other Red Guards, the good ones, protected our house.' But Lao Sheh was beaten so badly that his wife had to go to fetch him home

*In China many writers, painters and artists also hold administrative and political posts. Lao Sheh held about half a dozen such posts.

from the Ministry that night. 'I found a trishaw to bring him home, at two in the morning.' The next morning, however, although he was bruised all over, Lao Sheh insisted on going out. Two days later his body was found, in the Taiping lake. 'But I do not believe that he killed himself, though everyone says he did. I believe that he was killed,' said his wife to me. 'And now I am demanding justice.'

If I write this today, it is not to justify myself in not going back. There is no justification for pusillanimity, for a certain art of calculating one's chance of survival. I did not have the courage of Hou Paochang and Lao Sheh; yet I too loved China and its people. But I had suffered too much already in Old China,* from the feudalism, the intolerance which was also part of that wonderful people, the other face of its tolerance, humanity and greatness. I did not believe that there would not be recurrences of savagery as I had seen – and endured – in the past. Today in China everyone reads Lao Sheh and speaks with sorrow of his death. At least it has served a purpose; never again must shocking things like that happen in China. Never again. This is the cry of all the people, and that is why I have told here what is no secret. But in my spirit there will always be, like a cigarette burn, a small blackness when I think of Lao Sheh; and I shall always remember the way he looked at me in Hong Kong, bowed and then turned away, as I stared at his sure and certain back, so eager, so young . . .

In early March, with the spring drizzle, came Ian's first letter since late November, and from Saigon. 'My dear, this is to tell you that I love you.' I took the letter with me and climbed the hill and looked at the grey sea with a baleful cloud raining upon it.

'I can never go back to emptiness . . . there is nothing but the happiness of loving you.'

Now that I had won, I did not know what to do with this gift of life, and my hands and arms and body were sore from having clasped so long the black stone of solitude.

*See *Birdless Summer*.

I went back to the Andersons and sat in the living room, in the invading darkness.

'Why are you sitting in the dark?' asked Sheila, coming in with a happy crowd of dogs, Dainty and the Bassenjee, Lotus of the Nile (Sheila had begun rearing Bassenjees, the first to do so in Hong Kong).

'Ian has written. He's coming back.'

'Oh good!' Sheila said emphatically. 'You *must* ask him round as soon as he's here.'

I went out again in the immense night and said to the night the only thing I could say: 'I have survived.'

Spring came with honeyed fingers, cloyed us with sweetness; again the magic of resurrection in that fraudulent and so true marvel, the word, adding weight and colour to unreal substance. Lovely spring, seamed with delight, a dazzle we contrived to think perpetual.

And perhaps the abrupt destruction in that year's end was its final immortality, saving it for ever from disenchantment and corruption. For now, knowing myself slightly better than thirty years ago, I know a weary half-bitterness would inevitably have consumed our passion. I never said we had a future together, only a present.

May was burst of blossom and the swamp of body's juices; the wide sea and the wonder of being so childishly young, Ian at thirty-seven and me at thirty-three. And of course the letters, the letters, twice a day. Never had bird been so bird, nor rose so luminous. Sheathed in clearness, the racing midnight moon cloaked our walks; shifting dawn candled the itinerant seller of beancurd milk with the glance of discovery.

And at the end of May, Ian went back to Singapore, to that Emergency in Malaya which had started in 1948, which was getting worse, which was proof of 'Red aggression' in South East Asia, and was used to justify colonial reoccupation. Hong Kong talked panic talk but went on making money and building, building frenziedly. It was not threatened, and knew it.

In May the post of Casualty Officer at the Queen Mary Hospital fell vacant, and I applied for it. Firstly in order to get back to medical work, and secondly because, as I had been told by my almoner friends (how staunchly these anonymous, cheerful, vital and hardworking women of the Social Welfare Department stuck by me), the job came with a government flat attached to it. A flat. Yungmei to be permanently with me . . . I applied and was accepted. But alas, I was a woman and therefore not eligible for a flat before completing a probationary period of six months; and if I married I forfeited a permanency and the government pension, and possibly also the flat.

I could not stay with Sheila and Andy; they were leaving Hong Kong to retire in Canada. As Casualty Officer, I would have a salary slightly higher than the one I had enjoyed so far, with a regular yearly increase if I went on the 'permanent' list by staying unmarried. I took the job.

June and a Sunday. Balmy weather and Yungmei and I went swimming at Repulse Bay and then had lunch at the Repulse Bay Hotel with Julia and Roy Gabbott. Roy Gabbott was one of my first cases in Casualty. He had come in during the lunch hour while I was munching my luncheon peanuts. 'I've been bitten by a rat,' he said. At the time there was rabies in Hong Kong and Roy wondered whether he should have the injections. We had had accidents with anti-rabies injections, notably with a policeman, who after the third injection had become totally paralysed from the neck down. 'Have a peanut,' I said to Roy. 'You won't get rabies.' Julia was Chinese, an able painter, and we got on well. She had by then two children, and a third was expected.

The beach was littered with orange peel and plastic and families arrayed for the usual snapshot fusillade. As we sat at a table overlooking the bay, eating American fried chicken, someone from the next table bent over: 'Korea, they've started shooting. It's war.'

'Oh no, it can't be,' said Roy mildly.

'Oh yes it is, it's the end of the world. Armageddon.'

If there was a war Ian would have to go. He always went. War wouldn't be war without its correspondents writing it up, in fact *creating* the war for their newspapers, its profile and shape and dimension and reasons or unreasons. Within six days Ian's cable came from Singapore: I am going to Korea.

And so to the airport again, to see him emerge with a few of his colleagues, all in a nonchalant bustle of preoccupied people. Ian detached himself from the crowd, looked at me. 'You're smaller than I remembered.' 'I'm an illusion.' Lame. And then on to his small, cheap, Chinese hotel. 'I could wait for you for five years instead of two,' he said. His wife, apparently, had now fixed a limit of two years. As he told me this his face glowed, he was happy, with a set goal, conquest of time. 'The pillows stink,' I replied, sniffing. 'You'd better lie the other way round.' 'But that's where people put their feet,' said Ian, shocked. 'But they change sheets between two lots of people,' I replied, and he found this so funny he could not stop laughing.

Then it was time to go to Al's place (Al was the most important correspondent of a prestigious American newspaper), where a party for newsmen going to Korea the next day was being held; and it had all the lineaments of a heavy State Department briefing but I did not say so, not knowing the words, only the feel of something ponderous and contrived. I was reading the Chinese *Takungpao* newspaper as well as the English paper, and the enormous difference between the two versions of what went on made me understand why the correspondents now elucubrated and hypothesized and surmised and juggled facts like puzzle pieces. There was an exchange of 'hard' and 'soft' facts and unfacts, and Ian said, 'I simply wag my big long ears.' Al spoke heavily of the dangers of complacency. We returned and a cloud thick as beancurd came to wrap up the evening and it rained a little, and Ian fell asleep suddenly and inexorably; he had not slept much for a week. And then it was dawn.

Dawn, and I thought of Ronsard: 'In the midst of war, in a

century without faith, and among a thousand troubles, is it not great folly to write of love?'

Dawn still star-faint, and the airport, and Ian once again turning to smile his bright, diffident, heartrending smile: 'Take care.'

'You take care. If something happens to you they might turn you into a hero.'

He laughed again and then was gone, and my astonished heart said, 'Well now, that's that. I don't think I'll see him again.'

And for a moment I simply hated him for making me suffer, whether in presence or absence. There would always be a war, I thought, for Ian to go to and me to wait for, and nothing really but this for him, and I would have my paper universe, letters and letters, a verbal crust upon my cake of life.

The prices of gold and rubber soared: fortunes were made. Some wealthy families left Hong Kong for Brazil, Canada or California. Taiwan was protected by the American Seventh Fleet; Hong Kong harbour bristled with men-of-war, grey in the grey heat, embodiment of heat. Contingents of British Tommies, later to go to Korea, arrived to reinforce the Colony's defences. Women were enrolled to make bandages and to practise first aid. Sheila persuaded me and I learnt to drive a truck.

I dreamt of Ian laughing, it was a bird, and someone said, 'You must cage it', but I could not.

In the evening the sun peacocked and pecked at the windows: I took Yungmei out for swims and walks. Two American senators came to dinner with Sheila and spoke with great dash of throwing atom bombs on Peking. Why on Peking? 'Because it's all coming from there.' 'If Korea goes, the whole of the free world will be under the communist boot.' I winced at the jargon, but shadows grew grim and immensely tall, and I was afraid.

So I filled notebooks with recollections; desultorily, not knowing that one day I would use them. I wrote to Ian in my notebooks since I did not have any address; where would one write: care of Korean War? Would we really have a life together? More than ever, I thought it could not be; but that was unfathomed sea, grievous love; and I would always turn away from tragedy, to watch the lilac evening begin a storm.

Casualty work was exactly what I could do. Though looked down upon by the more snobbish housemen in medicine and surgery (because Casualty did not lead to better jobs, it was a dead end), it was for me occasion for my talent in diagnosis. Everything came to Casualty. Rare cases of leprosy, lupus, tetanus, enlarged spleens from long-term malarias, syphilitics, tuberculous meningitis (mostly children, and very common in Hong Kong), accidents and suicides, homicides, fishermen blown up by the dynamite they used for fishing, early cancers and late cancers, pneumonias and jaundices and brain abscesses and the insane. A suicide who had swallowed 180 sewing needles came, was operated on, and then convalesced in the Casualty jail (there were four cells in which would-be suicides were placed, since suicide was a crime in Hong Kong). I had an advanced leukaemia presenting as a swollen knee; a woman of sixty-five without any fever but with a board-hard stomach; I diagnosed her as peritonitis, and though I was jeered at, she was an aseptic peritonitis. She had swallowed an aspirin which had gone through her stomach and lodged outside her intestines. I had a ruptured oesophagus and several ruptured livers and spleens, and a fulminating cancer of the retina (the patient came in with a story of two days of blurred sight; he died nine days later). Everything uncanny, impossible and fantastic came to Casualty. The dressers of Casualty were seasoned men with tremendous experience. We got on splendidly; they knew far more than many young doctors, and they also knew how to save lives. Lysol swallowing, however, was their bugbear: 'If you wash them out, you never know if you're going through the stomach,' they said, and wielded the stomach pump with extreme care. They were cheerful, devoted and immensely courteous to the patients. They *liked* people; and in Casualty we truly did what we could to get bad cases accepted in the wards.

Each time I filled a sheet with the results of my examination and with a tentative diagnosis. Casualty also set simple fractures and was empowered to take X-rays in cases of suspected tuberculosis or suspected bone and head injuries. I also had 'waiting' beds, for doubtful cases, but using these was at times difficult. It depended on the houseman or the medical assistant. At the beginning the houseman deliberately challenged my diagnosis and threw people out whom I had sent in. I sent up to Surgery an acute appendicitis, very typical; the assistant in charge sent the man home with a laxative. The patient died that night. I became very angry and rang up the assistant. He complained to the professor of Surgery, who made a rule that there would be no admissions of patients to the Surgery wards unless the Casualty Officer's diagnosis was checked, in Casualty, by his house surgeon. But this measure, intended to humiliate me, filled me with joy; twenty, thirty times a day I would call for the house surgeon to come down to 'diagnose a case for surgery'; and if he did not come down I filled the corridors of the surgical ward with patients 'waiting for the house surgeon'. Within a week, very quietly, that rule was done away with, and from then onwards, and as I proceeded to discover some very nice cases, I was increasingly accepted. Even Cherry came down one day from the heights of her Department of Internal Medicine to tell me, 'That was clever of you, diagnosing that leukaemia . . .' Within three months my reputation was as 'a medical officer right on the top of the job'.

The Casualty matron was a splendid woman, Mrs Reynolds, from South Africa. I have never seen anyone less apartheid-minded. She invited the dressers and me to tea at her house, and she was heroically patient with the sick crowding in (up to ninety a day).

In another encounter with some department professor known for his bullying methods (my predecessor had resigned from Casualty because of him) I lost my temper, and seizing my pen, wrote a blistering letter, *in red ink*, to the said professor – and was hauled up in front of the Medical Director (government service), who informed me of my crime. It wasn't having made the correct diagnosis, neither was it writing a letter, it was . . . using red ink.

'Don't you realize that in Hong Kong red ink is only to be used by His Excellency the Governor?' said he severely.

'Next time I see HE I'll ask him why,' I replied.

The Director sat back, and then we both laughed.

Summer blazed into August, and it was very hot; one evening I was asked to a small party. The radio was on, but indistinct, and someone turned it off. 'What was it?' 'Oh, something about Korea,' said the man casually. I had no premonition. But the next morning when I came down to breakfast with Yungmei, and Sheila opened the newspaper, she screamed, 'Oh, Suyin!' I took the paper from her and there was the banner headline saying that Ian had been killed; his jeep had blown up on a landmine. He and two other newsmen had died immediately.

I went to work. Mrs Reynolds came and put her arm round my shoulders and the dressers were very subdued. And then, after a while, I did not feel well at all; quietly a young Chinese houseman came down and did my work for me that day, and I went home. Mrs Reynolds gave me a brew of something with opium in it; useful, for I had nervous diarrhoea. I walked back across the heat-dimmed upland, along the stone path we had so often walked together, Ian and I, and the sea was glaucous with indifference. I was back at work the next day. And then Ian's letters started coming from Korea. One by one they came, and though I knew him dead, this protracted counterfeit of his presence blunted my perception of his death. How could he be dead when that most vital paper reality, his writing, the words that were his, were there under my hand? For three weeks they kept on coming, one by one, and by the date I knew when it was the last. And when the last had come and I knew there would be no more, I took my typewriter, put a sheet of paper in it, and began to write *A Many-Splendoured Thing*.

CHAPTER 2

Hong Kong: September 1950 to February 1952

During the weeks and months which followed, while the actual event was still a wound and a blindness, both kindness and cruelty were dealt out to me. Both fed my typewriter; since all I presented to such injury was transient silence, or inept retort, not the significance of precious earth in which my tree of words would grow. Foreign correspondents came back from Korea and took me to lunch, being decent, kind men. And a woman said in a restaurant, 'Too bad some of them won't come back.' Her luminous eyes watched for my wince.

Kindness – heaped and running over or unobtrusive, always healing, came from Sheila, Andy, the Pans, the dressers, the almoners, the Chous; but also from people like Professor Ryde, Chancellor of the University, and Gordon King, who clenched his teeth and came down to Casualty to ask how I was and teetered like a nice clumsy bear and crushed my hand. Cherry came to tell me that she had heard (from her very British friends) that Ian's family had cabled for his body to be disinterred from Korea and sent to Singapore for burial. With the war raging in Korea, this could not be done, and Ian was cremated locally, his ashes then sent southwards.

In my mind an imaginary dialogue: 'Oh, Ian, you so hated aeroplane trips. They could not spare you a posthumous one.'

Ian's reply: 'The Happy Hunting Ground. Your little Ian is in Heaven tonight, wagging his ears and thinking of you.'

'Oh stop it, it's you they're trundling and you know it.' I could not stop laughing. Cherry went away.

Sheila and Andy now left Hong Kong for Canada, and in October sold their house, which had been my asylum, blessed home for many months. Ada Chung surfaced once again and suggested my becoming the living-in matron of a small dormitory for female students of Hong Kong University. The girls were all from Malaya; Malaya did not yet have a medical school, and so the Malayan Chinese sent their children to Hong Kong to study medicine. No salary, but free residence; the only condition: looking after the moral welfare of the inmates. Ada was pious and a widow, and under the double burden of Confucianism and Christianity she stressed how important it was to see that no male hovered around the dormitory after ten at night.

I was matron until March 1951; the absurdity of my position seemed so evident, yet no one commented openly. As keeper of the girls' morals, I was provided with a long list of forbidding regulations. But from the start I assumed that there was no point in making sure that my twelve girls were *virgines intactae*, for the simple reason that they all came from good, conservative Chinese families; that they had their own very sound sense of self-preservation and a great pride; a shrewd lot, collectively supervising each other. They would make quite sure that until their weddings there would be no gossip about them. They knew only too well what disgrace would attend a moment's faltering. And if by chance there was default, there were quiet and discreet ways of becoming a virgin again . . . So what was the use of supervision?

The English matron of the far larger, fatuously luxurious dormitory for women students up the road had a much harder task because she chose to snoop. In addition to the rules which I blissfully ignored, she had a further set of restrictions. She told me how 'rebellious' were her charges, and of the troubles she had.

'How do you keep order, my dear?'

'I treat my students as ladies and they behave as ladies.'

She then reported me to the Chancellor. Ryde asked me to 'drop in', but within minutes we were both laughing.

In February 1951, I became a 'permanent' employee in government service and was allotted, in March, a government flat, to share with another doctor. And as usual hazard, chance – or God – provided me with a sharer in the person of Mary Mostyn, my other friend from the Royal Free Hospital besides Cherry. I had made many entrancing bicycle excursions through the English countryside with Mary; her mother was a Yorkshire woman and fed me most wonderfully. Mary Mostyn, Cherry Heath. Both had decided to come East. I like to think there was, in both of them, a fundamental English romanticism, a spirit of adventure. But I think it was also my being in Hong Kong which decided them. Mary had become a Quaker, and was posted to China in 1949. And she had landed, of all places, in my own province of Szechuan, in Chengtu! But she arrived there only four months before Szechuan was liberated by the Communists. In January 1951 she became part of the exodus of missionaries from China. 'Any atrocities?' was the first question she was asked (as were all other missionaries) when they reached Lowu. But Mary had no atrocities to relate; she described to me the liberation of Chengtu, which she had seen. Like a maelstrom with a notch, it started with jubilation in the streets, millions of people streaming forth, and red flags; narrowing down to her filling in forms in order to get out; and being treated very kindly, for Mary had no racism and was liked by her Chinese colleagues at the hospital where she worked.

Mary had of course met Marian Manly during her stay in Chengtu. Marian Manly continued to run her small midwifery school and hospital where I had worked in 1939 and 1940–1. She and Mary had watched together the rice come in in bags from the countryside to feed the starved city after Liberation, the hoarders compelled to unload their stores at fixed prices; the city dirt cleared, the relief and exhilaration of the populace, the excellent behaviour of the People's Liberation Army.

Liberation was, for Mary, a real and solid thing; but not so for Marian Manly. She looked upon it with anger, with frustration, since it had all happened outside Western missionary effort, and dedicated missionaries like her found themselves suddenly aimless, unwanted. Some of the missionaries like Earl Wilmot, who had very quietly conducted seminars for pro-communist sympathizers under the bland title of studying the Bible, rejoiced, even when they knew they would have to leave. But Marian had put her heart into the small hospital, it was her life, she knew no other . . .

Marian was irritated by the great noise, day and night, the singing, the marching, the drums, and the dancing and the flags. She saw the people she had helped, because they seemed so incapable of anything but disorder, suddenly orderly, with astonishing capacity for discipline and organization and running things themselves. One morning as she came into her class, there, above her desk, on the wall, hung a large picture of Chairman Mao Tsetung. Had she been wise, she would have realized that this was the way her students, who liked her, were complimenting her, identifying her and her teaching with the Revolution. But she did not understand. 'What is this? We don't want any politics here,' she shouted and tore the picture down.

There was, of course, an uproar. There was a meeting; the students, the midwives, the cook, the amahs and even the patients, all collected to discuss the case, and since Marian refused to put up the picture again, they had to call the public security bureau, newly installed. Marian behaved badly, so she had her hands tied with a rope as she was led to the bureau, where she was incarcerated for nearly a week. She then apologized and was released; and she was given an exit visa.

Mary and Marian reached Hong Kong at the same time. I went to see Marian at her hotel; she wept a great deal. 'They're morbid, they're fanatic . . . it's no longer the China I knew.' I felt she had been treated with fairness, considering the insult she had so thoughtlessly dispensed – but she would not agree.

'Look, what would happen to me if I tore down the American flag in an American school or the picture of Jesus in *your* church?'

'That's quite different,' she said.

'No, they've discovered national dignity through Mao,' I replied.

She stared at me and the tears rolled down. 'I've kept all your letters, all of them,' she said. She could not forget that we had collaborated on *Destination Chungking*; and now she felt that I was far from her. I did not speak to her about *A Many-Splendoured Thing*.

Marian wanted to be a writer, assiduously typing short stories, poems, even beginning a novel. But the simplified ghosts she dealt with were declined by publishers, except for one short story, exceedingly romantic, of which I only remember that the heroine was built like a lotus with crimson lips. But Marian had discovered my talent for writing, and we had laboured together on *Destination Chungking*. In the end it had become almost her book, in that she read it out to people, she had elaborated and softened and embroidered the writing until it became a beautiful veil drawn over events too appalling in their reality and in my first draft. I think she did her best, and the times were not for brash-tongued horrors minutely described; America still expected coy and bashful female writing; coyness being regarded as exotic authenticity.

Marian Manly is still alive, and in America, where I saw her in 1965 when I went on my first lecture tour to talk about China. She still will not accept the Chinese Revolution. 'They are pagans . . . nothing they do can be any good.'

But history, whether we like it or not, shrugs off the notions of Good and Evil. Only enduring and success count, alas, for history; and good work well done has an immortality of its own.

Today, in 1978, in my province of Szechuan, in the city of Chengtu, the quality of the teaching which went on there, given by American and other missionaries, is recognized. The midwives trained by Marian Manly hold her memory in affection. I would like to say to her, 'You see, Marian, one must wait. And wait. One cannot compel gratitude, but gratitude and love will come. If only one can wait.'

Mary, Yungmei and I moved into the flat, which was luxurious, with three bedrooms and two bathrooms, a living room and a veranda. Mary Mostyn was provided with a job in the Medical Department. Yungmei now went to day school. I typed at night and worked in Casualty by day. We were going towards summer and the season of suicides (summer by drowning, Lysol swallowing in the winter) and of hatchet wielding. August was the month when they reached the year's high; tempers ran short in the heat and the Cantonese took their choppers to each other. I remember one woman brought in almost exsanguinate, her scalp crisscrossed with dozens of gashes; I gave her a drip and stitched frantically, catching spouting arteries, while two dressers close-cropped her long hair. She did well, and complained bitterly that we had disfigured her by scissoring away her tresses.

Writing was now a frenzy; not solace or opiate, but compulsion, insidious mastery of the white page waiting. As the book grew, I could not bear to be away from it. It became a great joke with all my friends. 'Let her get on with it, at least it makes her happy.' Mary Mostyn, to whom I showed a few pages, thought the style clumsy; Cherry was not interested. Someone else called it verbal diarrhoea. I eschewed all parties. Only the Pulitzer Prize winner, Keyes Beech, back from Korea said, 'The lady can write.'

The book was taking shape. I sent a few pages to Jonathan Cape in London. 'If it's no good, just put it in a drawer and forget it.' I got a contract by return mail and a letter from Jonathan, 'If you can keep it up, I think you have a splendid book,' I got piles from too much sitting on a hard chair, and had to be operated on; it was most painful, but I sat up in the hospital bed on a rubber tyre and went on typing . . . and then, one night in late July, it was done. The next day I was down with 'flu; I ached all over and I was very feverish. But my body had waited until the word END. I thus got further acquainted with its potential, its capacity for slogging. I was very sick for four days and very miserable; and then I was cured.

During these months of work-glut I was not without other troubles. Yungmei caught a cold, was feverish for some two weeks, and then spat blood. I was frantic. For I always remembered that time in England when she had had a primary tuberculous complex; and though I had been assured that she would get over it, I was now frightened that there was a recurrence and a deepening of that initial tuberculous infection. Dr Hsu, the hospital paediatrician – who happened to have been a classmate of mine at Yenching University in Peking in 1933 – examined Yungmei carefully. Nothing untoward appeared on the X-ray. We put Yungmei to rest and on Rimifon, and for almost a year Yungmei, though going to school half a day, was under his care. He pronounced her clear in September, but I remained on watch, uneasy. I would never be free from anxiety about her health. I kept her as much at rest as possible; and at meals stood over her, pushing food into her. She did not have to walk to school but took a bus from door to door. She was entirely off gym or sports, and she grew well, and put on weight. 'Don't worry,' said Dr Hsu, 'she is well, she will get over it.' But I would have Yungmei examined every six months and I weighed her every fortnight.

'What the child needs is stability.' Thus, with pursed lips, some friends. 'But this is what I am working for, dammit, for Yungmei's stability,' I said.

Regularly, and even red-eyed with lack of sleep, I took her on Saturday afternoons to children's parties; with a round of families whom we now frequented. Yungmei was well-adapted to Hong Kong and has kept friends of those days, and still visits them when in Hong Kong. But I think one is inclined to feel more responsible and guilt-ridden if things go wrong with an adopted child than with one's own offspring.

I was also worried about my family in China. I had had no news of my father or of Third Uncle since the summer of 1950, the beginning of the Korean war. Scare stories about China were prolific in Hong Kong. I met a Mrs Yu, a great friend of a friend; Mrs Yu was from Szechuan and had just escaped to Hong Kong, or so I was told. Mrs Yu came to see me one night, greatly agitated, her hair all frizzled and awry, to tell me that Third Uncle was in jail as a counter-revolutionary and would no doubt be executed. She had the news, she said, from her brother, who had a friend who had just escaped from Szechuan. 'And my father?' The corners of her mouth turned down, her hands dropped. Who could tell? 'He must also be in grave danger, I think ... the Communists are killing *all* those who have some property.' She put her hand on her chest, breathing asthmatically with self-induced excitement, and told me of people being beaten to death. When she left (I still remember those short hurrying legs, the buttocks planted so extremely low), I was thoroughly miserable. I wrote to Jonathan to tell him what had happened ...

Reports of purges in China. They were true, and there were purges; the campaign for the suppression of counter-revolutionaries started in December 1950 and it went on through 1951. Certainly nearly a million people must have been either executed or condemned to lifelong jail. There were so many Blueshirts, Kuomintang spies, dope pushers, pimps, bandits, assassins, Secret Society gangsters, black marketeers, heroin dealers ... And then came Land Reform, and gruesome pictures were published in Hong Kong of executions of landlords. I was very disturbed, thinking about my family. The Pans were also worried. 'I have a brother in Peking,' said Francis.

Casualty was a haunt of the British police investigating cases of assault, battery and murder. The Casualty doctors had to give evidence in court. This my predecessors shunned, and for good reason. The doctor's evidence was meant to conform to the police's opinion of the malefactor's crime. I remember one particularly burly British police officer who came in one day dragging a dwarfed, shrunken Chinese man with a face like driftwood from the sea, and insisting that the almost skeletal prisoner had aimed a heavy blow at the policeman's private parts. I was so stupefied that I looked at him open-mouthed; he insisted on my inspecting his genitals for evidence of 'contusion'. In court several days later I denied having found any trace of violence. All such cases made my dressers uneasy. On the one hand, to give evidence against another Chinese, and in a foreign court, was not done; if the man charged was a Secret Society man and the doctor's evidence sent him to jail, the doctor would be 'marked down'. On the other hand, not doing what the British police demanded also brought trouble.

It was with a local police officer that Leonard came to Casualty. Leonard Comber was an Assistant Superintendent in the Special Branch in Malaya, on leave in Hong Kong. The case brought by his colleague in the Hong Kong police was a man with his forehead sliced and an eyelid hanging by just a thread of flesh. I stitched him up; he swore that the wound was due to his inadvertently having fallen out of bed (it was certainly the result of a Secret Society gang fight). Leonard remained when his friend went away with the prisoner, and told me he had just returned from a police course in the United States. The Americans were studying the Emergency in Malaya, and the special methods the British used in preventing the population from helping the jungle guerrillas.

Leonard asked me to dinner at the Peninsula Hotel. He told me about himself. He came from south-east London. His father was a typesetter; his mother, during the Depression in 1929, had scrubbed floors; they had saved and skimped to give Leonard an education. The war had come and Leonard, while soldiering in India as an officer, had learnt Urdu and Hindi; now he studied Cantonese and was learning Mandarin. He had a great talent for languages, and enormous obstinacy. He had joined the Malayan police after the war because he did not wish to return to England; but he wanted, above all, to study languages, to go to university. He wanted to escape the throttling class distinction from which he must have suffered very acutely in England.

I told him very little. What was there to tell? I felt sympathy for him. He had been hurt by the condition of his birth, had struggled and would fight on. I admired that. What could I say? That for so many years, due to Pao, I had been like one dead, and that Ian had come, and I was now alive, and now I would never die in myself again, never again? I don't think he would have understood that I had remained alone and without a man for so many years, until Ian . . . that it had been impossible for me to have sex relations with a man until Ian.

What I did not know then was that this condition of mine, total repugnance for sex, would recur and recur, again and again. Sex would always be impossible unless there was love, a climate of love, a whole world of feeling and tenderness in which the body's act was submerged, necessary and evident. I did not think that Leonard was built that way; for him sex was very definite, a necessity, apart from love. I suppose this is what people call 'normal'.

I listened to Leonard because he did not give me the usual 'we must fight communism' clichés, but spoke intelligently about the Emergency and its injustices. 'We'd really no business to come back to Asia. It will all be over, sooner or later.' His words were flat, but his mind was lucid. 'We promise them independence, then we break our word and try to mess things up so that we have an excuse to stay.' He had seen Partition in India, and its horrors. He was definitely a strong character; everyone, including Mrs Reynolds, liked him. Yungmei liked him very much, and he set out to conquer her. He was at his best, delightful, with children. I think an unplotted, well-meaning conspiracy to make me marry Leonard began then, and among the conspirators I must rank an eminent Jesuit, Father Ladany, of Hong Kong.

It was a few days after Ian's death that Father Ladany had come, tall and dignified and admirably versed in Chinese. In an hour the scholar had entranced me. Owner of uncommon intellect, Ladany spoke with eloquence and restraint. He had humour, zest and knowledge. He suggested a Mass for Ian's soul, and I agreed. Sheila and I attended. Through the months of Yungmei's illness, Ladany had come to see her. 'She is a charming girl, but she has no imagination at all,' he

said. 'You, on the contrary have too much.' It was pleasant
to relax by having an argument or creating one with him.

'Father, I was in my bath and I *think* I've solved the
problem of the Assumption.'

'How, my dear Doctor?'

'Oh no, I haven't, there's a snag.'

'Perhaps another bath,' said Father Ladany, pretending
to sound hopeful.

With him came Father John Turner, a delightful
Irishman, a mystic and poet. I never showed them anything I
wrote, neither did they ask to see; they gave me charm, good
conversation. They were priests and they only wanted my
soul for the Lord God.

When debate on the Fathers of the Church or the
mysteries became wearying, there was Father Turner's Irish
voice, liquid with poetry. But it was Mary Mostyn who
entered the Catholic Church, and then Ladany set out to
convert Yungmei. My turn came indirectly. A reconversion;
yet it was not entire because of that abstemious demon in me,
wary of absolutes, even when I would hunger for the
unshaken bliss of perfect belief. But I could put on a good
show of trying, not for faith, which I never understood, but
for conformity, which I can deal with. And the occasion for
exhibiting conformity would be my marriage with Leonard.

Leonard went back to Malaya and wrote to me: could I come
to Malaya for a few days? This brought up the matter of my
passport, which would expire in January 1952.

I had already worried about its expiry in April 1951. It
would have been easy for me to have it renewed. It was a
diplomatic passport, and through Francis Pan I could have
had renewal by the Kuomintang for another ten years.

But I did not want to go to the Kuomintang. I wanted
nothing to do with Chiang Kaishek. Whatever my
misgivings about what was happening in China, I was not
going back to Chiang Kaishek. And the People's Republic of
China did not issue passports – not to people in Hong Kong,
nor even to Chinese in China. The only way out was to apply

for a British Hong Kong pasport; for which I was eligible, having been more than six years in England and Hong Kong. But here my reputation as a 'Red' (that communist dance poster – my heedless talk!) went against me. I was interrogated at Special Branch by a friendly young man, who asked me many questions, to which I replied candidly. I told him I wanted nothing to do with Chiang Kaishek, and he nodded understandingly.

The weeks went by and then one day I went to lunch again with the Granthams, and Alex bent towards me.

'How is your application for a passport getting on?'

'I don't know, I haven't heard.'

'I'll see to it.'

The next thing was that I had tea with Austin Coates, the son of Eric Coates, who was also a 'government servant' in Hong Kong, in charge of the New Territories. Austin was an art connoisseur, a collector of antiques, and would later write some most enjoyable books.

'My dear, you should have seen the files on you!' His hands curved up and down a pyramid of files. 'A Red, a pro-communist, a fellow traveller! The Special Branch was just going to turn you down when they got a little note, a little note, my dear, from HE himself! About you. What is happening about Dr Han's naturalization? I would like to see it dealt with quickly . . . My dear, Special Branch almost *collapsed* . . .' Austin giggled.

I was again called to Special Branch, and was interviewed by a short, competent man radiating reluctant appreciation.

'Tell me, what do you think of the Chinese communist leadership?'

'I think they are honest, I think the people of China want honesty . . . I think this revolution had to be . . .'

'That is all, thank you.'

I now saw myself stateless, perhaps thrown out of Hong Kong, clutching Yungmei (Yungmei by now stateless as well, since she was not yet twelve, and still on my passport) and getting on a boat to nowhere. One such stateless person had commuted for forty-two days on the boat between Hong

Kong and Macao, denied landing at either end . . . Two
weeks later I heard that my application had been approved.
All due to Alex Grantham's use of red ink.

Now I could go to Malaya for ten days, on a Hong Kong
travel document, because the passport would not come for
some time. 'I'll look after Yungmei,' said Mary, so off I went.
Whisked through customs, driven to Johore Bahru across
the Straits from Singapore to Malaya, I was at once
overwhelmed by the intensity, the effulgence of Malaya's
plant life; every leaf colossal, succulent; a passion of growth,
and no bare rocks anywhere.

I went to Penang and stayed with the parents of one of the
girls who had inhabited my dormitory. The Teo family was
of the wealthiest; but to preserve his good luck Mr Teo had
never moved from the old and rather dilapidated house
where he had begun to make money. There was no
bathroom, and I had to use chamber pots or piss on the
flagstones of the toilet, which slanted to a small runnel. But
there were six enormous cars, Mercedes Benz, Rolls-Royce
and Cadillac, for the family's use, crowding the front courtyard.

Mrs Teo was absolutely delightful. She had a porcelain
complexion because she kept out of the sun, under a parasol;
and she had only one hand. The right one had been severed
by her Indian cook in a fit of anger as she stood over him and
criticized his cooking. He had wielded the hatchet and
slammed it down upon her wrist. Mrs Teo was a typical
Nonya, a felicitous product of centuries of intermarriage
between Chinese and Malay; she wore a *sarong kebaya*, and
spoke Malay, Chinese Techew dialect and English. Her
glazed artificial hand was covered with a white glove. She
was always afraid I had not enough to eat; so whenever I
came in or went out, two maids in the kitchen served me
some delicacy to consume.

Leonard asked me to marry him. I told him that I did not
love him. And that I would marry him because everyone said
Yungmei needed stability, and because it might work out,
but if it did not work out he must let me go.

'Are you still thinking of going to China?' he asked.

'Yes, of course. I'll never give up. But at the moment I might become an error of the Revolution, and there is no point in becoming just a mistake.'

So now I put away those months of love, saffron glory, waking every morning with the taste of hope and joy, sunflower to the sun. Perhaps I felt that I must sober down; in me always contradiction, ambivalence, and of course necessary compromise. How much enchantment can one create? Perhaps it was true I wanted too much . . .

The surprising thing was that I did not think of myself as a writer, even though I had written a book and it was being printed. Both Leonard and I were agreed that I would continue as a doctor in Malaya. I think I did not mention my book to him until after we were married; not subterfuge; I simply did not think of it.

Everyone was elated; Father Ladany, Mary and Cherry, and as for my Chinese friends, the Chous and the Pans, they said, 'If you are sure you will be happy, then of course we are happy.'

Cecilia said, 'Leonard is nice but he is not your type. Ian was your type.' I left quickly, not to break down.

In December I began to plan my wedding, and Mrs Reynolds gave me a beautiful piece of white Chinese satin. Father Turner and Father Ladany would officiate at the ceremony. This time I would have a proper Catholic marriage ceremony and I chose the spot, Our Lady of Lourdes at Pokfulum, a small chapel hidden away, and miles from the city. And since I invited the Granthams, the Public Works Department was busy for days building a road to the chapel so that Their Excellencies' car could drive up.

'There'll only be a few friends,' I told everyone. By the time I had finished inviting my few friends I had 150 persons on the list, and another 100 came along anyway. Now everyone was nice to me, and I basked in this solacing popularity.

Father Ladany insisted that I go to confession, to start clean. So I did; and after days of trying to pray (rather unsuccessfully) I went to an Italian priest. 'Come on, speak up,' said the priest a bit impatiently. But so much had happened since I last was kneeling in that little grotto of a confessional, way back in Peking when I was twelve or thirteen years old and angry because neither animals nor unbaptized babies were allowed in Paradise. I told him I had had lovers.

'Yes, yes,' he said, bending his ear towards me.

'I also got married.'

'Married in church?'

'No, a Chinese civil ceremony . . . it was during the war in China.'

The priest exploded. This was wrong, extremely wrong. How could I marry without the Church? It was a heinous sin.

'Well, I'm getting married again, in Church,' I said and almost added, 'just for the kick of it.'

'You have greatly sinned, so you'll say a whole rosary for penance,' he told me, and muttered absolution.

I rose, and then I knew I was only play-acting, fascinated by the outcome of a few almost theatrical gestures . . . but that's life, when one makes things happen.

We were married on February 1st, 1952, at four in the afternoon. I was given away by the Chancellor of the University, Dr Ryde, sprightly and handsome in a marvellous grey suit. Father John Turner officiated but no one heard a word of his; because a Chinese friend who was a singer had volunteered herself and another friend to sing, and they sang so loudly, their voices filling the church, that Father Turner started shouting, but in vain.

Father Ladany stood quietly on one side, looking powerful and benign. The Granthams came, and almost everyone who was anyone; I had arranged a reception at the Hong Kong Hotel and I spent all the two thousand dollars which I had saved in the last few months, and had seven dollars left in the world. But two days later Yungmei and Leonard and I were on board ship for Singapore.

On the ship, in that porous sleep pricked by the restless

stammer of the sea, I dreamt about Ian for the first time since he had died.

He was alive; he had not died, but he was in a faraway, inaccessible country; a movable Antarctica (distinctly, there was ice, ice that reached inside my chest and fingered my heart); or perhaps it was an unreachable African kingdom with no roads and only high mountains. I did not know how to reach him, and he, he had forgotten me. 'Oh, why then did you pretend to be dead?' I cried at him as an immense emptiness swallowed me whole and I woke sobbing and sore with the bruising inside my chest.

Several times, at intervals of three or four years or so, the dream has recurred. It is always the same and always it hurts because I can never remember that it is a repetition of a dream. I know that whatever I did to exorcize Ian was futile. But did I really try to exorcize him? Through writing a book about him? Was this not too a kind of resurrection, trying to wrest him from the grave in Korea? I do not know the answer to these questions.

One comes to the end of people, to the end of things. There is an end, somewhere. It is when life goes on, opening new doors, new avenues. Even if, in the end, they lead back to that porous sleep which the trains of my childhood, the ships of my youth, sieved with the restless rumour of an onward march.

CHAPTER 3

Malaya: 1952–1954

At the end of March 1952 I knew that I was pregnant and that I was going to have another ectopic rupturing, requiring surgery. That sudden unbearable jab in the belly, that heaviness in the loins, the rhythmic throb above the pubis . . . My second Fallopian tube had burst, and it was just as it had been in 1943 in London, when I had been married to Pao and had my first tubal pregnancy.

By that March I had already started working at the Johore Bahru General Hospital. There was a great dearth of doctors because Johore State was reckoned the most dangerous of all the states of Malaya in the number of ambushes and attacks by jungle guerrillas.

Johore Bahru hospital was immense, spread within acres of rather unkempt shrubland. Its mile-long corridors always saw the few doctors and nurses jogging at a fast clip along their emptiness. They all acquired sore feet, and little supervision was possible through the enormous wards, where voices echoed and the light was cathedral dim. Patients sauntered in and out; families brought baskets of spicy foods to typhoid cases. It killed them off, but it was hopeless to try to forestall the relatives. One ward had become, by night, a gambling hall. I acquired seventy-odd beds to look after, in which lay children with diphtheria, meningitis, beriberi and pneumonia, almost side by side. I also cared for an annexe in which on my first day a woman, bright auburn and screaming with cancer of the pancreas, held hands with a snow-pale girl dying of aplastic anaemia.

Besides the wards there were about a hundred cases to see every morning in outpatients, from eight to twelve. No proper examination was possible. Sometimes the dead remained quietly in bed for a long time before their trespass was accidentally noticed by a nurse on the gallop.

Heroic nurses! Chinese, Indian, Eurasian and some European (at the top of course!). All of them with extraordinary devotion. There were no Malay doctors at the hospital; only six Malay doctors (mostly in private practice) in the whole of Malaya. Nursing was not allowed for Malay women. No woman was allowed to 'touch' a man or to be in his proximity; this was *khalwat*, the law of Islam.

The Malay patient was also a rarity at the hospital. The ordinary Malay lived in the rural areas, the *kampongs*; he did not come to town; he stuck to the *bomo* (magician); the bulk of our patients were, therefore, Chinese and Indian, with an occasional Malay official. Each doctor was on call one night a week for emergencies; pretty soon two of my colleagues left (one from exhaustion, the other felt he was going crazy) and I was on call two nights a week.

Now my belly clanged its alarm. I rang up Dr Pink, the hospital gynaecologist. It was six in the evening and the sun crumpled its gleaming aluminium foil into the Straits of Johore, and suddenly dusk and the sea breeze were there with cool, enchanted fingers. Dr Pink, bespectacled and enthusiastic, rushed in. 'Lass, how do you know?' 'Second time running. I want you to operate.' Pink blushed with pleasure. Mary Mostyn drove back from Singapore. Mary had come with Leonard and me to Malaya, and obtained a job at SATA, the Singapore Anti-Tuberculosis Association. She lived with us, and went across the Causeway to the city every day. I telephoned Leonard, who rushed back and started making us all tense. We went to the hospital, where a Tamil nurse fragrant with smiles prepared me for operation.

I recovered swiftly, and enjoyed as usual the enhanced perception of convalescence, when all small and daily things become unexpected pleasure, gifts of wonder. In the garden of my days those recoveries are like passing a bush of roses, a swoop of fragrance, sudden delight.

As Assistant Superintendent, Special Branch, Johore, Leonard was assigned the top floor of a rather splendid Spanish-type house. It made me aware of Malaya's chequered history of invasion: the Spaniards and the Portuguese had come here. A village near Malacca sheltered the descendants of the conquistadores, speaking old Spanish, living in abject poverty as fishermen, intermarrying into total decay . . . The Chinese had come when their large commercial junks sailed across the Indian Ocean to Africa, to Zanzibar and to Mauritius, trading in rhinoceros horn and elephant tusks, porcelain and silks. The rise of the Spaniards had driven both the Chinese and the Arab merchants from the oceans of Asia; and later the Dutch, the French, the British occupied South East Asia.

Our house had walls of ochre, a red-tiled roof, a patio with a fountain, much gracious ironwork and an enormous living room with hand-painted beams. The windows were large, glassless apertures hewn out of the thick walls, with wooden shutters. On all sides the evening breeze, and at times a storm wind, poured in. The trees of the unhesitant forest advanced upon us in a massive sovereignty of leaf. I never tired of the terrifying ferocity of growth, exacerbation of the living cell, a shout of green in the hum of silence. Jacaranda and banyan and tulip tree, peepul and flame of the forest and so many others, they helped me to recover as I lay reading the history of South East Asia, of the extraordinary old kingdoms, of Singhapura, the Lion City, Singapore. I walked, tasting grass with my feet; hostile, sharp, no velvet sward but an emerald swamp set with a million small vicious spears, and beneath it the bulbous termite mothers, breeding and breeding the white soldier ants that devoured the wood and the books, and reduced houses to a quiet fall of dust.

The Emergency. We lived and breathed it; it penetrated our pores, we chewed it with every mouthful of food. Its formless pervasive threat held gaunt shape in my unquiet mind.

Leonard fed me chicken essence, which came in crates of twelve times twelve jars; gifts, from the local Malayan Chinese shopkeepers, as was the magnificent rattan furniture we had in our living room and sundry other 'gifts'. 'Every Chinese feels insecure; he can become suspect at any

time; he placates with proffering . . . it's traditional.' Not
bribery, of course, just tradition. Special Branch was The
Power of the Emergency. Feasts, by the local Malayan
Chinese Association members to Special Branch; much
jollity (what better way to hide one's fears than under
chortling laughter), enormous quantities of brandy-ginger
ale and stengahs* consumed from sundown to four in the
morning.

And yet so quickly, behind the back of the *orang puteh*, the
white man, bitterness, rancour would surface. 'Emergency
. . . no British, no reoccupation, no emergency . . .' The
'reoccupation', a word used not only by the Malayan
Chinese, but also by the Malays. They uttered it
nonchalantly; threw it with scarce breath upon the intimate
air.

To our house came a stream of people; a small party
would mean at least a hundred guests, if not two hundred.
Singapore University historians and professors and
economists; Malayan Civil Service officials brimming with
Brahminic condescension; Chinese scholars, Chinese
businessmen; and later students and schoolchildren.

I remember such parties, introduction to the land, as a
blur of lights, a hum of talk, the gurgle of drink from an
enormous punch bowl into which I would keep pouring
bottles of gin or brandy, in which floated fresh pineapple in
chunks, and mangosteens and rambutan. And the talk, so
much of it sieved, sifted, discarded, search for the bright
nugget, a sudden illumination.

Parties. With the University of Singapore élite; the
professors, the lecturers; British expatriates, and some with
great talent. Echoes of England, and good music, the classics
streaming out incongruously under the jacaranda, and
Chinese ayahs distributing plates of cold cuts and salad, and
the perfume of frangipani which went unheeded among the
talk of new books and shows in London; and then all of a
sudden of course the Emergency, and raised voices and

---

*Stengah: whisky and soda on ice.

arguments, and bad temper almost surfacing until talk turned to Siamese cats and their ways . . .

Parties. With Special Branch. Much bonhomie, and here there was fried rice and other dishes dubbed Malayan (in reality Chinese), and oh, how smoothly the liquor flowed, and how efficient once again the services of those silent white-clad ones, the Chinese servants (and many of them the ears of the jungle, perhaps). And here again the Emergency, a theme repeated strenuously, unendingly, the speakers wishing to convince themselves, almost, or perhaps they were convinced and this was their effort at converting me? 'The Malay is a good chap . . . he's happy and loyal, and he's satisfied with what he's got . . . the Chinese . . . they're untrustworthy and treacherous . . .' Round these words glided the Chinese servants. Special Branch was there, was necessary, to protect the good people against the bad ones, to stop South East Asia being overrun by communism. It was so simple.

Somerset Maugham nights, sensuous, velvet, tropical, with that small stir of darkness and silence; and the human voices, pathetic for all their assertiveness. And lurking in the darkness beyond the gardens the Malay police, on guard, watching, lest the silence turn suddenly into dangerous ambush and the liquor into blood.

In those years in Malaya I was to learn all the Malayas, the British, the Chinese and the Malay, and this through the Emergency. I read, and I travelled, and above all I met people. People, people, a never-ending procession of people. I went up to Kuala Lumpur, the capital of Malaya, to see the man whose reputation in South East Asia then equalled that of General MacArthur before President Truman fired him. General Gerald Templar was a professional military man, doing a job in the only way he knew; and of course for him the Emergency had to be simply the Goodies versus the Baddies; but he knew better, knew that the social order must change, and said so.

I went down to Malacca to visit the *Baba* Chinese, for here the Chinese had established themselves since the fifteenth century, and had intermarried with the Malays. I saw the venerable Tan Chenlock, older statesman, descendant of many generations of Chinese settled in Malaya; who spoke Malay and no Chinese but was proud of his Chinese ancestry and kept his old and lovely house filled with Ming furniture and priceless porcelain. I heard his mellow bitterness regarding the 'reoccupation by the British' and the unfairness of what was now being done to the Chinese in Malaya.

I went down to the Malay *kampongs* to visit Hajji Ma,* a Chinese Muslim. 'The only way is intermarriage,' he said. I would sally forth whenever I could along the tarmac roads which gashed the broccoli jungles. Large cars with protruding guns would whizz by, for it was considered unsafe to dawdle; and no rubber planter or Special Branch officer went at less than seventy miles per hour.

It was the Japanese conquest of Malaya in 1942 which spurred national independence. The white man's myth of invincibility was shattered by the Japanese victories.

The Japanese favoured the Malays, recruiting them for police and militia work in order to suppress the restive Chinese population of Malaya and of Singapore. The Malay sultans, the aristocracy, and the Malay bureaucracy, which had been created in the 1930s by the British, collaborated with the Japanese. It was the Chinese who formed the battalions and fought rearguard actions and died while the British made a getaway from Singapore; who would organize jungle guerrillas and jungle bases, swooping on Japanese garrisons, ambushing convoys.† A Malayan People's Liberation Army, which was communist-inspired (as were many groups of resistance both in Asia and Europe

---

Hajji: honorific title in Arabic denoting a man who has made the pilgrimage to Mecca.

†Spencer Chapman's splendid book, *The Jungle is Neutral* (Chatto and Windus, London, 1949) details the courage and heroism of the jungle guerrillas.

during the Second World War), was created; the bulk of its members were Chinese, although there were some Malays and Indians and Eurasians among them. When Japan was defeated the contingents of this army paraded in Singapore's victory march, and their leader, Chen Ping, received the OBE in 1945.

But the British military administration which took over in 1946 at the end of the war had orders to restore the colonial status quo, albeit in another form. 'They did a great deal to wipe out the first enthusiasm with which they were greeted,' a historian commented. It was inevitable that the returning British should do precisely what the Japanese had done: lean heavily on the Malay police and militia trained by the Japanese. Former jungle guerrilla leaders were systematically arrested and jailed.

A scheme called Malayan Union, which would have resulted in direct rule by the British, failed when massive demonstrations by the Malays took place, showing very clearly their desire for independence. Another scheme was now set up which was unfair to the Chinese element of the population, for by 1947 the West feared that not only China but also Indonesia and other South East Asian ex-colonies would become communist or communist-influenced. The spectre of a Red China utilizing the Chinese in South East Asia as its advance guard for conquest was the catalyst in the creation of this new plan.

The scheme was based on two assumptions; the first that the Malays were the true 'sons of the soil' whereas the Chinese were 'outsiders'. The second was that in order to counterbalance the economic power of the Chinese, legal power must be given to the Malays; in other words, the administrative posts throughout Malaya would be reserved to Malays.

This caused great protest from the Chinese in Malaya; the Malays had come into Malaya – as they themselves averred – around the eleventh century, from Yunnan province in China; and the Chinese had made their first settlements three centuries later. But the bulk of the Chinese had come in the nineteenth and early twentieth centuries, with the development of tin and rubber in Malaya. They had become workers, rubber tappers and traders. Some of them had indeed accumulated vast wealth, but the majority remained smallholders, shopkeepers, repair-shop owners and small manufacturers. As for the Malays, apart from the aristocracy, the bulk of the population were farmers in the *kampongs*, their rice production at a primitive level.

According to the 'sons of the soil' theory, citizenship would be automatically granted to the Malay in a new Federation of Malaya, whereas this would not be automatic for the Chinese. Yet around 20 per cent of the Malays in Malaya had come from Indonesia or other Islamic or Arab countries within the last three decades, and were not born in Malaya. Thus the citizenship criteria became appurtenance to Islam and to the Malay culture rather than strictly the 'sons of the soil' theory. But, ran the argument, the Malay had 'no other home', whereas for the Chinese, their spiritual home would remain China. The counter-argument was: How do you want the Chinese to become loyal citizens of Malaya when you start by racially discriminating against them?

According to the citizenship regulations now drawn up, the Chinese could not become citizens unless they could give proof that both their parents were born in Malaya, that they were of 'good character' and intended to reside permanently in Malaya. In addition, they must have an adequate knowledge of Malay. No such adequate knowledge was asked of any British resident in Malaya, who acquired Malayan citizenship easily, and was even able to hold two passports, one British, the other Malayan, for a considerable time.

By 1950 the population composition of Malaya, together with Singapore, was 41 per cent Malays, 44 per cent Chinese, and 15 per cent Indians, Eurasians and others.

Without Singapore – with its almost 80 per cent Chinese – the percentages were 45 per cent Malays, 38 per cent Chinese, and 17 per cent 'others'. English administrators calculated loudly the results of such rigged citizenship. Of the one and a half million Chinese in Malaya, about 375,000 would be automatically eligible for citizenship were the rules stringently enforced; the others would have to show proof before being granted citizenship, and a good many would become suddenly stateless; in danger of being thrown out or placed in concentration camps, behind barbed wire.

The effectiveness of this scheme for debarring the Chinese from citizenship is all the more remarkable when one recollects that no identity cards had existed in colonial days; and that many of the Chinese in Malaya had mothers born in China. By custom the Chinese continued right up to the Japanese invasion of 1941 to send for brides from China, for until the mid-1930s, the British colonial policy admitted very few Chinese women to Malaya; only man-labour was wanted. Hence few Chinese could prove that both their parents were born in Malaya.

'If we left, there would be a bloodbath,' said the British. There had been racial clashes, in 1945 and 1946; in 1948, the Malayan Communist Party committed the grievous crime of executing some police officers in reprisal for mopping-up operations practised by the now British-led, erstwhile Japanese-trained Malay police, against former guerrilla leaders. And so the Emergency began. It would justify the suspending of all rights, giving the police (Special Branch) total power to arrest, search, detain anyone without trial and indefinitely, to disband all trade unions, arrest trade unionists, ban demonstrations, mete out the death sentence for 'possession of dangerous weapons', which included school penknives, to apply censorship in all its forms, to impose curfews, to shoot suspects on sight.

The division between the races was increased by the Emergency, becoming almost total through the 'resettlement of Chinese squatters', known as the Briggs Plan. This purported to remove Chinese 'squatters' (which meant smallholders cultivating vegetable plots and rearing pigs) from certain areas so that neither food nor recruits would be accessible to the guerrillas who had returned to the jungle.

Whole villages, in some cases villages established for a century or more, in which Malays and Chinese had lived peacefully together, were now sundered, the Chinese taken away and put in 'new villages' behind barbed wire. Over half a million people were thus removed from their fields, market gardens and the vicinity of small towns.

I started my knowledge of Malaya with rubber. A pullulation of rubber; all the roads lined with rubber trees, a landscape of broccoli monotony displacing the jungle, soaked in perpetual shadow, buzzing with stinging insects, all the way up Malaya, rubber trees. There was a boom in rubber owing to the Korean war. Rubber was a big dollar earner, and this paid for the Emergency. With Chinese farmers removed from their fields and market gardens, the cost of food and meat had shot up; but the income from rubber allowed for purchasing food from outside. Luckily the trade unions were not operative and rubber tappers could not protest at their wages.

I visited the Dunlop Rubber Estates. The manager was personable and articulate, with a charming wife. They made me warmly welcome. I do not subscribe to stories of whisky-swilling rubber planters; most of them are sober, able, hardworking, and stengahs at sundown is an important ceremony, solemn like saluting the flag. The Dunlop manager did not conceal the fact that the whole point of the Emergency was 'to keep our vested interests in Malaya'. Independence would be handed to those who would protect and guarantee those interests. I watched the rubber tappers, stray ghosts and silent in the milky jungle of trees as they went from trunk to trunk, slicing the bark with their curved knives, and latex, the white blood, dripping into the tin cups.

Dunlop Estates built neat huts (behind barbed wire, to protect their tappers). They showed me a nursery for toddlers: an edentulous Tamil woman surrounded by about twenty small children sitting under a tree. 'The weather does not bother them; they're used to it.' There was even a small clinic, visited once a fortnight by a government nurse. Eighty per cent of the rubber tappers were Chinese, twenty per cent Tamil (southern) Indian. 'The Malay is lazy . . . when he's been paid he just disappears until he's spent his money . . . The Chinese are the best workers . . .' The Rubber Institute issued a pamphlet; with more efficient planting, double the latex could be produced, and the years needed for the maturing of rubber trees could also be shortened. Rubber was King, was Romance, was Wealth.

Dunlop was a good firm, thorough and treating the tappers well. Though there were patrols of Malay police, they were not allowed to ill-treat and to rob the rubber tappers, as happened in other plantations I saw, where the tappers' huts were appalling; where there was no clean water to drink.

I stayed for a short time with a Chinese rubber tapper, a patient of mine, on a small plantation near Johore Bahru. The family rose at three in the morning; three of the five children went with their parents into the darkness of rubber, their heads shrouded in black cloth to ward off the myriad stinging mosquitoes. They ran from tree to tree; two hundred, three hundred trees . . . the tapper was paid by the load of latex he tapped; and there was a rush to bring it around to the factory in pails; rain spoilt it, as did too much lingering; he had to use his children and his wife to help him. After that the children went to school, 'but they don't learn very much'. Of course not; they were tired out. I had so many exhausted children to see in those years. 'Give him an injection, Doctor, so that he can work tomorrow,' implored the mothers.

Up to Kuala Lumpur to listen to the aristocratic Unku Aziz, a Malay economist trained in England. 'Eighty per cent of the rubber in Malaya belongs to the British, not to the Chinese; 10 per cent is in small plantations belonging to individual Malay tappers, whose trees are old, and who have no means of replacing them.' Unku Aziz had taken up the cause of the rural Malay. 'The economic power of Malaya is in the hands of the British. But the Chinese hold the web of the trade; the fabric of the cities. The Malayan Communist Party has not analysed the Malayan revolution properly. It cannot be achieved without the Malay peasantry.'

Tin. Mined in Malaya for almost four hundred years, and first by the Chinese, Malay's tin is the purest in the world, 99·9 per cent pure after furnacing. In the nineteenth century, when the British first came, two-thirds of the tin mines then open were in Chinese hands; the profits were shared with the Malay sultans. By 1950, 80 per cent of the tin produced was from British mines.

I walked round tin mines; saw the gravelly hills of an excoriated land, dropping to a lake in its middle; buckets hauling out the soil, dredges working with great raucous screams. I visited the small, derelict mines of private owners for sale . . . they could not compete against the big companies. Here again all workers were Chinese, some Indian; no Malay workers in the tin mines.

I was taken to see a 'new village' by no less a person than the man in charge of resettlement. Mr Winslow was tall, imbued with the importance of his task. At first there had been a bit of trouble in Johore because people had been dumped in cleared jungle spots without food, shelter, clothing . . . but now everything was provided for them, said he. It took us four hours by jeep to get to the new settlement. The dirt road was a new red gash across jungle. There, at the edge of a fetid mangrove swamp, between the thrusting mangrove spikes like a field of spears for miles, the jungle rearing its sombre menace behind and the barbed wire manned by a police post, was the 'new village', spreading itself into the swamp. Four hundred beings, including children, huddled there; foot-deep in brackish mud. There were some atap* huts with rusty zinc roofs, obviously brought from elsewhere. I shall never forget the pale and puffy faces: beriberi, or the ulcers on their legs. Their skin had the hue of the swamp. They stank. There was no clean

---

*Atap: palm leaf used in making local huts.

water anywhere. Mr Winslow, standing on a box (brought with him in the jeep to keep his shoes from slithering in the mud during the talk), admonished them sternly in Malay; a Chinese interpreter translated in Techew dialect. The villagers had been guilty of passing food to 'bandits' and so they had been transported here. Now they must work hard to redeem themselves. 'What will they work at?' I asked. Expansively Mr Winslow gestured, showing the swamp and the jungle. 'They'll find something, they always do . . .' I tormented him on the way back with questions of food supplies, medical care for the four hundred grovelling on that lick of mud . . . I drove to other 'new villages' and after a while I established a weekly medical visit to one village, behind barbed wire, not too far away from Johore Bahru.

'Do go and see how happy the Malays are . . . they may be poor but look at their smiles!' A pair of nice British liberals; young civil servant with good taste, young wife doing tie and dye work, collecting Malay silverware. I went off in my miniature Fiat to Kelantan, to the north, where the population is almost totally Malay. I walked along the Beach of Passionate Love in Kota Bahru, nicknamed locally the Beach of Passionate Flies because of their enormous numbers. Here the Japanese had landed in Malaya in 1942 and had been welcomed most enthusiastically by the Malay population.

Now I was not driving through the infernal monotony of rubber plantations but through the Malay *kampongs* with their unkempt rice fields and limp, dying rubber trees and patches of jungle, and I was appalled. Appalled at the beautiful big-eyed children and their lassitude, their thin legs and the ulcers; the pallor of listless women, the obvious evidence of tuberculosis and hookworm and malnutrition . . . . True, they smiled; true they were charming, and hospitable, and infinitely courteous. I fell in love, in love with the Malay people, but I was ashamed because I knew they distilled pathetic helplessness, and it is so easy to love pathetic, helpless people. I could have wished them less lovable, more vigorous; self-centred and busy and uncaring, like the Chinese. This clutching at the compassionate heart . . . how shaming for the compassionate. Beguiling, mild and half-starved . . . and within them the converse fury, ferocity, fuelled by religion – Holy War.

Indeed, the Malay peasant was much worse off than the Chinese; even the Chinese behind the barbed wire of the 'new villages', for by dint of extraordinary courage and survival techniques, and also that efficient collective help of Chinese communities in which every person in times of stress is looked after, within a few years, a good few – not all – of the 'new villages' had become livable. With shops and markets; better off than the hopeless, charming, rural *kampongs* I went through with their markets at night selling such few, poor things. I saw the Malay fishermen in their bowed *prahus*, and the catch they brought back, sold for so pitifully little, grabbed by peremptory middle men, and those middle men Chinese. No wonder, no wonder it could be said that the Chinese exploited the Malays, as in Africa the Indian middle men were resented for exploiting the Africans. But the real overlord, the Great Beneficiary, his face was not seen.

I called on Dr Burhanuddin. He was an Arab, a Koranic scholar, and astonishingly influential because all of Islam was astir with a new definition of religion from Cairo. And in Cairo was the El-Hazar University, perhaps one of the oldest universities in the world, the legitimate fountainhead of Islamic thought and the mainstay of the creed.

Dr Burhanuddin was not only preoccupied with religious concepts. He was also very aware of the social and economic problems of Malaya. 'There is nothing more strenuous or less rewarding than the growing of rice paddi.' The Malay peasants had been 'protected', their land being reserved for them for paddi planting by the British colonial power. 'They were not deprived of land, as happened in the industrial revolution of Europe, and driven to the factories. But nothing was done for them. They have no machinery, no fertilizers, no scientific know-how. The Malay peasant is imprisoned in his feudal village, under his landlord, in his deprivation . . .' I had a good look at the Malay rice fields. How uneven, how stray the planting, how inefficient the cropping and harvesting; and in the end only enough for subsistence, not enough to enrich the peasant. 'But they don't want to grow more,' a British university lecturer in agronomics had told me loftily. 'The Malay doesn't know thrift, not like the Chinese. That's why he has to be protected.' And protection, said Burhanuddin, was the root cause of the inability of the *bumiputra* ('son of the soil') to compete in his own land.

Nik Kamil, handsome, intelligent, educated in England and then at the special college for aristocratic Malay administrators, invited me to a marvellous dinner in Kota Bahru. 'We have no racial feelings against the Chinese . . . if all Chinese became Muslims, there would be no problem in Malaya.' This I have come to believe was true. Islam barred intermarriage on religious, not racial grounds, and the only way out was intermarriage. I would meet so many Malay families who had adopted Chinese children, girls especially; so many Malays proud of having a Chinese mother. Not race, but religion was the barrier between the races. But the set-up of the Federation, based on racial discrimination, made even Islamic conversion well-nigh impossible for the Chinese.

The Federation of Malaya, today renamed Malaysia, is still based on the powers of Special Branch, on the Emergency. The Internal Security Act, which allows arbitrary imprisonment without trial, has been retained. But the fundamental problem of the *bumiputra* also remains. Despite many schemes devised to create a class of Malay urban entrepreneurs by forcing all business companies investing in Malaya to have Malay participation, to nominate Malay directors and managerial staff, the *bumiputra* in the rural *kampongs* do not get their fair share of the wealth, and the gap between city prosperity and countryside poverty still exists. Therefore a smouldering Emergency goes on. But the composition of the forces which oppose the present establishment has changed. It is now chiefly Malay. A rising of famished Malay peasants took place in 1975 and again in 1976. In one instance, when the Malay peasantry demonstrated in protest because they were starving, they were tear-gassed by the Malay police.

I am glad that, willy-nilly, I became involved so early in this complex story, not through any love of politics, but because this was the very stuff of the air which I breathed. For me it was an unshrouding, divesting me of thinking only in terms of China; making me aware of so many other cultures and peoples, and opening another door to bring me towards a certain universality.

Trivia also helped: Leonard had to resign from his English swimming club because I was not allowed to dip in the pool with him (colour bar). Other pinpricks; the hallmarks of an era now gone. But these small practices freed me totally into the new world of South East Asia. A world which enriched me with love and knowledge and indignation; with fury and delight.

The Emergency also affected my plans for Yungmei's schooling. There were Malay schools, Chinese schools and English schools in Malaya, and in Singapore. There were three times as many children in Chinese schools as in English schools; but the Chinese schools had many problems. They were regarded as the hotbeds of communist infiltration; and Special Branch swooped upon them regularly. In the years to come I was instrumental in saving a handful at least of young adolescents from arbitrary detention and three to five years in concentration camps. The Chinese schools were in general not government subsidized as were English and Malay schools, but funded by the Chinese community clubs, associations and chambers of commerce. The overseas Chinese of South East Asia also built and funded universities in China for their children's higher education. This pattern was accepted until, in 1949, China became 'Red', and all intercourse with China was considered a legal offence and a crime. Youngsters going to China were refused re-entry to

Malaya. A witch-hunt began against graduates of Chinese universities who had become teachers in the Chinese-language primary and middle schools of Malaya and of Singapore. Many of them were deprived of a living for suspected sympathy with China. Anyone possessing books or magazines from China was liable to be automatically detained, without trial, under the Emergency regulations enforced, and for a minimum of two years. Regularly, during my eleven years in Malaya, I would have books seized and destroyed by Special Branch. Such books as *Red Star Over China*, by Edgar Snow, were considered subversive.

Malay schools catered only for Malay children, and all of them were religious schools, where the pupils chanted the Koran, in Arabic, and went on chanting it for many years. Most of the Malay *kampong* children never reached any higher educational level; but those who did came from aristocratic families and attended English schools. Some of the Malays who had strong Arab ties went to Cairo, to El-Hazar University, and others went to London to study, usually law.

Obviously, it was dangerous for Yungmei to go to a Chinese school, and impossible to go to a Malay school.

I sent her to an English convent school, but I provided, as I had done in Hong Kong, a Chinese tutor three times a week. In the English schools eight out of ten of the teachers were Chinese (English-educated) and 80 per cent of the schoolchildren were Chinese, the rest Indian and Eurasian, with a sprinkling of Malay girls from the nobility. The teaching in these English schools at the time was colonial; it bore no relation to what really happened in Malaya, or in any other part of Asia. But at home there was constant and ardent argument, a stream of disputation, every problem was debated aloud, and I was giving Yungmei a double education. Yungmei's Chinese tutor was an excellent man, headmaster of a small Chinese school, who taught and spoke good standard Chinese. Of course, this did not go without demur from Yungmei. 'It's too difficult . . . others don't study Chinese.' 'People who only know one language are one-eyed,' I retorted, and told her how long, how bitterly I had striven to educate myself, and succeeded. If Yungmei today is not alienated when she goes back to China, it is due to the teaching she had in Malaya.

'I must tell her she is adopted.' The Singapore Anti-Tuberculosis Association, with its team of able doctors, pronounced her totally well. This was the right time . . . but still I hesitated. It seemed to me that I loved her so much, that she *was* my daughter, no one else's . . . our lives had been so unsettled, yet so much together . . . was it right to disturb her now? And in China we did not tell children they were adopted; it was not supposed to be traumatic for the child not to know, on the contrary . . . I gave myself reasons, and kept pushing away, day after day . . . adoption meant more, not less loving, she must know that I cared.

Yungmei was converted to Catholicism and duly baptized. For a while our house was covered in religious pictures; they blossomed even in the bathrooms. But this fervour ended as suddenly as it had begun. One of the nuns at the school, speaking against the heinous sin of family planning in the catechism and morality course, argued that 'God will send a plague, or a war, if there are too many people'. This upset Yungmei. Another item which made her less fervent was the problem of babies. Yungmei came back one day to tell me that I had lied in telling her that babies came from their mothers' bellies. The Mother Superior had told her they were found at the foot of trees . . . But abruptly a Malay schoolmate of Yungmei's age, thirteen, was withdrawn from school. 'Fatimah's gone to have a baby. She'll come back when the baby is born.' Fatimah was a high-born Malay, so the nuns did not say anything. Yungmei was convinced by Fatimah's rounded belly. But the fact that at twelve she had preferred authoritarian conviction to cold reasoning worried me. I realized she would always be far more trustful, and therefore vulnerable, than I had ever been.

A Many-Splendoured Thing would come out in England in
May 1952. Jonathan Cape wrote to me; he seemed worried
about the way it would be reviewed; and certainly a great
deal of hostility was exhibited against it. Chief among the
critics were *The Times*, of course, and the *Observer*. A
correspondent of some fame who had been Ian's great friend
felt my book destroyed a myth he had propagated about Ian;
devoted to his family, happy with things as they were. He felt
it bad for Ian's children. 'I have done what all writers do,
write about their love and praise it,' I said. Of course it was
'bad', but I did not claim to be 'good'. Leonard was superb.
He suggested that Jonathan ask Malcolm MacDonald, at
the time High Commissioner for South East Asia, to write a
foreword. Jonathan did write to Malcolm, and he accepted
and sent a foreword to Cape's for the second edition. (The
first had sold out much too rapidly . . . 'Every third woman I
see on the London buses is carrying your book under her
arm,' wrote Jonathan. And this despite the adverse reviews.)

Copies now began to circulate in Singapore and a swell of
protest arose. At least a dozen persons appealed to Malcolm.
He must not write a foreword! It was an insult, not only to
Ian, but to all the British in Singapore.

Malcolm wrote a little note asking me to go to see him. I
drove to Bukit Serene, one of the Sultan of Johore's
residences, where Malcolm lived. It was on a small hillock
just outside town, sloped with green sward, seemingly true
English sward, kept so by the feverish weeding of at least a
score of women and the scythes of another score of men. For
here the grass grew visibly, audibly, by the inch during the
day.

Bukit Serene looked like a Walt Disney fantasy castle with
turrets and cupolas and marble terraces and shimmering
green-tiled roofs and pink-hued walls. Malcolm had
redecorated its splendid marbled interior with glassed-in
cabinets containing his collection of Chinese porcelain and
ceramics. He would give away 430 priceless pieces to
Durham University when he returned to England. I sat in the
living room and Malcolm came in, an unassuming, short

man with a nice smile and a soft voice. Perhaps wrongly, said he, he had been told that the book was about Ian Morrison.

'It is, it's about Ian and me.' He looked at me, and a smile began. I said, 'You can take back your foreword if you want to.'

'Not on your life,' said Malcolm, 'it's a splendid book. I wish someone would write a book like that about me.'

From that day onwards Malcolm and I were friends: having a deep and undemanding friendship and trust. As the years went by I appreciated his talents and skills more and more, even when we were on opposite sides of an argument. Only Premier Chou Enlai, among the men I have known (and I have known many ambassadors, diplomats, politicians and statesmen), surpassed Malcolm in a certain winning patience and a quality of serene, cold thought in the midst of conflict and controversy. Like Chou Enlai Malcolm could grasp swiftly the small middle ground which could be enlarged into something like agreement. The two men were similar also in a reasonableness of exposition which rallied even the hostile; and in a certain gift for life, a liveliness and humour, a grin and dash about them, the illumination of an unforgotten, minute detail ignored by everyone else.

Malcolm certainly did not have Chou Enlai's immense stature or his ideological dedication to a cause; but he is the same kind of person in a different environment. Malcolm was committed to the England he knew, and served her well, and was not appreciated as he ought to have been, because he fought steadfastly against stupidity, pig-headedness, intolerance, but somehow these always prevail when it comes to distributing the rewards. Both Chou Enlai and Malcolm had an incredible capacity for work; Chou even more than Malcolm. Both made themselves instantly available to ordinary people; but Chou Enlai went on growing and his work is of great significance in history. Malcolm's task was to liquidate the British Empire with the least amount of trauma, keeping a British foothold, British interests and the Commonwealth. And this, too, has its importance.

Malcolm created liaison committees between races in Malaya, worked against both British diehards and native diehards. 'You make even neo-colonialism palatable, Malcolm,' I would say, teasing him, and his eyes would be a little sad. He was staunchly anti-communist, but was accused of being soft on communism because he was not rabid. Special Branch hated him; the Malayan Civil Service diehards gossiped about him; later, in Kenya, Malcolm would again bring harmony and conciliation in an explosive situation. He would be the first to break down the colour bar, to invite Africans as equals to places reserved for whites only.

In Malaya Malcolm was accused of 'placation' and 'compromise' and 'selling-out', not only by rabid Englishmen, but by even more rabid Americans. One of them, a newspaper correspondent with some literary pretensions, even purported to see *my* influence in the 'disastrous' decisions Malcolm took to hasten independence in Malaya and in Singapore. And the fact that he had so many Chinese friends, that he turned somersaults in the streets, stood on his head at parties, was anathema to this 'serious' American (who was enthusiastically pro-McCarthy). 'If we can make it stick another ten, fifteen years here in Malaya we'll be all right,' said Malcolm. 'I don't want to see a mess of blood here, as at the Partition of India.' Where the mess of blood was concerned, Malcolm was, alas, quite right, and so, despite the injustice, I would understand and admire his view and actions.

By the end of summer 1952 *A Many-Splendoured Thing* was a best-seller in England. I was involved in Malaya, in hospital work, in so many things, I did not even want to read the reviews. I received many most joyful fan letters. Young lovers wrote to thank me, old people too. A pair of crofters from the north of Scotland, seventy-four years old, wrote, 'That's still the way we feel about each other . . .' Lansdowne, who has become a most famous painter of birds, sent me his first kingfisher; others wrote music and sent it to me. Reminiscence is a jade; it has to be handled firmly. I let Jonathan run everything, ignored accounts and royalties for over two years. I was already planning another book, which I began in 1953; it would be on Malaya.

Locally the uproar over *A Many-Splendoured Thing* was fearful, although it only affected the British. But then they had so little to talk about! With dreadful repetitiveness they rehashed old gossip. In Hong Kong no conversation was complete unless it contained some well-worn anecdote about Emily Hahn, the American writer (author of many novels, including *China To Me* and *Miss Jill*) who had fallen in love with an English officer and had had a child and written about it, and this twenty years after Emily Hahn had not only survived the affair but married her Englishman! It would be, I thought, the same with me. In twenty years, at their coffee clatches, the *mems** would be rehashing Han Suyin.

A reputation as a loose nymphomaniac was now established for me by some of the more indignant. I was told this by Lily Abegg, correspondent for the *Neuer Züricher Zeitung*, who came to Malaya and stayed with me. 'You are a knight, a *chevalier*, you are pure,' she said after some days with me. 'That is why these dirty people hate you.' But I had no time for introspection, for self-scrutiny.

Jonathan sent *A Many-Splendoured Thing* to Little, Brown, whose editor was Ted Weeks. He declined it. His reader had reported that 'nowhere does the heroine appear physically attractive', a somewhat puzzling literary judgment. Weeks had not bothered to read the book himself. It was the writer Nora Waln who persuaded Weeks to take it.

I had met Nora Waln in England in 1943. Her reputation as a writer on China, because of *The House of Exile*, stood high. *Reaching for the Stars*, her book on Germany, was for me much more true, even agonizing, but people had not reacted well to it. Nora was in 1952 still writing the book on China she told me she had started in 1943. 'Our great mutual

---

***Mem:** name given to English women in Malaya at the time. Abbreviation of the Indian *memsahib*.

friend', wrote Ted, meaning Nora, 'has a major book . . . about China coming out . . .' But I knew she could no longer write about China. No one could without going to China, and Nora had not been for twenty years.

The waste of Nora Waln's talent brought me unwillingly to face a decision. Would I be a writer or a doctor? If Nora shredded her talent in the kitchen shredder, as I had seen her do, would I lose mine through the stethoscope round my neck? And did I really *have* any talent? All I knew was that I had not intended to be a writer; I still wanted to be a doctor. And sitting down to begin my next book, the words came, the images; but also I felt lost, bereft, without the contact of people, the children, the sick.

I discussed this with Emily Hahn, who now came to Malaya to write about the Emergency, and stayed with me. I had seen her once in 1951 in Hong Kong when she passed through, and this was because Ian had been enamoured of her face, so I had wanted to see it. She quoted poetry, and had a roguish bounce to her; her soft luminous eyes belied the hardness within. For Emily was never life's victim; her adolescence had taught her to regard all women as her natural enemies.

On the day that she arrived the Grand Prix for motor racing was going on in Johore Bahru. The Sultan of Johore and his son were car collectors and speed addicts. The Sultan had raced in his youth; and one day his car had been overtaken by the car of the Tiger Balm* king, Aw Boon Haw. The latter's vehicle, a splendid Rolls-Royce, was painted to resemble a tiger, and its protuberant lights were the tiger's eyes, fringed with painted lashes. The Sultan was enraged. He speeded up, overtook, rammed the Tiger Balm Rolls, took out his revolver and shot out the tiger's eyes. Aw Boon Haw felt that his whole spirit, his tigerishness had been destroyed . . . On Grand Prix day the Sultan and his family were on the grandstand when the racing began. The schools

*A famous ointment made up with ephedrine and selling in South East Asia. The Aw family is one of the wealthiest in that region, owing to Tiger Balm.

were on holiday and Yungmei and her schoolfriends were rushing in and out of the house, elated by an accident: 'There's blood all over the stones.' 'How bloodthirsty children really are,' remarked Emily. She then advised me to give up doctoring. I did not take her advice; it seemed to me a betrayal of my twelve-year-old self. I had wanted then to be a doctor; and I had become also a writer. But it seemed to me I would exhaust the child within me and her freshness should I give up medicine. I went on doctoring by day and writing by night.

This would have been impossible had I not had servants. Ah Lai, the cook, came from Hainan Island, as did all cooks to Europeans in Malaya. He had a large, uproarious family; his wife and his wife's sister did our laundry. Ah Mui the maid was an s.e.p. (surrendered enemy personnel). Daughter of a rubber tapper, she had been captured in armed action by a Gurkha battalion and turned over to the Special Branch. After much interrogation she had 'come clean', betrayed. Ah Mui was a most charming girl with a round face and large eyes and a fetching manner, given to soft sighing and smiling in turns or together. She moved gently, with grace, and regularly disappeared, going to the jail as a stool pigeon. Into the movable array of servants I did not inquire too closely. How disagreeable is accuracy when service is efficient; for never were we left service-bereft.

Other s.e.p.s, male and female, came and went, visited, chatted, served the meals, cut the grass, made the beds, ate and talked. I could hear them through the open windows, and in the evening they caught the breeze with jollity and a blaring radio. I paid the bills when presented, only grumbling when they rose too high. Ah Lai managed parties for 150 with ease, produced the required crockery and glasses. I never asked where they came from. Ah Lai was Chinese, and therefore took full responsibility, and inquiry was an insult. Our only real disagreement was over Australian tinned butter. We never ate butter, but it appeared on all the bills and in vast quantities. I do not know how much of it went to the jungle guerrillas but I smelt the

air and I knew; and one day I shouted, 'Not so much butter!'
The bills came down.

Ah Mui returned from her stool pigeon sessions in jail to
tell me bits of her life as a rubber tapper, the bitterness of
resettlement (her family was taken from their home near
Klang and settled in another mangrove swamp. The
resettlement officials seemed to favour mangrove swamps as
sites for 'new villages') She was nineteen years old,
inhabited by a vague, unverbalized resentment; which she
expanded by ineffectual sweeping and tapping of cushions
into place. She sloughed off her small treacheries, but this
was the condition of her life; and she was pampered because
she was such an eminently good stool pigeon, extracting
facts from the most obdurate communist sympathizer.
There was no compounded deceit in her, but always she
would be deceived by her own betrayal.

Through Ah Mui and all the others, through my travels in
Malaya and the medical care I brought to the 'new village' I
had adopted, I began to see Malaya. And I wrote of what I
saw. My book smelt of the jungle and the swamp, the
secretion of people's lives; the rubble and the waste. The
book would come out in 1956 and I called it: . . . *And the
Rain My Drink*. It is still in print, and still today it is high on
the list of certain American universities as the best book on
Malaya, on what the Emergency was like.

Leonard reacted to my success with something like
euphoria. He became less cautious. His enforced resignation
from Special Branch could have been predicted the day he
married me, I think, and he now hastened towards that
conclusion. Two high-up people in Special Branch came to
our house: Leonard received them in shirtless defiance,
which I thought unnecessarily provocative. He was
considered a 'security risk', and would be transferred to
some out of the way place. 'You wanted to get out of Special
Branch, now get out,' I said. After some hesitation he did.
Within a week our telephone was ripped out; notice was
given us to leave the house. I had to give up the job at the

hospital; without a telephone, I could not function.

Suddenly the rent of the few houses available went up and up . . . the usual squeeze. But we managed to find a small house in a hollow, hot and the neighbours abominable. The man beat his dog to death; regularly beat his wife and children; one child also died one night, amid great lament. 'We'll stick it here until we find another and better house.'

Leaving the hospital was necessary though sorrowful. I could not remain on call at night; it was too exhausting, especially with my writing. I then discovered how nice, friendly, unimpressed by the 'dishonour' of leaving Special Branch were my colleagues and the nurses. The Chinese nurses accompanied me to the annual Topekong ceremony. Johore Bahru was actually a great trading centre for the Hakka Chinese* and had been founded by them in the seventeenth century; the temple then being erected to honour their 'leader', who once a year was taken out in a palanquin into the streets of what had been his city. All the Hakkas of Singapore came for the ceremony of the Topekong to Johore Bahru.

Dr Pink, who had operated on me, came often to call and Dr Nayar, the pathologist, asked me to tea. Nayar was a Brahmin Indian and as such could not touch corpses. Yet he was in charge of post mortems, one of many such bizarre touches which made Johore Bahru General Hospital such a wondrous institution. He directed autopsies with a long wand, and two Chinese helpers did the slicing up. Then there was the affable, wistful Dr Holmes, a Welsh nationalist. One of the last cases I had to bring to his attention as head of my department, was a dead man, head neatly split in two by an axe. 'Heart failure,' said Holmes. As I protested, he explained. Such 'incidents' might lead to a Holy War; the man, a Chinese, might have been 'accidentally' hit by a Malay. No one wanted an unneeded pogrom. Dr Holmes

---

Hakkas: a particular minority among the Han Chinese. See *The Crippled Tree*.

came very often to our house, and inveighed against Special
Branch and the Emergency. He would leave Malaya quite
abruptly one day, and I never found out why.

I was approached to open my own practice by Mrs Wong,
who had been a nurse at the Johore Bahru General Hospital.
Mrs Wong, fat, jolly and practical, offered to partner me in a
venture on the main street of Johore Bahru: a pharmacy
below and doctor's rooms above, my own practice. She
would assist me, we would go halves on fees, and there would
be, to pay her back, the profit on the drugs sold by her in the
pharmacy. This was the usual arrangement for young
doctors going into private practice.

Mrs Wong was very efficient; within a week she had a
house along Jalan Ibrahim Sultan, a qualified pharmacist, a
young boy to sweep, clean, fetch and carry. But there were
still some snags, such as the repainting of the rooms and
plumbing to be installed. 'All will be ready in three weeks,'
said Mrs Wong. And suddenly I felt exhausted. I decided to
go to Bali for a fortnight or three weeks.

Off by aeroplane to Djakarta, and then in another small,
rickety hopper to Bali. It was surprisingly full of rather
sweaty Dutch who kept up a running commentary on how
terrible everything was. One woman sitting next to me told
me I would find the Indonesians not quite human, and the
Chinese far cleverer.

We landed in Den Pasar, and I made my way to Sanur on
the motorcycle of a German sociologist who was on a world
tour to study ancient customs. He was going, like myself, to
stay with Le Mayeur, a Belgian painter who had lived in Bali
for three decades. Malcolm, who knew him and regularly
purchased some of his paintings ('because he's such a
delightful fellow') had suggested my staying with him.

Le Mayeur came running out on the beach when he heard
the motorcycle; he loved visitors. His house was of stone,
and great clumps of pink and red bougainvillaea in blossom
dotted his sandy garden. He was still strong and healthy,
though seventy, and around him his dogs leapt and barked.
His wife, Polok, came out, hands in prayerful welcome. She

was truly beautiful and had been, in her childhood, a great dancer.

Le Mayeur gave me a room full of splendid old carvings interspersed with some of his paintings; sun and sea and bougainvillaea and slim golden girls in light and shadow. 'My house is Bali and Bali is my house. You don't need to see anything else,' said Le Mayeur firmly. Every morning an indefinite number of lissom relatives of Polok glided about the sand paths of his garden, tenderly setting down offerings of flowers in coconut shells and cooked saffron rice for the gods. 'The Balinese don't like to live near the sea; they think the sea is evil, but they like me to stay here to protect them from sea demons.' We went swimming every morning; the beach was grey and silver sand, volcanic lava. We sluiced at the sweet water well in Le Mayeur's back courtyard. Every evening eight Indonesian soldiers came and sat with us while we ate, and played with their guns. They were detailed by the government to protect Le Mayeur, for President Sukarno (who liked his paintings) had decreed that he and his house were 'national monuments'. 'He got the idea about national monuments from the Japanese,' said Le Mayeur, who endured his protectors with equanimity.

Mr Vreelander and his wife came to the house. Mr Vreelander was Dutch and represented Shell. He was enamoured of Bali and the Balinese. He was stuporose all day, dreaming of night. At night he woke and lived to watch the Balinese dance. And now I wanted to join him in discovering Bali, much to the ire of Le Mayeur. 'Just look at my paintings, *there* is Bali.' Mr Vreelander's wife was a timorous Dutchwoman who went swimming with a large bunch of keys tied to her waist. She hated Bali, she hated the beach. 'Even the sand is black here. It makes me feel so dirty.' She brought plastic cushions to sit on. 'I have to lock up everything. They're such thieves.' Le Mayeur told me that he had heard from Polok, who had it from her relatives, that Mrs Vreelander counted the sugar cubes remaining after breakfast and tea every day, and then locked up the sugar bowl.

I went to call on Theo Mayer, a Dutch painter who lived
beyond the first range of hills in a beautiful house overhung
with white dove-orchids. He painted dark, large, gloomy
canvases. From his terrace there was a fabulous view of the
valley, bestarred with glistening water patches; and oh, the
softness, the pastel tints over all; here was not the raucous
green of Malaya but a gentle medley of hushed jades and
browns and mellifluous beiges; along the paths would walk a
daintiness of cows, delicate on slim legs with jet hooves and
luminous brown eyes. Flotillas of ducks gathered round a
bamboo pole with a tuft of white feathers at the top; how or
why this tuft managed to keep the ducks from straying I shall
never know.

On the third night we managed, Mr Vreelander and the
German sociologist and I, to escape Le Mayeur. Thence-
forth I too went stuporose by day, soaking in the sun
and the sea and with a perpetual smile of sleepy enchantment
upon me. We went to one village or another; on the
German's motorcycle (with sidecar three could manage) or
by Vreelander's jeep, and sometimes trudging on foot, until
we heard the music of the *gamelan* coming through the trees
and then we trod the night, walking in ecstasy of expectation
towards the laughter spreading in the satin dark, the music
and the lamps. Vreelander knew a great deal about Balinese
dancing. The German sociologist took notes. The village
would make us welcome and we would sit on the ground or
on a flat beam above ground. The dancing proceeded.
Perhaps I saw then the best dancers of Bali; little girls
moving in rapture, in brocade, in ritual, all below puberty,
for they would no longer dance when their periods came. We
would return home very late, still enchanted and not sleepy;
the dogs would bark and Le Mayeur, vigilant and
unsleeping, would rush out, torch in hand. 'Ah, there you are
at last.' He recuperated us. The next day he would say, 'Why
go there? I can always ask the dancers to come here . . .'

In a great hush of smiles the Balinese walked, small-boned
and beautiful. But then I came nearer; and I could see there
were many sick children. I went into the compounds and

always a child lay sick in the darkness within the hut, dying
enormous-eyed, and always there would be *bomos* chanting,
and the blood of cocks to ward off Evil. So many must have
died in the silence and softness of the island.

One day Le Mayeur did give a feast, and dancers came. We
sat on the beach and ate suckling pig, cooked on spits above
the pewter sand. A *gamelan* orchestra performed and a
famous male dancer danced the Kebiar; a wonderful,
unforgettable Kebiar. But then Polok seized two carved
wings of painted wood and danced; she had been a famous
Legong dancer when a little girl; the Balinese were very
polite and clapped and laughed gently but Vreelander was
indignant: 'It's not done for a grown woman to dance.'

We went another night to a cleared space ringed with trees
to watch the Monkey dance. But how poor, how very poor
the villages were, more so as one went inland to higher,
smaller valleys. My eyes picked out the sores, the
mutilations. And there was the caste system; there were
Untouchables here, in this archaic Hindu island, just as in
India; and when we went to see the Chokoda Agung, the lord
of the community, at Ubud, a famous centre of Balinese
wood carving, he was as hefty and stout a landlord as one
could wish for, waited on by many servants crawling in and
out, bent to the ground.

I have not been back to Bali. Le Mayeur is dead, and the
beautiful and wise Polok has married again. I am told,
however, that Bali has not changed very much; although
there are many tourists, the Balinese continue to live in
another century. The painting and the carving for tourists
has nothing to do with the temples, or with the worship of
the gods. I could detect, even than, a hint of ironic artifice as
the dancers strove to catch a pristine golden fervour which
had once made their gestures grandiose, magic against evil.
But even today their non-nubile children still dance
themselves into immortal goddesses, casting most potent
spells upon the land. Too well they know we come to watch;
but they have sundered themselves from the acts they
obligingly perform for visitors. What is delighted trance

becomes routine gesture eliciting tourist money, but it does
not corrupt them . . . or does it? Perhaps Le Mayeur was
right to create his Bali, for himself. 'Bali is Bali. Don't go and
spoil it. Look at my paintings instead.'

I had been in Bali ten days when Mr Dean arrived. He was
neatly dressed in a suit, walked on the beach in good leather
shoes and was Vreelander's superior. Vreelander took him
to see the dancing by night, but Mr Dean got cramp sitting
on his heels listening to the *gamelan* orchestra.

Mr Dean spoke to me of oil. He was single-minded and
romantic about oil. Creased with heat and sweat, he was
impervious to discomfort when he talked of the vast
underground wealth of Indonesia. Then he decided to leave.
'There is a ferry from Bali to Java, crossing the Straits,' said
Mr Vreelander. We would take the ferry. I decided to leave
with Mr Dean as my time was almost up and I wanted to see
a little of Java. We said goodbye to Le Mayeur and Polok
and set off at dawn by jeep for Gilimanuk, and saw from its
promontory the sea amble its green and blue waves like tiles,
sliding them one upon the other, and the sun burst out like a
dancer upon them. Mr Dean perspired gently as we waited
for the ferry; Mr Vreelander was then struck with a most
wonderful and disastrous idea. Instead of waiting for the
ferry (which might or might not come, one never knew), why
not take a sailing boat? Then we would be sure to get to the
other side.

I do not know why Mr Dean said yes to this scheme;
perhaps the sun dancing the Kebiar, the growing heat and
the enticing coolness of water. We embarked in a boat with
six men. After about an hour we could still see the coast of
Bali. We then saw the ferry boat advancing upon us, going to
Gilimanuk. Its swell tossed our boat. Mr Dean clenched his
teeth.

After another hour of vainly trying to catch the breeze we
saw the ferry boat again; it had left Gilimanuk and was
chuffing Java-wards. Its wake tossed us again. Mr Dean
swore, volubly. 'That Vreelander . . . what a rotten idea . . .'

I suggested that we might all do a little rowing; the Balinese laughed obligingly and while the sail hung limp, began to row . . . By late afternoon, when the ferry had crossed us twice again, the wind picked up. Mr Dean's choler had expressed itself several times, but now we sat hungry, thirsty, mute and red-eyed while the sea sparkled unruffled and the Balinese talked cheerfully, laughed and rowed. After the sudden sunset we went on and finally landed on the coast of Java in deep night. A European employee of Shell was waiting for Mr Dean on the dock. We were driven to a hotel, and I slept soundly in a vast bed under a large mosquito net, and came to breakfast to find a good many Dutchmen and Dutchwomen seated before blue and white willow pattern plates with cheese in large slabs on white bread, sugar on butter on white bread, honey and jam on butter on white bread . . . oh, those pounds of flesh which billowed under the thin dresses around me; all this white bread transformed into flabby motion.

Mr Dean appeared, still angry. 'That Vreelander . . . he'll hear from me.' The car would take Mr Dean across Java to Surabaya, and he gallantly offered me a lift. We went through green, green Java, the dense crowded villages, the splendour of the paddi fields, and of the trees, but Mr Dean's conversation was all about the evils of communism. How could one, he asked rhetorically, prevent the workers, say in an oil company, from becoming infected with the Red virus? He gave the answer. By establishing a system of social security. All stores, the canteens on every plantation or oil field, or in every factory, should be company owned, so that the workers need not leave their place of work at all; everything they needed would be there, including schools, hospitals, shops, recreational facilities. All the needs of the workers would be directly satisfied by the companies employing them. There would be adequate protection against 'subversive tendencies', and that meant barbed wire and patrols, if needed, organized by the company. And a provident fund, docking a portion of the workers' earnings for security and health and for their old age and good behaviour, and to make sure they paid their debts and did not squander all they earned.

I do not know whether Mr Dean has been able to organize this concentrationary paradise, and sometimes I wonder what has happened to Mr Vreelander.

I started private medical practice in Johore Bahru in the summer of 1953. The Chinese merchant community sent me a large rectangular mirror engraved with the words HUA TO IS BORN AGAIN. Hua To was a most renowned surgeon and physician of the third century A.D. My first visitor was Dr Ismail, the sole Malay doctor in Johore, and also a politician. He would give up his doctoring when independence came in 1957 and become Minister of the Interior.

Dr Ismail looked at the shiny new autoclave I had bought. He said kindly, 'You won't have any patients. People don't like women doctors.' By the end of the first month, I had twenty patients a day and by the second forty to fifty a day, more than any other doctor in Johore Bahru.

Mrs Wong was happy. 'People have seen you work at the hospital; they know you came at night to see the babies.' I had indeed sat up one night because a baby had been admitted, who had died within six hours of heart failure; I had not diagnosed him properly; only afterwards did I realize that he had had acute beriberi, which seemed absurd, for his parents were well-off. The mother came again to the clinic, fat, apparently healthy, with a baby with a rigid neck – beriberi presenting as meningitis. This time I was not caught. I administered vitamin B and the effect was miraculous. Because of this, I gained a great reputation. I got another mirror, inscribed STAR OF SALVATION.

Now I had time to take histories, to examine the patients properly. This was not always easy. Just as in Hong Kong, patients deployed great ingenuity in not telling the truth about themselves; it took much contriving to get beyond prevarication. But Mrs Wong and another nurse whom we soon acquired knew three languages and nine dialects between them. I charged only three Malayan dollars for complete examination, including urine and blood. Very soon my peculiarity (examining urine and blood; apparently none of my colleagues ever bothered) became well-known and I acquired a fascinated clientèle just for that. My colleagues, all men, charged ten to fifteen dollars when they gave an injection. I charged five. I went visiting patients at home for my usual three dollars. It taught me much about actual living conditions. Thus a baby eight months old, dying of anaemia . . . it had hookworm; the mother, a rubber tapper, left it on a mat on the earth floor of the hut. My wealthy fat woman ate only boiled noodles, nothing else. Hence beriberi in the babies she bore. I discovered mild diabetes in a woman married fifteen years, and sterile. I put her on a diet and anti-diabetic pills and within three months she was pregnant. The child was a beautiful boy. After that lucky miracle, I could do no wrong.

Many of my patients were infected with modernism. Anything out of a tin was better than fresh food. They gave their children vast quantities of English biscuits and sweets and soft drinks. Rotten teeth and gum abscesses were extremely common. The children liked me because I was 'the doctor who does not give injections'. Some of my colleagues, pressed for time (an injection is mystically worth more in fees), would resort to the needle unnecessarily.

Now I had the later afternoon to myself, and I could write at nights. Sunday was my free day, except that I went to the 'new village' I had adopted, about fifty kilometres away. At the time there was still curfew at night outside town limits. The cars and jeeps of British planters and police whizzed by me, sometimes with guns sticking out of the back, the occupants giving horrified glances at my car. The pretence of 'terrorist attack' still went on, but I knew I was safe. 'Only bad people get killed, Doctor,' Ah Mui, my stool pigeon maid, had told me on those occasions when she dreamt herself back in the guerrilla camp in the jungle. And now I became too successful a doctor. My patients increased phenomenally. Occasionally some rubber tappers from a distant village would get together and hire a small bus, collecting relatives and would-be patients on the way, and would arrive at my door. Especially on festival days, or at lunch time. 'We knew you would be at home, so we came.' And since there was curfew, and they had to be home before dark or would be in danger of being shot by the British or Malay soldiers on patrol, I had to see them.

CHAPTER 4

Malaya: 1954–1956

We had settled in the small hot house in the hollow. Leonard did his best to find a job. We lived on my earnings as a doctor. I did not touch my royalties. We acquired a family of Siamese cats, bluepoints, and Binky, a perfect mongrel with a hyena-striped coat, which Yungmei had brought home. My love of cats, stifled since childhood, came back; for a short time almost a mania. When cat 'flu decimated our seventeen Siamese, we went round with kittens snuggled close to our chests, feeding them glucose water with droppers. All the kittens were born in Binky's large basket; and Binky tenderly cuddled them while the mother cat looked on, purring pleasantly.

One morning, when I went to Yungmei's room to wake her up, she said, 'Mummy, I coughed up some blood last night.' She showed me her toothmug. In it was a dark brown clot. She had not wakened me, but waited for the morning. Then all the worry and anxiety which I held within me about her health came up again; I knew her tuberculosis was not over, despite the X-rays and the tests.

'Don't worry yourself sick over her, she'll be all right,' said the specialist reassuringly. I said it was impossible not to worry. So back she went to bed, this time in a first-class room at the hospital; she had tutors to give her lessons while she rested, and further tests were made. This lasted some two months, while she was on an anti-tuberculous drug, as she had been in Hong Kong. I was by then quite sure that there was something seriously wrong with her lungs. Everyone assured me that it was not serious; and Yungmei herself did not want to rest; but I saw how her cheeks went rosy in the evening, and was worried, and she hated me for worrying so much.

Not only was I concerned with my practice, and with writing and Yungmei (and also somewhat about Leonard's future), but I had also, in that year, 1954, become drawn into the educational problems of Malaya.

The University of Singapore was set up for the English-educated young of Malaya. It applied the government policy of graduating Malays, even if they did not reach the required standards. The bulk of the students were, of course, Chinese, since 85 per cent of Singapore's population was Chinese and only 6 per cent Malay, the rest Indian or European. The Chinese resented this favouritism, but endured it for fear of 'no job later'. Exclusivity to every job in the administration and all liberal professions went to the graduates of English-speaking schools. But since two-thirds of the children of Singapore attended Chinese-education schools, and for them no jobs were available in government offices, the medical profession, law, engineering or architecture, the injustice was flagrant. I lectured on this, but the English-educated were afraid, and the professors blandly countered with arguments about the low standards of Chinese education. This was inaccurate. For the most brilliant scholars were those who first attended Chinese schools then switched to the lower standard at English schools.

Not surprisingly, in 1953 the Chinese communities of Singapore and Malaya began to plan for a local university to cater for the Chinese-educated, since it was now impossible for them to go to universities in China without being jailed or deported. Nanyang (the Southern Seas) University was conceived by the Chinese Chamber of Commerce, led by the Hokkien Club (also called the Millionaires' Club). The Chamber had protested in 1951 at the law arbitrarily passed making English and Malay the only languages valid for official documents of any kind in Singapore and Malaya. In January the Hokkien Club held a meeting and decided that since an 'English' university of Singapore had been set up to cater for the English-speaking minority, there must be a Chinese university to cater for the Chinese-speaking majority – logical, but for months I saw staid Englishmen at the Cockpit Restaurant and other haunts of Singapore's whites foam at the mouth and gibber when the Chinese university was mentioned.

It was this plan which led to my being solicited to talk at Singapore University. 'Why on earth is a university for the Chinese-speaking necessary?' 'Why does the élite have to be English-speaking only?' I countered. 'Nanyang University is a typical exhibition of Chinese chauvinism,' said one choleric Englishman. 'What about English chauvinism at Singapore University?' Of course the wrecking of Chinese culture was designed to 'counter communism', and to prevent the young from being indoctrinated through the language medium. The British staff of Singapore University and the government administrators seemed quite certain that an English education would preclude communistic ideas.

In February and March 1953, 270 Chinese associations and clubs throughout Malaya had joined in the scheme, and Nanyang University was born. Everyone gave money; the millionaires some millions, the pedlars of the Singapore food market a week's earnings every month. How many oyster omelettes, sliced crab, noodles of all kinds went into Nanyang University? The trishaw pedallers of Singapore and Malaya pedalled for three days and turned in all they earned for Nanyang University, and theirs was the greatest sacrifice, for they were so very poor. Rubber tappers flocked to give; they knew that their children would never have a chance to go to university; but it was a gesture of cultural identity. It was incredible and magnificent, and it must be remembered.

In Jurong on Singapore Island a site was bought and building began. I was, by then, researching into Malayan Chinese literature. My contacts with Chinese scholars in Malaya had made me discover that there existed an extensive body of essays, novels, criticism and poetry by Malayan Chinese authors, different in content and feeling from Chinese literature proper. There were two excellent Chinese newspapers in Malaya and Singapore with a wide coverage of world events. There were some very good journalists who spoke superb English and Malay as well as Chinese, and I had had some lively meetings with them.* An incessant cultural ferment within the Chinese community, and much creativity, but all of it totally ignored by the British, and of course thoroughly suppressed by the Emergency as 'subversive' . . . Some years later I would collect, and help to publish the first compendium in English on Malayan Chinese literature. Meanwhile, students would bring me slim volumes of verse and novelettes, all of them anti-colonial, full of verve and spirit, if not always technically perfect. I kept them carefully; their possession meant imprisonment. Some of the writers did go to jail.

And so the image of the Malayan Chinese who had come as an illiterate labourer to wield a spade and build the roads and plant the rubber and mine the tin, and had suddenly become a crass, cupid, still uncultured 'millionaire', was totally false. Indeed, many had come as labourers, and some had become millionaires. Such people as Tan Laksai, head of the Hokkien Club, and Lien Yingchow, who mimicked for me the way he had shovelled to build the roads, and Li Kungchiang, who had worked his way up from a clerkship in a rubber plantation to a vast ownership of newspapers and business enterprises. These millionaires funded scholarships, subsidized newspapers, schools, and welfare societies and libraries; and were intensely concerned with the education of the young. Many of them had painstakingly learnt to read and write. Some, like Li Kungchiang, managed to do so in three languages.

I supported the project of Nanyang University from the start, but after the first year, added a condition to my support. Nanyang should incorporate the Malay language in its curriculum and open its doors to Malays who wanted to study Chinese.

Today, hundreds of European students go to China to study Chinese; hundreds of Americans study Chinese in

---

*Some of them went to jail for 'subversion' later.

American universities. But at the time, the idea of Malays studying Chinese seemed ridiculous and incomprehensible to the British (though curiously not to the Malays themselves), and also to a good many overseas Chinese, including some of the millionaires of the Hokkien Club. It became very evident to me that the overseas Chinese were, because of the war with Japan, resentful and suspicious of the Malays, just as the latter were being harangued by some of their more fanatic religious leaders to kill the 'infidel' Chinese. Something must be done about it; and it seemed to me that the Malayan Communist Party, although it preached unity of the races, had failed to tackle the problem, and even denied that it existed.

My support gave rise to an invitation to the Hokkien Club in Singapore. I went up the steps of the unimposing building; upon them, waiting for me, stood some second-magnitude businessmen. The Club was spacious inside, and contained a swimming pool as large as a miniature lake crossed by a series of pavilions linked by a zigzag bridge; the zigzags possibly prevented the demons from following the millionaires when, to discuss big business, they repaired to the cool pavilions in the lake middle. The renowned Tan Laksi came out from an inner room to greet me. He was clad in simple, loose trousers, his loose top open upon his inner shirt – which was the same as that worn by any ordinary worker in Singapore – and on his naked feet he wore the kind of sandals that were to be had in Change Alley for a dollar. The other members of the Club were similarly at vestimental ease, thus flaunting their labour origins. Courtesy tea was served in minute cups, Hokkien fashion, while Tan Laksai fanned himself with a coolie palm-leaf fan and surveyed me obliquely. He had a massive bullet head with a crewcut, and a very extraordinary face; simple and shrewd, bulldoggish with massive jaw, and yet wistful. I liked him; he had great power, and honesty. And now he was angry. He had had enough of being bullied.

There were journalists and scholars and teachers there, as well as the likeable Li Kungchiang, far more subtle than Tan

Laksai, with more vision. He was thin and his hair stood up in a mop. We developed a great liking for each other, aided by the fact that shrewd Malcolm also had immense regard for him. We were to meet several times during the next few years, always with a large concourse of people so that Special Branch would not accuse us of conspiring. Li Kungchiang told me how puzzled he had been, when young, by the use of English words. Thus to find the inscription POST NO BILLS on a wall had nonplussed him. Post was to mail, bill was a bird's beak. Why should one be enjoined not to mail birds' beaks?

After an imposing banquet Tan Laksai led the way to the coolness of the middle pavilion in the lake, and there talked of the necessity of Nanyang University. I responded. The next day Special Branch had all the information and had approached Malcolm to try to curb my enthusiasm. 'They seemed quite upset,' said Malcolm. The Chinese newspapers published the exact version of our conversation the next day. Tan Laksai, and Li Kungchiang even more so, were denounced by an American correspondent as 'Red agents'. Tan Laksai had some connection, through his father-in-law, Tan Kahkee (a millionaire founder of universities in China who had returned to China to avoid detention), with his native province, but certainly none of these millionaires were communist-inclined. It was, however, the fashion of those days to confuse the urge for cultural identity with communism. For those were the days of witch-hunts and Joseph McCarthy, as manifest in Singapore as in Hollywood.

At the second or third dinner at the Hokkien Club, I ventured to touch upon the admission of Malays to Nanyang University, and felt the immediate drop in temperature. Lien Yingchow meaningfully shook the ice cubes in his brandy-ginger ale, and an alert young secretary asked me what I was writing at the moment. Tan Laksai fanned himself with his cheap coolie fan. After a decent pause he began to speak bitterly of the terrible things that Malays had done to the Chinese under Japanese rule: 'We fought for the British, we died, we were tortured . . . We came here and we made things grow where nothing grew, and Malaya is wealthy because of us . . .' I listened with profound respect on my face.

Now the Board of Directors of Nanyang University had to find a chancellor or university president who would pick out staff, professors, lecturers. Within the Board was a strong pro-Kuomintang wing, which had the blessing of the American Consulate. The Americans thought the British weak-kneed, and the important pro-Chiang Kaishek lobby in America also became interested in Nanyang University. An anti-communist Chinese university in Singapore might not be a bad thing. It might offset the appeal of the jungle guerrillas; it might also, in the long run, offset Malay 'leftist' tendencies influenced by the Communist Party of Indonesia. For despite the sedulous repetition of the 'loyal Malay' theme (loyal to what?), none knew better than the British that the Malays were also nationalists, sharing a common culture, language and script with Indonesia; and that the Islamic world, from Algeria to the Philippines, was effervescent. There were fears of pan-Arab, pan-Islamic movements affecting Malaya. *Utusan Melayu*, the Malay newspaper, reported favourably on upsurges against colonial domination in Iraq, Syria and Algeria, and Egypt's Nasser was immensely popular.

The choice of an anti-communist chancellor for Nanyang University fell upon Lin Yutang, author of *My Country and My People*. Lin Yutang had lived in America for a little over two decades. A two weeks' trip to Chungking during the Sino-Japanese war had been his only wartime excursion in Asia, but he was in Taiwan in 1953, actively denouncing Communist China, and participating in the formation of an Anti-Communist League which had the backing of Chiang Kaishek, and of course of the CIA.

Tan Laksai was none too pleased with the choice. Lin Yutang arrived in Singapore with his family; his daughters and son-in-law were also given jobs in Nanyang University. The Lins were provided with a bungalow by the sea and a Cadillac or two. Lin Yutang then started to recruit staff, and

I received a little note from him, asking me to drop in for a talk.

There was a mat with WELCOME written on it at the front door and in the cool living room orchids hung from the ceiling in fenestrated pots. There was some extravagant carved furniture and jades, kindly loaned by the Tiger Balm king's daughter, Aw Hsiang. Her father, Aw Boon Haw, had mansions filled with priceless jades both in Singapore and in Hong Kong, and I had visited them with proper clucking awe. Rotund and charmingly effusive, Mrs Lin greeted me; Lin Yutang had impish bespectacled eyes and in spite of his small size was truculent. 'Now I want you to tell me all about the situation here in twenty minutes,' he commanded. I began to speak, but Lin's attention span was short. That creeping glaze, that fixity of face which denotes a mind turned off, already astride another subject . . . I cut my exposé down to five minutes, and he nodded sagely. 'Mummy,' said he, turning to his wife, 'we must get around to see something of Malaya.' 'If it's safe,' said Mrs Lin. I assured her it was, and mimicked Ah Mui, my former maid. 'Only bad people get killed, people like police officers.' They looked stunned. 'Will you have some cawfee?' said Mrs Lin.

We then talked of the book Dr Lin would write about South East Asia, of the bastion that Nanyang University would prove against communism . . . Lin Yutang had already announced this as his intention. He then asked me to be Professor of English Literature at Nanyang. I shook my head. I did not know anything about English literature. 'But you write English,' he exclaimed. 'Not English literature.' I did not want to teach Dickens and Thackeray, worthy though they might be. 'I'd rather be the college health physician; all the students admitted to the University should have a medical examination.' He agreed, but when I had gone summoned a press conference and told them, 'Han Suyin has accepted the post of Professor of English Literature at Nanyang University.' This appeared in the *Straits Times* the next day. I wrote to the *Straits Times* to deny it, and to explain that all I could do at the moment was to offer my services as college health physician.

My denial led to another interview with Lin Yutang. He was a bit ruffled. 'Why don't you give up medicine?' As a professor I would have ample time to write. 'We'll see to it that you don't have more than six hours a week of teaching.' I tried to explain my idea of literature; that we must create an Asian type of literature; we needed something other than nineteenth-century English writers . . . but his mind wandered again, and I left.

Throughout the rest of 1954, while Nanyang University was a-building, I did not approach him again. Lin Yutang made pronouncements, called press conferences, gave talks revealing a blithe unconsciousness of the situation in Malaya. He declared a university a place of leisure, with time to smoke a pipe and to browse. To the rickshaw pullers who had gone hungry, sacrificing three days of earnings to build Nanyang, this was fury-rousing. People began to dislike him intensely; and the students of the Chinese high schools mounted campaigns against him and called upon the Board of Directors to force him out. In this Lin helped them greatly. For his idea was to start with a budget of incommensurate dimension, more in keeping with the requirements of a wealthy American university than one funded by the people of Malaya. He offered his recruited professors transport by air for themselves and their families, and transport for their household goods. He demanded luxurious bungalows for them.

The Hokkien Club was holding meetings in great perturbation. They contemplated in baffled silence the bills which Lin Yutang kept sending in. They received protest delegations from the students. By December, Lin's relations with the Board were very strained. He then took action in ways considered un-Chinese, and above all discourteous. Thus he summoned a press conference of Western newsmen (Chinese journalists were absent) to make his disagreement known to the English newspapers; to them he complained that the financial outlays provided were insufficient. This was considered gross betrayal by the Chinese, who in Malaya as elsewhere prefer to settle all disputes within their own community, without resort to the press, especially a foreign press. When questioned by a journalist, Lin said that Malaya and Singapore were 'outposts of civilization', hardship areas calling for increased financial recompense. By publicizing the quarrel before the Board had finalized its meetings, Lin Yutang had made his sponsors, and in particular Tan Laksai, lose face. In early 1955 Lin Yutang and his family were quietly paid a very large indemnity by Tan Laksai personally, and returned to America.

In the summer of 1954, at last, a specialist in tuberculosis came to Malaya, Beryl Wilberforce-Smith, a tall attractive Englishwoman. It was due to her that Yungmei's tuberculosis was at last cured.

Beryl had worked in many parts of the world in her chosen field, and had great experience. Her arrival was due to Lady Templer, who was launching a campaign for the prevention and cure of the disease in Malaya. For it was indeed prevalent; it caused great mortality among the Malays, who had apparently no resistance to it. Lady Templer was behind a scheme to endow Malaya with a large tuberculosis hospital (forty beds to start with) about twenty-five kilometres outside Kuala Lumpur. Beryl was called to Kuala Lumpur, but after studying the scheme told Lady Templer that she thought this was not the best way to tackle the disease in Malaya. The building was miles from anywhere; the patients would feel isolated; their families could not shoulder the expense of travel from the *kampongs* . . . much better have, all over Malaya, a series of small bungalow-type annexes to hospitals. Lady Templer was not too pleased with Beryl's suggestion, and the hospital, which cost a great deal, was built and opened with much pomp. I asked Beryl to take Yungmei in hand. She examined her most carefully, took X-rays from many angles, and finally discovered a small cavity at the back, well-hidden, behind the clavicle. Meanwhile, at last, a big campaign to give BCG to all schoolchildren and to extend this to the *kampongs* was being launched throughout Singapore and Malaya.

Yungmei was now on streptomycin, but Beryl advised that she should have an operation, a lobectomy (the cavity was in the upper lobe of the right lung). This radical removal held a good chance of total cure. I took her advice; Beryl wrote to Mr Cleland in London, one of the two surgeons renowned for lung operations. At the time lung operations were not yet very common but the mortality rate, high some years previously, was down to less than 4 per cent.

In these circumstances, I felt justified in selling the film rights of *A Many-Splendoured Thing*. Ted Weeks had written a few months earlier to Jonathan Cape of an offer by Twentieth Century-Fox for film rights. But I had turned down such demands. However, I was now to go with Yungmei to England; I did not know how long I would be away; meanwhile my clinic would have to be taken care of by another doctor.

Mrs Wong and I searched for a replacement and we found a very nice girl, Dr Low, who had been a student in Hong Kong and was now a graduate doctor. She gladly took over while I was away. Malcolm, who came in frequently to see Yungmei, arranged for a passport for her; and in December 1954 we flew to London, arriving on a day so dreary, so cold, so foggy, so dark, that both of us began to weep. Oh, for the green eternal summer of Malaya!

Mr Cleland, the surgeon to whom Beryl had written, received us the day after we arrived. He wanted to operate almost immediately, but I insisted that Yungmei should have a few days' rest; I knew she was very tired by the cold. For the next four or five days we never saw the sun. Yungmei slept solidly, woke up and slept again. On the Sunday every food shop and restaurant was closed in the vicinity of the rooms we had in Kensington. I searched that morning for some hours for food and eventually took the Underground to Oxford Circus to buy some sandwiches; I could not take Yungmei out in the cold. I then realized that I had forgotten how difficult simple things were in England at weekends; in

Malaya the Chinese shops and restaurants were open every day and late into the night. By Monday things were better; breakfast could be had at the restaurant downstairs. On the Monday, Yungmei entered hospital for her operation.

'We were in time,' said Cleland happily. 'The cavity was full of pus; had we waited, there might have been a generalized infection.' For the next few months Yungmei would be on streptomycin: for the next few years on regular check-ups. After she left hospital I administered the injections and she took them well; in fact her recovery was uneventful and swift, and apart from a neat scar which scarcely shows, she would now lead a normal life, swim and dance and travel and study and marry and have a child.

During these months Yungmei showed herself stoical and good humoured; with immense fortitude. I knew that, whatever happened, in the end all would be well with her; and though in the years to come we would have our usual share of disagreements, yet I think that she is built to surmount, to survive woes and hardships, as I am.

I sought out the friends I had known when I had been in England bewtween 1942 and 1948, both as a diplomat's wife and afterwards as a medical student living in a basement and hard put to make ends meet, raising Yungmei and studying medicine. Isobel Cripps and I met frequently. Since the death of her husband, Stafford Cripps, she had become most active in promoting good race relations in the Commonwealth. Margaret Godley – who had stood by me so staunchly when I was running away from Pao – also helped very much. She sat with me throughout Yungmei's three-hour operation; and then moved us from inconvenient Kensington to a large room in a quiet hotel in Mayfair. The restaurant was just one floor below, there was Sunday breakfast, and I could bring up Yungmei's tray to her bed.

John Coast and his charming Indonesian wife, Luce, came to see Yungmei, and soon she was walking, slowly, but a little more every day.

Suddenly in London, beneath all the activity, the bustle and tremor of success, Yungmei's convalescence, suddenly again there was China for me. What could I do about this obsession, my obsession, which I would not understand until, almost twenty years later, a Chinese intellectual would say to me, 'But this is what has always been: our only religion, our only love, is China, and that is why China has persisted, endured, survived, and is reborn again and again, throughout the millennia.'

But in London then I had no answer except torment, and then it was that in order to escape inner conflict I consciously began to move as two people, between two worlds, whose actions and thoughts need not have any link between them. Suddenly my life in Malaya, my doctoring, my marriage, became for me ferocious dismay. The more I appeared ensconced in my Malayan niche, the less I was substantial; the more dutifully involved with Yungmei's illness, the more dreaming like a rebellious refugee of going back, going back . . .

Throughout these weeks I had also been working on my book on Malaya. The time had come to type it; my hand was sore with writing. At Cape's, Wren Howard now looked after me. Blue-eyed, diffident, humorous, he twinkled amiably all the time. My dearest Jonathan had had a bad stroke in the autumn of 1954, and had not yet recovered. Wren Howard was helpful. 'I'll get you someone.' And so, one morning, into my room at the Mayfair hotel came a beautiful sprightly girl with shining dark hair and dancing eyes. 'I am Menina Mesquita,' she said.

Menina had been Jonathan Cape's secretary. I do not think the word secretary applies; she was far more than that. She had enormous flair for books and writers; and she had typed *A Many-Splendoured Thing* for Cape's from my manuscript.

Now I began to dictate parts of . . . *And the Rain My Drink* to her. She responded with such delight to a good sentence that it stimulated me; she never wanted less than perfection. And so those bleak cold days of January and February were also days of happy endeavour, while Yungmei recovered strength and I put food down her four times a day and walked her round the park, and at night boiled needles in a saucepan over a small gas contraption which the British seemed to favour (it ran on shillings) and with tremulous hand gave her the streptomycin injection.

Meanwhile I also tried an approach to the Chinese Chargé d'Affaires in London for permission to go to China. But I was turned down. A meeting could not be arranged. Patience, I thought, the day will come. Nothing can stop me, neither the Special Branch, nor even the Chinese themselves. One day they will understand me. One day, and I also shall have understood the Revolution then, and then all will be good, rounded out harmony. But first, let me get Yungmei back to Malaya, healthy again.

In March, while Yungmei was with Isobel Cripps for a week of milk and cream in England's beautiful countryside, I went to Paris to see my brother, who lived in France. I met him at the railway station and we sat in the downstairs café of the Hotel Voltaire, which Cape's had recommended to me (none of my English friends seem to know anything about comfortable hotels; Hotel Voltaire was . . . well, perhaps Voltaire had lived there and nothing had been done to it since).

We talked a great deal, and I was sad for he had accepted his state, was satisfied with his ruined, peaceful life. My brother had had great trouble; his wife had become insane while he was still in China, teaching at the Jesuit college in Tientsin. 'I took her to Lourdes but it did no good.' Because of the sick woman whom he loved so tenderly he had given up everything, his career, further study; he had returned to Europe, where she foundered totally and died. He went on teaching, brought up his two sons, adopted a daughter, and insisted he was happy.

And then, of course, he started about my mother; and like Marianne, he was unquenchable. Again and again, and all over again, as the afternoon paced itself out of the sky and the windows of the Hotel Voltaire, and in the frosty twilight the people of Paris hurried and jostled. I saw two policemen drag a black man between them, and everyone turn away, and somehow it was also Mama out there . .

Oh, what was this enormous pain that Mama had inflicted upon her children? How could it cripple my brother, so beautiful and intelligent, so much? I saw ourselves, he and I, doing geometry and algebra problems under the lamp in Peking, just for the fun of it; both bent over the table corner arguing about the solution and Mama suddenly riffling our books off the table. 'It's time to eat.' And his piles of science fiction magazines, called *Amazing Stories*, which he kept in a corner of his room; almost forty-five years later I would find again some of the stories such as 'The Moon Pool', reprinted, which I first read when I was twelve. My brother could not release himself in uproarious laughter, jeer at himself in defiance. 'I'm bad, okay I'm bad. So what?' I would say. But not he. No acceptance of wickedness for him. Always he had to have good reasons for what he did. There are no good reasons for anything, I thought, never entirely good reasons for anything, nor is evil entirely vicious. And so when in doubt laugh, and wait, and don't use words to corner reality. I suppose he had made happiness of a sort for himself, especially when he told me with so much satisfaction that he had burnt all Mama's letters, save one scrap . . . which he proceeded to read to me and which twelve years later would be the start of my book, *The Crippled Tree*. And sitting there, in the soiled, greasy air of the hotel café, I knew we would be leaving each other, we were rapidly getting so far apart, receding from each other even as we promised to keep in touch, even though he said, 'I have loved you so much, Sister.' I gave him all my royalties from the first French edition of *A Many-Splendoured Thing*, I do not remember how much it was, and we spent two more days together, and I was fighting against a bone-melting compassion; for he sucked my hard-gained strength from me, and I had to discard pity and go on with tough bones.

André Bay of Editions Stock, my publisher in France, admired the Chinese Revolution; which was not the fashion then. The French Communist Party, I was told, had attacked me . . . but I never found out (or tried to find out) what they wrote about me and my book. *Le Monde* published extracts of *A Many-Splendoured Thing*, and it was a great success.

And then it was mid-March and Yungmei could travel. We left London for Switzerland and a few days in the crisp, delightful spring. Helmut Kossodo, my German publisher who lived in Geneva, put us up at a delightful small hotel on the lake; the swans came gliding by under our window and Yungmei was transfixed by the sight. A Swiss businessman I had met at a diplomatic party in Singapore, Mr Egon, invited us to visit him; we went to Zurich, stayed at the Storchen and shopped in the beautiful shops of Limmatquai. How tidy, how honest and precise the Swiss! How fabulous the clothes! We revelled in the fastidious good work, the good food, the cleanliness of the rooms, the comfort . . . Mr Egon took us to his house for dinner; and then invited us to spend a few days up in the Engadine, at his mountain chalet.

Mrs Egon wore no make-up, her hair was dragged into a thin bun on top of her head, and she shut her mouth grimly and looked at Yungmei with dislike. Her particular brand of racism was not overt but it was unrelenting. My Hong Kong Jesuit friend, Father Ladany, was a rollicking sybarite compared to Mrs Egon, who was convinced Sin began just outside Zurich, and that the whole of Asia was one vast orgy. I learnt later of (and saw with my own eyes) postcards she sent to poor sweet Mr Egon with skeletons and death's heads and graves, inscribed SIN IS DEATH!, when Mr Egon was on business in Bangkok, Hong Kong or Singapore.

Nevertheless, having planned to see the famous Swiss mountains, we decided to ignore Mrs Egon. 'I think she's just born that way,' said Yungmei wisely. We had dinner with the Zigglebecks, who lived in the quiet unostentatious way of the truly wealthy of Zurich; their house was all smoothness and dark polish and valuable furniture and antiques and old masters. Mrs Zigglebeck was in Moral Rearmament, and Mr Zigglebeck was simply in high precision armaments, including a new type of very lethal gun. Mrs Zigglebeck tried to get me to go to a Moral

Rearmament meeting up in the mountains at Caux. It would be excellent, she said, if Yungmei and I attended, for we would meet people from all over the world, gathered there to save the world. Yungmei ate stolidly. I said no. 'You will feel inspired in your writing,' said Mrs Zigglebeck. 'My mother does not need inspiration, she just writes,' said Yungmei.

Up to the Engadine, and the first shock of genuine postcardy sky and snow, the health, health, health of skiers . . . Mr Egon went skiing with a very nice Swiss couple. Mrs Egon pursed her mouth and told me that it was very difficult for men to remain without sin, but it was up to women to see they did not sin, and women who dragged men into sin should be punished publicly. 'You mean stoning?' I asked. We had a beautiful room and shared a huge bed, Yungmei and I, and a maid in starched apron and cap brought breakfast with a curtsy, but I could not find a bathroom to wash in. Every morning we were supplied with two large jugs of hot water. 'Ask HER,' said Yungmei. I tackled Mrs Egon. 'Oh,' she said, 'you want to use *our* bathroom?' 'In Malaya we bathe *at least* once a day.' Very reluctantly, she led me to the bathroom, and so Yungmei and I had a bath. 'We'd better not stay too long. I don't think we can have another bath,' said Yungmei.

On to Rome, and just in time for Easter. We hired a horse carriage because Yungmei enjoyed feeding sugar to the horse, and it was the best way to see Rome; every day now she was better, rounding out, firm and rosy. I wanted to give her a good time, to make up for the suffering she had endured.

To Naples to see Vesuvius; but Vesuvius had blown its top off and only some smoky holes glowed redly, and Yungmei was quite disappointed. We then boarded a Danish ship in Genoa for a leisurely return to Malaya. The sea air, the rest, would be good for Yungmei. When we docked at Penang a policeman was there, asking Yungmei, 'Are you back from China?' I explained we were back from London and showed the tickets, but the police officer obviously did not like Yungmei's Chinese face and would not let her land. I then had to invoke Leonard, Special Branch, Malcolm MacDonald. Finally we landed and took the train for Johore Bahru. It ran through the night and the jungle; the rain started; the heavy, insipid, noisy rain of Malaya, soaking the trees and erupting from the drains, and we were back, back in the heat and the green. 'I'll have a lot to tell my friends,' said Yungmei. She had maintained a steady correspondence with some of her schoolmates, sending dozens of postcards; hers was the age of passionate friendship. We came out of the train and there was Leonard, in shorts and shirt, wearing the half-assured, half-fearful expression which was his face to me. And immediately I knew that, alas, he would always remain a stranger, unloved, despite his very great devotion, despite his qualities. And that I could no longer live with him.

We now moved into a large airy house on the hill slope, with a garden full of frangipani trees. I kept five cats, two marvellous amber Burmese with green-yellow eyes, and throughout South East Asia sold the kittens I bred. Everywhere I found cat addicts, and for years sustained correspondence about my cat progeny with people in Malaya, Thailand, Indonesia, even Ceylon. I got rid of Auntie Hsu, my servant, tactfully paying her three months' wages. She fried everything in coconut oil and had a very frizzy perm; but the worst thing was that she insisted on frying the cats' fish.

In her place came Lao Chieh, Big Sister Lao, and until I left Malaya nine years later my life was smooth and easy because of her.

Lao Chieh came one morning to my clinic with three of my patients, her friends, who had persuaded her to 'help the Doctor'. She had a lovely classical face, a long pigtail down to the back of her knees; she was slim and tall and straight and she belonged to the sisterhood of silk.

There is a famous district in the province of Kuangtung, in which all the nurseries where the silkworms are reared, and the mulberry trees which provide the leaves for their food, are owned by women. And so that this wealth of silk and its labour should not fall into the hands of men, who would exploit the labour of women and their adroit fingers and reap the profit, the women live in sororities, and form their own couples, vowing love and sisterhood to each other. They wear their hair long in a virgin pigtail all their lives. This lesbian society, which is also an economic system, is accepted and respected. But in order to perpetuate their numbers the women must breed girls; and for this a man is needed. The sisterhood has devised its own system to prevent marriage being used to enslave them.

When a girl is of marriageable age, a man from another district is recruited by the matchmaker; and the marriage ceremony is celebrated. But at night, in the bedroom, another girl, bought for the purpose, takes the place of the bride in the marriage bed. The next morning the sorority makes sure that the marriage has been consummated (by inspecting the sheets) and then the real bride, still *virgo intacta*, serves morning tea to her in-laws and goes away, never to return except when the man dies, when she will wear mourning and perform the funeral rites. All the girls born of the substitute woman are accounted hers, and she will take them away and rear them as her own in the sisterhood.

Lao Chieh had two 'sisters', who came and went in our house. One of them had married and had therefore cut her hair and wore a bun, but this did not seem to damage the sisterhood. The sisterhood was highly thought of in Johore Bahru. Most of the women owned some land, or shops, or houses, even if they were mere 'servants'.

Lao Chieh took charge of me and my house. When one is lucky enough to have a Big Sister, one does nothing, except pay the bills. Lao Chieh decided what food Yungmei and I should eat, and she was a superb cook. She told Leonard when and where he must drive her on her afternoon off. She told me everything that went on in Johore Bahru and gave me advice about my patients. On her first inspection of the house she had sniffed at the mattress on her prospective bed.

'It smells of coconut oil.'

'I'll buy you a new one, Big Sister Lao.'

'No, don't go to that expense for nothing. I don't know if I'll stay.'

After three months, she said one morning, as she put down the breakfast, 'I think you'd better buy a new mattress.' She dosed me with Chinese medicine when I was tired or unwell. 'Your body is a Chinese body, you don't take well to Western medicine.' She made strengthening chicken soup for Yungmei. She hired and fired gardeners and laundry women. Our first gardener was a Tamil; he turned one end of my garden into a sago plantation. 'I was wondering when you would find out,' said Lao Chieh, and fired him. She bred orchids and planted trees. The only time I needed to put my foot down was about Hamid. He was a young boy straight from the *kampong*, a Malay, recommended to me by one of my Malay women friends, Che Katijah, who was a member of the ultra-conservative Pan-Malay Islam Party. She was Hamid's aunt by adoption. Because of Che Katijah, whom I loved dearly, I stuck by him when Lao Chieh would have fired him. I paid for driving lessons for him, and after a while Lao Chieh got used to him, and he would take her in the car to market and to see her friends on her day off. 'He shows his teeth all the time,' Lao Chieh said of him. 'He is just happy,' I would reply, and so she hurled a great deal of invective at him in her atrocious Malay, but Hamid only laughed cheerfully, and all was well.

Of course Lao Chieh fell in love with Yungmei; she would contemplate her with ravishment when Yungmei picked nimbly the cheek of the fresh, delicious garoupa she had prepared. 'Your thousand gold pieces* knows the best part of the fish, not like you, always thinking. You don't know what's at the end of your chopsticks.' But she did care for me, deeply, though she never said it; and late at night, after I had typed myself sleepy, I would find my bedroom smelling of fresh jasmine; Lao Chieh had plucked the white flowers and placed them on my pillow, and I would sigh with

---

* Name given to girls in China.

pleasure and fall asleep so quickly, knowing all was safe because of Lao Chieh.

It was on Lao Chieh's advice that I purchased, cheaply, a piece of land on the same hill slope, just in front of the house we occupied, and built three small bungalows on it. There was a marvellous view of the Straits of Johore, and we were neighbours of the Sultan of Johore's eldest son; his peacocks came to parade in our garden every afternoon. My bungalows were designed by a Chinese architect friend, Kee Yeap, from Singapore. He was inspired by the graceful Malay houses on stilts, and created airy, beautiful structures. 'You very lucky, Doctor,' said Mrs Wong, 'Lao Chieh give you big face everywhere.' The houses were ready in 1957 and we would live in one of them and rent the other two to agreeable families, one Chinese and one English.

Outwardly in that year of 1955 all was well. My clinic prospered, Leonard found a temporary job and went on studying for a London University course; Yungmei was a heroine in her school, with accounts of her operation and her European travels. I finished my book on Malaya and sent it off to Cape. Ted Weeks annoyed me again with suggestions for cuts, which I refused. But I was absolutely unable to sleep with Leonard. It was physically impossible.

Pretty soon I was informed by a charitable English-woman, and also by an anonymous letter, that Leonard had a 'mistress' – she was the buttock-cheeked salesgirl of a certain shop selling cosmetics. This relieved me greatly. I had now relapsed into that state of sexlessness which was mine before Ian; but Leonard, of course, was different. He was a normally constituted man, a healthy, well-sexed man. I had once inquired, out of curiosity, from a newsman how many times a week he found it necessary to perform. 'At least three times,' said he.

But the trouble was that Leonard really cared for me; that it was me he wanted, and my total indifference irked him. Our relations thus became extremely difficult and since he did not understand my complete block, he thought I was behaving in a way calculated to enlarge his inferiority complex. He tried jealousy scenes. 'Don't insult me,' I said. 'If and when there is someone else, I shall certainly tell you.' But this was not the kind of situation he could explain to himself, or that I could explain to him. How does one explain a total inability to function sexually? Of course I knew the cause. It was Pao. He had wounded me mortally in that respect; until the end of my life I would suffer from relapses.

Meanwhile I felt disagreeably restless. I had finished my book, I was working too hard, I did not sleep well, and I was afraid Leonard might try to make approaches. We had many short, sharp quarrels.

I received a letter from Cousin Pengju in Hong Kong. He wrote about Premier Chou Enlai and Chou's invitation to all Chinese intellectuals to return, even if only to see what had been done in China since Liberation. I felt parched and withered with that inner drought which compels me to go to China as a thirsty beast goes to water. I had to go back.

Christmas Eve. I had decorated a small tree, placed presents for Yungmei and her friends below it; and asked Leonard to return early because this was Yungmei's first Christmas free of tuberculosis. There was also a present for him. Gestures. Routine, accomplished with compunction and no pleasure. All part of that façade self which I had conjured up, that brisk mother and wife self which I wrapped myself in as a magician in his cape. Meanwhile, I knew something would happen that Christmas Eve ... almost, I willed it to happen.

'Let us see if he will come back early.'

Leonard had tended to stay out late at night; and this could be expected. He would return and watch me as I looked asleep and did not stir. He would watch me at breakfast; and I would not give him a chance. I never even inquired why he was late. But now I had mentioned the fact, obliquely, by asking him to return early. What would he do?

Leonard did not return until one o'clock. 'Where have you been?' said I. 'That's my business,' he retorted, braced for the showdown. And so we went into our parts, as if rehearsed. 'You're not a woman, you're a thinking machine,' he said. The ritual of a quarrel. I think he hoped – most reasonably – for anger, tears, then reconciliation and catharsis to end, as normally as possible, in bed. But this would not be. I had not prepared the script that way.

One afternoon in early January 1956 I drove to the hairdresser in Singapore and had my hair cut short. Until that day I had kept my hair long. It was thick and fell to below my waist; everyone commented on my beautiful hair, and some men slavered when they saw it, when I unloosed it to go swimming. Now it was strewn on the linoleum floor of Miss Peck Poon, the hairdresser, in great sheaves. Miss Peck Poon giggled as she gathered it tenderly. 'I can make at least three wigs out of this, Doctor.'

She then cajoled me into having a perm; and since I was determined to do the worst, I acquiesced. I looked at the lamentable result, an Afro-American dandelion. Even Miss Peck Poon was worried. 'You look different,' she said.

Ignoring Leonard's perturbation, I took an aeroplane ticket to New Delhi. Malcolm had moved to India in late 1955 and had invited me to visit him. With Yungmei healthy, Lao Chieh better than me at looking after her, I could go away. I had by now a permanent assistant, because the clinic was too much for just one person. But patients fell in number drastically when I left. 'I've kept my disease for you to look at, Doctor,' some used to say to me reproachfully when I came back. Nevertheless, I was beginning to detach myself from medicine.

And so to Delhi, to be the guest of Malcolm and his Canadian wife, Fiona, in their house and splendid garden, in the superb winter of north India. Squadrons of parakeets in battle formation swooped across the lawns, the drongos were more cheeky than in Malaya; jackals screamed at night and came into the suburbs of the city. And oh, the beauty of India! A totally different beauty from the untiring loveliness of China. China is pastel and nuance and discovery, and India hits you in the eye, flaunts everything; India is show and riot and gaudiness, extravagance and surfeit of everything. Indian skin changes hue with anger or happiness; India is audible, visible, melodious and raucous and garish and monstrous in its open cruelties; tinsel and gold, horror and marvel all at once. Mind-jolting in its profligate splendour.

Malcolm entertained well and much; and to the British High Commission came the Prime Minister, Jawaharlal Nehru, in admirable pure white with a rose in his hand, looking with a pout on his lips and moving eyes both moody poet and disgruntled lover, and yet with a prick of asperity somewhere. He started immediately talking about *A Many-Splendoured Thing*, which Lady Mountbatten had given him to read. 'I think great loves should be kept private,' said he. Perhaps he had known Ian well, and felt too near the impact of his death. 'In that case literature would be much impoverished,' I replied. For about three seconds Nehru stopped twiddling the rose he held between his fingers. As a result of this brief passage of arms, our relations, though amiable and friendly, would always harbour a twinge of strain.

He then asked me what I thought of India, but answered it for me. 'It's full of tragedy and comedy, laughter and tears.' 'You are a poet, Your Excellency,' I said, courtier-polite. He expected some tribute and nodded. After dinner Lady Mountbatten sat next to him, and kept patting his hand to make a point. But it was the Maharaja of Patiala who won my heart that day. He was the tallest, most handsome man I had seen so far. Among the maharajas and maharanees a-glitter with diamonds and rubies and emeralds whom I met then and was to meet at other dinners, he stood out not only for personal good looks, but also for a kind of simple common sense. I learnt of Patiala's woes; his father had left him encumbered with something like five score (or perhaps more) widows and ex-wives, all to be looked after by the present Maharaja, his son.

Vice-President Radhakrishnan had a most magnificent turban – I wondered how this confection was held together;

invisible pins, he told me. His grandeur depended on this headgear as well as on his extraordinary gift for lengthy verbal jousting. He talked philosophy solidly for about two hours, and the next day a large case full of his books arrived for me to read.

In the garden the crows swooped down at tea to wrest sandwiches from our hands. 'I must learn about this country.' Everything has the same largeness of dimension as China; big, and bigness stretches. The largesse of great size . . . I went wandering in Old Delhi and its oily, rancid misery. 'I must learn about this country.' How big Asia was, how little I knew about it! And not only me, but so many Asians like myself! We had been more cut off from each other by the Western colonial period than from Europe and America; and now the time had come to know each other. 'What a wealthy country you have!' I exclaimed when I had been there some days. 'You have so much of everything . . .' 'That is exactly what Chou Enlai said,' replied Indian friends happily. Yes, India was rich, rich, so much more wealthy than China in resources; but even then I could see its primal fault, squander, waste, everywhere, in everything. Even the poor wasted, they wasted effort, energy, they made so many unnecessary gestures. Then it always irritated me to see the women trailing their sarees in the dust; such beautiful sarees, so much work in them and all the hems in the dust; and the way things were not kept working, and above all, the inefficient tools of labour. It was only after going back to China that the full *meaning* of this neglect of implements of daily labour struck me as the unforgivable crime.

I had tea with the Health Minister, a prim and proper spinster in white homespun. We discussed family planning; she approved of continence, and the teaching of the safe period to women by means of beads. I felt these ploys for denatalization were somewhat precarious; but no, said she firmly, in India they could be effective.

I went to small parties thrown by the New Delhi intelligentsia because they had read my book; but they had also read *The Waste Land* and T. S. Eliot was almost a god.

Among the younger diplomats I met Tikki Kaul, just back from Peking, where he had fallen in love with a Chinese girl. But members of India's diplomatic service are not allowed to marry foreign women. Tikki shook his head, sighed, and returned to Delhi. He was writing a book, but not about thwarted destinies. A very intelligent, able, deft diplomat, he would have a brilliant career as Ambassador to Moscow and Washington, which only came to an end when Indira Gandhi was deposed in 1977.

I told Malcolm that I wanted to go to China; and that I had come to India for that purpose. I had had no news of my father, not even through Hong Kong. 'Of course one must have patience, but I feel in my bones that it's time to go and have a look.' Malcolm agreed. 'I don't think China and Russia are really alike,' he said. He then invited the Chinese Ambassador to lunch. The Ambassador and his wife came; they were both portly, grizzled, and both had been guerrillas in their days of strength. The Ambassador had been a Long Marcher. I talked to him about returning to China for a visit and he said, 'Of course, you should certainly go to see what has been done.' A polite formula, and noncommittal. Not all overseas Chinese were welcome to return, I knew. And as for myself . . . Nevertheless, I presented myself at the Chinese Embassy the next day. The Ambassador was not available. The secretary was a severe young man, less than helpful. What was the purpose of my visit to China? I told him I had read Premier Chou Enlai's call to Chinese abroad; anyone who wanted to return to the motherland could do so, even if only for a visit. The secretary's stiffness increased. What were my qualifications? I told him that I was a doctor. But the story of my life was so eminently complicated that he obviously could not grasp any of it, so after attempting a short biography I gave up. He handed me a form to fill in and said he would send it on to Peking. 'When shall I know?' 'Three to four weeks, perhaps more.' I did not tell him that I was Han Suyin, which is my writer's pseudonym. This would merely have upset him even more. I gave my real Chinese name, my father's address in Peking and his profession, and wrote on the form that I wanted to visit my family. Always I felt worried that my connection with Pao might have caused prejudice against Papa and Third Uncle, although Cousin Pengju assured me that this was 'improbable'.

The French Ambassador asked me to lunch; he was erudite, passionately devoted to Indian mysticism, and advised me to go to Kathmandu. I heard a golden bell ring in that word. Kathmandu, Nepal. Malcolm's office cabled the British Ambassador in Nepal, and four days later I flew to Kathmandu.

The airport was handkerchief-sized, but all the Himalayas stood watch on it, and there was the primrose smell of snow in the air. Men with plaited hair and turquoise and coral earrings hung over the rickety airport barrier to watch our aeroplane land. And there was Judith Tollington, the wife of the British Ambassador, Boyd Tollington, brown and nutmeggy and eager and affectionate, come to meet me.

The British Embassy was a rambling mansion of modest demeanour, in marked contrast to the imposing white stucco and stone Buckingham Palace-type palaces of the Ranas, the ruling caste. Boyd typed all his reports himself on a small old typewriter, for the Foreign Office was then in a crisis, enjoining its diplomats to economize. 'We're a bit forgotten here because nothing very nasty ever happens in Nepal.'

Judith gave a party and a treasure hunt; the European community of Kathmandu came, including Boris Lyssanovich of the Royal Hotel and his beautiful Scandinavian wife, Inge. Boris was a giant of gaiety and Rabelaisian humour, bestriding his world with imperishable joy. His career, first as a ballet dancer, later running clubs in Calcutta, now as a hotel manager in Kathmandu, was interspersed with unbelievable episodes; unbelievable unless one knew Boris, when everything became credible . . . anything could happen when Boris was there. He had just emerged from jail, where he had been placed for reasons bureaucratic and confused, and was very proud of the parties he had thrown while under duress.

Boris could arrange anything. He conjured up the best Moët et Chandon champagne on a Himalayan peak; organized a banquet with ostrich eggs, elephants' paws, Boston clams and caviar without batting an eye. 'Ask Boris,' said everyone, and Boris obliged. He had a scheme for installing a dairy farm; another to cut the transporting of beef on the hoof from India across the passes (the animals were skeletal when they arrived, from the long walk). He wanted to lay a golf course up at 3,000 metres; he wanted to build a chain of hotels in Nepal. Boris was not wrong in these schemes; today Nepal is very much part of the tourist circuit, and many of the impossible things he then planned now exist.

How poor Nepal was, at first glance: in the medieval way Europe of the tenth century must have been poor. Yet it was almost impossible to be gloomy there; altitude seemed to prevent it and the Newaris, the real inhabitants of Nepal (as distinct from their masters, the Ranas, who had conquered them and stayed a class apart), were such a gay and singing people and beautiful to look at. Addicted, like the Balinese, to festivity and honouring the gods, they were superb carvers of wood, and in the past centuries Nepalese had come up to Szechuan and even up to Peking to carve wood-latticed windows and stone pillars and arches. The streets of Kathmandu were glossy mud, shining with offal and cow manure; the garbage was thrown from the windows of the sculptured wooden houses with their projecting balconies; hence the stout black umbrellas everyone carried, hooked on to the shoulder. So Europe must have been, even up to the seventeenth century.

Holiness was greatly about, in magnificent and somewhat decrepit temples, which abounded; every street corner had its holy place, its holy stones, lingam and shrines and perpetual conjuring of malefice. The rulers, the Ranas, looked physically different from the Newaris, who were more mongoloid in appearance. They built themselves replicas of English palaces and piled the rooms with Victoriana brought on the backs of porters across the passes. Like Tibet, Nepal wanted no wheels, for wheels brought change. Hence no roads until 1956.

But now a road was to run from Kathmandu through the foothills of the Himalayas, and on down to the plains of India. This road was being built by the Indian army, more specifically by the Madras Sappers. Another road was going to be built by the Americans, running lengthwise across Nepal, skirting the mountain ranges. And yet another one was contemplated, to be built by the Chinese, linking Kathmandu across the Himalayan passes to the Tibetan plateau and to Lhasa.

'King Mahendra of Nepal is a far-sighted man; he wants his country to come out of seclusion, to be modernized and play its role among the emergent nations of Asia,' said Boyd. He then added that, as a treat, he had arranged to take me on the Indian road.

'It's going to be rough. Much of it is still being bulldozed into shape,' said Boyd. 'I shall introduce you to the engineer in charge. I hope you don't mind, he's quite dark,' he added, a little nervously. Perhaps Boyd had met with a colour bias in other guests . . . it was so prevalent at the time, and accounted so natural. Even in Singapore and Malaya, even among the overseas Chinese and the Eurasians, the colour bar held sway. Lao Chieh deplored the fact that I went out without a parasol. 'You'll get so black,' said she. Among the Eurasians it was even worse. I knew at least two families who kept their darker children locked up in the bedroom when there were visitors, only showing off the light-complexioned ones.

As for India, never have I seen such a colour-ridden society! From my first day in Delhi I was secretly appalled by the advertisements in the English newspapers for marriage partners, specifying that the complexion must be 'light'. Small wonder that Boyd feared that I too might nurse a colour complex.

In the sunny afternoon of my third day in Kathmandu I went with Boyd and Judith to a Rana's palace for a wedding festival. Avoiding cows, holy men in contemplation, holy stones, and sundry other sacred obstacles, Boyd manoeuvred the car past the gates into the palace grounds, basking in the joy of a small, light rain that laid the dust. 'Awfully lucky sign,' said Boyd. The palace had ceilings painted blue and pink and green, with holes gouged into them for ventilation. And by the grand piano in the middle of the largest of the three reception rooms stood a tall man in Indian army uniform, with a glass of whisky in his hand. 'Do let me introduce you to the Colonel,' said Boyd. 'He's taking us on the trip I told you about, along the road he's building.'

Oh, I thought, what a marvellous, marvellous looking man! How beautiful, how beautiful he is! He was indeed very dark, almost blue in the darkness of his skin. But it was the most gorgeous, sensuous, satin chocolate colour in the world for me. Then and there I fell out of frigidity into the most blazing need to put my hands on him, to hold him, to want him to make love to me. Heaven – how was this possible, and so swiftly? I stared at him and my legs were unsteady, and all the juices of my body started to pour.

We shook hands. He smiled, and then I knew that if I wanted to have him I must not be too eager. He was a diffident man, unspoilt, and probably many women threw themselves at his head and he avoided them. I do not know how I could tell this, but it all came, affirmation, certainty. So I put on a timid look, and went off immediately to speak to other guests. And of course, as I went from room to room, it was not very long before I found that he was following me, although he, too, was very busily speaking to other guests . . . How silly, I thought, how silly and yet it was not silly, that we should both behave like adolescents in love for the first time.

Boyd and Judith and I had a very early breakfast the next day, and then the Colonel arrived in his jeep, and the morning became a shining glory, and all the world was full of laughter. Boyd and I got into the jeep and the Colonel drove up the road, which soon lost its tarmac and became an earth road, then a meander of boulders and crevices as it began to zigzag, mounting the soft and treacherous foothills shifty with the rains of summer. The sun beat down hard and after some hours, pausing at a bend when we had soared some 1,500 metres higher than Kathmandu, we saw the whole chain of the Himalayas, the peaks of shining ice, and among them Everest. When night fell we reached the Indian army camp, some 3,000 metres up. It was now bitterly cold, but in the common room for the Madras Sapper officers there was a great log fire burning, and the Colonel kicked the logs, and then looked at me, and then went back to kicking logs with immense concentration. He was jittery; his colour had changed, he looked darker now in the light of the fire. And suddenly the tales of Krishna, the God of Love, so dark that he is blue, came welling up, and I felt that all my skin was glowing with life, and I had a thousand eyes and ears; I could hear the fire lick and swallow the wood logs and the tiny bursting noise of sparks. But still it was not possible to talk.

We slept in separate small tents and I was wretchedly cold; an icy wind swept through the camp and my face was covered with cold sand, but I did not dare get up and ask for more blankets, lest the Colonel think it forward of me, so I froze until morning.

Morning; and after breakfast we had to return to Kathmundu, and what I was waiting for then happened. 'Now you will drive the jeep,' said he, turning to me. 'Oh!' exclaimed Boyd, involuntarily, by no means undisturbed. I sat in the driver's seat and we lurched and bounced abominably, jumped rocks and dived into holes and rolled a mere few inches away from the precipice edge, only saved by the Colonel swiftly turning the steering wheel. 'That was close,' said Boyd in a faint voice. We were now both distraught with love, but still we had not said anything to each other except 'Oops, sorry', when I nearly overturned, and 'Better sound the horn round the bends', and 'Now we'll stop for tea', when we thought Boyd had had enough of my driving.

Judith saw us return and immediately she knew. She came to hug me that night as I lay in bed.

'Oh, my dear, my dear . . .' she said.

'He's nice,' I said.

'I sometimes feel our only responsibility towards ourselves is to be happy,' she said.

'His name is Vincent . . .' I broke off lamely.

Vincent. Because he was not a Hindu but an Indian Catholic, and Catholicism in India is said to go back to the Apostle St Thomas, whose bones rest in the crypt of the cathedral in Madras. Vincent came from Madras.

He had asked me to dinner for the next evening. He had also invited Boyd and Judith, but they said that they had another engagement. We went to the Yak and Yeti, Boris's bar at the Royal Hotel; and Boris took one look and knew. 'Altitude sickness,' he announced to the ceiling as he served us solidly packed drinks.

'Are you really a writer?' Vincent said.

'Yes I am.'

'And you are leaving tomorrow?'

'Yes I am.'

'Shall I see you again?'

'I don't know.'

He kicked the logs in the hearth of the Yak and Yeti and Boris threw us one look and smiled ecstatically.

'All I know is that I want to be a woman again. It is very difficult for me to be a woman sometimes. Make me into a woman again.'

Many weeks later, Vincent would tell me of Boyd's consternation when he had received Malcolm's cable announcing the arrival of a 'Chinese writer, female' in Kathmundu, to be entertained.

'I'm sure she wears glasses and she's probably quite old,' Boyd had said gloomily. 'What does one do with a Chinese writer, female?'

'Let's take her on the road. Maybe she'll leave more quickly,' Vincent had said to him helpfully.

And that is how it had happened.

He was at the airport the next morning with Judith, seeing me off. We had made no plans; how could we? I only knew that there was ache and glow, and what did tomorrow mean in front of the Himalayas? He stood looking at me from outside the aeroplane, and then rushed in (the pilot was his friend, and went on revving to oblige, delaying the takeoff). 'I'll come to see you in Delhi,' said he.

Then I was back in Delhi, and Malcolm himself opened the door (Malcolm often answered the door chimes without bothering the servants). 'Suyin, you look absolutely glorious,' said he. 'I am in love,' I said. 'Oh, how happy I am for you, Suyin.'

I spent the next few days not quite knowing where I was, exuding radiance, since several men suddenly fell in love with me (I disengaged tactfully). I also went to the Chinese Embassy, but there was no news of a visa. I went to Agra to see the Taj Mahal, and along the road the vultures were feeding on carcases of dead cattle. I nearly bought a very large emerald, then desisted. And on the sixth day the secretary brought me a telegram: 'The mountain is coming to Mahomed. Will be in Delhi. Tomorrow. Vincent.' Which was enough to make me quite incoherent, dissolving into smiles as I walked on the street. By the afternoon of the next day there was no Vincent. At 5.30 I went to the prim secretary. She disapproved of the stream of 'natives' whom Malcolm invited; a stream which had swollen to a small flood by my being there.

'Has anyone called for me?'

'Oh, some *dark* native came a little while ago, but you were having tea with HE, in the garden. I told him to ring up or call later.'

I could have strangled her. But before murder was done, the telephone rang.

'It's the same fellow, I think,' said the secretary.

'I'll take it.' It was the same fellow. 'Come, here and now,' I said.

And within half an hour he was there and I was out and we held hands in the taxi, and there was no future, no future, only the small fragment of time now, and that was a marvel like Everest. Vincent also trod on air, caught his finger in a taxi door the next day: he had himself closed the door on it. 'I'm going crazy,' he announced. I went back to the Chinese Embassy. No visa. We persisted in doing the usual things, knowing that everything was no longer what it was; there was no logic, no future, only this.

'What shall we do about it?'

'There is no need for plans, is there?'

'It just is.'

'Yes, it is.'

No visa. I rang up Tikki Kaul and explained to him that I wanted to go back to see my father in China. Tikki Kaul had been a diplomat in Peking and had excellent relations with the Chinese Embassy. Would he intercede for me? He did. At last I obtained a visa for one entry, valid for the end of May. 'Everything will be arranged when you get to Peking,' said the visa officer, less rigorous now, but still baffled. And now I had to get back to Malaya.

We went to Benares for two days. Benares, where dirt and fervour were conjoined, and the smell of ordure and sanctity indistinguishable. But there was the Ganges, ample magnificence, and the funeral pyres and their blankets of flowers, and death had no dominion over all. To Calcutta, for one day and one night at the Great Eastern Hotel, and then I was off, back to Malaya.

'When shall we meet again?'

'I'll manage something,' I promised.

'I'll wait for you,' he said. 'Even if it is ten years.'

'Only ten years?'

'Twenty then,' said he recklessly.

Never did he reproach me for going away. And yet how was it that I could, with my new love and all its enchantment beckoning, how could I still go away? But then perhaps there is no explanation, except that all my life I shall be running in two opposite directions at once; away from and towards love, away from and towards China. Forever sidetracking myself; and in the end garnering both sides of my coin of life.

Back to Johore Bahru, and immediately Leonard: 'Oh, what's happened to you? You've changed.'

'I am in love, Leonard.'

He laughed. 'What nonsense.'

'It is not nonsense.'

'It will pass,' said he confidently.

'Oh no, not with me,' I said, 'I set like concrete.'

'I know this kind of thing,' he began. 'It happens in every marriage, but it shouldn't affect marriage.'

'I'm not built that way, unfortunately. I want a divorce.'

He laughed again, then lost his temper and threw a little soup at me, but it was not very hot.

I went to a few parties, and said I was going to China at the end of May to see my family, and this created an enormous commotion in the press. Li Kungchiang asked me if I really intended to go. 'Of course.' 'I think that's the future,' he said. 'Come back and tell us about it.' Then there were dramatic banner headlines in the *Straits Times*, for no one dared to say: I'm going to China. My letters were opened by the Special Branch, and plain-clothes men followed me. 'I'm going with my eyes closed to the politics,' I said grandiloquently to an American who came to interview me, knowing that silly semantics reassure people.

I took precautions. If Malaya denied me re-entry, I might enter Singapore; I even put money down for a small bungalow in Singapore, which I could then claim as my house . . . And then, when all was neatly in place, I felt I must see Vincent again. 'Perhaps it was the Himalayas, the sun and the snow. Perhaps I won't like him when I see him again.' So I flew to Kathmandu for a week, for King Mahendra's coronation in early May.

I remember that week, for it was the beginning of another book, *The Mountain is Young*. I remember the dawn like pink candy-floss and the thousands of little pink and white radishes being washed in the river, and side by side with them the ablutions of brown, gaunt, holy men; everything transparent, and the childish sun lording it over all and the earth laughing. I remember the painted elephants and the dust under their feet, the tawdry and the magnificent processions, and Vincent and I going to Pagan by jeep and up in the hills, and what words did we have when there were no words, only this exultation of the mountains and the sky?

After five days Leonard turned up. The encounter was unpleasant, though unavoidable. I had to leave anyway, so I left with Leonard. He thought he had won; but when we arrived in Calcutta, I told him that it was all very simple. I wanted to be free, Vincent or no Vincent. 'You promised to let me go if I wanted. I want to be free.' But at the same time, knowing that he had no funds, and no job, because of me, I arranged for a living allowance, and we still went on living in the same house.

'I'll wait for you, whether you come back from China or don't come back,' wrote Vincent. And he had said, 'You are always with me now, until I die.' And so I left him, and I went to China, carried also by this renewed strength and beauty bestowed by love.

Four days after leaving Calcutta I was in Hong Kong, to cross the border to China. People came and entreated me not to go. It was too dangerous. I would be shot or jailed. Some others came to take photographs of me. I was pursued right up to Lowu, the border railway station between Hong Kong and China, by a persistent American television reporter. 'We want to film you in case you never come back,' said he heartily as he pointed his apparatus at me.

Francis and Cecilia did not panic. Francis merely said, 'Well, you must go, of course, to see your father.' And he asked me to take a letter and a leg to his brother, who was in Peking. The brother only had one leg, having lost the other in an accident some years ago. Would I take an artificial leg, the latest model? I would. I also bought two bicycles, some watches and other gifts for my Family. And thus one morning in May I crossed the border between Hong Kong and China, holding the artificial leg under my arm, returning home.

CHAPTER 5

China: 1956

The barbed wire at the border looked theatrical, for as I crossed the bridge leading to China, grass-cutting women in black, with grandmotherly cackle and bare feet, sauntered into Hong Kong. They did not produce passports and were not checked. Daily they came and went between these two universes. 'Please enter,' the Chinese Liberation Army soldier on guard at the bridge said politely to me. He had tennis shoes on. The customs official was meticulous. No taxes to be paid on the artificial limb and he suggested that I should wear a watch and use a Parker pen. 'Then we shall only tax the remaining ones: you'll save some money.' As for the two bicycles, surely I was going to ride one? He need only tax one of them.

The China Travel Service young man who took care of me was eager to learn more English. How young everyone was! An overwhelming impression of youth; among the train attendants, the people who carried bags and hauled loads, the few police (unarmed). And then the familiar churn of wheels began, train lullaby cradling my childhood back to me as we ambled among the jade green fields of May, dotted with Hakka women with black-fringed hats and their feet absent in water. I remembered denuded mounds and hillocks, dilapidation and ruin. Now the villages were neat and the houses new; everywhere there were trees, all of a size, six-year-old trees flapping small, young leaves like children's hands . . .

Canton, now renamed Kuangchow. Entry into the station to music and young men wearing white shirts and neat trousers. No rags, no beggars. I was taken to the Love the Masses Hotel; a Yugoslav youth representative and some overseas Chinese came with me. My room was on the fifth floor, looking down upon the translucent Pearl River. The hotel was clean, whereas I remembered it filthy when I had stayed there in 1938.* The breeze flowed in and threw itself upon my bed. All night I would hear the frolicking water slap its freight of small sampans. The fishing junks clacked their sails as they went out to sea; ferries hooted reassuringly above the gurgle of the peopled stream.

I walked about Kuangchow, met more overseas Chinese from the train. They had come back to stay; they were going to build themselves bungalows in areas where repatriated overseas were housed. Most of them came from Indonesia. In 1958, and up to 1960, many hundreds of thousands would leave Indonesia; the Chinese government sending ships for their repatriation. They would start rubber and coffee plantations in the south. 'If you go to Peking, go to the Hsinchiao Hotel. My uncle has put some money into the building,' said one of them to me.

I read the newspapers pasted on boards along the main street. Achievements and production. I went to a cinema and saw one-third of a Russian love story. I came out in the evening and the Cantonese strolled by, clicking wooden slippers, that incessant tap dance which vanished when they switched to rubber and plastic sandals by 1964. A health campaign was on, and slogans everywhere enjoined people to refrain from spitting. People went on spitting. Accustomed to dire threats of fines and punishment in other countries for refusing to obey orders, I asked the young China Travel Service man, 'Why don't you punish people who spit?' 'But that would be oppression,' he cried. 'We believe the masses can discipline themselves.'

Acrobats in the People's Park; an exhibition of Polish painting, children roller-skating, couples with young babies in the open-air restaurants . . . such security, such tranquil enjoyment of the balmy warmth, I had never seen in China, never without being interrupted by clawing hands, diseased bodies, hungry faces . . . 'Lady, lady, open your compassionate heart . . . I have not eaten . . .' But now it was not so.

*See *Birdless Summer* and *Destination Chungking*.

I remembered the streets as dreadful corridors of want; now they were calm and safe.

At dawn the Pearl River was solid pink and the sun heaved itself out of its seabed and light seized all the earth. Then I was on the train to Peking, and again young trees were everywhere. The attendant went round with a fly swatter, trying to look murderous; there were no flies. Every station was clean, with flower pots, and among them always the nice young face of one unarmed policeman in white, standing to attention. And this was not for tourists, since at the time there were no tourists; few people from the West went to China then.

The loudspeaker on the train never stopped dispensing exhortation, encouragement, warnings at each station to leave no luggage behind, and achievements in production. A perpetual self-congratulation, a little boring after two days. My companions in the compartment, two men and a woman, were amiable. I said I came from Malaya, and they talked about production and achievements. They reeled off satisfactory statistics; they were well-informed. Never, I thought, had I seen such a network of information at all levels. Unanimity of effort, unanimity of explanation, explanation repeated in a hundred thousand places at once; including the running trains.

At Wuhan we crossed the river by ferry (the bridge would only be built three years later). A gnarled peasant sitting opposite me picked up the book on my lap, one of those I had purchased at the Hsinhua bookstore in Kuangchow. Entitled *Story From the Old Mulberry Tree*, it was about Land Reform: well-written and unsparing, noting the brutalities which had taken place when peasants had been aroused. The peasant leafed through it, read a sentence aloud and replaced it on my lap. He could read. That was the miracle which kept me entranced for the next hour. Suddenly I saw the immensity of what had been done . . . peasants travelling in trains, who could read.

We rolled through the plains of Honan and I craned at Sinyang, my birthplace, but could not see the house on the hill where we had lived. Chengchow and the Yellow River, and the loudspeaker waxing excited, and the bridge, my father's pride and pain, and the car attendant going round locking the lavatories . . . no excreta in the noble stream. All the familiar stations and their names, and I thought of my mother's children buried here, their bones in the yellow earth with so many, so many millions of other bones. I thought of the locust plagues, and the famines, and the floods, and the droughts I had seen. And now there were young people washing the train, and flower pots, and outside in the fields the peasants wore clean white T-shirts, and there was peace.

In the late afternoon, a greyness on the mauve horizon; the battlemented grey walls of Peking with their crouched monumental gates. By the wall's base pyramidal piles of coal balls, made of coal dust and clay, and donkeys laden with them in baskets trudging into the city. The loudspeaker now went berserk with joyful recommendations. 'Beloved passengers, we are approaching Peking . . . leave nothing behind . . . please be careful as you go down . . . please take care of the children . . .'

Music, and the train sliding to a stop and Third and Fourth Brothers running along the platform . . . I came down and there in a small group, his eyes screwed up to see better, was Papa, Papa, oh so beloved, a little thinner but well, and everyone round him smiling as if something good had been achieved. We greeted each other, cousins and nephews and nieces and aunts by blood, and by affection, using the correct and appropriate names of family relationship and courtesy. And Papa said with love, 'Your dress is so thin, you'll catch a cold.' And Aunt Ting exclaimed, 'Ah, how much your father has waited for this! Now his face is like spring!' She had a plug of paper in her left nostril; she was being treated for a cancer of the nose. She would live another fifteen years. Papa smiled and introduced me to two people in sober clothes standing diffidently behind the family group. 'These are Comrades Li and Wu, of my organization; they have come to greet you. The organization has sent a car to take us home, and then to bring you to your hostel.'

'We welcome all intellectuals from overseas who return to serve the country,' said Comrade Wu, a jovial man, pumping my hand.

'I came back to see my father,' I replied, smiling noncommittally. 'May I stay at home with him?'

'We made arrangements for a hostel,' said Comrade Wu, 'but we can study the problem.'

I did not protest; it was now arranged that I would first go home with Papa and then proceed to the hostel for the night.

Home was, of course, smaller; part of the veranda partitioned off since another family now lived in what had been our living and dining room. Papa had kept the two bedrooms and the bathroom for himself. The kitchen was now in the outhouse where our rickshaw puller had lived; the veranda, glassed in, was the congenial living room.

Hsueh Mah, our servant, beamed and screamed. Her front teeth protruded more than ever. 'Big Miss is back, Big Miss is back, oh what a happy day!' She stomped around, ineffectual, taking up a lot of space trying to pour tea. I went in to wash my hands and I saw mother's large trunk in Papa's bedroom. She had come with it from Belgium in 1913; it was the one she always packed with winter clothes when she threatened to leave. Now she had gone but the trunk remained; perhaps it was too old, perhaps left to remind father she was still there. Oh, the dreadful tenacity of things; memory traps to ambush us.

First Uncle's daughter Ping, Fourth Sister in our generation, arrived and shook hands with everyone. She was a Party cadre in charge of education in the eastern sector. In her teens she had run away from middle school to the Communist base at Yenan. It was a most hazardous journey, through the Kuomintang lines, with their concentration camps and tortures for the young like her going to Yenan. She had taken part in the guerrilla wars against Japan; she had married another guerrilla and borne five children and lost three – she did not know where they were – whom she had had to leave with peasants when the guerrillas moved camp. 'There were bad people who sold our children behind our backs,' she would tell me years later. Like so many, so many modest heroes, the core of the Chinese Communist Party, and the reason why it succeeded, she had no time for self-pity or for reminiscence, until twenty years later, in 1976, when at last she began to tell me a little of her life.

But now she came in, portly and self-assured, and I only saw a glossy, managerial woman. She assumed a stance of 'teacher' towards me. I was a responsibility. Educating and remoulding into correct thinking such people as myself, come from the capitalist world – with gentleness of course, but withal firmly, not giving up until the teaching penetrated – was quite a task. It took us time, Ping and I, to become fond of each other; to realize that, in a way, we were both as domineering; but that I managed it with less frankness. She had the greater moral courage, the unflinching dedication.

We ate some noodles and chicken that Papa had prepared, for he was a good cook with a light, swift hand. On the wall hung a picture of Chairman Mao, looking debonair; below it was my father's 'model engineer' certificate, framed and with a big red satin flower pinned to the frame. It was all untrue about his having been in jail or ill-treated. 'How is Third Uncle?' I asked of Third and Fourth Brothers (who are Third Uncle's sons, and technically my cousins in the Western style). 'He is well, but very busy.' All private companies, factories, shops, were being nationalized that year. Many were going 'semi-public' as joint companies with the state. Third Uncle had managed many companies. 'I intend to go to Szechuan to see him.' 'Our government always give intellectuals returned from abroad the opportunity to see the achievements of socialism,' said Comrade Li graciously. I understood that I had spoken out of turn.

We smiled and burped with satisfaction. Then I was taken to the hostel on Hatamen Street. I was greeted there by the man in charge, Comrade Liu, most affable and solicitous. 'Welcome, welcome,' he cried, and took me to a very nice room, where I slept, after having stared at the ceiling for a very long time.

The next morning I went down to breakfast at 7 a.m. The refectory (the word leapt out, for there was such a school ambience to the hostel) held round brown tables with eight stools to each. Some people were finishing breakfast, others just beginning. There was white steamed bread and gruel and pickles and tea, copious and hot. At my table sat a couple, husband and wife. They smiled at me and we introduced ourselves. They had returned from America to serve China, they had read of me, seen my book and recognized me by the photograph on the cover. They belonged to an illustrious, scholarly family; I had known Mr C's uncle and his father, both professors in renowned Chinese universities; both were now in the United States.

'How long have you been here?'

'About four months . . . we read Premier Chou Enlai's appeal to intellectuals to return, so we came back . . . It was difficult to manage; the Americans are not letting people like us out of the States.'

'But no work has been assigned to us yet,' said Mrs C. 'We are being re-educated politically.'

Mr C nodded towards three people sitting at another table. 'They've been here longer . . . one is a sociologist, the other two are students who have not completed their studies abroad. Some people are snapped up very quickly, especially scientists, engineers, mathematicians . . . but others have to wait.'

'It's also a question of class origin,' said Mrs C ruefully.

'But that's getting better,' said her husband.

I swallowed the words with little sips of gruel. 'What is your general impression?'

'At first we felt strange . . . we were not used to many things . . . everything is so organized here . . . perhaps too much, although they try hard to be kind.'

'We had a walk in the park last week. They took us marching four by four,' said Mrs C laughing.

'Now, dear, you must remember, they don't know how

people react to small things . . . but they mean well, they're so anxious, they *want* to do well . . . it's shaming to us, really, how painstaking they are . . . And we came at a bad time. There was a big campaign on, against hidden counter-revolutionaries. Of course it hit the intellectuals. They were checked and rechecked. It was . . . unpleasant,' Mr C said.

'Do you regret having come back?' I asked.

'Oh no,' they said together. 'It's our country, for better, for worse. We sacrificed a great deal. We had good jobs in American universities; we threw them up to come here.'

They did not look at each other, but I felt them most conscious of each other then; their love wrapped round them close as one skin. They had done this together and would stand by each other, for better, for worse . . . and suddenly I could not swallow any more.

I felt hemmed in and constricted, shrunken and curtailed; and this came as a sudden realization as I sat there at breakfast. 'I have difficulty in breathing,' I said.

'We felt the same at first. We're not used to what they call mass movements, we're used to a capitalist society . . . It takes time to get accustomed' – said Mr C.

'To tutelage,' I cut in brutally. Mr C winced. 'To being controlled and checked at every turn,' I added.

'That isn't the whole picture,' they said. 'The peasants, the workers, they don't feel choked; they've got oxygen now . . . it's our class feelings . . . they make us feel guilty.'

'Guilty!' I echoed. 'Choked with guilt.'

We sat there and knew it was so.

Class guilt; not for particular sins individually committed, but for what we had omitted to do for our people. A sense of turpitude. Possibly, I thought as I tried to swallow, only the Chinese intelligentsia would feel that way. Because they had been for 2,500-odd years the administration, the establishment, the possessors of knowledge, and knowledge was power. The Chinese intellectual felt more responsible than any Western intellectual would ever do towards his own history, his culture, his society. In the Revolution the Chinese intellectual was still the lynchpin of whatever China would become. But he also represented the past, with all its misdeeds, its arrogance, and in this dreadful ambivalence he would remain for a long time, until the New Dynasty was stabilized . . .

All this went through my mind as the gruel slipped past my gullet. Since waking that morning I had felt choked. Not terror, fear or outrage as in the old days, but guilt. And in my case it was almost unbearable, and my reaction was physical, nausea, because suddenly it put me right back where Pao my husband had tried to root me: in añ unnamed, incoherent, morass of guilt, abasement without respite.

I got up and it seemed to me that I would topple, lose my foothold, fall, because I could not feel the edges of myself. I had lost me.

Twenty-one years later, in the *People's Daily*, I would read that Mr C's old mother had come from America to stay with her son and daughter-in-law and their children. The old lady was received by Chou Enlai's wife, Teng Yingchao. Now they would be together, with children and grandchildren. The Cs must have had their good years and their bad ones; their love for their country helped them to survive until at last all was well again.

There would be others, so many others; writers of renown, artists and teachers and scientists, greater in knowledge and dedication and dignity than I would ever be. I followed them through the years, and they never reproached me for not having joined their ranks. 'You were more vulnerable than we were,' they say gently. They talk of the bad years they survived, and of those who did not survive them. Some of them, it seems to me, enjoy the recollection of what they surmounted; as all hardship becomes, in memory, joyous adventure.

Perhaps the Chinese intellectual, conscious of his value as the knowledge bearer, transmitting the enduring civilization which he represents, has fashioned an extra dimension of fortitude, a larger limit of personal endurance. I am forever conscious that my friends traverse the centuries. Their conversation refers to what happened to some poet of the sixth century A.D. They quote a philosopher of the Han dynasty; refer aptly to a neat treachery performed twenty centuries ago; and all this in a way which does not occur in any other culture I know. Allusion to the classics gives them an amplitude of examples; the very names they give their children are references to lyrical lines from famous poets. Thus their own living is forever witness to a universe of multitudinous lives; in which they take their place and find serenity. Through their span of years their predecessors remain alive in the great ocean of time which rocks us all. They bear witness not to one era, but to many.

And now the Revolution has wrenched from the intelligentsia the power, which was exclusive education. They have had to remould themselves, change their views on society and their role in it; and as Mao Tsetung had already said in 1942, thought-remoulding is a very long, very arduous and painful process. But their main and traditional concern remains towards that culture-nation which is China and her people; the transmission of knowledge to the new society to come. But this new society – how was it going to treat them?

Comrade Liu inquired how I had slept; told me there would be a meeting after lunch, and asked me to criticize him. 'I make a lot of mistakes. People like myself, not cultured, never saw an intellectual until now, when the Party gave me the task of looking after them . . . Chairman Mao says we must unite with intellectuals, who are valuable and also re-educate them . . .'

'There are a good many here.'

'Indeed, from many countries; they are different in their habits from us, but patriotic . . .'

'They need readjustment.'

'Even so, even so,' said Comrade Liu, abashed, for I had spoken too quickly; and who was I to say that others needed readjustment? I wondered whether Comrade Liu was gauging the real readjustments that I needed.

'You seemed to enjoy breakfast, you have many of our

habits,' said he charitably, thus pushing me right back into my difference. If it was a task to cope with pure Chinese returning from abroad, how much more difficult would a Eurasian prove to be? What new problems would I place upon Comrade Liu and others, whose job would be to remould my thinking? And how would they know what I really felt? And what were my feelings really worth? Would I be able, as they were, to give up everything, literally life itself, to fight and to die so that human dignity should come to those who had none? The answer was no. I despised myself then, and this was unbearable and made me sick.

I walked out with gentle suffocation wrapped around me, feeling culpable and disobedient and guilty. And Peking was so beautiful and beloved and well-remembered. I loitered in the streets, peaceful and clean despite the dust of the spring wind. I went to my father's house and no one followed me.

Papa worked half a day only, and only because he wanted to. He was entitled to a full pension, and the leadership* in his organization offered him a car, and milk three times a week. Papa refused the car. 'Our country is still so poor, why waste petrol?' He took the bus to his office, a long ride of over forty minutes each way.

Papa had bought mooncakes for me, going to the Muslim shop in the western city that made the best and most flaky ones. When I was a baby he had named me his little Moon Guest. I told Papa I did not want to be re-educated, my skin crawled at the thought. He said, 'You must not show temper.' 'But I don't like to be under tutelage.' 'One must be patient,' said Papa, plucking at his hairless chin. 'Things will be better now, I think. The last campaign was very harsh, but I was not criticized. It's mostly writers who get into trouble. And that is due to the Hu Feng case.'

*The word leadership refers to the Party committee in charge at the level at which the individual is employed.

I had read a little about the Hu Feng affair* in Hong Kong, but there was so much exaggeration in the reports of the Western press, and the Chinese press itself so suddenly and so virulently started denouncing him that I could not understand why this 'counter-revolutionary writer', once a member of the Communist Party, had been so powerful as to compel the Party to a major drive to sift 'hidden counter-revolutionaries' throughout the administration and intellectual circles.

Papa gave me some old newspaper clippings about the Hu Feng case. I read while he cooked lunch and Hsueh Mah screamed and hovered and interrupted. Then I went to stand outside the front door of our house, to watch the peasant horsecarts returning to the countryside, empty. They came into the city by night; I would wake to hear the soft step of horse and mule and donkey hooves, and a great sweetness would come over me. The peasants brought fresh meat and vegetables and fruit to the markets of Peking every day. Now the animals were sleek, with shiny coats; some had a cloth stretched behind their back legs, fastened to the cart, to collect their dung. No more flogging and whipping, which had been my childhood agony. Did security also bring kindness? And the peasants sitting on the carts' arms nodding drowsily, they were well-dressed and well-fleshed.

Opposite our house there had been a well with a windlass of pear wood. The windlass made a special sound when the pails dropped down the well; *humph*, *humph*; and it sang *loo*, *loo* when the well man wound up the wet rope of the pails, and water would come spurting out, so icy pure and sweet; for beneath Peking was much underground water. Papa, in the 1930s, had drawn up a plan for tapping and using this water. 'It's not done properly at the moment,' he had said.

*Hu Feng was a Communist Party member and a writer. He began to challenge many of the official policies. This resulted in the general campaign against 'hidden counter-revolutionaries' in the Party, the administrative and intellectual circles, from July to November 1955.

Note that the word 'intellectual' in China denotes anyone who has some learning, and includes schoolteachers. It was reckoned that there were five million 'intellectuals' in China in 1956–7.

The wife of the old man had large, floating breasts, always exposed, and a child hung at the right nipple year after year. Mama hated her, but I thought her very beautiful; she laughed and she had magnificent teeth and a clear ivory skin. How she laughed! Like the water.

But now the well was covered over. 'There are taps in every house in our road,' said Hsueh Mah. 'No need to fetch water in wooden pails any more.'

The door-bell rope which traversed the veranda shook; the bell tinkled; it was our neighbourhood policeman. He had come to pay his respects to Papa; he did this once a month. Now he welcomed me, accepted tea, and chatted with us. Hsueh Mah told him that I had looked for the well. 'It seems it was there only yesterday.' 'Ah, don't look at today with yesterday's eyes,' said the policeman. He was so young, with that great candour about him which many young people now had; so scrubbed, neat and clear-eyed that he looked like a brand new toy policeman. Papa said that he was a very good young man, respectful of his elders.

Papa now took a little time to explain a few things to me. But it was no swift, machine-gun explaining. He said a few words, let them sink in, like water into soil. 'They really have done so much, pulled the country out of squalor and chaos . . . I can forget their pettiness and their suspicion when I see all that has been done. But they turn up everything; they want to know every single thing in one's life. They don't trust us.' Why should they trust us, I thought. Even Papa had been under so many administrations, had kept trains running under so many warlords; had worked (although he had also been jailed) under the Japanese when they had taken north China . . . The new government had inherited more than three million bureaucrats from the Chiang Kaishek administration; they could not let them starve; they had been confirmed in their jobs. But of course the Kuomintang must have had agents among them. To ferret these agents out of their various and manifold burrows would be a long and unpleasant process.

'Some people cannot stand the incessant questioning, the

meetings. They commit suicide,' Papa said. 'But I only had to write my autobiography twice more, because of your husband, Tang Paohuang.'

The Party had sent people to search for intellectuals, scientists, engineers and artists, as soon as Peking had been liberated. Papa had been taken to hospital and given the best of care, had recovered. The engineering bureau where he had been assigned to work (at a top salary) asked him to help. 'We need you, we need all those like you who can help us put the country together again. Is it not a shambles?'

'It was Marshal Yeh Chienying who was in charge at the time,' Papa said, 'and the first thing was to get the coal mines going. Without coal, no electricity, no locomotives, no heating and no industry . . . But the Japanese and the Kuomintang had destroyed the coal mines. I was sent to Tatung, to the coal mines there.' Papa was not alone. His old engineer friend, Hua Nankuei, and our external uncle, Uncle Liu of the stentorian voice and huge frame, all three old men, shouldering knapsacks, went off to Tatung on the edge of Mongolia. They toiled like youngsters, ate *kaoliang* (rye) gruel, slept on the beaten earth. 'When we needed machinery the People's Liberation Army got it for us. Yeh Chienying himself came down to see our work; he provided us with army greatcoats against the cold. The soldiers worked with the miners, repairing the shafts. Truly, it was wonderful . . . we were very enthusiastic,' said Papa, falling into newspaper stereotype. It was the new vocabulary, a phraseology of enthusiasm and struggle and achievement, which transformed one's expression of feeling and possibly the feeling itself, since the way people talk affects the way they think.

The coal mines began working again. Papa and Uncle Liu and Hua Nankuei were named 'model engineers' and officially congratulated. The railways started running, and a new railway was built within two years, 1950–2, between Chengtu and Chungking, in Szechuan. 'It's the railway that I came back to build in 1913,' Papa reminisced, laughing and creasing his eyes. In 1952, when the first locomotive, beflagged and all its loudspeakers singing, had rolled into the new station in Chengtu, where crowds danced and beat drums, an old engineer, overcome with emotion, had knelt and kissed the steel rails. He too had wanted, all his life, to build a railway for his country.

I went back to the hostel in Hatamen Street after lunch, and then it was time for the meeting. A bus took us to a large new brick building. We marched in two by two, regular as a school snake. We sat in rows of chairs. To one side were five or six chairs, similar to ours; there the officials would sit, not elevated on a platform, but in a friendly manner, by our side. I was next to Mr W from Indonesia. 'This is my fifth meeting,' he said. 'There's one almost every month. The officials change, but it's always the same thing . . . they are helping us to progress in our thought-remoulding.'

In filed four men, one of them with face clad in thick spectacles, which radiated benevolence. He reminded me of Father Ladany, especially the shrewd mouth. He welcomed us in quiet, measured tones; praised us for returning to join in the country's reconstruction; and said that if there was anything on our minds we must speak it without fear. The Party welcomed criticism. Chairman Mao repeatedly emphasized that the people must be listened to; he and his colleagues were there to help us in every way.

(Suddenly the word 'help' gave me a disquieting feeling. Had not my cousin Ping, Fourth Sister, the night before, held my arm and said, 'We must help you . . .'? I was allergic to soul-fingering.)

One person spoke. He said he had many difficulties in understanding, but would strive hard to dispel his doubts. He realized he needed more help. Another said that despite a great deal of help he found it difficult to throw away past burdens and turn around,* although he knew he would feel much better when he had done so. Several other people said

*The expression 'turn around', in Chinese *fanshen*, means to change one's attitude, behaviour and thinking. It is a process of rejecting the old self and acquiring a new personality. The words 'born again' now used so much in America, convey exactly the same idea of conversion.

more or less the same thing. The bespectacled official nodded encouragingly; he did not fidget, but sat upright, untired, letting each person talk as long as he liked while the afternoon lengthened drowsily, endlessly, and I listened to a magpie call in the camphor tree, and was filled with fury and that suffocation familiar since breakfast. Perhaps the index of boredom was the measure of successful remoulding, I thought wickedly. One man talked sheer nonsense for twenty minutes. 'He's mentally deranged, from Indonesia,' whispered Mr W. He could whisper without seeming to move his lips. The unhinged man was listened to with the same attention as others and then gently led away, sobbing, to the garden outside by Comrade Liu. Spectacles then looked around. Did anyone else wish to speak?

Had Papa been there, had I been in a normal state of mind, I would have kept quiet; even found it humorous. But I must speak or stifle; something in me would not keep still. I said that I felt suffocated. I did not like tutelage. I had come to learn facts and ask questions but I did not want to be thought-remoulded. I did not think it would work with me.

Not a muscle moved on the official's kind lower jaw; nor did his glasses glint more fiercely. Round us the silence settled like an implacable velvet smother. After what seemed a long pause but was probably not more than ten seconds, the official said that the meeting was ended, it had been productive, he wished us all 'good progress, perseverance and success' in our own efforts to alter our world point of view. He then shook hands with everyone as they filed past him, and when I came up he said with a kind and terrible gentleness, 'You are certainly of big landlord origin.'

Bad origin. Good origin. There were five 'bad origins', which meant that in any mass political campaign, anyone from one of the five bad was due for special attention: landlords, rich peasants, reactionaries (counter-revolutionaries), hooligans or asocial elements – thieves, pimps, dope pushers, for example – and 'bourgeois elements who refuse to be re-educated'. For the next twenty years, this classification of 'origin' would wreak a great deal of harm in China.

And of all bad origins the worst was to be of big landlord issue. On the bus I felt like a leper, and did not inflict myself upon anyone, although Mr C heroically did not avoid me.

In the late afternoon I went home to Papa. Sitting with Papa was a tall, thin-faced young man, from Szechuan, Wang Wanchun. He was a journalist working on the *Peking Evening News*. He came from a wealthy family, but he had renounced all his property and was classified as 'enlightened intelligentsia'. He told me very humorously, as I mentioned a little about the meeting, that during the campaign for ferreting out hidden counter-revolutionaries in 1955 (which was the campaign Mr and Mrs C had talked about at breakfast), he had been rigorously grilled. But in the end, after a great many accusations which he rejected, he had said, 'Comrades, I do have many failings and defects; but I love my country.' And suddenly everyone had let go, and the Party cadres in charge had concluded the meeting and he had been left in peace ever since.

Wanchun and I were to become very good friends; and my friendship was perhaps the cause of his death eleven years later.

Pretty soon, in came Comrades Wu and Li from Papa's engineering institute; I think they had been told about my outburst because they were so solicitous, inquiring about my health, until I began to feel indeed grievously ill. Why, oh why did I buck like a wild pony instead of trying to find out what it was like to be remoulded? Was I certain that my thinking was so healthy and correct? Comrades Wu and Li assured me that Papa was *not* classified as a landlord; they smiled reassuringly. We sipped tea and they said that Papa was being given a full holiday, as long as he liked, to be more with me. I then said, 'I am sorry that I did not tell you this straightaway, but I know Madame Kung Peng; she is at the Department of Information of the Ministry of Foreign Affairs. I think she would like to know that I am here; we were at university together.' 'We shall certainly pass on your request,' said Comrade Li.

I went back to the hostel to sleep with a little jingle in my mind: 'They want you to be docile, but you happen to be hostile.' Hostile – of bad class origin – but on the streets people were laughing, and strolling, and there was palpable cheerfulness and ease, and the children, oh, how beautiful were the children now, so beautiful and healthy. No more infanticide, no more selling of little girls, no more baby corpses wrapped in newspaper on the streets. At last there was order and peace; and the people were no longer miserable; they were free of disease and famine . . . there was no sense in a freedom which did not first assure the fundamental needs of man . . . so what was the matter with me?

The next day was study day at the hostel. Everyone read books or sat at tables and wrote in notebooks. Comrade Liu suggested I have a rest. I went to the Eastern Peace Market, and rediscovered all the little shops of my childhood. They were all there, including those in the alley where carved jades of all kinds and colour were sold. After lunch with Papa, Comrade Wu came to the house to tell me that Kung Peng indeed remembered me, and asked me to go to see her at five o'clock.

I went back to the hostel to dress and Comrade Liu came in with a book on Peking for me. I said I knew Peking, I had grown up here. 'Ah, that is why you're *almost* like one of us,' he said delightedly. 'I shall try to be more like you, with your help,' I said. Comrade Liu blushed greatly, for he was most modest, and he wrung my hand with such affection that I felt I had been stupid and arrogant at the meeting.

The block of flats where officials of the Foreign Ministry lived, including ambassadors and vice-ministers, was in Paofang Hutung. Kung Peng's flat was very small. The higher Party officials did not dwell in luxury, although they went to official parties in large black Zis cars with drawn curtains (the cars were from an official pool). Kung Peng greeted me with genuine happiness. 'You used your own name, so we did not know that you had arrived, although I expected you.' She had seen the foreign newspapers, which had made a great stir about my going to China. I had not written to her, thinking she would be informed.

We talked a great deal, and I find in my early notes of that day (May 21st, 1956), that as usual when I was with Kung Peng I was over-exuberant. I talked about the need for new words and expressions for the adjustment of new ideas; I thought both the jargon of the West and that of Marxism as I had heard it stale and inadequate. At this time the West had nothing to offer China except hostility, the language of prurient enmity. 'As for the propaganda from here, it's appallingly childish and has no influence or impact.' 'Is it so bad?' replied Kung Peng. 'Perhaps for someone as sophisticated as you are, but we get letters from many people, praising us . . .'

We strolled in the courtyard. Kung Peng's little daughter was there with her nurse. A doctor had told Kung Peng that the child was backward. 'Not at all, she's perfectly normal,' said I. The girl grew up beautiful and intelligent; and Kung Peng always felt grateful to me.

Kung Peng's mixture of honesty and detachment, genuine affection and care, patience for my many quirks . . . how can I ever describe them without a wild sense of loss? For so many years I would need her, need her, while I made my way so painfully through the unknown universe of the Chinese Revolution; a world not as it was represented: unilinear, unidimensional, both in the West and in China's propaganda, but infinitely complex and multitudinous; a wholeness made up of a million contradictory aspects; subject to swings and crises, each of which overlapped its contrary; magnificent in its achievements and colossal in its errors and failures. I sought clearness and Kung Peng said, 'You yourself must think it out.' This was the greatest boon of all; her trust in my ultimate lucidity. Meanwhile, she gave me the gift of time and space and silence, and so many encounters; argued for me against the Party cadres who were infuriated by the unorthodox, non-conformist me. Thus was

I privileged; and if I feel like a thief, having purloined so
much from living, then I must thank the bounty of Kung
Peng who gave me to hoard in such great measure
knowledge to last me all my days.

The restaurant we went to was the Kang Lo, also known as
the Three Tables; literally only three square tables, a small
room, and most excellent food, renowned throughout the
city. Alas, in 1959 the restaurant ceased to exist. Perhaps
now, when restaurants are being resurrected, it will open
again. The reason for its closure was that it encouraged a
'bourgeois' aspect of life.

Kung Peng's husband, Chiao Kuanhua, was relaxed and
friendly. He had great charm, and with wine we talked (I
talked too much) until very late at night. I said many things
that I have now forgotten; and I found Chiao's mind so
swift, so arrow to its mark, that it was necessary to ask him to
slow down and explain himself. Perhaps it was this great skill
and intelligence which lost him in the end. One day when I
was visiting them, as I did several times in the course of the
next few weeks, he pointed to a rather awkward Chinese
picture on the wall. 'See that beautiful curve, how the willow
bends?' I wondered why he thought I did not understand
anything about Chinese painting. He was always aware of
himself as brilliant.

But at the time they were a happy couple, and well-
informed, since they both worked in the Foreign Ministry
under Chou Enlai and read all the outside newspapers. Kung
Peng accepted immediately that I had come for a visit; and
actually at no time asked me to stay. I think she realized the
many difficulties I would have; and it is even possible that,
after due consideration, had I brought up the matter, she
would have asked me gently to remain 'outside'. Many
overseas Chinese who did not apply to return were refused
for one reason or another.

Kung Peng said that I should move to the Hsinchiao
Hotel, which housed journalists and minor diplomats and
was the centre of all the 'news' filtering through Peking's

grapevine; and so I moved there. I managed to spend a great deal of time with Papa, who grew younger and smiled all day. Many people came to our house, relatives and friends, and Chinese journalists to interview me. At weekends, and sometimes late in the afternoon, Third and Fourth Brothers came with their wives, Jui and Shuan. Together we walked a great deal in the parks.

Third Brother had been in America for six years, studying at the University of Minnesota; he had graduated and been offered a job in research. Then the Korean war had started. The American government did not allow Chinese scientists to return to China. Third Brother pretended no interest in 'Red' China, abstained from correspondence and went for a holiday to Brazil. In Brazil he got in touch with a Szechuanese friend who had emigrated there in 1943. The friend helped him on a very roundabout journey to Scandinavia, to Finland, to Moscow and thence back to China. Being a physicist, he had been immediately welcomed to a position at Peking University. Third Uncle had married him off to Jui before his departure for the United States, and she waited for him all those years, staying in Chengtu with Third Uncle and Third Aunt. Jui was a very beautiful girl, with a delicate skin, and was working in the Chemistry Department of the University of Chengtu.

As to Fourth Brother, he had studied in England, and had straightforwardly travelled back to China.* For the first few months he had been the government's guest, and had been taken to see many new achievements; but in one political campaign against bourgeois ideas among intellectuals, in 1953–4, he had been violently criticized because he wore English trousers (plus-fours). 'But I had no other clothes,' he said. Third Uncle arranged a marriage for him; and despite the new advocation of freedom in courtship and romance, the young in China still bowed to tradition, and preferred proper parental introduction. Fourth Brother married at his father's suggestion.

*The UK government recognized the People's Republic of China promptly in 1950.

Shuan was an excellent choice for Fourth Brother. A calm girl with great courage; very devoted and clever, with a good brain. Owing to his work, which brought Fourth Brother to Manchuria in 1960, they were to be separated for almost seventeen of the next twenty years; and at the end were most deeply in love with each other.

Fourth Brother loved beautiful things; he collected a great deal of old furniture. In that summer of 1956, we spent happy hours buying furniture for Papa. I acquired some beautiful Ming chairs and a rosewood table as a present, and Papa was pleased. Alas, during the Cultural Revolution, all Fourth Brother's carved bookshelves and other antiques disappeared.

I asked my relatives, 'Did you feel strange when you were first back?'

'Yes,' they said, 'not accustomed . . .'

'As if not enough oxygen?'

Third Brother laughed. He always laughs when he does not wish to show perturbation. When during the Cultural Revolution he was condemned as a 'bourgeois' intellectual to keep the stove of a cook going, he laughed.

After laughing he said, 'It's better at the University. We are all high-class intellectuals and the movement there is careful and easy; I think the Party people in charge do understand that they must not press us too hard . . .'

'But it is not like this everywhere,' said Jui. 'In some places it was very bad. If you have a bad leadership, Party cadres who hate the sight of you, then it is not good at all.'

'But can't you tell them?'

They looked at each other. When does criticizing a Party cadre become criticizing the Party line and therefore the Party? How can one stand it if one is accused of being counter-revolutionary?

We talked and talked; and Papa said, 'Up on top, no trouble. Down below, the lower cadres are pretty hardworking. But it's the middle cadres.'

'Commandism, bureaucratism, sectarianism, sit down and give orderism,' chanted Fourth Brother. The last campaign, from July to November 1955, against hidden counter-revolutionaries, had been extremely unpleasant and strenuous. 'Meeting after meeting, no rest . . . people became exhausted . . . There are suicides each time there is a campaign. The cadres sometimes go on and on. It's gruelling for them and for us.'

But how could the middle cadre be anything but rigid and unbending? He was the transmission belt for orders and their implementation from the top to the bottom. Upon him rested much responsibility and far too much work. He could not take decisions easily; and especially when, at the top, there were divergences and crises. 'And then rectification in the Party. The cadres do not have a good time. And they don't get the salaries or the privileges which we, as intellectuals, are getting,' said Third Brother. There had been two major Party rectifications in six years, and every time the middle cadre had to go to study sessions and meetings, criticism and self-criticism.

I said that, with such political campaigns going on, there would be a tendency to focus on the odd man or woman, the slightly different individual, as a 'target'. Both Party cadres and the people in the organizations would look out for a potential black sheep in their midst; someone more isolated, more vulnerable, who could be attacked safely and could not retaliate easily. My family had not thought of it that way. 'It's true that sometimes they do pick on an overseas Chinese,' said Fourth Brother, 'but it's not the policy of the government. However, some overseas Chinese have such different habits, and they have more money too, and they spend it . . .' 'That's exactly what I'm talking about,' I said. Would I be able to stand being the natural target for criticism, a horrendous example of bourgeois tendencies and decadence? I knew in my bones it would happen. I was too exuberant, too impulsive, and also too striking in my looks. A natural target. And what good would it do to me, after I had been picked ragged by 'the masses' – who would easily find in my past life so many examples of immorality and other vices – what good would it do for the Party leadership to console me, and say, 'Comrade, this is to educate the masses'?

There was the young overseas man doing translation work; held up as an example of bourgeois defect because one day, trooping out of collective enjoyment at a cinema, he had broken away from the group to buy an ice cream from a pedlar at the gate of the cinema house. Another person, taken for a group march in the park, four by four, had lingered behind and started taking snapshots: typical bourgeois individualism. There was a girl who kept flower pots on her balcony; she brought a pot to the office and set it on her desk . . . small things, trivial things; and the smaller and more trivial, the safer to criticize and pick up in a campaign . . .

There was also the danger of beauty, and its outlandishness. A beautiful person would draw the lightning. Not everywhere, but should it happen that one of the Party cadres in charge had a hatred of beauty . . . This fear of loveliness, and the desire for its destruction, is very common everywhere in the world. I was told of one Party cadre who, in the movement for thought reform of 1953–4, said that 'all beautiful things must be abolished'. He was, however, unable to carry this out, for it was pointed out to him that his own wife was very pretty.

And all this had nothing to do with socialism. It was still Old China, still there; feudal, medieval, rigid Old China, as I had known it, but now it surfaced again, trying to survive by assuming righteous, moralistic 'anti-bourgeois' attitudes. And now it deployed massive political pressure; it crushed non-conformism more efficiently than ever. In the process, people did get hurt. Perhaps, with a sense of humour and enormous courage, one could get over this constant attrition. But I knew that I would be broken, very swiftly. I had suffered too much in the past with Pao. And the effluvium of past distress now came up. I was responding to it by feeling restricted and choked.

On May 22nd Third Brother gave me a report to read. It was

a draft report on the Hundred Flowers, not yet in the newspapers but circulating for discussion in the universities and among the intelligentsia.

The words Hundred Flowers came from an old saying: 'Let a hundred flowers blossom, a hundred schools of thought contend'. Now Chairman Mao had resurrected this saying. It indicated a change in attitude towards the intellectuals. After the campaign to ferret out hidden counter-revolutionaries in 1955, Chou Enlai and Mao (but especially, it seemed to me, Chou Enlai) had become very much aware that the campaign had engendered such terror among the intelligentsia that many refused to function at all; nothing could be got out of them except total acquiescence. 'In my newspaper,' Wanchun told me, 'there is an old scholar in charge of the historical section. He was so harassed and criticized that now he won't say anything; he just nods his head and mutters "Good, good, very good", whatever is said to him.'

Chairman Mao had now condemned the sectarianism and high-handedness, the brutality of some of the Party cadres conducting the campaign. Premier Chou had been even more outspoken; and since November 1955 had held meetings with intellectuals and scholars, and also with the representatives of the eight non-communist parties which funtioned in the Political Consultative Conference.* Most of the intelligentsia, the engineers, doctors, scholars and scientists, belonged to these parties; unless they were, of course, Communist Party members. 'There are far too few intellectuals in the Party . . . there's going to be a drive to get more of them in,' said Third Brother. 'Anyway, the Party leadership at my university has already told us that the intellectuals are no longer suspect. They are considered sufficiently well remoulded politically.'

'Does that mean no more thought-remoulding?'

*Eight non-communist parties were admitted by the Communist Party in a 'United Front' in 1949. The Political Consultative Conference, a body distinct from the State or Communist Party is the instrument whereby they express themselves.

'It means doing it much more . . . softly . . .' said Fourth
Brother. 'Though of course it all depends where one is.' In
his organization, there was little pressure. 'It depends
whether the leadership is intelligent or not. But so many of
them are just good guerrillas; they've fought so many years,
and they don't understand the minds of the trained,
professional scientist, or scholar, or writer . . .'

'And we are also very complicated!' said Wanchun.

Anyway, the Hundred Flowers was to promote freedom
of expression in the academic disciplines and especially in
science. Also in art and literature; but the more we pored
over the draft, the less we understood what the limits to this
freedom were. For there must be limits. 'Too much
searching for counter-revolutionary thought has just
paralysed so many brains; now they have to be defrozen,'
said Wanchun. ' "Learn to listen more to the masses," that's
what Chairman Mao has said.'

'But who are the masses? I hear a lot about mass
movements; it means rousing the people to perform, to
criticize, to condemn . . . but who exactly are the people?
Are you the people? Would I be the people, part of the
masses?'

'Yes and no.' In every unit, there was the leadership or the
Party committee in charge; they had to define the political
line and watch over the carrying out of the work to be done.
Then there were the authorities, professors, experts,
engineers; who were part of the leadership in the technical
sense, but not in the ideological sense. Then there was the
ordinary rank and file of the employees, the workers. In a
hospital, for instance, the man who cleaned the toilets was
one of the employees, and therefore part of the masses, and
would join in the mass movements of the hospital together
with its authorities, the doctors, and the nurses and all other
personnel. 'That is why the professional people who are
experts are both part of the masses and not part of the
masses. They are when they criticize others in campaigns to
eradicate counter-revolutionary ideas; they are not when
they are criticized themselves.' The Party leadership was

supposed both to lead and to guide the masses, and at the same time accept the criticism and suggestions of the masses, and put themselves at the service of the masses.

'This is dialectics,' said Fourth Brother. I said that I thought the way it worked out was usually that someone, the Party secretary, for instance, just laid down the policy and everyone acquiesced. My relatives and Wanchun grinned, and said, 'You're learning very fast.'

The Hundred Flowers was to reinforce the rights of the intelligentsia to conduct their own research, and to do their work unhindered. 'It is for the good of socialism,' said Third Brother. 'But who decides what is good for socialism and what is not?' There were two trends in the Party; one for total arbitrariness, clamping down on everything; the other for the intelligent use of people, for moderation and listening to contrary advice and opinion. Mao was always enjoining Party members to listen to contrary opinions, to criticism; had for years tried to curb bureaucratic tyranny. 'But it recurs again and again. Premier Chou Enlai understands the problem well,' said Third Brother.

'But will there not be a tempest, a tornado rising from the hearts of the intellectuals, or some of them, when the pressure is released through the Hundred Flowers, and they start to speak up?'

'Third Sister, you open your mouth far too wide,' said Third Brother, laughing cheerfully and long.

Third Brother's wife, Jui, had had the worst time of all our Family. Land Reform in Szechuan had been particularly harsh and prolonged and bloody because Szechuan landlords were the most oppressive; Szechuan had been the last bastion of Chiang Kaishek's domination. The structures of the old society were still very strong there when the Communist armies came into the province in November–December 1949.

Cleaning up the opium-growing areas had taken three years; cleaning up the Chiang Kaishek gangs, who fled to the high mountains, and proceeding with Land Reform, had been very difficult because the peasants were at first so frightened that they would even protect the landlords. Jui saw it both from the side of the social revolution, for the poor peasant, and of course from the side of her own class, the owners. She described the panic, landlords knocking their heads on the ground, begging the investigation teams to take away their lands and houses, but not submit them to the judgment of the people; landlords offering their wives and daughters to Party cadres . . . Despite the Party injunction not to beat or torture landlords, the poor peasants, when aroused, would do so, suspend a landlord by the thumbs and beat him to death. 'There was so much furniture, and silk and books and valuable things, littering the streets, that most of the city lanes became impassable.'

And then there were the Secret Societies, especially the Brothers of the Robe, very powerful in Szechuan. Sometimes they bribed the Party cadres; sometimes murdered them. So deeply implanted were the Secret Societies that years later, during the Cultural Revolution, they would make a return.

During Land Reform in 1950–1, Third Uncle was in Chungking, and Third Grandfather, the head of the clan, and responsible for land ownership committed suicide by jumping down a well, so terrified was he. No one was there to answer for the accounts and the clearing up of fields belonging to the ancestral hall of the Family in Pihsien, and to remove the Family graves, which took up good land, to another site. Jui then came forward, in place of Third Uncle and in place of his eldest son her husband, Third Brother, who was then in America. She would represent the Family two or three times a week at the people's court. The case took eight months to clear up. Jui was never harmed physically; but it was a great strain having to stand for hours in court and listen to the accusations launched by former tenants; and she became very nervous.

When Land Reform was over there was the movement against counter-revolutionaries; but the Family was not involved in it. Then there was the movement against the three evils in the Party (corruption, waste and bureaucracy) and the five evils among the national–capitalist class, tax evasion, theft of state property, cheating on government contracts and stealing of economic information. Third Uncle was a national–capitalist. His case lasted for months; Jui had to answer for a certain amount of rice which was unaccounted for. Was it hoarded rice? In Chungking, at the time, the businessmen had organized a 'Thursday Dinner Club', devoted entirely to ways and means of defrauding the government. Third Uncle, was, luckily, not of that club. Finally the Family was cleared.

Then in 1953–4 there had been the campaign to change the ideas of the intelligentsia. Jui was an intellectual since she held a position in the Chemistry Department at the University of Chengtu. Because her husband was in the United States, and there was at the time the Korean war, some silly colleagues of Jui (not the Party) tried to make her divorce her husband. She refused.

Then Third Brother came back, and Jui became pregnant, but remained in Chengtu while Third Brother went to Peking to join the Peking University staff. Unlucky Jui. During that year, 1955, the Hu Feng affair erupted, followed by the campaign to ferret out hidden counter-revolutionaries. And since Hu Feng had many adherents in Szechuan, the drive there was most drastic. And because Chairman Mao had made a casual remark that *probably* 10 per cent of the intelligentsia in the administration and the Party harboured counter-revolutionary feelings or thoughts, such was the literal-mindedness of the middle cadres (and can you blame them?) that some were determined to expose at least 10 per cent in each organization as counter-revolutionary, to show they were not slacking . . .

Writing out one's biography. Again and again. Meetings. In thirty days, twenty-nine meetings. Accusation sessions. Struggle sessions. People encouraged 'boldly to accuse each other without leaving any face to anyone'. Everyone called to account for every minute event in his life; until at last condemnation would centre on the few, and then meetings to criticize and to struggle against these few.

Meanwhile, Jui's belly swelled, and one afternoon during a meeting she felt the pains come on. But the comrade in charge that day did not know that she was pregnant, for Jui was intensely modest, and concealed her bulk behind a desk (the meetings were held in a lecture hall of the University). She asked to leave as she had a 'headache'. 'We have a most important meeting . . . no one can leave,' said the cadre firmly. The meeting went on, and Jui could no longer bear it and she began to groan, while round her some of her colleagues stirred uneasily. And finally one bolder than the rest tiptoed to the cadre and whispered in his ear. Upon which, thunderstruck, he rushed for an ambulance and Jui reached hospital just in time. And to make up for this, Jui was cleared totally and sent to Peking to join her husband. But now Jui would not believe that things would be better. 'If a Party cadre has it in for you, it's no use, he will pick and pick at you until you have no way out.'

'It's a class struggle,' said Fourth Brother. 'That's why we feel so helpless; it's a different class in power today.'

But now a new policy: 'Let a hundred flowers bloom, a hundred schools of thought contend . . .' Now things were going to change. 'Is it because of what has happened in the Soviet Union?' Khrushchev's denunciation of Stalin in January 1956 was known in China; it circulated 'within', in the Party and administration newspaper and in documents. Everyone in China knew of the speech denouncing Stalin. No, said my relatives. The speech against Stalin was in January 1956, but already in November 1955 Premier Chou Enlai had started discussing a new policy for the intelligentsia, holding meetings with the eight non-communist parties. It was probably Chou Enlai who had called a halt to the campaign. We surmised, speculated, argued. The Hundred Flowers called upon the intelligentsia to speak up; called on the Party to listen to criticism. How, how much, how soon, we did not know.

During most of my two month stay I felt as if I was careering full speed on an enormous roller coaster, going up and down artificial heights and canyons at dizzying speed, and with my insides not following suit. The alternation of exhilaration and depression which fragmented my days and nights; the almost ecstatic joy levitating me, followed by deep nausea and utter prostration; I cannot explain, even now, why my reactions were so violent, so physical, so inescapable. I needed Kung Peng very much; felt lost without her, sought her out and often missed her, for she was very busy. I could not describe to her what I felt, only say, 'There are many contradictions fighting in me.' The word 'contradiction' was not only acceptable but understood. It was a useful word in this new political shorthand I was beginning to acquire.

Kung Peng arranged for me to see everything I wanted. I had a nice chauffeur, Comrade Ku; a demobilized People's Liberation Army man who had driven a jeep in the Korean war and took me everywhere in a Czech car. When I felt too near vomiting I went to the Western Hills to watch the summer burgeon in splendour, the wanness of long winter vanish. I went to the Temple of Heaven and to the Peihai Park and to the Summer Palace, and also walked miles and miles, trying to get a grip upon my unhinged body.

I visited the tuberculosis sanatorium in the Western Hills; a palatial spread, where Russian methods of streptomycin inhalation were used. I saw the ordinary, and very crowded, tuberculous clinics, not show places, in the city itself. Tuberculosis was still rampant; it was impossible at the moment to care for everyone. The workers were treated at government expense, but 'We cannot do this for everyone in China,' said the directors. I visited the children's hospital, which filled me with joy. I went to the cancer hospital . . . I think I visited all the hospitals in Peking. And it was for me, as a doctor, fabulous. Something had really been done, and most effectively, about all the main epidemics and scourges which had ravaged the population. The result was an unbelievable lowering of infant mortality and just as impressive a rise in the population growth rate. Until 1949 the growth rate had been around 4 per thousand; by 1956 it was over 32 per thousand. No more cholera, no more smallpox, and venereal disease being eradicated . . . I visited the opium treatment centre for the rehabilitation of opium addicts. 'The biggest problems were the heroin and cocaine addicts under the Japanese,' said the doctors.

I went to the Yung Ho Kung, the old Tibetan lama temple in Peking, and just as when I was a child, the halls containing statues in erotic poses were locked. In the past, a bribe to the priest would open them; now bribery was impossible, and they remained closed.

I duly delivered to Dr Pan Kuangtan his prosthetic leg, going to his institute to meet him. He beamed fatly, had a throaty, false laugh. Pan Kuangtan had been very much criticized because he held pro-American views. His exuberance ill concealed lingering shock. However, he would live on, and his children are today employed as university staff in China. Pan Kuangtan declared he did not need the new leg, for the wooden stump he wore was enough. He looked very much like Francis Pan, his brother.

Professor Cheng Chento, Vice-Minister of Culture, invited me to dinner. At the table was Kung Peng and the writer Lao Sheh whom I had met in Hong Kong, and also the writer Hsiao Chien, whom I had met in England, where he had studied for some years. Professor Cheng was no obsequious, terror-stricken man. He went right into the problems of writing. 'We had no life at all under Chiang Kaishek. Now we have security, official positions, good houses and good salaries. But too many things have happened too swiftly for our minds to grasp.' He thought re-education through thought-remoulding good. 'But some of it is excessive. We hope there will be more flexibility.' Many writers found it difficult to write, although they produced inspired journalism, adequate reportage. They felt frightened because this was a new society whose bearings they had not yet understood, whose motivations they could not fathom . . . On and on went the Vice-Minister of Culture, who was not a communist but belonged to another party; and Kung Peng did not interrupt or protest. I felt greatly encouraged; if this was what the Hundred Flowers meant, there was hope.

Lao Sheh looked very fit, glossily happy. He had not suffered during the counter-revolutionary campaign; but then his class origin was good; he came from a very poor family. He told some delightful anecdotes about his time in England. He had produced an excellent play, and was now a People's Artist, honoured and respected. I would go to visit him in his very beautiful house; he collected antiques, ivories and priceless furniture. He also grew chrysanthemums of rare kinds, and his Japanese friends would give him some very exquisite plants. He was Vice-Chairman of the Union of Chinese Writers, but also held a dozen other positions in various friendship associations, besides being a delegate to the National People's Congress.

As for Hsiao Chien, he was also an official in the Union of Writers, and most enthusiastic about everything. He agreed with Professor Cheng that some writers found it difficult to create, but thought this was a question of time. 'We are all bourgeois intellectuals; we took certain things for granted.' I saw Hsiao Chien several times, in private talk, in the days that followed. He told me about his own remoulding. He had found it difficult, but not insuperably so. He had been greatly helped by a revelation during Land Reform when he went with many other intellectuals to the villages to help the peasants become aware of class struggle and denounce their landlords. Hsiao Chien found that a landlord who had been his friend, whose hospitality he had enjoyed, was an individual who owned six male and six female concubines, some of them mere children. 'I was appalled at myself. I had never inquired into his private life . . . I called myself the friend of such a monster!'

Dear, amiable Hsiao Chien! With his round face and appealing eyes, eyes with that opaque anguish which I had seen emerge, like a creature rising from muddy water, in the eyes of Nora Waln. I thought his ardent conversion a little too swift to be true, and alas, in 1957, he seems to have made inapposite attacks upon the Union of Writers and sundry other political targets, and was labelled a 'rightist'. 'He got changed too quickly,' I would say later to Kung Peng. 'The colour didn't stick.' Hsiao Chien was unjustly labelled; he would be rehabilitated, but it would take a great many years.

There was a reception with many eminent writers at the Peking Hotel. I met Tsao Yu, China's Chekhov, shy, his thick spectacles a wall between himself and the world. But such talent, such perception behind that uneasy vitreousness! His plays had been for me major events, and he was writing another play. In 1969 I was told by a Party cadre that he, Lao Sheh, Pa Chin – the latter an author from Szechuan, whose wonderful Balzacian novels had been a revelation to me when I was a student – were counter-revolutionaries. But this was the summer of 1956, when the Hundred Flowers had just begun, and in that year all three of them were honoured, and under no stress.

Suddenly there was a stir of excitement. The fabulous and eminent Madame Soong Chingling, widow of Dr Sun Yatsen, had come to the reception. Soong Chingling exuded glamour; she had a flawless, creamy skin, and her hair was bright jet. The eldest of the three Soong sisters (the second none other than Madame Chiang Kaishek), Soong Chingling was, I think, the most beautiful of the three. She had stuck with immense loyalty to her principles, and was a great and honoured personage, a symbol of the Communist Party's determination to carry out United Front policies with non-communists who were loyal in serving their country and its people. I had already met Madame Chiang Kaishek during the war, in Chungking.* Soong Chingling had exactly the same voice, a beautiful voice, with faultless and melodious diction. Both had been educated at Wellesley.

'Why don't you make up your mind to stay here?' she said to me straightaway. Round her the air shone with her vitality. I could not reply; I merely smiled.

Then I met Mao Tun, the Minister of Culture, the famous

*See *Destination Chungking*.

writer of *Midnight*, the launcher of so many literary magazines in the 1920s and 30s. He was a genial, simple person with great courtesy, a humble person with a slight nervous tic, which he would lose in the following years. We discussed the Hu Feng affair. Mao Tun said that Hu Feng's crime was that he *organized* cliques of intellectuals against the Communist Party. There were always contradictory tendencies in all human endeavour; writers had to struggle against themselves and depict these struggles, said Mao Tun. I asked him how it was possible to distinguish between genuine criticism, which was welcomed by the Party, and counter-revolutionary statements, which got one into trouble. Mao Tun smiled with great delicacy and replied, 'They are being distinguished now.'

Mao Tun ascribed to Chairman Mao and to Premier Chou Enlai the new policy of the Hundred Flowers. 'It's too early to draw conclusions, but I am in favour of it,' said he. He told me that of the 18,000 people employed in the Ministry of Culture, only 3 per cent, or 540, were doubtful. He then gave me his speech at the second conference of Chinese writers in 1954 to read. It was full of useful hints. 'Many authors are confused ideologically and their standpoint is unsteady . . . there are objective reasons why literary work is lagging behind reality . . . The heroes of our fiction are drab, colourless; there is monotony and crudeness of literary form, not taking pains with language and structure . . .' 'Perhaps this comes from being salaried officials,' I suggested as respectfully as I could, and the Minister of Culture threw back his head and laughed happily. 'True, too comfortable a life sometimes makes the writer lazy . . . We have some writers who expend most of their effort considering whether a theme is proper or not.' He said the state paid for writers' travels; they had summer bungalows in the hills where they could retire to write. Mao Tun was scathing about 'political critics who drive writers to impotence by hurling political epithets at them.' He said these critics did not understand anything about writing. 'In the West, too, critics just say anything; but then they contradict each other,' I said. I added that some of the journalists I had met at the big reception for writers had the notion that in the West all writers were capitalists. It was not so; some of them were labourers; and others had gone into coal mining and other manual jobs to acquire the experience and feeling for a novel. Mao Tun knew all this; for he, like Tsao Yu, like Pa Chin, like Lao Sheh, was very well-acquainted with Western literature.

I asked Mao Tun about Ting Ling, the woman writer whose book *Sun on the Sankan River* had been awarded a Stalin prize, but who was now in political trouble. Mao Tun professed not to know all the details because the case was still being studied. In fact, Ting Ling would be officially excluded from the Party and dubbed a 'rightist' in 1957.

Then an interview with Kuo Mojo, the distinguished, erudite poet, critic, archaeologist and head of the Academy of Sciences (founded that year). Kuo Mojo was from my province of Szechuan. He had immense learning, knew German and French and had done a great many translations from Western literature. He was in Japan for many years, he told me and 'indeed I grieve that I did not participate fully in the liberation struggles of my country. But then I am politically very backward.' He was not a communist (neither were Tsao Yu, Mao Tun, Pa Chin, or Lao Sheh), but he would be admitted to the Party that year.

'One must see beyond the transient, the instant capture of events.' He was frank, and commented on the writer's difficulties. 'It is the propensity of the mind to resist tutelage,' said he, 'yet all history has been made by the contradiction between those in power and others. There are contradictions, of course, between the Party and other sectors of Chinese society. The important thing is to construct a strong, prosperous and socialist China.'

'The writer's business is the landscape of the human heart,' I said. Kuo smiled. 'The human heart . . . such an indefinite and changeable affair . . .' He loved miniature gardens, and said they made him think of the human heart 'fashioned by drought and a drop of water; a tree clinging to the ridges of a rock . . .'

Kuo went on talking of China's needs for modernization, of the impossibility of practising socialism unless there was also some measure of abundance through 'the release of the productive forces'. The sunlight through the window sculptured his cheekbones and ear with the hearing aid glued to it; his delicate hands occasionally moved to mould a sentence. I remembered that he too, like Lu Hsun, had been a doctor of medicine before becoming a writer. He gave me facts. In areas where there had been 'the wrong leadership', productivity had declined. 'It is also bad when people dare not speak up.' There had been an obsession which had seized some Party members about the counter-revolutionary insurrection among the intelligentsia. 'Two photographers belonging to a newspaper were arrested because the flash bulb of one of them exploded accidentally . . .' 'It's also ignorance,' I said. The Party had grown from four million to ten million in six years; many cadres were inexperienced, yet administrators were needed. In December 1955 Premier Chou Enlai had begun to fashion a twelve-year programme for China's advance. 'We need science, science . . . a million technical scientists at least . . . our most urgent need is to create more intellectuals, not less.' One should be careful that the levelling process would not become self-defeating. There were at least ten thousand Chinese scientists and other 'brains' abroad; in the past six years one thousand had come back; and this one thousand had made a great deal of difference and had contributed already very much to China. 'Our policy should be to learn from everybody, to open doors.'

He agreed that badly handled, the intelligentsia could not function, would sink into passivity. 'Some research workers were accused of sending secret messages because the Party cadres could not understand their scientific equipment.'

I was very grateful to Kuo Mojo for giving me so much time and speaking so openly. He was a man who understood his era, its potential and its limitations. He knew the immense trajectory in time which Chinese writers had to

perform, and how vulnerable they were. Far more so than
scientists. Scientists were immediately useful. But writers
dealt with human beings; they conveyed ideas; so they were
also dangerous. 'Engineers of the soul', they were now
called. Their task was to fashion a human spirit ardently
loving socialism . . . how could they do it unless they
themselves were convinced?

Some weeks later, in Szechuan, I was to read in the local
paper Kuo Mojo's speech on the Hundred Flowers. Kuo was
Deputy for the province of Szechuan to the National
People's Congress: his speech was the most concise and also
the most accurate explanation of what the Hundred Flowers
really meant to the scientific intelligentsia. It would help me
a great deal not to fall into the error into which so many fell;
of considering it an attempt at liberalization followed by a
clampdown.

To Peking University, once known as Yenching, my own
university. Again the chic, elegant willows scrutinizing the
narrow water at their feet. Twelve thousand students by
1958, instead of the mere eight hundred we had been. Two
young and beautiful women professors took me round the
campus and told me most remarkable things. Already the
spirit of the Hundred Flowers was at work. Already articles
in the newspapers, critical of bureaucracy; critical of
insufficient care in the factories leading to accidents . . . The
professors told me that a system of 'progressive classes'
utilizing criticism and collective study had been started in
1953, at the time of the great campaign for thought-
remoulding among the intelligentsia. But it would now be
given up. Students must have self-reliance; they lost it with
too much collective study. Research was important and
promising individuals should be recruited early in the
various disciplines. Too many meetings were bad for study,
injurious to the health of the students. They left no leisure
even for rest. 'We have had breakdowns. We hope to change
all this.'

'There is no need to carry on more intensive politicization.
Our intellectuals are already changed, they have truly

reformed themselves mentally,' said the professors. How astonishing, their blithe confidence that in six short years, 2,500 years of mandarinate, of élitism, should be changed! That was not possible, I thought. And even though I was *also* on the side of the élite (was I not one of them?), I could not forget what they had not done for the Chinese people.

To the Peking library: 4,200,000 books; chiefly on science, says the librarian. *How to Win Friends and Influence People* is banned because it teaches a typically opportunistic, bourgeois attitude. But now the library must be enlarged, books must be purchased 'from everywhere . . . we must study even from our enemies'. The librarian is quoting Mao, but I do not know it; because Mao's particularly important speeches of that year would not be printed for over two decades.

A morning with the Minister of Justice, Madame Shih Liang. She is a diminutive, frail, small-boned person, so tiny that in her youth she failed to pass a physical examination during the selection for a magistracy. But she is a person of indomitable rectitude, and she went to jail, although not a communist, because of her stand against Chiang Kaishek's spineless compliance when the Japanese invaded China. Shih Liang was active in drafting the new laws, and especially co-operated with Teng Yingchao (the wife of Premier Chou Enlai) in the all-important Marriage Law of 1951, which is the chief document for women's liberation in China. For the abolition of infanticide, the protection of children, Shih Liang has laboured greatly. 'The Marriage Law and the Constitution of 1954 are enormous advances in women's liberation.'

Shih Liang tried not to be too technical. She explained that it was not easy to change feudal customs so deeply imbedded. 'The notion of law and legality is still quite fluid in our country.' The legal system must also promote the socialist revolution; it must therefore not follow the bourgeois codes. In short, a legal framework must be made for a reality which was in the process of transformation in the interests of the Revolution. The concept of law, as so many other concepts, needed to be defined and revised. 'Mistakes have certainly been made; but then Land Reform was like a hurricane, and so were the other campaigns . . . We are going through every case, rehabilitating as many as possible.' Over 1,300,000 people unjustly labelled counter-revolutionary had already been rehabilitated. 'The emphasis is on not carrying out the death penalty immediately; it is held up for two years in case new evidence turns up; and it may be postponed indefinitely.' Mao Tsetung had said that 'heads are not leeks that can grow again . . .' But of course there had been executions, especially in the 1950–1 crushing of counter-revolutionaries. Papa had told me how the lorries with their loads of the condemned rolled by the house at night.

I asked how judgment could be correct when one referred to the masses, whose passions were aroused by the recital of a culprit's crimes; and when was a mass not a mob or a crowd? Shih Liang explained that the Party's function at those popular trials was both to educate in class struggle and to restrain from physical violence. There had been excesses because Party committees, in launching movements in a hurry, were not acquainted with the situation, not clear about differential treatment. But the use of physical violence was abhorrent and severely condemned. 'And precautions are taken to avoid the culprits committing suicide.' But there were suicides.

Shih Liang had arranged for me to see the trial of an ex-counter-revolutionary, now on the way to reform, at the Bureau of Public Security. There was one judge, looking very young, and two assessors, one a woman. Hunched, but healthy-looking and burly, the culprit stood, and agreed he had been guilty of black marketeering, hoarding and passing information to remnants of the Kuomintang organization for about three years after 1949. He had been re-educated through labour. The judge, who tried very hard to make his gentle, suave face look grim and stern, discharged him with 'two years' supervision by the masses.

On to Peking's model jail, which contained a factory for making socks, at which the prisoners worked. Here was reform through labour and political study. I saw no young people; the average age of the eight hundred or so prisoners was around forty. 'We do not jail very old people, we place them under mass supervision but leave them at home. Unless they have no home; then we take them in but do not make them work.'

When I told Wang Wanchun that I was greatly impressed by the drive for women's equality, and the Marriage Law, he said, 'But not all Party cadres like it. Some of them are still quite feudal in their treatment of women.' For instance, there had been great resistance to allowing widows to remarry. It was still considered dishonourable; and that very year a poor widow would be pushed to suicide by her family, without the Party cadre interfering. Afterwards the All-China Women's Federation had intervened, and a full inquiry was held; in fact, it was through the Federation that women dared to protest against ill-treatment. The government backed the women fully.

The drive for women's equality was spearheaded by the women of the Long March, that small group of indomitable females who had survived, among them Teng Yingchao, wife of Premier Chou Enlai and Kang Keching, wife of Marshal Chu Teh.*

An afternoon with Madame Li Tehchuan, Minister of Health. Not a communist, Madame Li was the widow of the Christian marshal, Feng Yuhsiang; I had a photograph of Papa and me taken with him when he came to ask my father for rolling stock for his troops.† Madame Li was a cheerful and amiable person with a smooth, unlined face.

She received me in her house, and spoke of the great campaigns against epidemics. 'We could never have done it without the people's backing.' Over 180 million people had been vaccinated against smallpox in the first two years after

*Chinese women retain their own names after marriage. This does not apply only to professional women but to all, including housewives.
†See *The Crippled Tree.*

Liberation, and now there was no smallpox in China. We talked of family planning and Li Tehchuan waxed voluble. Unlike her prudish colleague in India, she launched into detailed descriptions of methods. 'We'll try all the methods, Chinese and Western, old and new.' The Western world was laughing at China because someone had advocated the swallowing of tadpoles as a contraceptive device. 'We've tried it, but it doesn't work.' However, the ancient books did describe oral contraceptives (at that time the pill had not yet been invented in the West), and Li Tehchuan would have them tried. There was also a rather heroic way of avoiding inseminating a woman, which was practised in China in the past. It consisted in the male pinching off the vas at the moment of ejaculation. 'Of course it demands discipline,' said Li Tehchuan brightly.

Her grandson came in, a very beautiful child, and suddenly Li Tehchuan was a doting grandmother; she hugged him in open love. 'At one time we thought every child must be brought up the same way . . . but we must let children develop their own personality, not turn them into robots.' The newspapers had just published a cartoon showing Chinese youngsters, differently clad, entering a big book spread like a tent, labelled MARXISM–LENINISM, and coming out the other end all looking alike.

'We think families must be kept together. We encourage mothers to keep their children with them at night – but we provide nurseries and kindergartens for day care. In this way the children are at home, but the mother can be liberated for work or study.' I was to see the development of nurseries and kindergartens through the years; and on this point of caring for children there was no doubt that China was ahead of many countries in the world. I wrote an article on my meeting with Li Tehchuan for the *Observer* in London, and it was published.

A few days later I saw men in Central Park queuing up for condoms at a booth. The charge was one cent (half an American cent) for a packet of ten. At night, in many parks, open-air films on childbirth and on contraception would be shown. This was really an assault on the Chinese traditon of prudery, and my Chinese friends in Hong Kong would not believe me when I told them. Francis and Cecilia, a devoted couple, blushed when I told them that now a man called his wife 'my loved one', and so did the wife call her husband. 'Shocking,' commented Cecilia.

A visit to the ballet school of Peking to see Eileen Tai. Eileen Tai, or Tai Ailien, was the sister of my dear friend Phyllis. Phyllis and Eileen were overseas Chinese born of a wealthy family in Trinidad. Both girls were of strong character; Phyllis went to Singapore and Eileen to London, where she studied ballet under Madame Rambert, and Jacob Epstein was so taken with her face that he made a sculpture of her. Phyllis was one of the exceedingly few Chinese who got out of Singapore when the Japanese came; and only because of an English family with whom she was friendly and who warned her in time: 'We're going, Phyllis, drop everything and come.' Somehow the English family had managed to get her on the evacuation boat (for British whites only). All she carried was a towel in her hands and her diamonds in a paper bag. She loaned me those diamonds in London, when I had to go to Windsor Castle to be presented to the King. Back in Singapore, Phyllis had told me, 'Try to see my sister Eileen, she's in Peking.' Eileen was intensely patriotic and had gone to China during the war against Japan, and remained there at Liberation. She was now running the ballet school in Peking. She was a small woman, with a spirit like a flame. 'We now have fraternal Soviet experts to teach us ballet,' she told me.

Eileen would train ballet dancers until 1966. Then, like so many others, she was made to 'stand aside' as unfit to teach and as a 'bourgeois authority', when Chiang Ching started to manage art during the Cultural Revolution. Eileen was not harmed, though harassed and subjected to humiliation. She stayed at home and drew a diminished salary. When in October 1976 Chiang Ching and her acolytes were arrested, Eileen Tai heard about it from a painter friend of hers who lived in the same compound. She put on her ballet shoes and danced right down the main avenue of Peking.

Now Eileen Tai put on a small ballet rehearsal for me and some other visitors who had arrived. My chauffeur Ku, who had strolled in, was amazed. 'How can they dance on their toes? It must be very painful – as much suffering as bound feet in the old days.'

Dinner with an illustrious lady, Madame Ho Hsiangning. Madame Ho was the widow of Liao Chungkai, who had been a revolutionary of the first vintage, and a close friend of Sun Yatsen. Ho Hsiangning had an oval face and piercing, lively eyes. A painter and a poet, she was also Chairwoman of the Overseas Chinese Affairs Commission, and chairwoman of one of the eight non-communist parties. She was seventy-eight when we met, but looked fifty. We talked a great deal of the overseas Chinese and their problems, and the difficulties they experienced. The Kuomintang in Taiwan was trying to capture them, promising them 'protection'. A policy for the overseas must be very clearly laid down. Madame Ho said there had been cases when overseas Chinese returning to China had met with difficulties, for instance, payments made to old retired people by their offspring working abroad might sometimes be held up. 'This is due to ignorance of the conditions,' she said. We discussed *jus sanguis*, whereby Chinese born anywhere are Chinese if the father is Chinese. On the whole, concluded Madame Ho, overseas Chinese returning to China were given privileges in order to give them time to get used to conditions.

I would meet this sagacious woman again ten years later, in 1966, at the start of the Cultural Revolution. As I think of her, of Shih Liang, of Soong Chingling, of Li Tehchuan, of so many others and of the immense work they did for their people, I feel grateful that I had the luck to meet and speak with them, for each one of them gave me spirit to live by.

Dinner with Uncle Kang of Szechuan, who was in Peking for the National People's congress due to open that June. Uncle Kang and others of the Kang family were big businessmen, Third Uncle's partners in banking and commercial enterprises.* Uncle Kang was now also some kind of financial adviser for the province of Szechuan and a representative at the Political Consultative Conference, which was holding a meeting at the same time as the Party Congress, (some delegates of the one held seats on the other body). He and the other national–capitalists with him talked at length about the Hundred Flowers. They were obviously hoping for a new start. 'A great deal of potential talent has not been employed for political reasons. It's time for it to be used,' said Uncle Kang. It was part of this extraordinary country that is China that Uncle Kang went on, in his new role, serving his country, and died peacefully of old age.

A visit to my dear friend Yeh, the editor of *Chinese Literature*, a monthly magazine. Yeh, a man full of humour, a gentle and learned man, had spent some years in England and had written a best-seller in English.† He did not shout about his convictions or lack of them; he just performed to the best of his ability. 'Of course we must extend the scope of writing. Until now we have not really begun to describe what has happened in recent years. There is no depth to what we write because we don't quite understand ourselves what has happened . . . so it's just a formal description of outward events.' As for being remoulded, Yeh agreed that it took time but said, 'The thing to do is to plunge into the new without reservations, without looking back over one's shoulder.' I admired and respected him for saying this. Truly, it was diving into an unknown sea, never to return as one had been, but metamorphosed, having suffered a sea-change . . . But what would this sea-change mean for me?

The peonies spread their splendour in the parks, acres of them languid in the fragrant air. So used had I been to rapine and decay and dirt that I could not get over the restoration of beauty and of temples and palaces. It was enchantment. But

---

*See *Birdless Summer* for the Kang family.
†*The Ignorant and the Forgotten* (Sylvan Press, 1946). He published two more books in English, *The Mountain Village* (1948), and *They Fly South* (1948), both by the Sylvan Press.

in me turmoil continued. Scarcely did I feel exalted by some noble human achievement than its antithesis, some stupid and brutal act, would again plunge me into distress. Thus I heard of a man and a woman working in the same organization who had had a love affair some twenty years before, but since had gone their separate ways and married happily. However, in the course of a campaign this ancient love story had been raked up; not by the Party, but by their own colleagues, other members of the organization. It was written up on posters hung in the main hall of the office where they worked. 'Boldly criticize each other, discarding the hypocritical politeness which tries to offend nobody' was the quotation (from the *People's Daily*) which prefaced this revelation of 'reprehensible bourgeois immorality'. The result was three suicides: the woman, her present husband (loss of face), and the former lover.

And yet so much cruelty was being inflicted upon so many people in the 'free' world. In America, with McCarthy, guilt by association was current, and there were suicides, and ruin for many artists and intellectuals; and in Malaya 500,000 stateless were behind barbed wire. But those cruelties did not affect me so much because I did not relate to them. They were 'outside', not within. Here in China I was all the time thinking of myself in the same situation. 'Supposing I do stay; I too shall have my love with Ian exposed and made ugly . . . and perhaps, who knows, I shall be persuaded it was a dreadful thing, and revile it . . .' And this made me quite sick. I think it was actually the pivotal factor which made me decide to wait for more dust to settle. For I never gave up the intention of returning to China; but it was a question of the right time. This Hundred Flowers opening did seem the right time; but one had to see how it would turn out.

The argument that there *was* a private life, that not all personal matters were political and that sex relations especially must not be held up as examples of villainy – how often I would have angry debates over this! 'There is too much nitpicking,' I said to Kung Peng. But where lay the difference between political and non-political, between private offence and public guilt? This was a matter of legal definition, and a legal code was still being fashioned.

Meanwhile guilt lay upon me like a poisoned itch; the guilt of class. The realization that with all noble emotions to the fore, such people as I had thrived upon the prolonged and terrible misery of the Chinese people; and that with all their faults and pettiness, and the 'mistakes' and wrongs perpetrated by Party cadres, the Chinese Communist Party had undoubtedly done more, in six short years, to free, both mentally and physically, the enormous majority of the Chinese people from oppression and misery than we had ever dreamed of doing.

Yet there was also that stranglehold pressure to reveal one's naked soul, to become transparent like a clean glass window, to repudiate one's crimes or sins ; to confess and to be redeemed, accepted, no speck of spirit opaque, no corner of the mind unturned; established in a bright new house of living.

I talked with some intellectuals who had been sifting through their own lives, punctiliously, and was suddenly gripped by the sensation that I was Alice going through the Looking Glass. A depersonalization, almost unbearable. 'I shall have a nervous breakdown if I don't control my imagination.' I got up at night to walk, walk in the streets, walk to the park in the quiet, safe night. No one could have walked so safely in the night in Old China. I saw romantic couples demurely walking in the alleys, and in the park, sitting on an artificial rock, above an artificial pool, a pretty girl singing to herself. She was a factory worker on night shift, and her face shone with that extraordinary innocence which was the hallmark of the young in New China. She came here to sing, she said, especially on moonlit nights, before going to work. 'Only six years ago my whole family were beggars; now I am going to night school and I work in the textile plant.'

The foreign guests at the Hsinchiao Hotel provided me with

moments of amusement and even illumination. There was the Englishman who worried about getting his shoes properly polished. 'The only place where they're done just right is Calcutta. Nice city, Calcutta.' There was the Polish expert on porcelain who said, 'I'm not doing good work. The Chinese have far better patterns than we have.' He borrowed Cyril Connolly's *The Unquiet Grave* from me, and sighed: 'We have no such good books now.' When I asked him about Khrushchev and Stalin he paled and walked away.

Delegations from fraternal socialist countries marching in to breakfast made the words 'groaning board' a vivid reality. I watched with wonder the pyramids of cakes and bread, the hillocks of butter and jam, the battalions of plates with fried eggs (three each) laid out on the tables, which the delegates contrived to engulf.

There were the newsmen, some with the most bizarre hypotheses about China. They speculated and made up stories; they were either from fraternal countries, in which case they were privileged with travel and interviews, and described everything in paradisial terms, or they were the few, rare representatives of the Western press. Correspondents of Reuter's and Agence France-Presse were accredited to Peking and somehow managed to do sound work without much help. There was Claude Roy, at the time a leading communist, with a delegation from the French Party. 'Han Suyin, why do you not become a communist?' he asked me sternly. 'I'm like St Thomas, I have to see and to touch . . .' In the last two decades Claude Roy has changed; he now spends a great deal of time excoriating what he has worshipped. Whereas I, having clung to honest doubt, have always felt my solitude shared by those who have no need foolishly to burn, who hold the privilege to change their minds, but not their love.

There were the embassies. The British Embassy asked me several times to lunch and dinner. I think the Chargé d'Affaires felt that I might be brainwashed. He gave me a series of horrifying articles by Robert Guillain of *Le Monde*, describing all China as one vast antheap of 'blue ants'. Since then Guillain has been back to China and explained with inimitable French elegance that 'ants' are hardworking and praiseworthy insects . . . Nevertheless, the articles influenced me; I rushed to Kung Peng with them and asked her if these horrors were true. Then I read them again; and I was not so impressed.

To the Indian Embassy, to meet R. K. Nehru, the Ambassador, and his very able wife. Both admired China. R. K. Nehru was very happy about the Hundred Flowers. 'Unless this policy is implemented, advance will not be so fast.' Intellectuals were always much afraid of re-education, 'yet all life re-educates us constantly . . . it appears tyrannical when it has to be done consciously instead of just happening by circumstance.' He laughed at his Western colleagues and their 'obsolete' ideas of freedom 'based on the affluence they derived from exploiting us, India, China . . .' He agreed with me that some of the Chinese intelligentsia were afraid that the Hundred Flowers was only a flash-in-the-pan contrivance. 'There is a great deal of resistance within the Party to it,' he remarked, 'but Chairman Mao is all for it . . . In China there are not enough competent cadres to go round.' In India the British had left a framework of laws and had trained judges and lawyers to carry them out. But in China everything had to be created anew, including not only a legal system but the very notion of law. 'There are not enough seasoned administrators . . . Those that the Communist Party have who know anything about running cities are mostly ex-Kuomintang bureaucrats . . . No one can be sure of their loyalty . . . I have just written a fifty-page memorandum to my government on the present situation.' Matters of jurisprudence interested him greatly; and he had had many talks with Chinese officials about them. They had agreed that 'mass movements are necessary in the first years of a revolution, but out of them must be born laws and regulations . . . to improve the people's democratic legal system.' A penal code, a civil code, the law of criminal procedure – all this was being studied, and the Indian Ambassador was immensely interested. He was sure

that the Hundred Flowers was a step towards drawing up
clearly the rights of the individual, and the creation of a legal
system. There must be more intellectuals in the Party, to
overcome 'that small peasant mentality . . . so many in the
Party are peasants . . . wonderful people, but knowing little
about running institutions.' Chairman Mao himself had told
the Ambassador that it was essential to raise the educational
and cultural level of Party cadres, 'which is pretty low,
considering that they've come through decades of
fighting . . .'

I had other good Indian friends in Peking; among them P.
N. Sharma, the photographer, who was, at the time,
exhibiting his photographs to crowds in Central Park, and
Natwar Singh, a young Embassy secretary, a delightful
companion for rambles, and a devotee of the English writer
E. M. Forster.* He was learning Chinese, but appeared in no
hurry to become an expert. Both were to help me a great deal
during the subsequent years of tension between India and
China.

I also enjoyed impressively stimulating conversation with
Jacques Locquin, the French representative of Agence
France-Presse. He was impeccably logical, and he
manipulated theories so deftly that it dazzled me. A
revolution, said he, was made with what is best and what is
most vile in man. It devoured, decanted, sifted, churned and
changed, and spared no one. 'In fact, our world has already
changed; but our politicians are not aware of it.'

'Why don't you write down your shock, your alternance
of happiness and dismay, when you get back to Hong Kong?'
suggested Jacques. 'I will,' said I. And I did, in an article
entitled 'Peking Revisited', which I would produce for
Holiday magazine in America. But I could not write a book
on China. Only when everything had fallen into perspective
would I write. At the moment I felt too flayed, too raw. 'I
think that we are only seeing the beginning of the Chinese
Revolution,' I told Jacques; 'I think China will have to

*Author of *A Passage to India*.

invent a new pattern, all its own, for socialism. Meanwhile, it'll take at least twenty years to disentangle the Old from the New, the recurrent obscurantism disguised as revolutionary advance.' I did not know then how accurate these words of mine would prove. I would have forgotten them, but that they are in my notes of that time.

I went to see Kung Peng and she appeared angry with me. This was because in the course of my visits some remarks of mine, deemed 'unfriendly' by middle cadres, had come to her.

'You make statements attacking us,' she said.

'I don't attack, Kung Peng – I state what I think. If every time one says something the cadres don't like one is dubbed reactionary, then no one will ever speak the truth.'

Kung Peng nodded: 'Some comrades at a lower level are not used to anything but acquiescence.' It was difficult for them to recognize 'constructive criticism'. She was upbraiding me; she was trying to tell me to be careful.

How does one tell the truth and yet avoid offending susceptibilities? The problem is worse in China, with its long tradition of 'face', than perhaps anywhere else. Any official in China, whether communist or not, was simply not accustomed to being contradicted.

Kung Peng said, 'How could you marry such a feudalist as Tang Paohuang?'

'How did I know he was a feudalist? It was wartime, he had spent three years in England at Sandhurst, he sounded immensely patriotic, and I married him because of a common ideal: to fight to save the country . . .'

Suddenly the terrible bitterness, the harrowing anger of the past came back. I had then plumbed, I thought, the ocean of China's feudalism. How profitable, how truly beneficial had been those years with Pao, though I would keep the scars of this great battle all my life! Now I did understand to the marrow the medieval mind, its total absence of cause-to-effect logic, its subjectivity, its intolerance, its emotional composition. That is what made me so cautious now, about

New China, because in the air I could still sniff the mustiness.

I was back to that searing time, when I was just seventeen years old, in Yenching University, and had been denounced in the Students' Association newspaper because my sister was going out with her American fiancé and I had walked with both of them to the cinema one afternoon, and the fiancé, being American, had asked a friend of his to be my 'date' at the cinema . . . Kung Peng, and others who were now officials of the government, had then been in Yenching, prominent leaders of the Students' Association. 'What did you do to me then?' I cried. It was twenty-three years later, but the wound they inflicted upon me then would never go away. 'Did you try to find out? Did you come and talk to me? No. Arbitrarily you denounced me. On the walls of Yenching University I was denounced, when I was having such a hard time trying to save money to study, when I wanted so much to be Chinese, to be Chinese . . . it was you who rejected me. You never gave me a chance, did you? What do you call that but feudalism?'

'We did not understand you then,' said Kung Peng.

'And how do I know that it won't be the same again? I *know* it will be just the same again. Someone will dredge up that story, and embellish it. Trust some man who was a student at that time, who is a middle cadre today, whom I possibly irked, or ignored, twenty, twenty-three years ago – trust him to use the next 'mass movement campaign' and to paste it on wall posters all over the organization where I would be working, and to have me up, standing to defend myself, against all my co-workers . . .' And no one could protect me against this since every unit, every organization, ran its own meetings, with its own cadres and its own 'masses', solved its own problems, condemned or cleared its own people. I had heard enough to know that malice, jealousy, pettiness, envy, vindictiveness had not disappeared. They were present, they were there. Only now they were daubed over with political jargon; the fuelling force for political condemnation; not always, but sometimes. And I was target enough, for I was so different, so different . . . not only because I was a Eurasian, but because I wrote. And *A Many-Splendoured Thing* was, in China then, a bad book (for McCarthy and his ilk it was also a bad book).

'Believe me, Kung Peng, I love China, but China to me means the Chinese people. It will take at least twenty years before all these confusions of the mind are sorted out. Twenty years. I believe that in twenty years China will be democratic. But until then . . .'

And Kung Peng did not contradict. She did not attempt to persuade me to stay. 'You must come back again next year,' she said, thus audibly promising me a visa. And so gently led me back to quietness, out of pain and anger. And later I was to know that Kung Peng would come out boldly for me, to address many people who were irate with me and wanted to throw me out, and would tell them to let be; tell them the story of my life. Not once, not only that year, but many, many times through the years, she would fight for me against the witch-hunters, the sectarians.

And now Kung Peng is dead; she too suffered, suffered greatly from the witch-hunters, the sectarians, all disguised as 'revolutionaries' . . . But she was a staunch, a dedicated woman, and she never gave me a hint of what she endured because she was a very loyal Party member. To be able to manage one's sufferings and fears without inflicting even a suspicion of them upon others, is not that true courage?

So many of my friends, so many, have that courage, obstinate and valiant as heartbeat itself. And although I realized that I could not stay in China then without betraying things that mattered to me – including my love, my love, a many-splendoured thing – yet I would also not betray my friends, who had given everything they were, everything for China.

CHAPTER 6

China's Hundred Flowers: 1956

I turned in my bed, and staring at me was a dinosaur, smacking its jaws. But it was the Hsinchiao Hotel waiter knocking at my door to wake me up. Papa and I were to leave early, for the seaside resort of Peitaiho, about five hours away by train from Peking. That is where Mama used to take us for a month in the summer, leaving Papa to swelter in Peking during the dog days of July and August.

In the train a policeman came up to me to ask for my papers, and Papa showed him our travel permit. Afterwards a group of suspicious young train workers (the Masses' Committee) came to chat with me. They were polite but thorough in their questioning. I told them I came from Malaya, and that I was a doctor, and had returned to China to see my family. It was not the clothes I wore but the fact that I spoke Chinese that had disconcerted these good people. Had I been a Westerner, people would have muttered 'Soviet expert'. Had I been speaking in French with Papa, I would have been a foreign traveller – but 'You look like us, you speak Chinese, but you're different'. Hence the questioning.

In Peitaiho, the local Party organizers insisted on taking me to beauty spots I knew well and telling me totally inaccurate stories of how the resort had been reserved 'only for imperialists and their running dogs'. That Papa had a house there placed us in a strange category. The Party man pointed to a beach: 'Chinese were not allowed to swim there.' It was true that few Chinese came to Peitaiho, but I had seen little boys from Chinese families swimming everywhere.

Papa's house had been taken over by the government with compensation paid to him. But Tiza's house had been confiscated since she had not claimed it. Here Papa felt more at ease to speak to me about Mama, and as we walked with small steps along the well-kept sand roads, he sighed a little. 'We are old now. Perhaps I should try to go outside, to see her again.' Because of the new policy of the Hundred Flowers, Papa had begun to hope that a demand to go abroad, to undertake a study tour, might now be accepted. But Mama was in America; and Papa could not go there from 'Red' China because the Americans would not allow him to enter unless he pretended to be a refugee and against present government, and this Papa would of course not do. I had to arrange a midway place for Papa and Mama to meet. I said I would ask David Marshall, now the Chief Minister of Singapore, who was a friend of mine and an able lawyer, whether he would let Papa come to Singapore.

Actually, the day before leaving the seaside, I had sent a telegram to David Marshall. A young journalist had called, obviously on orders from a superior. He asked me whether I knew Marshall. 'I do.' 'Do you think he might like to come here for a visit?' 'I think he would.' I told the journalist that prior to becoming Chief Minister, David had asked me to be his Health Minister, and I had refused. The young man was nonplussed, but too polite to ask why; he looked at me steadily and I clearly got the message. 'I can send him a personal telegram, just from me, suggesting that he might like to see Peking.' And I cabled. David would come to Peking later that year, and greatly enjoy himself filming the yellow roofs of the Forbidden City. David could help Papa to stay in Singapore; I would try to get Mama out of the United States so that they could meet.

I visited in Peitaiho a hospital for mental cases. But everyone was reluctant to call it a mental hospital: it was 'for cadres who are overtired'. The only mental illness which was acceptable was neurasthenia, and throughout the years innumerable were the cases of neurasthenia, transient or permanent, that I would hear about. There is something very Victorian about this coyness; one thinks immediately of the word 'decline' which covered so many cases of tuberculosis and cancer in the nineteenth century.

But inside the hospital the doctors were brisk and modern. There were around 70 per cent of cases of schizophrenia, they said, and the majority of the two hundred patients were under forty years old. I asked about nervous breakdowns and psychoses. One of the Party cadres objected to the word breakdown. 'Our cadres do not get enough rest. Their health is affected,' he said.

I saw the deep sleep therapy rooms. They were very comfortable. One patient sat up; the blinds were drawn and he was happy in the semi-darkness, and he talked. He had worked too hard at the time of the big floods of 1954, which had threatened to submerge the city of Wuhan. He had not slept for many days, and in the end, while behind him his comrades toiled to raise the last foot of the earth dyke, to stop the surging waters, he had been swept away . . . he had been rescued, but had become very panic-prone. And then there had been so many meetings, and sometimes his heart beat so fast and loud that he could hear nothing except its drumming. He had sharp, quick movements and needed, said the doctor, another three months of rest. 'We try all forms and modes of therapy, both Chinese and Western; also the Chinese breath control exercises.' On the terrace, some patients were shadow boxing. I asked about homosexuality and again the Party cadre stiffened.

'There is none in China.'

'But there is. It is mentioned in the old Chinese novels, for instance, in *The Dream of the Red Chamber*.'

'But it does not exist under socialism.'

The doctor kept quiet. It was, said the cadre, a perversion due to the social system. In fact, most mental diseases were ideological in nature. There would be no recognition of homosexuality as anything but a disease due to 'ideological causes'. But then everything was being redefined, both in jurisdiction and in mental disease; new concepts of insanity and of delinquency were being worked out. Thus rape was not only a common law crime, it was also a political sin; asocial behaviour labelled 'bad habits inherited from the past society'.

When Papa went back to Peking, I went to Wuhan by train and from there by aeroplane to Chungking, to see again Szechuan and Third Uncle.

In the train, a most unusual sight: in one of the compartments a Russian, drinking and hugging a Chinese girl. He came down at the stations, still hugging and fondling her. Round him were four 'companions', all Chinese. The whole train stared. Never, never would this have been possible, had it been anyone but a Russian ...

Some weeks later I was to hear from a friend the remark that the Chinese were getting very angry because the 'fraternal' experts raped interpreters or other women working in their offices. 'But no one can say anything: one man who complained was punished for indiscipline.'

I was met at Chungking airport by Comrade Kao, who was not a Szechuanese but a northerner and obviously hated the heat of Chungking. I was lodged in a fantastic new building, a Temple of Heaven grotesque, which functioned as hotel and assembly hall for meetings, and where the kitchen was a hundred metres away from the dining room. It was pretty grim for the waiters, who had to run up and down flights of stairs with the dishes. In Peking Uncle Kang had termed the building 'extravagant'; it had cost too much.

I would witness a big criticism meeting in the main hall; I was on the balcony, too far away to see or hear clearly, but a group of people seemed to be accused of some crime or other; they were standing with heads bowed, and people were getting up, pointing and talking at them. I asked Comrade Kao about it and all he said was, 'You should not have been looking.'

Third Uncle, with his daughter, Third Sister, and her husband Lin Jugao, came to dinner; this had been arranged by Comrade Kao. 'They can come here, it is more convenient.' Comrade Kao did not wish me to walk about Chungking. Third Uncle was well, not a whit older, and seemed cheerful; but then he had good manners, and would appear cheerful even under duress. Lin Jugao was a representative of one of the non-communist parties.

Comrade Kao (who insisted on being present) frowned at him, but no one cared.

'What do you think of this building?' asked Lin Jugao. I was just going to say how awful it was when he added, as Third Sister coyly tittered, 'She is one of the fifteen architects who designed it.' Third Sister said, 'Shut up', fondly. I said, 'How interesting . . .' She had, however, only designed the balconies and the concrete mouldings on the stairways.

The next morning, before Comrade Kao was astir, I went to see Third Uncle. I had asked Third Sister where he now stayed when we went together to the toilet. Third Uncle lived in a new small house not far from the enormous hall-hostel. He was dressed in a light gown of grey, he had summer slippers of woven fibre upon his feet, and at once he gave me a pair. 'You'll be more comfortable.' Then he moved towards the cupboard where he kept his tea boxes; he brewed and we sipped, as always, he discoursing on tea. But his mind was not on tea; he let it be known, in small hints, that there had been some 'inconsiderate' times, but that now things were moving 'appropriately', and 'anyway order and peace have been restored so that the future is limitless'. 'Of course, *our* Szechuan is a most important province; and it has to be managed properly.' He reminded me of the poem written in Chengtu on one of the pavilions in the Wu Hou Sze Shrine: 'Should you wish to rule Szechuan, think, think, and think again'.

'The new cadres come from other provinces. They do not always understand our character,' said Third Uncle. But luckily there were many Szechuanese among the commanders of the army: there was the great Chu Teh, and Chen Yi, and Teng Hsiaoping and Lo Juiching, and Nieh Jungchen, all of them Szechuanese, all of them veterans of the Long March and Mao's companions. 'Szechuan is the heart of China, China's treasure box,' said Third Uncle. Then abruptly he opened a drawer and took out a parcel, long and slim, wrapped in cloth. He unrolled the cloth; there were papers. 'These are the rubbings of our gravestones. We had to remove the graves.' He stopped. I think he was very sad.

'Take them. Keep them. And also the book of our generations.' This book, which each family in China draws up, lists all the family members, generation by generation, but the one Third Uncle gave me contained only the names of nine generations, albeit the names to be given to thirty generations from the time our Ancestors arrived in Szechuan from our original Hakka home in south China, Meihsien.*

I put the rubbings of the gravestones and the book of generations in my bag and Third Uncle inquired about Papa, and before I could say anything he was saying, loudly, 'Yes indeed, the government has given us all security in our old age,' and in came Comrade Kao, puffing and a little irritated by my absconding.

'We have to visit many places,' he said crossly, 'we are late.'

He looked round enviously. The walls of the room had been covered with fine white paper. 'What a big house, and very expensive . . . it's very big for just one person.'

'I am expecting my loved one, and my youngest son and his wife next month,' said Third Uncle.

We left, Comrade Kao and I, and on the way Comrade Kao said, 'We cadres have a very poor life; only thirty *yuan* a month, and too much responsibility and hard work . . .' One could see he felt life was a bit unfair; here was Third Uncle, an arrant bourgeois and a capitalist, with fine accommodation and fine silk garments, and possibly ten times the salary of Comrade Kao, not counting the interest on his investments, at $3\frac{1}{2}$ per cent. And Comrade Kao was from the north; his wife and five children had stayed there. He had come with the army in 1949 and had been in Szechuan for all of those seven years since Liberation, and, 'I am not used to the food or the climate. Sometimes I get quite unhealthy,' said he, and described the way his bowels let him down.

The steel works of Chungking, which had been a private company (set up to make the rails to build that railway planned way back in 1903), were now nationalized, and I

*See *The Crippled Tree*.

spent a very happy day there with the director, a Szechuanese. I inquired about the workers' health and accommodation; was shown their new brick dormitories, up a small hill. 'It's gruelling, climbing up that hill in hot weather,' I said. 'But there's no other space. All of Chungking is ladder streets climbing the many hills,' said the director. In 1972, I would again visit the steel works of Chungking. And the same director would greet me, with much emotion. 'We remember your visit in 1956; you asked so much about the workers, their welfare . . . we circulated your remarks . . . the workers were moved by your concern . . .' The director himself had been under duress during the Cultural Revolution; sent back to manual labour; but in 1972, with the return to prominence of Chou Enlai that year, he had been reinstalled, and the steel plant was working again. In Chungking, as in all Szechuan, there had been a lot of fighting, almost civil war, in the Cultural Revolution.

Comrade Kao complained, 'I couldn't understand what you were saying,' because he did not speak Szechuanese well. He then duly took me round many places I knew, but also to the house where Chou Enlai had lived when he was working in Chungking, keeping the United Front liaison going with Chiang Kaishek. Kung Peng had also stayed there; she was then working with Chou Enlai, and that is how we had met, in January 1941. I looked at the small, hot house, with its tiny rooms; the desk, the beds with their neatly rolled blankets. Another Party cadre in charge, also not a Szechuanese, tried to tell me all about the bombings of Chungking. 'I know, I was here, I was bombed.' But he went on giving me totally inaccurate figures.*

I went to see the jail hewn out of rock where the (American) OSS, together with Chiang's hateful security service under Tai Lee, subjected Communist prisoners to torture. Since I had personally seen someone repeatedly beaten and then walked round, I knew that it was true that

*See *Birdless Summer*.

torture was used. But once again there was some exaggeration in the dramatic way the Party cadre presented the facts, as if he had to force me to believe them.

Then by train to Chengtu, on the railway which had been completed in 1952. It was a night flooded with moonlight, and the small villages clustering under their bamboo fronds looked delightful in the silver radiance. We reached Neichiang, the sugar city, where I had spent some weeks with Tenth Sister, at the local branch of the Meifeng Bank. Now the Meifeng Bank had become the People's Bank, but the government had kept all my relatives in their jobs; so that Second Brother and his wife, Ninth and Tenth Sisters, and many cousins further continued to serve the bank.

Chengtu, and a clean railway station, and to greet me some Szechuanese cadres as well as northern cadres. I felt slightly guilty of provincial chauvinism because I was happy to see cadres of my own province. Of course, during the Long March the Red Army had replenished its numbers in Szechuan, hence the training of seasoned Party members from my province; but the bulk of the Red bases had been in the north, and that is why there were so many cadres from the northern provinces all over China. They were hardworking, honest, but occasionally no match for the agile-brained Szechuanese.

I went to the university, where I had so often been in 1940 and in 1941. On the way to the university we passed the site of Marian Manly's former midwifery hospital. It no longer existed. In place of the small wood and brick building rose a new block of flats for workers. Chengtu was now becoming industrialized, I was told, and 'many workers from Shanghai have come and more will be coming to start industrial projects'. As a result of the influx of young workers, the same phenomenon of population increase was happening here as in Chungking. 'The first thing workers do is get married and raise a baby or two. They have never had such a good life.'

I thought of Marian as we went past, her tears when we had met in Hong Kong after she had been expelled from China, weeping her heart out because she was no longer wanted. 'I must write to her, tell her I have come here.'

At the university I met professors I had known in the 1940s: Dr Huang of the Dental Department had cared for an awkward wisdom tooth of mine, coming out late and impacted; and Dr Yu, the gynaecologist, I had seen when I was working as a midwife at Marian Manly's hospital. Both had humorous, harassed faces. They had obviously been through some gruelling criticism meetings, but now all was well, and they continued working. The university and the hospital and medical school were expanding. Many more thousands of students were expected in the years to come; they would provide the staff necessary for medical care in the whole of south-west China. Already medical teams from here went to Tibet and Tsinghai, out of the way regions. The enormous drive against venereal disease among the national minorities (very prevalent, especially in Tibet, where it was the cause of so much infecundity among women) had produced good results. 'We hope to eradicate both gonorrhoea and syphilis,' said Dr Yu. Of course, this also meant changing social behaviour, laxity in morals, prostitution. The custom in Szechuan of selling one's wife for 'temporary employment' to government officials from Nanking and Shanghai, during the last years of the Chiang Kaishek regime, had disappeared, and so had the selling of girl children to the brothels, which had been closed.

At dinner that night I found the doctors gentle but stubbornly forthright. 'Of course interference with scientific work is not good; the Party must learn to listen to the masses,' said Dr Huang. The Dental Department, and in fact much of the university, had been started by Canadian and American missionaries, and staffed by them for a considerable number of years. But no one could refer to this fact for the time being; there was a violent reaction towards acknowledging that 'colonial imperialism' had left a little knowledge and training behind. And of course, among the very nice Party officials at dinner, there was the usual intransigent bureaucrat who told me quite inaccurate stories about the hospital and how it had catered only for the wealthy. But he had such a narrow vocabulary, such a paucity of words, that I suddenly understood how difficult it was for him. He was a poor peasant's son, and in a drought had seen his sisters and mother die of hunger; he and his father had become beggars. 'Wealth' to him meant simply enough to eat.

I launched into birth and death rates. Already in Peking the response when I made inquiries about death had been 'Nobody dies now', or 'Very few people die now'. And here it was the same. Oh, my China, I thought, my throat suddenly seized with love and nostalgia, still so involved with the totem and taboo of words! The word death had always been taboo; now it had become almost anti-socialist! There was such a big hoard of ancient symbols and myths to dispel: a new metaphysics was in the offing; and how could the cadres be blamed for thinking that fervour was truth, as in pre-scientific Europe? China had not yet accomplished her industrial revolution, or developed the scientific logic that goes with industrialization.

Dinner with the intelligentsia of Chengtu; the writers, among them the famous Li Liuju, whose book *Sixty Stirring Years* would provide me with so much information for my own book, *The Crippled Tree*. I inquired about Pa Chin, another Szechuan author, but he now lived in Shanghai. Li Liuju spoke at length, because I asked him, of the Secret Society, the Brothers of the Robe, of their beneficent and then nefarious role in the province. I also met Szechuan opera artists and went to the Szechuan opera with my cousins, and to drink tea in teahouses with the writers, and to discuss gastronomy while eating at the old Kokochuan restaurant. 'All the good cooks are being taken away from Szechuan to serve in the hotels in Peking.' 'Then we must train many more.' 'But the young look down upon the art of cooking.'

Enchanted strolls through the Chengtu I loved so well; to find the busy street of silversmiths and craftsmen almost deserted. 'It is reorganization of small commerce . . . they will now enter co-operatives.' But the temples were kept and repaired, as everywhere else, and the harvest was good. Szechuan was providing rice for other provinces in need of rice. 'We have a surplus this year.'

At that time it was possible for outside visitors to read the local press; something which was changed in 1960. I never found out why. In the *Szechuan Daily* I read complaints against commandism and corruption, against shoddy work (a report that 35,000 water carts were unusable in Shantung province, so badly had they been joined together). I read of Party cadres pushing the peasants to fulfil quotas irrespective of the quality of the harvest; giving wrong orders about planting. The Hundred Flowers spirit was certainly catching on in Szechuan. Clearly, it was not 'liberalization' in the sense of sharing or relinquishing power to another party; simply a demand for greater co-operation from the intelligentsia in accelerating progress by speaking the truth about the many problems impeding China's advance to modernity.

I visited the National Minorities' Institute; thirty-five million people, fifty-odd national minorities. 'We've found some new ones; so small, only a few hundred individuals, still in the Stone Age,' said the director. The problem was, how could one construct an artificial language for them? 'Some of them count no further than two.' But here in Chengtu the bulk of the students were from Tibet, being trained as cadres. A Tibetan typewriter had also been invented. 'We aim to have 2,000 Tibetan accountants for the co-operatives which will come to Tibet at Land Reform,' said the director.

Up to the mountains, beyond Pihsien, our ancestral home.* On the road back, I watched the human labour, the human labour of Szechuan, people pulling and tugging and carrying ... when would that stop? And there was a coffin being carted away on a small cart, pulled by two men roped to it. Of course funerals were now furtive affairs. No one ought to die in a country six years old. One-third of the

---

*See *The Crippled Tree* and *Birdless Summer*.

population of Chungking city, I had been told, was under six years of age. At the steel mill, two hundred children were born each month. Ten thousand two hundred workmen, but with their families they numbered 70,000. There never were enough living quarters. The steel mill must expand to ten times its size in the next ten years but the area for dormitories only three times . . . In the rural co-operatives there were children, children, children . . . 'Szechuan is very prolific,' said the Szechuan cadres beatifically. 'No child dies of hunger now, everybody lives.' Obviously family planning here was going to be difficult – a difficulty made worse by the fact that in the villages every baby received a full adult ration in rice, meat and oil from the day he was born.

I returned to Peking, and at the Party for the British Queen's Birthday I saw Premier Chou Enlai.

Chou Enlai looked no older than when I had last seen him in Chungking in 1941, fifteen years ago. His eyes, the most startling feature about him, were lustrous and moved quickly; everyone found him irresistible. 'What a man,' sighed a matron near me. People were being introduced to him by the British Chargé d'Affaires. Chou himself walked up to shake hands with ambassadors, and then Kung Peng pushed me forward and Chou Enlai, who never forgot anything said, 'Ah yes, you applied from India.'

I said, 'Prime Minister, I heard you speak in Chungking in 1941.'

I saw him turn inwards, groping in his store of memories (I think he had total memory and total recall).

'You couldn't see me, there was such a huge crowd. You were talking to the people.'

'Ah yes,' he said, and then someone else came up and Chou went round the rest of the party, which ended with a toast to the Queen. His coming to the British Embassy was of great significance, the correspondents said. It meant that China might 'liberalize'.

Some days later was the opening of the third session of the First National People's Congress. It was held at the back of the beautiful Peihai Park, and I remember the Tibetan delegates, in sumptuous scarlet and saffron robes clicking their beads and walking round the lake; the Uighurs and the Yis and the Miaos and so many other representatives in their own colourful embroidered garments and ornamental headgear; the many temporary restaurants to suit each minority, with various kinds of food; no pork for the Huis (Muslims), but then one-third of the city of Peking was reckoned 'Muslim', and almost every street had a Muslim restaurant. Representatives of overseas Chinese in ties and Western suits, and delegates from factories, and intellectuals, all walked about, admiring the beautiful pomegranate trees in pots which lined the avenues.

I still have some of the speeches that were distributed at the Congress – one by the representative of the national minorities, mentioning 'shortcomings' and errors, but also lauding the fact that at last the minorities were no longer treated in a degrading manner as in the old days, and that health and education, besides economic benefits, were theirs. There is also a speech by the representative for the overseas Chinese praising the patriotism of those who returned to China. Most of them were labouring people, and the money they had sent their old parents from abroad should not be interfered with ... The spirit of criticism promoted by the Hundred Flowers seemed to belong among the routine sentences of praise ...

The correspondents of Reuter and Agence France-Presse, and I, had received invitations to attend the opening session of the National People's Congress (not, of course, the committee debates). I am certain that this was at Chou Enlai's initiative. It showed that China had nothing to fear; it got rid of this bogus 'secrecy' which plagued all communication. It indicated that China would open herself to the world and its nations, and learn from all countries to accelerate her own progress. However, some Western experts persisted in regarding the whole Hundred Flowers in a romantically wishful manner; as a falling away from 'communism', and a 'thaw', a change of purpose. This was confusing goals and aims with methods. If I have stressed this, it is because today, in 1979, China is back in the spirit and exaltation of the Hundred Flowers and all the bright hopes of that year.

There is, however, a major difference. In 1956, the bulk of the Chinese people were still illiterate; the intelligentsia was reckoned at five million, or 1 per cent of the total population. But by 1979 a new intelligentsia has grown up, derived from the sons and daughters of peasants and workers. Even in the hamlets of faraway Szechuan, the young can read and write, hold meetings, and if these meetings were streamlined for acquiescence, there have been so many crises, so many abrupt reversals in the last twenty years, that now even the partly educated insist on thinking and arguing for themselves.

On that afternoon in June 1956 in Peking Chou Enlai climbed on the rostrum and spoke. He looked happy, his eyes shone. He had delivered the previous day a speech on external policy which contained all the elements of an 'opening' upon the world. Now Chou Enlai gave a speech on internal policy that was so contrary to all that was current and habitual in Western minds about China and China's system that it held me spellbound.

I sat with Jacques Locquin of Agence France-Presse, occasionally translating for him. But my attention was riveted to Chou and his words, and the translation I made was inadequate. Locquin, however, was so fired by what I told him that he immediately sent a cable to Paris; to which there was no response at all.

Plans for scientific and economic advance; a total reshaping of the economy, and above all, *decentralization*, the regions being given more power of their own, with less central rigidity. The adjustments to be made between the individual and the group, between the small group and the larger collectivity; between the Party power-holders and the people – all these Chou talked about. The need for the intelligentsia, for non-communist parties to continue in their useful work of providing through advice and criticism a necessary foil for the Communist Party; the need for destroying the bad habits of commandism and sectarian behaviour in the Party; the need to listen to criticism, even if it was unpalatable . . . an electrifying speech, and the faces of the listeners showed their elation, their excitement. Chou managed to pack into that hour the sensation of a new set of policies, the search for a framework to broaden the basis of consultation.

As in 1941, when I had heard Chou Enlai speak in the streets of Chungking, because the crowd was so large no hall could contain it, I was moved by some quality in him beyond eloquence or rhetoric. He was not gifted with oratory; but he was immensely impressive through his deep sincerity, the reasonableness and the simplicity of what he said, which everyone understood.

What Chou Enlai said implied a departure from the accepted theses of how to run a socialist state. And yet I was to discover that he was not its sole originator; it was a combined effort, with Mao Tsetung as the visionary behind it; for Chou's speech was an interpretation of a speech delivered by Mao in April of 1956 to Party secretaries and state ministers and leaders from all over China. Neither was Mao's speech an individual creation; it was based on work done, for more than two years, by Chinese economists and statisticians and social science researchers probing and studying to discover what was the best, the more effective way to *accelerate* development in such a backward and poor country as China.

But none of us, at the time, knew of Mao Tsetung's speech, or of the collective effort that had gone into gathering the material for it. In fact, Mao's speech, which was to be called 'The Ten Major Relationships' was not to be officially published until twenty-one years later, in April 1977!

I have always been puzzled by this extraordinary delay. I think it was a regrettable error; for had this speech of Mao been known earlier, many things which harmed China might not have happened. I was able to obtain an 'illegal' version of it in the mid 1960s.

Chou Enlai's speech was the foundation (so frail, so chancy at the time) of the democratization of China. Twenty years would go by before its meaning would take hold.

The next morning I was surprised to discover in the *People's Daily* only a terse half column of summing up. Perhaps I had missed the main speech? But I checked with Locquin, and he confirmed: 'It hasn't been printed yet . . . But if Chou Enlai's speech means anything, it means a democratic, socialist China, along the pattern of Yugoslavia, refusing the Soviet yoke.' We were both elated, but also puzzled, because neither of us had enough solid material to go on. And when, later, I spoke to some Party cadres about it, I discovered frowning and tight mouths. Even Kung Peng was to say to me ten years later, 'We did not realize the importance of certain things said and done in 1956 and 1957.'

I suppose I could have guessed, by the very composition of the Party, that there would be strong and obscurantist opposition to those more generous, libertarian impulses. But I was not at the time as knowledgeable about the history of the Chinese Communist Party as I later became. And Western experts were of no help to me in analysing what was then going on.

Why was so little publicity given to Mao's important discourse, 'The Ten Major Relations'? Why so little about Chou Enlai's major speech in that June? I would try to figure it out in the following months.

In his April 'Ten Major Relations', Mao Tsetung had criticized in mordant terms the methods used by Stalin in Soviet agriculture. At the time, Mao was also beginning to have doubts about Khrushchev; the way the latter had proceeded against Stalin did not appeal to Mao, although Mao and Stalin did not like each other. Perhaps Mao was already becoming suspicious – there is evidence to bolster this view – of Khrushchev's real intentions in promoting in Russia what looked like a 'liberalization' and was spoken of as a 'thaw'. The word used today is détente. But was the whole purpose merely a softening-up directed towards the United States, to make the USSR acceptable to the US as an 'equal partner' in the sharing of the world? After all, the episode of Yalta, where Roosevelt and Stalin had divided Europe, and even attempted to divide China, must have rankled very deeply with Mao Tsetung.

There might be another reason why these documents were withheld.

Ever since the early 1930s Mao Tsetung seems to have been concerned and perturbed with the problem of physical liquidation or purges within the Communist Party. He had almost been a victim, himself, of the sanguinary liquidations which had been practised by the then leader of the Party, Wang Ming, a man trained in the most rigid Stalinist orthodoxy. Mao realized that Soviet Russia had never made clear the distinction between acceptable 'contradictions', that is, differences of opinion but within the limits of promoting the good of the socialist system, and 'enemy contradictions', that is, through opposition and rejection which could not be treated otherwise than by physical force because they sought to overthrow the socialist system.

In 1956 and 1957, Mao Tsetung was to do what I consider to be his major work in illuminating this problem. He would make 'acceptable' 'contradictions among the people', which must not be dealt with by force, and many divergences of opinion. He hoped thus to avoid the massive Stalinist purges.

It was this issue which, in June 1956, all unknown to me then, I was hearing debated – and sometimes violently opposed – in Peking. It was on this foundation that Chou Enlai's speech rested.

Mao would also then aver that Stalin had been wrong in assuming that, once a communist party had taken power, the socialist state was established and class struggle would disappear.

Not so, said Mao. In a socialist state, the struggle for supremacy between the former ruling class – the bourgeoisie or the feudal aristocracy – and the toilers still goes on for decades, even for centuries. But the forms and shapes it takes are different. Even if former exploiters are deprived of power, the ideas they have engendered, the habits and behaviour which germinate within the environment they have created still continue, and they permeate *all* the classes, and new exploiters are born.

But in early 1956, Mao Tsetung was not yet quite sure of these theories that he was elaborating. Only in 1977, when I mentioned again this problem, did I acquire from a high Party member confirmation that this assumption was correct. Mao therefore hesitated, and his speeches were not published although they were circulated within the Party, and discussed. It seems, moreover, that a good many Party members did not agree with him. Some – how many we shall never know – thought the whole experiment of the Hundred Flowers extremely dangerous. And so did the Russians. The Russian Ambassador was very forthright about it. 'We don't have this kind of thing in our country,' said he.

I asked Kung Peng whether I might have an interview with Premier Chou Enlai, and handed her six pages of wide-ranging questions. I then waited about ten days. During that time, I went to see Popovic, the Yugoslav Ambassador. Popovic was tall and handsome and spoke excellent French. Was it possible, I asked him, that China, like Yugoslavia, would go her own way? Would there be an alteration in the apparently indissoluble bond with the USSR? Popovic was too good a diplomat to reply in a direct manner to my astounding questions. He agreed that China was 'in a new tide of total experimentation' and that probably 'the Soviet model does not correspond to Chinese needs . . . National independence is of great importance to China as it is to us . . . a fact occasionally lost sight of by the Great Powers,' said he. He told me that a delegation of Yugoslav journalists was in China and was explaining the Yugoslav way to socialism to the Chinese; but so far nothing had come of it.

I also had an interview with Chinese newsmen, and one of

them appeared surprised that I should be both a doctor and a writer. He had a cataloguing mind. 'It's quite impossible. You must be one or the other.' We discussed the duty of newspapers; and I said I thought their function was to expose wrongdoing on the part of the government or its officials. I approved of two instances of bad handling being reported in the papers recently. The first report was on the high rate of accidents in factories caused by the 'killing' of machinery by running it too fast in order to beat targets. The second was about pigs, my favourite topic in agriculture. I don't understand agriculture, but I know about pigs.

Pigs too hastily collectivized, I said, had died, and brought the amount of meat for consumers right down. I had noticed the poor condition of pigs in the collectives. And I had been happy to see in the report that in one co-operative the pig population had dramatically shrunk from around 370 to 50 . . . The reception to my remarks was mixed.

I mentioned Yugoslavia. 'Should one not study what they are doing?' And then, suddenly, one journalist – a Party member, and in the committee leadership – lost his temper and started shouting at me. 'It is all very easy for people who have done nothing to criticize us . . . but we have carried guns and fought and died to build all this,' he cried, and the others kept quiet.

I went to see my childhood friend, Simon Hua. He was the son of my father's dearest friend, Hua Nankuei, the engineer who had gone with my father to restore the Tatung coal mines to working order. Simon had studied in Paris, where he, of course, had become a communist – the French variety, in fashion among the intelligentsia in France after the Second World War. He had married a charming and intelligent Frenchwoman, Irène, and they had come to live in China in 1951. Irène worked at the radio broadcasting centre and Simon in architecture. I congratulated Simon on the children's hospital he had designed. What was he doing now? 'Housing for workers,' said he, and his face clouded. He felt his talent was not being used properly.

I also met Rewi Alley, the indomitable and fabulous New

Zealander, who had arrived in China in 1927 and stayed on, and whose books and articles and poems are an extraordinary and massive compilation; a great treasure trove to help future historians understand the Chinese Revolution.

Rewi, ever since 1927, had been totally involved in that Revolution. Both in the early Gung Ho co-operatives – in which Americans played a part – and later. He owned a fabulous collection of books. He had greatly impressed Ian when both of them had travelled to the Buddist caves of Tun Huang and the Crescent Moon Lake. He talked quietly, and he knew everything. Every pulse and heartbeat of China. And oh, how much he set me straight, and in so many ways, through the decades which followed.

With Rewi I met the American doctor, now a Chinese citizen, the legendary Ma Haiteh, George Hatem. A Lebanese American, he had been in Yenan in 1936–7, the physician of all China's leaders, including Mao Tsetung. After Liberation in 1949 he had been one of the main figures in the drive against venereal disease in China – a drive so successful that 'we're working ourselves out of work', he would say to me.

With Ma Haiteh I would spend some hours of one night walking up and down, down and up, in the dust road trodden by the village carts in front of Papa's house, talking, talking . . . To him I revealed all my distress, my trivial and yet important hesitations, and it was he who made my spirit whole and healed me, for after that talk I no longer suffered from suffocation. The tremendous epic of the Revolution now came clearly to me. 'Sister, nothing under Heaven comes easily, and certainly not building a new world,' said Ma Haiteh.

And Rewi Alley would say, 'Take it easy, lass, take it easy', when I imprudently exploded verbally. 'China has a long way to go, lass . . . sometimes it's best to keep silent and to trust.'

A small black car with an unassuming young man in it came

to fetch me. We drove towards Chung Nanhai, where China's leaders resided; but the young man did not know the exact entrance, so we were ten minutes late.

I was going to see Chou Enlai in his own home.

Through the neat avenue bordered with oleanders to a modest pavilion, and there were Chou Enlai and his wife Teng Yingchao, and with them only Kung Peng.

It was like a visit to one's own family, so simple, with no protocol of any kind. In the living room, many books on shelves, but no antiques, no curios, no priceless furniture. Old worn sofas, rattan chairs, a worn and cheap carpet . . . At one time during the next three hours I had to use the toilet, and went through their bedroom. Small wooden twin beds, old blankets, no carpet on the floor, a washbasin, a desk with a lamp . . . Spartan. And this was no fake. Chou simply did not care for any material comfort.

'So you did not go to the Anshan steel works,' said Chou immediately. I had been offered a visit to the Anshan steel works; they were the pride of China then, set up by the USSR, but I had refused to go.

'I don't understand machines,' said I.

'I hear you do not go to the United States, although you are popular there through your novel,' said Chou Enlai.

'I don't go to the United States, Prime Minister,' I replied.

Chou glanced at me and that grin, which some newsmen described as utterly devastating, swept over his face. Appreciation, humour, understanding, and beyond that the very human touch of recognition . . . recognition that in himself also existed those impulses, those dos and don'ts, unexplainable.

Kung Peng said that I was 'very determined'. 'See how well she talks Chinese, although she had to fight for a Chinese education, and she has been abroad so many years.'

'We talk Chinese in Malaya,' I said.

Chou then asked about Malaya, and Singapore, and David Marshall. David had by then accepted the invitation to come to Peking.

'Now,' said Chou, 'you've given me a long list of

questions. A very long list.' I had questions about law, legal trials, people's courts and 'mass' judgments with the attendant risk of prejudice and passion; a question on the writer Hu Feng and the demarcation between expression of personal opinion and counter-revolutionary thought or behaviour; the ineptness of Chinese propaganda abroad, with its bombast and smugness; the low political level of criticism of individuals, in the mass political campaigns (in so far as I had been able to find out). There were questions about the plethora of bureaucrats, all non-productive, and the rising élitism among the bureaucracy, as exemplified by priorities, perks, such as travel on trains. There were questions on hygiene, and on the fact that too many meetings after work interfered with normal rest and were injurious to health. I asked about birth control, and finally I tackled the question of 'socialist realism' in writing.

'I'm not going to answer all of them,' said Chou Enlai. He would delegate Marshal Chen Yi to continue the conversation with me another day. Meanwhile, he gave me almost three hours; with measured clarity and conciseness he covered a vast amount of ground. His main theme was the long Chinese Revolution, with its many turns and twists and crises. How many times in the past people had said 'It's all over'. But true revolutionaries went on, despite setbacks and failures. And there had to be setbacks and failures; for how otherwise could there be advance? The future was still uncharted ground . . .

'But one thing is certain. We are going forward. There is no going back. The door to going back is closed.' Chou said this with great passion, with an almost lyrical rising of tone and an abrupt gesture, his eyes flaming. 'The power we have will not be lightly cast aside, not in the name of pseudo-liberalism, which will only lead to a tyranny like the one we have just emerged from.' For the future, and because of the needs of the country, 'we are prepared to go along even with people who disagree with us, provided they do not sabotage the socialist revolution.'

This was the United Front theory; a major concept of Mao

Tsetung, and one which had been practised during the war with Japan, and which had been an indispensable factor in victory.*

'You think there is no dissent in the Party; this is a common subjective view in the West; that the Communist Party is a monolith . . .' It was not so, Chou said. 'If you only knew how much we debate, discuss, argue . . . we often hold very different opinions . . .' Again there was a note of passion in his voice. There was always, he said, a lot of talk about individualism in Western countries, but it was in China that with progress, prosperity and security there would come the full blossoming of the individual . . . for how could there be 'individualism' when in so many nations of the world people still died of hunger, were exploited and had no security? The Constitution of 1954 had been a great step forward to ensure the rights of the Chinese people, rights which they had not had before. Had I not personally known what the situation was in Old China?

But the West (and I think here Chou meant chiefly the United States) found it 'difficult' to face what had been inevitable, the triumph of the Chinese Revolution. 'There is always a time lag in understanding the realities of history.' It might take a long time before the West accepted these realities, but 'We are patient. We shall never provoke a war. We want, above all, peace.' This did not mean knuckling under. He referred to his speech at Bandung in 1955 and how it had been welcomed by so many countries emerging from colonialist dependence. Bandung in 1955 and the Geneva Conference of 1954, which had seen the end of war in Indo-China, had been landmarks for Asia, Africa and Latin America. But the United States strove to ignore history, and was even contemplating the use of military force to maintain or perhaps extend her hold in Asia. 'This is wild dreaming,' said Chou with great composure.

As for Taiwan, it was China's territory, and 'No one on earth shall tell us what to do with our own territory . . . that

*See *The Morning Deluge*.

is infringement of sovereignty.'

The world of the enslaved had now risen; and there would be battles fought because national liberation never came except through struggles; but this did not mean provoking a war. Neither did it mean attacking others.

Some people thought that once socialism was established everything was like Paradise; others saw it as unredeemed Hell. Actually, 'we have no experience in socialist construction . . . we shall have to find the way which best applies to our own background and concrete conditions . . .'

I had heard through Peking's ever-busy grapevine that the Soviet Ambassador, Yudin, had reported to Moscow with great concern about the project of the Hundred Flowers and the new orientation. Chou did not reply to my hint about this. 'No one can stop the tide of history.' Then he went off at a tangent. What kind of life, what frustrations had the intelligentsia of China suffered in the past? 'Look at your own father, who came back to build a railway in 1913. He had to wait until 1952 to see it built. By us.'

Of course the remoulding of an intellectual was a very painful process, but had the Revolution been easy? 'Our intelligentsia is, however, progressing towards socialism.'

'Prime Minister, my rate of progress is exceptionally slow.'

Again that lightning grin, impish; Chou liked controversy, argument, spirit in others. He hated flattery, fawning, servility. Thirteen years later, one November night in 1969, he would tease me about my rate of progress. This was the night he introduced me, at my request, to the redoubtable wife of Mao, Chiang Ching.

Chou now described the composition of the National People's Congress, the highest organ of authority in China from the juridical point of view (but it would take many years until it would assume its proper authority, as it is beginning to do today). He showed me how the eight non-communist parties, which represented at most only 1 to 2 per cent of the population, held around 39 per cent of the seats. The policy was to retain the non-communist parties 'for a long time to come'. In the same way, urban votes, representing only 10 to 12 per cent of total votes in China, had been given for the time being eight times the weight of rural votes. Otherwise there would be a complete swamping of the intelligentsia in the cities by the peasantry in the rural villages.

We then spoke of the 'mistakes and errors' by Party cadres. 'I understand you have been collecting examples of such mistakes,' said Chou, again with that flashing smile. 'We do try to avoid them . . . and we always want to know about them . . . sometimes the top level does not know what is really happening down below.' I told him then what Jui had suffered in Szechuan, and both he and his wife listened sympathetically. 'Yes, such things do happen. We do try to rectify and reappraise, however . . . and we must not say a system is bad just because mistakes are made. How long has it taken democracy in the West really to function? And what is its true basis? I think you should study more deeply,' said Chou Enlai. 'I heartily agree, Prime Minister.'

Teng Yingchao then spoke to me. She was a small-boned woman, attractive in her youth and still intensely charming and deeply intelligent. As a student she had been a fiery and gifted orator. She and Chou Enlai had worked together since their student days; both had participated in the first cultural revolution of May 1919.* Teng Yingchao had been one of the pioneers to go among the women factory workers of Tientsin and Shanghai and to mobilize them in the massive demonstrations of the 1920s. She had also run night schools. She had done the Long March, although at the time ridden with tuberculosis. She had had a prize placed upon her capture by the Kuomintang; Edgar Snow has told, in one of his books, of how he helped to smuggle her out of a city and thus escape capture and probably execution.

Teng Yingchao inquired about Yungmei's illness and my life as a doctor. And then she gave me a great gift: she suddenly spoke about the Communist Party, but in such a

*See *The Morning Deluge*.

poetic way, with such deep feeling, that her words would stay with me vividly until today. The Party, said she, was not something created in the abstract; it could be likened to the white spume on top of the ocean waves. The ocean was the people; the white foam seemed to lead, but it was water-borne and water-bred and could not exist without the water below. 'This is our experience, those of us who have worked all these years for the liberation of the Chinese people.'

When I took my leave, I had felt enlarged, another dimension added to my thinking. 'China will be all right if there are such people as Chou Enlai and Teng Yingchao,' I thought. 'I indeed have a great deal to learn . . . judgments about China are so superficial,' I told Kung Peng.

Back at the hotel, Locquin tried to extract something from me but I was unable to convey the warmth, the intimate friendliness and concern which I had felt right through the afternoon with Chou Enlai. But the newsmen were all, anyway, favourably impressed by Chou. 'He is a formidable type, an extraordinary personality,' they would say, as did the diplomats. Chou did not suffer fools gladly. He would fall silent, his face would darken; he never shouted; but sometimes his hand shook a little with uncontrolled anger. He overworked himself every day of his life; he stretched his mind and those of the people with him to the utmost. Always he would demand facts, clearness, accuracy. 'We must stop using only percentages, we must use tangible figures.' Alas, the bureaucracy was stronger; and percentages went on being used, for many more years.

Several days later, Chen Yi saw me. Corpulent and jocund, his presence was not electrifying, like Chou Enlai, but he gave out such humour, such humanity, so much natural good temper, that I liked him immediately. Besides, he was from my province of Szechuan, and like all Szechuanese, he loved laughter, and had a great sense of humour (which northerners in China do not seem to have to such an extent).

Chen Yi had just returned from Tibet, where he had officiated at the installation of a committee, headed by the

Dalai Lama, for the autonomy of the region. 'I heard you were leaving soon so I came along,' said he. And indeed, it was he who had come to the hotel to see me, with utter simplicity and lack of pomp. Both he and Chou Enlai detested those immense coffin-like black Zis cars, with thick clouds of veiling, black and brown and white, shielding the passengers from being seen. Chou's car was a battered old one; he rushed in and out of it carrying his own briefcase. As for Chen Yi, he scowled at the curtains and took them down. 'I can't see a thing . . . In the past, in the guerrilla bases, any poor peasant could stop any high official on the street and talk to him . . . and now with those big cars, they don't even know who's inside.'

We started with laughter: Chen Yi made some jokes about football, the Szechuan opera, recited a line or two of poetry – he had been known to entertain whole companies of soldiers, when in the guerrilla bases, with his imitations of Chiang Kaishek. Now he made me laugh, imitating the bureaucratic officials. 'It's a style we've got to get rid of . . . we were infected with it when we came to the cities.'

But he had come to talk about the problem of Taiwan: there could not be two Chinas, or one China and one Taiwan . . . the United States was trying hard to make two Chinas, but 'we'll never accept that. And on this point Chiang Kaishek is not such a bad guy.' As I evinced surprise: 'One must always judge people dialectically; there is good in bad people, bad in good ones. Chiang is a turtle egg, but he also insists there's only one China. The Americans cannot twist him round . . . so Chiang and ourselves have the same policy, the unity of China. We merely differ as to who holds power in China.'

He almost hinted – but so lightly that I would not be sure – that should Chiang or other high officials in Taiwan become 'smart' they would be very welcome and be most amply rewarded . . . but there was small evidence that Chiang was very farsighted. 'However, we are not worried. We are prepared to be patient. The United States makes a great uproar and her navy runs hither and thither to contain us; of course, we must be prepared in case sudden war is launched upon us, but I personally think that who goes against the wheel of history courts defeat.'

We talked a little about Tibet; and the thousands of kilometres of road which had to be constructed in order to make it accessible. 'We are preserving the language and culture of the national minorities; but this does not mean there cannot be social change. The people of the national minorities have been cruelly oppressed in the past; they want to change.'

I told Chen Yi about Singapore and Malaya, and the setting up of Nanyang University. Chen Yi said that the question of the overseas Chinese 'was a problem still to settle . . . it is the cause of many headaches for us . . .' But China only wanted peace. It was clear that the last thing Chen Yi wanted was to interfere in South East Asia. 'However, when the overseas Chinese are persecuted, of course we must protest, and help them . . .'

My last three days in Peking, and who should I see on Morrison Street (named so by the British after Ian Morrison's father – although the Chinese never used that name) but my old friend, Hualan.

We stopped; fell into each other's arms. My dear Hualan, who had stayed with me when she studied in London during the bombings in 1944, and whose courage was awesome. When the shrapnel fell around us and I took Yungmei down with me to the cellar (we lived on the top floor in Welbeck Street), Hualan refused to go down. She was washing her hair. It was three in the morning.

Hualan took me to her home in Soochow Street. It was a lovely old house with a courtyard and very good furniture, much better than Chou Enlai's. Hualan's Polish mother, blue-eyed and fair-haired, fussed around me and poured tea from a samovar, and put jam in it, Russian fashion. Hualan's father was an expert in international law in the Ministry of Foreign Affairs. He was a great scholar, and had been an able diplomat, posted to Russia for many years; that is where

Hualan had been born, and with her sister and brother had spent her adolescent years. 'But we were back in China when Liberation came, and the Party sent people to ask me, "Will you help us?" and I said, "Yes, yes, oh yes, take me, hands and feet and all, I give you everything . . . everything." ' Hualan reverted to Slav syntax in describing the scene. She was devoted, utterly, to China, although a Eurasian. She was, in fact, very much like me, except that she was far less selfish . . . perhaps because she was not a writer. But never for a moment, during the many years that followed, and the many hours I spent with her through those years, would she reprove me for my doubts and hesitations. Until, at last, in 1978, she would say,'Well, my dear, in a way you were right . . . if you had stayed, I think you would have died.'

'No, I am not a Party member,' said Hualan, pouring me some more tea. 'I was asked to apply, but I thought I was unworthy . . . some people want to join the Party because it gives them power. But I don't want power. I only want to serve.'

I then told Hualan of my reactions; how happy I had been seeing the peace, the healthy children and all that was being done for the people. No more the long lines of gaunt and starving beggars everywhere; no more the terrible sight of half-skeletons with enormous loads climbing up those immense flights of steps, up from the river, in Chungking. Now there were conveyor belts. 'And yet I, who have always wanted this, have vomiting fits when I hear of some stupidity, some vileness, some brutality . . . as if it was possible to make a paradisial state all at once. And I feel . . . mortified, humiliated, diminished . . .'

'Because you are honest,' said Hualan. 'And you have had no share in all this. It has all been done without you. I think a good many of the intelligentsia also feel that way.'

She said that was the true substance of so-called liberalism; a certain hypocrisy. 'Preaching equality, but when it really comes, it's hard to take.'

I said there was something else. The constant harping on thought-remoulding. The relentless feeling of being controlled. 'And in order to propitiate the future, we have to become transparent, every bit of one's life known and recorded.'

Hualan shook her head with great serenity. 'No other way of keeping track of people. Think of the millions of bureaucrats from the old days we had to take over . . . we don't really know what's brewing inside their heads.'

I asked Hualan about Stalin, and about Khrushchev's speech denouncing Stalin. She was a little vague, or cautious. 'Yes, I've heard about this speech, but we're still studying it in my organization.' But she told me a great deal about Beria. 'Beria was a monster . . . and Stalin listened to him. Stalin did good things, but in the end he went crazy, he trusted the wrong people, he was out of touch.'

At the time, to me, the USSR was still Stalin, and I had been inoculated at the university in Belgium with a deep horror of Stalin and his deeds. What concerned me, however, was China. 'I was afraid we too might have a Stalin in China one day . . . but now I think we shall not.' 'No,' said Hualan, 'we shall not make the same mistakes. In fact, Chairman Mao and other leaders have talked about it.' But she would not give details. She confirmed, however, that Russian experts in China were 'high-handed, and some comrades don't like the way they behave with Chinese women'.

We then talked about what Hualan called 'the housecleaning', which meant the political campaigns and mass movements. 'One must never take criticism personally,' said Hualan. 'It is meant as an educational process.' She herself had been vilified because 'when I went down to the rural areas with my organization I would clean up the place where we lived. The others left chicken bones and bits on the table. I would sweep up the mess.' This had been called 'bourgeois' and 'typically Western' by some of her colleagues. 'But the people who reviled me are spoilt city people, they have servants at home, they still treat their wives in the old-fashioned way. They are always the first, in any movement, to jump up and denounce, to write accusations against the others.' Hualan was used to this kind of give and take, and in the end nothing was done to her. But I said,'I don't think I could put up with this constant harassment. Think of all the posters and juicy denunciations one could write about my life. I'd have a nervous breakdown.'

'Of course, that's just the point, there are nervous breakdowns,' said Hualan. She said it so casually that somehow it seemed part of the group therapy involved in these mass movements; there could be no remoulding of the person unless there was some kind of breakup of the previous personality.

'All of us have got something to hide . . . "To look at my body and my heart without disgust" . . . it's very difficult.' So many people tried to cover up. Then the masses had to be educated in political criticism. Sometimes they didn't really know what had to be criticized; they went round looking for subjects to talk about.

'When are masses only mobs? When do they become crowds? When is political criticism just nit-picking?' I asked rhetorically.

'The leadership of the party pays attention, not to let things get out of hand,' she replied.

'What you are saying is that we are all each other's keepers now.'

'Yes,' said she.

At the time Hualan felt that the intelligentsia itself was responsible for emphasis on trivial personalia. 'You know the Chinese intellectuals have always loved gossip; now they turn and hit and denounce each other and fabricate fantastic stories . . . some of it is quite shocking.' I could not believe that my friends could do this sort of thing. 'Not the good ones,' said Hualan, 'but there are cowards everywhere.' They did not have the shoulder feeling, she said, solidarity, as did the workers, 'And when they go into the factories, among the workers, or into the villages, among the peasants, it sticks out. They don't think the same way at all.'

Fourth Sister Ping and her husband invited me to dinner. And Ping strove then to make me stay. She had walked me round Peking's magnificent new zoo one afternoon, trying to talk me into staying.

'Since you admire what the Revolution has accomplished, why don't you stay?'

'Because, Ping, I would soon become a hindrance, then an embarrassment to you . . . I have very little to contribute, except another problem. And there are enough problems in China.' Had I been only a doctor, I do not think there would have been any difficulty; at least, no large difficulty; not until 1966 and the Cultural Revolution. But I was a writer, whether I liked it or not, and it is a disease, a perverse disease. 'I'd give you a lot of trouble, Ping.'

And where would I fit? Which niche, category, organization, label, would be mine? Suppose I was classified as a 'Western expert' since I wrote in English and had a British Hong Kong passport. In that case I would have a beautiful flat or house, and servants, and a high salary, and a car, and I would be given interviews and would go on trips . . . but pretty soon, I felt, I would begin to write the propaganda of which I had been so critical (and would continue to criticize, in letters to Kung Peng and other friends, for the next twenty years).

Were I to be classified as 'overseas Chinese', then I would have some privileges, and be with the Chinese; but the possibility of being picked upon in the political campaigns was somewhat higher than average.

Or perhaps I would be given employment in a university, teaching English; or at the Foreign Language Press, doing translation work . . .

It was selfish of me to choose myself and my daemon, but I did. I was afraid of losing whatever talent I had; and although I was certain that the time would come when I could write in China, and write freely, that time was not yet. 'I need time to remould myself, but nobody can do it for me. I have to do it myself,' I told Ping.

Then Ping gave up. Other friends, Party members, came in and we all talked about the Hundred Flowers. And some of them said, 'We fought for everything under Heaven; now others dream of sitting on everything under Heaven.' Very clearly, they were afraid that the intelligentsia would again make a bid for power, displacing the Party. And their feeling was quite understandable; for after all, they had sweated and slogged and fought and died . . .

A final meeting with Kung Peng, to say goodbye, and that I would come back next year.

'We are thinking of giving six visas to American newsmen to come to China,' said she.

'I'll tell them in Hong Kong. That will really make news,' I replied.

Kung Peng then gave me Mao Tsetung's latest book, *Socialist Upsurge in China's Countryside*, because I had said, 'The key is in the villages, isn't it? But I don't know enough about agriculture to say anything yet . . .'

'Let me know how you are. We like to have impressions from people outside,' said Kung Peng.

One last coffee with Hualan at the small coffee club in the Eastern Peace Market. This coffee club was to disappear in 1957.

And there, sitting at a table, were two American GIs, of those who during the Korean war had come over to the communist side. One of them was very homesick and his friend said, 'You talk too much, Pete.' All of them but one were to go back to the United States. The one who remained in China is very happily married to a Chinese woman and has five children.

The last evening with Papa. 'Don't forget about Mama,' said Papa. He was going to apply for leave to go abroad 'on a scientific tour'. I did not think he had much chance because he was old and the unit he worked for would invoke health reasons. But I could get him out, perhaps, and look after him in Malaya. Papa gave me a small box of mooncakes to eat on the train. 'I'll be back next year, I promise,' said I.

Back to Kuangchow, and to the cicada-loud night, and suddenly at the border I wanted to turn back. 'I'm staying. I'm staying.' But already I was being waved across the bridge by a very neat, polite soldier, and it was too late.

I was going back to the world I knew; but it had changed. Its ferocity clawed at me. I knew that in Hong Kong I would have trouble; for no one wanted the whole truth. Because the whole truth was a mass of contradictions. Everyone wanted a simple picture, in one world and in the other . . .

'How many years can I function as a writer?' I thought. And what does a writer have in the belly and the brain to keep him going? 'Twenty years,' I said to the hot sky, 'give me twenty years . . . in twenty years, I'll be ready.' Meanwhile, I would not cut the umbilical cord. I would grow, nurtured by China, by China. I would not give up.

And it was at that moment that I knew myself doomed. I would never be able to get China out of my brain, my cells, my bones. I would write in order not to die, trying to bring to birth things and beings in words. But it would be China all the time.

Back across the bridge, the barbed wire, I was assailed by waspish irritation and a sense of bafflement. A world fatuous and brutal, people cocooned in their preoccupations; and an alien sheen about objects, for now I looked at my Szechuan slippers, so comfortable, so beautiful in China, and in Hong Kong they were shabby.

'Oh, you have changed, what has happened?' said Cousin Pengju, full of concern, as his eyes expressed shock. 'You look so much older.'

'It's too much thinking, Pengju. I was upset inside.'

Pengju did not reply; doubtless he knew what I felt.

Now I felt guilty when asking the hotel waiter for service or my laundry, seeing servility spring into action. I felt lost among the street throngs, an avalanche of hurrying, resentful people. How they rushed. In China no one seemed hurried. One layer of skin was missing; I was no longer predatory.

There were the newsmen, reporters, journalists. They flocked, they rang, they clamoured. They did not want reasoned facts. Or ideas. They wanted something fit to print, which meant unfit to say. Sensation. 'Sure your father is still alive? You got a picture to prove it?' They were disappointed. 'What do you mean, you didn't see anyone starving?'

And how wrong I had been about the American newsmen in Hong Kong! The China-watchers who gathered at the Foreign Correspondents' Club preferred to exchange information among themselves and to build great edifices of assumptions based on the rumours that filtered from China into Hong Kong. But above all they were afraid, and I would find out why.

When I mentioned the six visas for American correspondents, the response was derision, anger. 'That's the best joke of the year.' 'They're fooling you.' 'You've been brainwashed. I didn't think it would happen to you.' 'You're losing your reputation as an objective writer.' 'Go and tell your Red friends, I won't shake hands with bloody murderers.' 'Why the hell do they issue their most important statements at night so I have to keep awake to listen to the news?' was perhaps the most amusing remark of the lot.

Oh no, no eagerness for visas to China. It was much more satisfying to accuse China of shutting the door and isolating herself. Much better to carry on this myth rather than remember that it was America which had put an embargo on China and which blacklisted anyone in Hong Kong trading with China. America was powerful then, and made herself felt everywhere, and everyone was afraid of the big witch-hunt which was being conducted not only in America, but also abroad, wherever there were Americans. Two at least of the correspondents representing American news agencies and newspapers in Hong Kong had been questioned by the Committee for Un-American Activities when it carried out an investigation of State Department officials who had been to China.

What I said was not reported as I said it; the six visas were not mentioned. However, I was asked by the London *Observer* for an article on contraception.

The American Consulate in Hong Kong sent two people

to lunch with me. I was frank with them but felt that we were not talking about the same things, though we used words which corresponded to some common meaning. In the end, they were not satisfied.

'Don't you think you ought to be more positive?'

'Positive about what?'

'About principles. You must take sides. You've got to choose. The fact that you're here shows you chose freedom.'

The word had a majestic roll about it, something like those sudden gongs in a Chinese opera announcing the entrance of a major personage on the stage.

The Americans were polite, but obviously puzzled. At that time they saw the world in such simple terms that my uncertain-footed pursuit of clarity appeared almost idiotic. How can the fisherman explain his passion for angling? I was the fisherman, sitting on the shore of the coiled and passionate and muscular torrent, the changing and shifting and undulating water, floating my life away. The substance I pursued was a shadow sometimes named Verity – Truth. I tried to read it, observe it . . . But the Americans asked me to produce a neat, encapsulated tin of sardines, clearly labelled. I could only tell them that I too had to change in order to understand China and the Revolution.

Francis and Cecilia came to tea with me in my hotel room. Then there was a knock on the door, and in came Father Ladany.

It was a council of cardinals which bore down upon me with austere disapproval. Never had Father Ladany looked more imposing as he folded himself carefully into a chair. And suddenly I had the experience of total dissociation. One me was here, watching him; the other stood, feet in the soft silver-grey dust, under the new trees of Peking.

'I am not pleased with you,' said Father Ladany.

'Oh.'

'You have come back from China and you have stated that religion was free there. Do you know what our Catholic brothers suffer at the hands of the communist regime? Han Suyin, when God in Heaven and the angels ask you: What have you done, what will you then reply?' He rearranged himself, and then: 'You have a grave responsibility. You must now make a statement, that religion is persecuted in China today.'

'I will not.'

I had entirely forgotten, while in Peking, to ask about Catholics and the Catholic religion. I had not been to church. I had visited my old convent school and talked to a very suspicious nun there. The school would cater for the children of diplomats until 1966, when it would be closed and the remaining six nuns expelled. But I had inquired about the Muslim religion, paid a visit to Peking's grand mosque in Ox Street, seen the Muslim hierarchy. And that was because, living in Malaya, a Muslim country, it seemed to me relevant, and I was involved in studying the impact of religion upon race relations in Malaya. I had not even called on the bishop who had proclaimed a Chinese Catholic church, and severed it from the overlordship of Rome. Yet he was a member of the Political Consultative Conference and of the National People's Congress.

Francis now interposed to say, 'I think Suyin needs a rest.' I felt I was being pressured, pressured. Throughout the night I was awakened by angry telephone calls from Catholics (not Chinese Catholics). Voices mouthing insults. It was not Father Ladany's fault. He would never do this.

Permission to bring Papa out of China was granted swiftly by the Singapore police. I wrote to Malcolm in India, giving him many details of my trip, and he asked me to come to see him in Delhi, which I would do in the spring of 1957.

CHAPTER 7

Periples and Perspectives: 1956–1958

In the autumn of 1956 Nanyang University started to function. Thousands of youths from the Chinese middle schools of the peninsula and the island sat for the three-day examination held in Singapore and the chief cities of Malaya. Loud jubilation and unsubdued publicity over the completion of Nanyang was exhibited by the Malayan Chinese Chamber of Commerce and other enterprises. The photographs of a British Labour MP or two, of the Governor of Singapore Island and other British high officials wearing chilling smiles while attending Nanyang University's opening ceremony, were prominently displayed. Tunku Abdul Rahman, who in 1957 would become the first Prime Minister of independent Malaya, declared that the setting up of Nanyang was a matter for the Chinese in Malaya to decide, but he hoped 'other races would be admitted' to the University.

As college health physician, I drove to Nanyang three times a week to make physical examinations of the students. That meant twenty-five kilometres on a new dirt road (later tarred) across jungle and brush, with here and there a small atap hut. Jurong, where Nanyang was sited, was almost unpeopled then; today it is the industrial heart of Singapore.

I had to discard my mini-Fiat and buy a stouter car for these trips to Nanyang. I acquired a Ford, low slung, which stalled in Singapore's torrential rains. As soon as my blue and white vehicle was sighted, bumper-deep in water, along the Bukit Timah Road, shopkeepers and trishaw pedallers would remove their slippers and come wading through the downpour with cheers to push my car on to the verge. 'Going to Nan Tah,* Doctor? What you need is a jeep.'

*Nanyang University was abbreviated in Chinese to Nan Tah.

Since my return from China, I had become quite popular, for I had dared what was unimaginable. The film of *A Many-Splendoured Thing* was being shown in Singapore. That it was possible to be both a ferocious 'Red' (me!) and successful with a made-in-USA movie astonished and overawed; increased my prestige as someone for whom obstacles to hinder ordinary mortals did not exist. I did not go to the première of the film. In fact, I did not wish to see it. It proved a seven-handkerchief tear-jerker, and stayed on screen in Singapore for thirty-six weeks. I received an amazing post from all over South East Asia; from demands to trace relatives in China, to offers of investment in ocean tankers, to solving amorous tangles. It was thought that I had become immensely wealthy. Little did people know Hollywood, or that all the money had already gone into curing Yungmei.

Yungmei was angry with me. 'The nuns say you are a communist.' Yungmei would always be easily taken in by conformity. But her schoolmates went to the film and cried and cried, so she continued as the school heroine, despite the great burden upon her of such a controversial mother.

In Singapore 1956 was a turbulent year. David Marshall, Chief Minister for a transient twelve months (1955–6), resigned. He had refused to give a guarantee that he would jail trade unionists or teachers with 'leftist' leanings, and the Colonial Office in London felt he was too weak to carry out what was now being prepared, a wholesale purge of the trade unions and the Chinese schools.

David talked to me at his house by the sea. He was bitter, and tossed his great mane of hair, and thought he would make a comeback heading another party, but he was not oblique enough, he was too visible and too audible; a whale flapping in the shallow mud-swamp of colonial politics. I liked him more than ever in his defeat; for he took it very well, but 'You'll never be a politician, David,' I said. 'Good intentions will always be your downfall.'

A small, quiet man with a round face, Lim Yewhock, became Chief Minister of a 'Labour Front' coalition government. He was very conservative, a great favourite of the local British and Americans. But he did not know that his role would also be transitory; for he would serve to carry out the big purge that the British had in mind, as a prelude to independence, both in Malaya and in Singapore. Without this purge there could be no independence for Singapore, neither could Singapore be 'safely' joined to Malaya.

Meanwhile, the astute British were already grooming for the future their best bet, Lee Kuanyew or Harry Lee. Lee Kuanyew, whose subsequent career as Prime Minister of Singapore fully justified the long-term and shrewd assessment of British officials, was English-educated. As his untiring hagiographer, the journalist Alex Josey, never ceased to write, Lee Kuanyew had been brilliant at Cambridge, where he studied law. In 1956 Lee appeared extremely progressive. His party, the People's Action Party or PAP, had come up very swiftly since 1954, and was now a force to be reckoned with. The PAP owned a left wing which comprised Chinese school-educated trade unionists and former Singapore Chinese middle school student leaders; people whom the Special Branch had jailed before, and would jail again, as communists or communist sympathizers. It also had a right wing which comprised most of the English-educated like Lee himself, who today continue to represent, as he does, the government of Singapore.

Because of its slogan, 'Socialism in Singapore', the PAP was massively supported by the workers, the trades union, Chinese school students, in short, a good majority of Singapore's people. Any party in Asia then that wanted to get on *had* to use two isms, socialism and anti-colonialism.

The Special Branch clampdown on Singapore's trades union and student unions began in September 1956, with daily arrests. The Chinese Middle School Students' Union was banned. The students barricaded themselves in the Chinese high school on the Bukit Timah Road, and were assaulted with tear gas and night sticks by the police. This led to the imposition of a twenty-two-hour curfew, which was maintained for four days. I drove just before the curfew, by night, along the Bukit Timah Road, returning from work. I saw the police charge. Two cars were overturned and burnt, not by the students but by Secret Society hooligans (who had come out to join the fray). Tear gas made us all weep, and a student offered me his handkerchief. 'Go away, Doctor, the police beat up anyone.'

Members of the left wing of the PAP were arrested, among them Lim Chingsiong, a young trade unionist, and the idol of the students of the Chinese high school (where he had been a student leader). Harry Lee was not in Singapore during the purge but resting in the Cameron Highlands of Malaya,* about six hours away by car. He came back when it was all over to demand Lim Yewhock's resignation and to make an excellent speech in the Legislative Assembly (November 5th, 1956), calling this a planned purge concocted between the British and Lim Yewhock. He thus enlisted enormous popular support while Lim Yewhock became the detested emblem of a 'colonial lackey'.

I attended a public PAP meeting held at the end of that year; I wanted to listen to Harry Lee speak. Cards for joining the PAP were being distributed at the entrance to the hall, and I took one, signing my name and paying two dollars. This thoughtless gesture would cause me much trouble later on.

Lee spoke very well, and I agreed with his thesis that 'In order to get independence, and unity between Malaya and Singapore, between the Malays and Chinese, the Malay government in Malaya must be convinced that the Chinese in Singapore are loyal to Malaya and not to China; that they have no intention of exploiting the Malays, but that on the contrary they wish to live and work equally and peacefully in Malaya as Malayans.' The myth of an overseas Chinese fifth column in Singapore was to be broken.

I asked Alex Josey whether I might meet Harry Lee, and it was agreed we should do so at the house of Rajaratnam, a Ceylonese Tamil, who is now the Foreign Minister of

*A cool, high mountain resort frequented by British high officials and wealthy Malays and Chinese.

Singapore. He had just published another short story of mine in a magazine of his which promptly folded up, and he was trying hard to hold down his job as newspaperman at the conservative *Straits Times* while also publishing and editing *Petir*, the PAP newspaper.

Alex and Harry arrived late, in ebullient mood. Alex was never drunk, though he could put down vast quantities of Tiger beer and remain beautifully vertical. Harry was not a drinker; even two beers would make him flush. He was now flushed, and took refuge behind a newspaper which he held up at arm's length so that nothing of him was visible except his legs.

I waited politely, making small talk, but the paper would not come down. Harry did not wish to talk to me. Perhaps because I had been to China, and he did not wish Special Branch to suspect him of *talking* with someone from China . . . After fifteen minutes in which he continued to prop up the paper Great Wall between us, by sheer muscle power and will, I got up without saying goodbye to the invisible Mr Lee, and went home. It had not been an unprofitable quarter hour. I had smelled the smell of single-minded devotion to power. No one would be allowed to stand in Harry Lee's way.

But my young Chinese students at Nanyang at the time idolized him and believed him a genuine 'socialist'. 'He is even learning Chinese now,' they said. Later, having endured beatings and torture in jail in Singapore under the PAP government, one of those students who got out would tell me, 'It was on our shoulders that Lee Kuanyew climbed to power.'

I started a medical clinic in Singapore, in Tangjong Pagar, the busiest part of the hardworking, restless city. My clinic in Johore Bahru was sold to a medical couple, man and wife, who did very well with it. I still occasionally saw patients at home at weekends, for some would not let me go, but I no longer went to the 'new villages' along the Johore road. Some of them had even prospered, owing to the all-conquering capacity of the Chinese for work, which could transform even a concentration camp, after a while, into a fertile market-garden! Even the mangrove swamps began to yield food through this endless labour of theirs. I used to stop and look at them, those work-obsessed people who created a new world out of the wasteland. A little help from the government went a very long way with them. Despite barbed wire, arrests, harassments, the rapacity of the Malay police, they did not stop making the land yield food.

The backers of my new clinic, which was called the Coral Drug House, were a Mr and Mrs Loke. Mr Loke was small, portly, round-eyed and disastrously optimistic. During the Japanese occupation he had made money selling vitamin B injections, and was paid in the existing paper currency. But the money became worthless when the Japanese were beaten and Mr Loke could only repaper a room in his house with the bank notes. 'What to do, Doctor, no luck is no luck.' He bounced back, however, and regularly came up with grandiose projects. One was to buy sugar, a lot of sugar, because the Suez Canal was closed and sugar was sure to climb in price. It didn't. Another one was to form a political party. Mr Loke got fifty votes, no more . . . Mrs Loke was the strength and soul and mainstay of the Loke family. She had five children. She was beautiful, sweet, hardworking, thrifty, frugal, and infinitely jealous when Mr Loke wandered to the Great World or the Happy World dance halls or came home with brandy-ginger-ale-laden breath (the Chinese drank brandy, the whites drank stengahs). Mrs Loke knew nine languages and dialects and besides attending to the clinic and pharmacy she employed herself as a hairdresser at night, to make ends meet, for Mr Loke was prone to impecuniosity.

I hired a nurse and a pharmacist, and all four of us women were photographed in front of our new clinic, and no one thought it strange that four women should run a clinic right in the heart of the working class district of Singapore. We were protected. The two 'benevolent' Secret Societies which dominated the area would never lift a finger against a woman doctor, a midwife, a nurse (or for that matter a child). Compared to what happens in Europe today, their behaviour was honourable and trustworthy. I knew my life, my car and my belongings were safe in 'our' district. However, having one day parked my car with my typewriter in it on a 'respectable' lane near the Legislative Assembly, I returned to find the top ripped and the typewriter gone. I was stupid enough to call the police. The police arrived; surrounded me and the area, blew white dust all over the car for fingerprints, delayed me for two hours, and of course the typewriter was never found. When Mr Loke heard of it, he exploded. 'Doctor, why call the police? Why not ask me? I would have asked a friend . . . he would have found your typewriter for you in twenty-four hours. Now it is impossible, no more face . . .'

I said I was very, very sorry, and would never again call the police. Never.

Of course the clinic prospered right from the first day. I had many cases, some of them, as in Johore Bahru, of great interest; and I had the services of an excellent laboratory which had been set up by an Englishman – one of those who had truly made Singapore his home. I had also the usual run of delicate problems. Homosexuality among the British troops quartered in Singapore; a couple of those cases came to me through my lawyer, Anthony Hills, who greatly pitied one he brought me, a beautiful and tongue-tied boy. At the time punishment meted out by the British to homosexuals was extremely harsh and the youth, sad and withdrawn, was almost inarticulate. Cases of virginity, or the lack of it. The usual mother-in-law irate because the morning after her son's wedding there was no blood upon the sheets she had inspected. Cases of forcible deflowering. Two 'aunties' bringing a young girl, shaking from head to foot, to certify she had indeed been penetrated; they wanted money from a businessman who had been presented with this virgin. I only hoped he had not infected her with gonorrhoea; for it was still believed that one could cure gonorrhoea by using a virgin.

The usual Secret Society fights. A man came in with his

face slashed right across by a razor blade. I stitched up, we all
worked very hard. He uttered not a word while we repaired
him. I should have reported him to the police. This was the
law, but he said he had accidentally cut himself and I left it
that way. Why send him to jail? Why get Mr and Mrs Loke
into trouble? Why? I was not all that convinced that the
representatives of law and order were less corrupt than
the representatives of wrongdoing.

Leonard persisted in refusing to divorce. He could not
believe that I loved Vincent. And why, if I loved him, had I
not joined him in India, but remained in Singapore and ran a
clinic and wrote books, and went to Nanyang University to
give lectures?

We no longer quarrelled; civility prevailed. Leonard
would continue living at home until 1957. But at that time
(only twenty years ago) it was not done *not* to quarrel, not to
accumulate grievances. English law on divorce made it an
offence to practise 'collusion' – divorce by mutual consent
did not exist. My lawyer, Anthony, pointed this out to me.
'As long as you live with Leonard, you won't get a divorce.'

Leonard obtained a job as Adult Education Officer in
Singapore. It suited him well; not only had he a remarkable
knowledge (far surpassing mine) of Chinese dialects, but
also kindness, real good-heartedness with ordinary people.
The Chinese and the Malays, faced with an *orang puteh* who
spoke their language and understood them, confided in him.

Meanwhile, plans for building my new house went ahead.
The architect, Kee Yeap, decided that instead of building
one large house, I should build three bungalows, staged on
the slope of the hill I had bought, all with a remarkable view
of Singapore and the arm of sea called the Straits, which
separated the island from Malaya. The houses had modern
uncluttered lines, wide window space, the use of black
marble on the floors to cut out the eye-paining reflection of
the sun, and pastel colours. People came from all over
Malaya to look, to photograph and to copy. One
enterprising travel agency ran buses for tourists to Johore
Bahru to come to see me and my houses.

I kept an enormous rain tree, so heavy and tall that it was a landmark, in the middle of the garden. It was far from the house because rain tree roots run shallow, and in a wind the tree can overturn. We had a special roadway inside the garden for the three houses, and the whole thing only cost 100,000 Malayan dollars (30,000 US dollars). It was worth five million in 1978. But more to the point, the design has been reproduced (sometimes with unhappy additions) all over Malaya.

I managed to free-float myself away for ten days with Vincent in Nepal. I had started my new book, *The Mountain is Young*, writing in the cool night, when a bliss of darkness or moonlight makes words emerge smoothly, like quiet fish. Vincent never asked me about China. I just said briefly, 'There is more dust to settle before I make up my mind.' He was less cluttered with formulae, being an inarticulate man, than most people. He could accept raw facts even when put into untoward words, or not worded. He guessed that I would keep China to myself until the proper time came to smear words upon a page or in the air. 'I hope you did not come back just for me.' 'No, I did not.' And so he gave me breathing space without words, in which I could fashion new words for new things. No one else ever left me alone about China; everyone wanted an arbitrary, total judgment; phrases, clichés; they could not understand that verbalizing was castration.

'You are my good earth, in which I can grow,' I told Vincent. Always this total easiness, and silence. 'Comfort me with silence, feed me with silence.' And so I grew well and young and beautiful and I said, 'I am going back to China next year, and the next, and the next, until . . .' Meanwhile I would wait and wander all over the earth, and always live in that crystal sphere of clear doubt because doubt is the most blessed thing alive. And the earthbound presence of Vincent would keep my feet on earth, and make dreams move and shape words; his absence as potent (even more so) than his presence, but unthinkable if not interspersed with presence. For only in absence is presence totally realized; but total presence, like total absence, is also somewhat a death.

Vincent's work in Nepal was almost completed. He would be given a prestigious medal by King Mahendra for finishing the road between Nepal and India in record time, but also threatened with court martial by his own government for having finished the work so quickly and within the budget allotted. Efficiency is always suspect to an Establishment, and one of Vincent's predecessors had distinguished himself by invariably reporting loss of equipment through white ant action, until some pernickerty accountant, looking up termites, discovered they could not devour the steel of bulldozers.

On the verge of the nineteenth century, at the time of his great-grandfather, Vincent's family had been fishermen in Tamil Nadu, a state of south India. I could visualize Vincent's ancestors in their catamarans skimming the terrible shark-infested waters for food. Of course they had become boat-owners in time, but they were certainly not considered high caste, like the Brahmins; and just as in China only 2 per cent of poor peasants could, within fifty years, become rich peasants, so in India a small minority of fishermen, by dint of frightful exertion, thrift and good luck, became boat-owners.

Vincent's family came from the fishing settlement of Royapuram, very near Madras. The Portuguese who landed there in the sixteenth century had converted most of Royapuram to Christianity. Today Royapuram is no longer by the sea, but inland; the sea had withdrawn, leaving its sand behind; and upon this sand is built the big church with its thirty-nine crosses (why thirty-nine I shall never know), its roof like the waves of the sea, its windows down to the floor, and – oh, how strong the caste system was – its place, within the Catholic church, for Catholic 'untouchables'.

Vincent's great-grandfather went to school; and after the Portuguese came the British, and his grandfather and then his father were educated; his father going to Cambridge, becoming a lawyer, and later chancellor of a university in Madras state. The whole family took up education; even his sisters went to university. And Vincent's father became President of the Catholic Association of India; the Catholics being six million, the second largest religious minority after the Muslims (sixty million).

From Kathmandu we flew to Delhi; Malcolm invited us and Prime Minister Nehru to tea. 'You will find Nehru disquieted about China,' warned Malcolm. As soon as he saw me, Nehru glowered in that skin-colour-change way which Indians have when they glower.

His chiselled features became dusky marble and I thought: What a broody Brahmin. Malcolm strove to make me speak of China but Nehru would not listen and changed the subject immediately. That night there was a dinner, and Nehru was there. I asked him in the meekest voice I could muster, 'Your Excellency, I've been reading up on the Hindu religion. Tell me, why is Krishna blue?' Nehru glared at me and replied, 'He is blue because he is blue.' I think Krishna was Dravidian,* as is Vincent, and Dravidians do turn blue under certain conditions of the weather and sentiment.

Instead of thinking about blue Krishna, the God of Love, I should have paid attention to Nehru's bad temper and Malcolm's hints; but I could not believe a quarrel was brewing between India and China.

In August of 1957 independence came to Malaya. In Johore Bahru a rumour spread that the Malays would come out with their krisses† and kill everyone. Some shops closed; some shopkeepers left for Singapore. A good many of the British in the town also went away to Singapore for that day. Johore Bahru was aglow with colour; the Malays came from the surrounding *kampongs* and their children were gorgeous, gaudy butterflies arrayed in silk and satin, pink and purple and green and blue, with trimmings of gold lace, the boys with small *songkoks*‡ of black velvet, the little girls with

---

*The original inhabitants of India, Dravidians are found chiefly in the south, especially in the state of Tamil Nadu.
†Krisses: Malay daggers.
‡*Songkoks:* Malay velvet caps.

enormous kohl-rimmed eyes and their hair plastered with coconut oil. How beautiful they were, and always with that grace and softness which I had come to associate with the Malay people. There was music everywhere, and the mosque was full of men rendering prayers of thanks to Allah. It was a brave and splendid sight, and I went to see my Malay friends and enjoyed multi-coloured sweets and being sprayed with flower petals and perfume, and late at night under the soft trees that held the darkness the people strolled, carrying their children asleep in their arms back to the *kampongs*.

Meanwhile in China the Hundred Flowers had blossomed and faded.

I had a letter or two from Papa, relayed through Hong Kong; Papa never mentioned in his letters anything except his own health. It was clear, however, that he would not apply to leave China in order to visit Mama. His organization thought him too old and frail to risk the journey.

I finished *The Mountain is Young* that summer of 1957 and an article on Nepal, and left for Peking in September, making the usual arrangement with a medical partner to take over during my absence. I stayed two days in Hong Kong, reading the Chinese communist press and asking Pengju what was happening. 'Is it true what the Western press says that a total reversal of policy has taken place?' 'I think you had better find out for yourself.' We talked at length about mutual friends, writers, who had not been accused of being 'rightists', although one expected them to be, while on the contrary several others were denounced as 'rightists' who had appeared most revolutionary.

Papa was alone at the station to receive me, and this time I stayed in our house with him. This total lack of attention to me was a boon. I had no programme at all. How often in later years I would try my hardest to have no programme, nothing to visit or to see, no one to recite at me long-winded 'brief introductions', which for so many years were unavoidable in factories, communes, everywhere.

I had left my Peking wardrobe, clothes bought in China,

cotton shoes, with Papa. And in trousers and a shirt looked local and went unnoticed. So unnoticeable that when inadvertently I wandered into the lobby of the Peking Hotel, where I had arranged to meet Fourth Sister Ping, I was promptly thrown out. I was not an Honoured Guest. I did not look like an Honoured Guest. And one evening, at the theatre, standing in the aisle to look for my seat, I was suddenly shoved aside. 'Place for the Honoured Guests from Outside,' said the man, obviously an interpreter, who had shoved me. He exuded self-importance. In filed five very large Europeans, undoubtedly some delegation of a Party somewhere.

Papa was plucking at his hairless chin, in pensive turmoil. 'I don't understand it,' he said, handing me a thick folder, all the clippings he had collected about the Hundred Flowers from the start in May 1956 to its climax in May 1957 and its crash in June. He gave me brief notes he had taken at the meetings organized by his own bureau to discuss and to implement the Hundred Flowers. 'I was also asked to criticize, to say anything I wished . . .'

Papa shook his head, as if stunned. The stunned look was on many faces in that September when the campaign 'against the bourgeois rightists who attacked the Party and socialism' was in full spate. Third Brother was at Peking University, where the students had had no summer holiday that year, but meeting after meeting to 'uncover the ringleaders' of the 'rightists'. Fourth Brother was just as busy with meetings in his organization. Only Papa had time, and my friend Hualan, because her Polish mother was ill and Hualan herself was recovering from a nervous breakdown. And as for writers, major 'struggle' sessions were going on in the Culture Ministry, the Propaganda Ministry.

I went to the Hsinchiao Hotel to see Jacques Locquin of the Agence France-Presse. He was dramatic. 'The students are pulverized, atomized, annihilated.' With him was a young Swede, one of the several dozens of foreign students at Peking University studying Chinese.

Third Brother emerged in October from the 'struggle meetings' against the rightists: Wang Wanchun, my journalist friend, Fourth Sister Ping and others also resurfaced. Everyone had had to participate in meetings, including the rightists themselves; many of whom had repented and claimed they had been misled by 'reactionaries' in their midst.

Until early 1957, the Hundred Flowers had not blossomed fully, despite official encouragement. The memory of the 1955 counter-revolutionary purge was still vivid with the intelligentsia. Third Brother had cautiously confined himself to saying he thought there were too many lengthy political meetings and that it was difficult to get adequate rest.

During those months, however, a good many scientists, writers and scholars had been taken into the Communist Party. The treatment of the intelligentsia had improved. Political meetings were shortened, there was an abundance of books in the libraries and greater facilities for students. The curriculum was changed, became less rigid, many students began to work on their own, and by the winter of 1956 they were holding discussion forums, writing papers on subjects they had selected, and crowding the libraries to read everything. 'No more forbidden subjects. Never have I seen young people so concerned, so astonishingly willing to participate . . . of course they were naïve, they did not know very much, but they tried . . .' Thus an old professor who dropped in to see Papa in October. Hundreds of literary and scientific magazines and periodicals, some of them with wildly heterodox views, came into print. 'There was even some pornography,' Wanchun told me. 'Handwritten, circulating underground.' Wanchun was too proper to elaborate. After all, *A Many-Splendoured Thing* was considered pornographic . . .

'My dear, one of the reasons why it all suddenly went wrong was the Hungarian revolt,' said Hualan. The Hungarian revolt of October 1956 had a great effect upon the Chinese students. 'At first it was a genuine mass expression against the Stalinist excesses,' said Hualan (whose job had been to translate all documentation on the subject). But later the revolt had fallen to 'unscrupulous counter-revolutionaries', who were 'agents of imperialism'. The ringleaders were the reactionary intelligentsia of the Petofi Club. The Petofi Club of Budapest was where the intellectuals gathered to drink coffee and apparently to plot against the socialist state.

The university students in China organized clubs and societies to hold debates, issue manifestoes and assemble in open-air meetings. At first most of the meetings appeared innocuous but increasingly, as 1957 went into the spring, some 'began to do very bad things. They ran amok.'

'Even we were startled, alarmed at what began to take place . . .' said Third Brother. The students demanded total abolition of government, councils of students running all institutes of higher learning. They wanted to stay with their families and only have jobs in the big cities. 'There was anarchy . . ' The most active and outrageous demands came not from students in the arts but those in the sciences, particularly physics. Third Brother taught physics at Peking University. He could not explain why this was so.

On February 27th, 1957, Mao Tsetung made a most important speech at an enlarged session of the Supreme State Council. Unfortunately, once again, this speech was not published at the time; it would only be published in June, and with some modifications, and by that June the reversal of the Hundred Flowers policy had taken place.

Because the speech was not published or tape recorded, the wildest surmises about what had really been said by Mao were current. Everyone heard what he wanted to hear. The 'small lane' gossip of Peking reported that some Party members present (top officials) were so hostile to the speech that they had walked out on it.

In April Mao Tsetung was to announce a rectification in the Party against the three 'evils' of bureaucratism, sectarianism and 'subjectivism'. This was a direct encouragement to the intelligentsia to criticize. It was specified that rectification would not be harsh, but 'gentle as a mild rain, or a light breeze'. The eight non-communist parties were asked to help the Party rid itself of these evils by pointing out instances of errors and shortcomings.

A writer I knew said to me, 'What the intellectuals forgot is that the Party has increased sixfold since 1949, is full of new members who are badly trained and quickly corrupted . . . being a Party member means to them power and privilege, and they'll fight to keep that. They cannot suffer anyone to criticize them.'

In March, to encourage more of the Hundred Flowers criticism, the respected Tung Piwu, one of the founders of the Party,* made a speech at a meeting of military procurators and presidents of military courts. He expounded the need to abide by the law. 'We have conducted mass campaigns . . . tempestuous revolutions relying on direct action by the masses rather than on law. But now the situation is different.' Tung called for a halt to illegal arrests 'without a warrant', and better control of juridical work. A system of laws must now be evolved, said he. Since Tung Piwu was President of the Supreme People's Court, Acting Chairman of the People's Republic of China, his pronouncements were weighty. But his speech of March 18th, 1957 was not published until October 19th, 1978!

By the time the month of May came round, the apprehensive leaders of the eight non-communist parties had plucked up courage and started a series of speeches, meetings and seminars. At least two leaders called for the Communist Party to share power and official positions with the other parties. The Communist Party was *not* the government; neither could it replace a government, they said. It acted arbitrarily and without consulting non-party administrative personnel in the government, who could only acquiesce.

Now followed, in the short space of eight days, a maelstrom of denunciations, of the Communist Party and all

*See *The Morning Deluge*.

its doings, by a great many intellectuals, including Party members themselves.

'The students went anti-Russian,' said Hualan. Since 1956 sporadic reports had appeared that some high-up party leaders had been critical of the USSR. The students denounced the inadequacy of the books and teaching on the Soviet model. Some Western-trained scientists complained of 'blind adoration' of the Soviet Union. Some traced the origin of the three evils in the Chinese Party to 'copying totally the Soviet Union'.

By mid-May there were not only student demonstrations throughout many cities in China but also a crescendo of attacks *against* Party cadres, both verbal and physical. In several places anyone who wanted to justify what the Communist Party had done was shouted down or threatened. Students beat up teachers and when the police tried to protect the teachers, they beat up the police. And then Petofi clubs cropped up, whose avowed aim was to overthrow the government totally. Members of these clubs began to travel throughout the country for get-togethers with other universities. 'Marxism is outdated' . . . 'The Communist Party has done nothing but evil' . . . Posters called for the killing of obnoxious cadres and mass uprisings against the Party.

Of course the anti-Party stance was not a universal phenomenon. A small percentage of the students argued for the Party, another small group against it and the majority, as usual, was in between.

'What did the Party cadres do?' I asked Wanchun.

'They listened, they took notes, they kept silent,' he replied.

During those weeks, the Communist Party had allowed hundreds of explosive newspaper articles, banner headlines on the front pages condemning them. One headline asked Mao Tsetung and Chou Enlai to vacate their seats; another wrote that the Party consisted of 'uncultured laymen' and should give up office to 'experts' who would know how to run things.

Wanchun agreed with my cousins, that the students

gradually lost the sympathy of the workers and of the
general public; especially when one of the clubs demanded
that the sons and daughters of peasants and workers should
no longer be admitted to the universities from the short-term
workers' schools which had been set up for them. 'Eighty per
cent of our university students are still of landlord, rich
peasant or city capitalist origin.'

On May 25th Mao warned publicly: 'All actions and
speeches against socialism are wrong.' These words were
propagated, within two days, among all university students.
'In our university the Party committee put up a prominent
poster: "All actions and arguments which ignore socialism
are wrong",' said Third Brother.

But it was too late for the groups which had called for a
'Hungarian situation' in China.

On June 8th an editorial in the *People's Daily* 'What Is
This For?' marked the landslide reversal. On June 14th the
magazine *China Youth* warned that even Communist Youth
League members were 'unable to distinguish between two
kinds of criticism'. One was well-meant, to help the Party
and socialism; the other was counter-revolutionary, to
attack the Party and to take power.

Then came the avalanche. Third and Fourth Brothers,
using words sparingly, laughed and shivered at once as they
spoke about it. Within three days, no more controversial
posters. Instead a deluge of lavish praise and oaths of
allegiance to the Party. 'The majority of the students turned
round,' remembered Third Brother. And so did most of the
members of the eight non-communist parties; and every
organization, factory and institute. 'Then started the
internal clean-up of each unit.' Each one searched among its
own staff and employees for rightists. And then the
confessions came pouring out. Within a day of each other,
the four major rightists had come out with letters of self-
accusation, apology, confessing their 'towering crimes'. The
nationwide anti-rightist campaign was on.

'There were also rightists in the Party,' said Wanchun,
detailing what had happened in his newspaper world. The

'three evils' rectification seemed laid aside; no more talk of gentle breeze and mild rain. From the end of August onwards every newspaper published excoriations of rightists, naming and labelling them; which meant that they had been condemned within their own organizations.

Papa said, 'A lot of innocent people will also be called rightists. That is bad.' Of course, he had also feared for himself; after all, he had written posters criticizing methods of work in his engineering bureau . . .

In the great tempest, the Family gathered, counting its members. First of all, Szechuan. Szechuan was the province where everything that happened in China happened more ferociously, took on an extra girth and weight and amplitude.

But Third Uncle was fine. He had not been labelled a rightist. Sixth Uncle was not so happy. He had opened too wide a mouth. In 1956 there had been massive complaints in Szechuan about low pay and overwork of schoolteachers. Sixth Uncle was labelled a rightist; and he underwent eighteen months of re-education through labour, returning to work in 1959, and living another ten years. He died of cancer in 1967.

Pan Kuangtan, Francis Pan's brother, was not a rightist. Francis would be very happy to know it.

But my friend Simon Hua, who had always been so revolutionary, was a rightist. I could scarcely believe it. Papa and I went to the Hua house; only his old father, Hua Nankuei, was at home. Old Mr Hua was Papa's best friend. They had worked for forty years on the railways together; together had been to the Tatung coal mines. Now wrapped in a fur robe, attended by two devoted servants, and waiting for his French daughter-in-law to return from her work, he spoke with great dignity. 'Yes, my son is now examining his errors in his thinking . . .' But the Party had sent an official to reassure old Mr Hua that no physical harm would come to Simon. 'Some foolish and irresponsible people went too far,' sighed old Mr Hua, 'and many will have to pay the price . . .'

Irène, Simon's wife, went on working as usual, taking the

situation with discipline and composure. Simon would do one year as an ordinary worker on a construction site.

Third and Fourth Brothers, Fourth Sister, everyone else in the Family was safe.

I still have the card on which Papa wrote down the names of the most prominent rightists. On the reverse is an invitation to Papa from the Vice-Chairman of the Academy of Sciences, to a scientific meeting in February 1957. It was at that meeting that the Hundred Flowers policy was discussed in the light of Chairman Mao's recent speech about it.

Now the speech had been published. I went out to the bookstore and purchased it. Its title was *On the correct handling of contradictions among the people*. It was Mao's famous February speech, only printed in mid-June, when the Hundred Flowers were already wilting with such precipitation. Was the printed version what Mao had really said, or were there additions? Jacques Locquin insisted there were additions, and that the whole thing was a trap.

Even today I remember my instant fascination, how gripped I was by this reading. I had tried, when I was a student in Belgium, to read some Marxist literature – my Belgian friends were so glib, so superior, so knowledgeable about politics, while I was so backward – and had found it insuperably dull and difficult. But not Mao's article. It became for me the key to coherence; coherence within the Chinese cultural pattern, of course. Mao was dealing with a situation which I not only understood but lived myself . . . from that time, I began to read Mao Tsetung.

Was the whole exercise of the Hundred Flowers a trap? Just a cheap, mean trick? Somehow this appeared to me highly improbable.

As October wore on, my strongest impression was of the numbers of rightists named. Although the newspapers always called them 'a mere handful', everywhere I turned I bumped into rightists.

Again, here, I was confronted with that obtuse literal-mindedness of the middle cadres, implementing policy to the letter. Mao's casual remark made some years previously that 'probably 10 per cent' of the people in higher institutions of learning and other such organizations harboured counter-revolutionary leanings still held sway. Now the anti-rightist campaign would seek to discover its 10 per cent of rightists. Out of about nine thousand students at Peking University, a neat eight hundred were labelled 'rightists'. Since Mao had said in 1956 that there were five million intellectuals in China, that would mean around 400,000 to 500,000 rightists.

Actually, no less a person than the thoroughly outspoken Marshal Chen Yi, China's Foreign Minister, would tell me personally some years later that 430,000 rightists had been so labelled and he felt 'it was too many'. They comprised Party members, students, teachers, artists and writers.

The 'unlabelling' of rightists proceeded, with rehabilitations, from 1959 onwards. By 1966 there were still around 130,000 of them whose cases had not been cleared; but a thorough review was undertaken after the Cultural Revolution, and by 1978 all of them were cleared.

I went to the coffee shop in the Eastern Peace Market where Hualan and I had met the American GIs in 1956. It was closed. 'All clubs are closed. Clubs are bad things,' said the caretaker. Literal-mindedness again at work. The transcendent ideogram, weighty with meaning beyond reason. How often in the years to come I was to be told by Party cadres, reasoning in the feudal manner of analogy, categorizing not by reason but by resemblance, that the very word 'club' denoted something bourgeois and evil; that clubs were usually associations for conspiracy since there had been that Petofi Club in Budapest . . .

In 1958 and 1959 an attempt to close all the teahouses, Chinese counterparts of the eighteenth-century English coffee houses, took place in my province of Szechuan, and was partly successful. Oh, shades of Boswell, and Li Po and Tu Fu, our great poets, and Verlaine too perhaps! I *needed* my teahouses; they reassured me that people could sit and talk and in companionship invent and create . . . even if, as a woman, I would never go to a teahouse, since they were strictly for men.

Small, enchanting restaurants which I suppose were also capable of breeding jollity and letting the imagination run loose – and the tongue – they too would be closed . . . It is possible that they were frequented assiduously by gourmet rightists, for as far as I know, all Chinese intellectuals are also gourmets.

A lengthy editorial appeared in the *People's Daily*, 'When a hundred flowers blossom, there are both fragrant products and poisonous weeds.' The 'poisonous weeds' were now being eradicated, leaving only 'fragrant products'. 'Pulling out too many weeds sometimes injures flowers,' said Papa.

The Minister of Culture, Mao Tun, had spoken against the indiscriminate labelling of the intelligentsia: 'Putting on them counter-revolutionary hats at will'. This was deemed acceptable. So were the criticisms of that great lady, Madame Ho Hsiangning, about the treatment of the overseas Chinese by some Party cadres – withholding remittances from abroad on the grounds that this was bourgeois funding. The Education Minister, Chang Hsijo, a charming man who spoke flawless literary English and could quote Shakespeare by the hour, deplored the neglect of historical and cultural factors. 'We apply foreign [meaning Soviet Russian] dogmas in dealing with everything . . . Cadres tell people what to do, never why they have to do it . . . dogma is their sole dictionary, their only support . . .' This was acceptable.

But to suggest giving positions of power to non-Party members, to members of other parties, to advocate rotation of rule among the parties, this was anathema. As Mao Tun would explain, the two slogans, 'Laymen cannot lead experts' and 'People other than Party cadres only have nominal posts', were not innocent verities. They were 'frontal assaults and side thrusts against the Party leadership'.

I went to see Kung Peng, but she was extremely busy. Two

weeks later she invited me to lunch. By that time, Locquin had become slightly overpowering. He attempted to influence me in his fashion. 'It's a dirty trick that has been played on the intelligentsia and you *must* proclaim it to the world.'

Kung Peng had bought small and delicious autumn crabs from Shanghai, only to be had at the time of harvest moon. She was wrestling with domestic problems, notably her bath which was old and losing its enamel; but she could not hope to get a new one, even though she and her husband were high officials. In the twelve years which followed she never got a new bath.

After lunch, she and her husband Chiao Kuanhua sat down with me. I referred to Mao's pamphlet, *On the correct handling of contradictions among the people*. 'It's really a most important work,' said I. Kung Peng appeared noncommittal. Two years later she would say, 'We did not realize how truly important this was at the time', thus indirectly confirming that there had been much opposition.

Neither had Kung Peng entirely liked my article 'Peking Revisited', published in America. Read collectively by some of her colleagues, it had been criticized because it was not all gush and praise. 'It's already difficult enough to have anything good about China printed . . . one cannot write for a Western audience as one does for a Chinese one,' I told her. In my heart I hoped the time would come when both China and the West would accept what I wrote.

Kung Peng started peeling fruit for me to eat, and I knew that she and Chiao wanted to talk about the Hundred Flowers. But I did not want to be briefed. No official explanations for me. I did not wish to go back to Hong Kong and have to say, 'This is what I have been told by such and such a high official'. I wanted to work everything out for myself, by myself, be responsible only to myself.

I left, saying I had another engagement.

I went to call on the Yangs. Yang Hsienyi and his wife Gladys, a beautiful, able Englishwoman, worked at the Foreign Language Press: both were scholars and superb translators. Their house was the meeting place for Chinese writers, painters, poets and also for many of the foreigners who came through Peking. But they did not wish to discuss the Hundred Flowers. Too many of their friends were being labelled rightists; among them a famous film director, some scriptwriters, a satirist or two, a few poets. However, they did see, as I did, the fundamental foolishness of challenging the Party in its holding of power, either directly or indirectly. 'Some Party cadres are geniuses at detecting innuendoes in almost anything one utters, even remarks on the weather can become matter for political scrutiny,' said Yang Hsienyi in his bland, dead-pan manner.

I asked them: Was the Hundred Flowers nothing but a trap?

The words 'Yes, it was a trap' had appeared in a newspaper article, which explained that it was the rightists who had trapped themselves. The Yangs did not think it was a trick to catch whatever residual counter-revolutionary thought or sentiment might subsist in the souls of scholars. It was an openly baited, clearly signposted test for anyone who used common sense and was percipient.

Increasingly I began to feel that a very few people, ignoring or brushing aside wary common sense, had done a disservice, not only to the intelligentsia but also to the development of objective and academic discussion and the expansion of scientific reasoning. They had not distinguished between their present role, which was to help the socialist system, and the old role of the Chinese intelligentsia, which had been for two millennia *the* ruling bureaucracy.

'All intellectuals always hanker for power,' said my Fourth Sister Ping, and many Party cadres.

I think that Mao and Chou Enlai (the latter especially) genuinely intended to use the recriminations of the intelligentsia to curb the evils of their own Party; to redress grievances and educate the cadres. But the repeated threats of bringing about a 'Hungarian incident' in China played into the hands of those in the Party (a silent but obvious majority) who did not want such an opening. The effervescence of the young was construed as the Party losing control of the educated youth, since even Communist Youth League members participated in some of the anti-Party demonstrations.

It was ludicrous to expect that a government like the present one in China, installed by a communist party which had fought its way to power through decades of agonizing suffering and two enormous wars, which had performed the extraordinary feats it had performed, including the Long March, would meekly allow itself to be displaced.

And from everything Mao had written and said, it was obvious that there was no intention of sharing *power* with the eight non-communist parties; they were invited to formulate suggestions to correct the flaws and defects of the ruling party, or as Mao had said, to become 'an opposition which would not oppose'.

There was also, most probable if not evident, pressure from the USSR. Right from the start, the USSR had been against that 'feeling of early spring', as some Chinese scholars called the Hundred Flowers. And in that November of 1957, Mao Tsetung was due to go to Moscow, not only to patch up certain discrepancies in views between himself and Khrushchev, but also for negotiations of importance on sharing nuclear knowledge, indispensable to China's progress and defence.

The May climax of the Hundred Flowers had revealed, even among the Party hierarchy, criticism and hostility towards the Russians. It was all very well for Mao to harbour these (unpublished) feelings, but now, with the student posters and the newspapers, criticism of the Soviet Union, demands to follow the path of Yugoslavia were out in the open.

For all these reasons the wilting had to be. But the Hundred Flowers would be revived four years later.

Meanwhile, a campaign for 'socialist education' of the people started that October. Eight hours per week of political study in all universities and in all organizations.

Which made everyone very tired.

In the countryside, the winter of 1957 saw very large water conservancy work being done, mobilizing tens of millions of peasants. The anti-rightist campaign went on among the collectives; for here too there had been trouble. Semiterrorist bands led by ex-landlords and their sons (some of them university students) had burnt storage barns and executed Party cadres.

The unrest had been stimulated by the bad weather of the winter of 1956, in which twenty-three million *mus** of land, involving seventy million people, had been affected by drought. 'We think there will be a vast push for getting wells and reservoirs and canals constructed; and it will have to be done by hand, since we have no machinery,' said the Yangs to me. 'We have plenty of redundant manpower.'

In one small factory in Peking there were 650 employees, of whom 200 were administrators, and 19 fully employed serving tea to the 200.

Chou Enlai had unofficially said there must be a cut-down in capital investment by at least 20 per cent, as the load was far too onerous and 'too many people were in nonproductive employment'.

'The bureaucracy will have to do manual labour.' Yang Hsienyi thought that city cadres would be sent down in large numbers to help in the villages, thus relieving the strain upon the cities, and also curing, partly, the 'three evils'. 'I might be among them,' said he. I looked at his thin, aristocratic face; obviously he was not full of joy at the prospect, but he added, 'Of course I shall go. I'll serve wherever they put me.' 'You're too valuable to your organization,' I replied, and he allowed himself a bleak little smile, took a gulp of wine, and recited a poem to the moon.

Through the remaining weeks, articles in the Party newspapers inveighed against the 'frantic attacks by the bourgeoisie'. 'The old tail has not been lopped off,' I read one day.† 'They still think they're the lords of earth.'

* One *mu* is one-sixth of an acre and one-fifteenth of a hectare.
†To stick up one's tail: to be arrogant.

Arrogance was, according to the middle cadre, the hallmark of the intellectual; but arrogance was precisely what the intellectual complained was the outstanding feature of the Party cadre.

'Of course they were traitors, since that imperialist Dulles has called them openly "brave men" . . .' was another current opinion among cadres of the Party. Any praise from the outside was evidence of active collusion with imperialism, the enemy.

Another campaign, to reassure the intelligentsia, to dampen the irate feelings of the Party cadres. Mao was photographed speaking to non-Party writers and artists in Shanghai. Raucous demands for strict punishment of rightists were played down. By 1958 some rehabilitations were taking place.

In the literary circles, fierce 'struggle meetings' were under way; of such complex and convoluted nature that even today, twenty years later, I feel unable to disentangle the whys and wherefores of these condemnations. 'Some of these writers have been feuding against each other for years . . . there are long-standing grievances between Party writers who have come from the guerrilla bases and the writers who remained in the cities and only joined at Liberation. Some of the seasoned Party writers are asking of their new colleagues: "You haven't been through the remoulding process – who knows what underhand games you were up to in the Chiang Kaishek controlled areas in the old days?" Writers have a natural disposition never to forget any detail of the past histories of other writers . . .'

The speaker was a writer friend of mine who ambled with me, speaking quietly. He asked me not to quote him. I would gather that a great deal of personal rancour between literary men (and how intense this becomes) must also have played a role in some of the accusations in literary circles that year.

I went to bid Kung Peng goodbye. She looked weary. The meetings against the rightists went on in her own department, and in the Ministry of Foreign Affairs. Twenty years later I would be told that at the time her own husband, Chiao Kuanhua, was under fire as a rightist, and that he was only saved by Chou Enlai's personal intervention.

'Whatever our enemies may say, we are not going to shed blood,' said she. 'The Chairman refuses to utilize violence, as was done in certain other countries. Heads are not leeks which can grow again.' We both knew to which other countries Kung Peng was alluding.

Vice-President Radhakrishnan of India came to Peking, and I went to a reception for him. I stood near the door and within a few inches of me Radhakrishnan walked in, and with him Mao Tsetung, and Liu Shaochi, and Chou Enlai and Teng Hsiaoping, and Chu Teh, and others. Everyone clapped, and they too were clapping themselves. Mao wore a pale grey suit. His presence seemed to abolish every other presence, for he conveyed power. He had a smooth, unwrinkled face and was taller than all the others, including Radhakrishnan, who did not wear a turban that day.

The Vice-President of India made an emotional speech in English; he spoke of the quality of mercy. Radhakrishnan had felt moved to utter a plea of compassion for the rightists . . . Mao made a speech in reply, and so strong was his Hunan accent that I understood very little of what he said. But the drift seemed to be an emphasis on non-interference between different systems.

Papa took me to his bank and opened an account in my name. He would put all his savings into my account. He also gave me all his patriotic war bonds. During the Korean war, the government had issued war bonds, and all of them were redeemed by 1961, with a tax free interest of 3 per cent.

Papa would not leave China. 'My organization thinks I am too old to travel.' Comrade Wu had come to see him on his birthday, with a bouquet of carnations stiffly tied and a bottle of wine. 'They try to show your father that they value his criticism highly,' said Wanchun.

'I'll be back next spring,' I told Papa. 'Look after yourself well this winter. We'll see what happens next year.'

Hong Kong. The usual barrage of newsmen. Jacques Locquin, perhaps because I had refused his advice, had sent an advance report, stating that 'Han Suyin alleges 99 per cent of the Chinese people are against the rightists.' I had said nothing so dogmatic.

I would repeat my view: there had been irresponsible and foolish statements made which had set back the cause of intellectual freedom in China; because the people who had made them had not kept in mind Chinese history and the traditional relationship of the intelligentsia to power. 'How do you want the workers and the peasants to approve them? They do not know them. They only know the Communist Party. And what have they have done in the past to help the peasantry?' Allowing self-expression was never meant to be liberalization, I said; it was merely a method to help the Communist Party reinforce itself, not to challenge it, replace it or weaken it.

Of all the newsmen, it was two Americans, one the representative of the *Baltimore Sun*, who reported most scrupulously and exactly what I had said.

March 1958. Singapore's heat bleached skin and mind; our shadows vanished as the sun dissolved in a heat-drained sky. Only the abrupt evening sea breeze came to restore bodies driven by work through the day. There was an epidemic of influenza and I was extremely busy. There was also an epidemic of abortions, and some were ugly. Abortion was a crime then, but many doctors performed it.

One morning a cable came from Hollywood, signed Balaban, inviting me to a presentation at the Hollywood Bowl in April. I rang up the American Consulate and was assured there would be no problem about a visa. Just as I was drafting a suitable reply which our errand boy would take to the telegraph office, another cable came, this time from Peking. It said that my father had died on March 8th.

I prepared to go to Peking, and set off for Hong Kong the next day. A cable from Walter Minton reached me in Hong Kong. (By now I had left Ted Weeks and Little, Brown.

Walter Minton of Putnam's was my new publisher.) *The Mountain is Young* was ready for publication, coming out both in London and in America that autumn. Could I come to America for the launching? I applied in Hong Kong for the American visa, but left for Peking without waiting for the outcome. Francis Pan would ring up the Consulate and inquire when the visa would be ready.

China Travel Service surpassed itself. A death in the family – the visa to Peking was there within three hours of my calling them. An aeroplane seat to Peking had been booked for the morning after my arrival in Kuangchow.

In the very few hours I was in Kuangchow I noticed a change. A quality of exhilaration in the air. Effervescence. Posters, flamboyant on every wall. Red flags and banners and trucks with workers standing in them beating drums as they rolled through the streets, announcing achievements in production. Wall posters against rightists, a procession of chanting young children with wooden guns, older children with spades . . .

And an explosion of women.

Women on posters, immense posters of women in factory clothes, in peasant clothes. 'We too can produce for the country.' Women calling to women: Come out and work! Build our country! Women and men with that smile to the fore, looking starry-eyed into the sky. Women, large-sized, brawny, and on the radio in my room the voice of a woman: 'It is better for a woman to have big hands and big feet. Big feet are beautiful, big hands are capable hands. A white skin is sickly . . .'

I was witnessing the beginning of the Great Leap Forward, which would take place that year.

Peking was still extremely cold when I arrived in mid-March, shivering, plunged into Arctic weather from the tropical moist heat of Singapore with the sun straight overhead. A shrieking sand wind from the Gobi Desert swooped upon the city and clawed at it, and tore the skin off my face. Yet even so, in the high wind, there were processions and marching, and drums, and exhilaration.

I went straight to Papa's house from the airport; noticing that there were more bicycles on the streets than the previous year. Hsueh Mah had shrunk upon herself, a dwarf bundled in Papa's cardigan, and she uttered long lament. Third and Fourth Brothers and Fourth Sister Ping came from work when night fell. They told me that it was on an afternoon with such a sandstorm, raging yellow, that Papa came home for lunch from the office. 'He insisted on taking part in the wall poster campaign.' The great campaign of wall posters which had been going on since 1956 had not stopped; on the contrary, there were many more of them, and now they were all directed towards the Leap Forward which was coming. How to produce more, more quickly, more thriftily; how to struggle for 'an upward stream' of achievement. Strangely enough, while some intellectuals had gone back into supine acquiescence, Papa had thrown himself into this campaign. 'How to do things better, it's my job to tell them how.' I do not know what wall posters he wrote. Only the organization and the Party committee in charge would know.

'Your father was very excited that day,' said Fourth Brother. Papa swallowed his food, then went to wait for the bus at the street corner to return to the office. The wind howled and threw great piles of sand in the air. It was difficult to breathe or even to see. Choking, covered with sand, Papa arrived back at the office, and spat out the sand in his mouth, and cleaned his nostrils.

A meeting took place. Papa rose to speak. He had just started to say, 'And we don't pay enough attention . . .' when he put his hand to his head: 'Oh, I'm unwell . . .' and then his face turned purple and he fell to the floor.

'The Party committee would like to tell you all about it. They have asked whether you can come tomorrow. They wish to offer you their condolences.' Of course I would go.

Fourth Brother came with me. He was, after all, almost Papa's adopted son. Rather than leave his brother without a male successor, Third Uncle had enjoined his son, Fourth Brother, to look after him, which he did most dutifully, giving up all his spare Sundays, as did his wife Shuan, to keep the old man company.

The Party committee head received me with utmost courtesy. He repeated what I had been told about the sandstorm: 'Very oppressive, your father could not breathe easily. We asked him to rest, not to take part in the meeting, but your father would not rest. He wrote so many wall posters, he participated in all the debates. Sometimes the criticisms he made were not apposite . . .' Here the Party leader tried hard not to frown a little. Undoubtedly Papa must, at times, have lashed out at the Party cadres, and it must have been hard to take. 'However, your father was a good man, most patriotic and devoted; we decided that he was an example for all of us in many ways, even if at times his world viewpoint was imperfect.'

The comrade then produced the doctor's certificate. A doctor had been there within ten minutes, but Papa had died instantly; a stroke had felled him. In view of his great merits, the Party committee had decided to bury him on Papaoshan, the hill where revolutionary heroes and people who have rendered great service to their country are buried. This was a signal honour, especially for a man like Papa, not a Party member, an old 'intellectual', and from a bourgeois background.

Ration tickets for a full set of funeral clothes had been obtained. Since 1954 cotton was rationed, as was oil and rice, pork and flour, to maintain stable prices. But for funerals, and also for marriages and for the birth of babies, extra cloth was always given. The clothes were made within twenty-four hours and Papa was dressed in them, and photographs were duly taken, so that every step of the procedure should be shown to me and I could judge whether it had been carried out appropriately. There were many wreaths, and at Papaoshan a small ceremony, as friends and colleagues and the Party committee representative paid their respects. Papa was even mentioned in the *People's Daily*, a great honour for a non-communist.

'We wanted to delay the ceremony until you had arrived,

but since you were so far, we did not know how long it would take.' I said they had done very well, and I was perfectly satisfied and very grateful. 'You have done more, far more than I ever expected. I thank you most deeply.'

Fourth Brother, Third Brother and Ping and I went to Papaoshan, and I saw the fresh grave. 'Should you wish a headstone, we can arrange for it,' said the keeper. We discussed the stone, its size, the words to be engraved upon it; it would cost a thousand *yuan*. 'We can afford it,' said Third and Fourth Brothers. As high-grade intellectuals, they had excellent salaries. I said, 'No, I will pay for everything.' By the summer the stone was laid upon the grave, Papa's name and a short biography engraved upon it.

Often in the years since then I have driven to Papaoshan, not only to sweep Papa's grave, but also to pay respects to other friends. I would stroll among the stone monuments on the slope of the hill where Papa was buried and stop in front of the grave of Agnes Smedley, just one row above that of Papa. 'Agnes Smedley, American revolutionary writer' and a hammer and sickle are engraved upon her stone, since she was an American Communist Party member.

Many times, too, besides visiting the outside slopes of Papaoshan, I would be allowed to penetrate the small rooms inside the modest building where lie the ashes of so many Party members.* Row upon row, upon shelves, they lie, nothing but the small casket, a name and a red star, and sometimes a photograph.

During the Cultural Revolution, a band of the May 16 group of Red Guards, the most virulent and savage of all the recruits of Lin Piao and Madame Mao, erupted into Papaoshan and started to destroy the 'graves of the bourgeoisie'. 'We shall scatter the bones of all those who have opposed Chairman Mao,' they chanted. The grave of a Communist leader of the 1930s† was broken up, but the family was able to take the coffin away with his bones and bury him privately elsewhere. This man had, indeed, been

*Cremation is currently practised in China, especially for Party members.
†Chu Chiupai: see *The Morning Deluge*.

guilty of an error of 'line', way back in 1928–9, but this was no reason to throw him out of the Papaoshan cemetery. Some graves, like Papa's, of non-Party members, had the headstones smashed. But the keeper of Papaoshan arrived on the scene. 'I told them to stop. I stood there and would not allow them to continue. "This is not the way to fulfil Chairman Mao's injunction," I told them. There were about forty of them, but I was not afraid. And they went away.' Thus the damage was limited to the outside. The band had wanted to go inside the rooms where the caskets were stored. Since the rooms are of modest size and have no bars, no heavy doors, it would have been easy to rifle among the small urns. 'They wanted to check whether there were any "traitors'" ashes there, but I told them, "Go away, you are doing no useful work here among the dead." And so they did not enter.'

Another headstone, with Papa's face upon it, done by a sculptor who is a friend of Shuan, has replaced the old one. We continue to visit Papa, and in spring my cousins' children also come to sweep the grave, to read aloud his engraved biography, and to bow. The keeper comes forward with two flower pots which we reverently place and leave for Papa, who loved flowers so much.

I began to sort out Papa's books, papers and clothes. The bank transferred Papa's savings and bonds and cash to me. The housing committee made no difficulty about Papa's four houses. His clothes were remarkably few, and Hsueh Mah asked whether she could have them for her son. Since she was wearing Papa's cardigan, I said yes. Ping said, 'Now Hsueh Mah must go back to her village. Her son can take care of her.'

Hsueh Mah wept heartrendingly. 'I have served Old Lady and Venerable Old Gentleman for so many years . . . how can I go back?' She knelt and knocked her head against the veranda's tiled floor. 'Do not send me away. I shall kill myself.'

When Liberation had come, Hsueh Mah had attended the meetings for equality between men and women. She went to the public security bureau and said, 'I want a divorce; I have been married against my will, and I was beaten all the time, and I have run away, and it is twenty-eight years ago. I don't want that old mule of a husband.' So Hsueh Mah wept, and clung to me, and said twenty-eight years, ah yes she had a son, but he would not look after her, and could she stay? And if I returned, she could serve me . . .

And so I said, Yes, she could stay. I would pay her thirty *yuan* a month, which was the salary of a worker, and she would be caretaker of the rooms in the house where Papa had lived. 'You are making a mistake,' said Ping. 'Hsueh Mah is afraid of village life because she thinks of the past. But her village is now quite well off. It even has electricity.'

But I could not bring myself to send her back to her village. So Wang Wanchun and Uncle Ting, who lived in one of Papa's houses, arranged to pay Hsueh Mah out of the rent of the houses, and to bank the rest for me, except the 20 per cent which the housing committee took out of the rents in order to carry out repairs.

During the next six years, until 1964 when she died, I would see Hsueh Mah become more and more rapacious, greedy for money. All the instincts of the peasant came up in her, and every time I returned to the house something was missing, until all the furniture was gone, and when I asked for it Hsueh Mah wept and said there were bad people who had taken it away. No one of course would comment on my silliness in allowing her to stay. It was my fault, and I had no way now of getting rid of her. Then I found out through Uncle Ting that it was Hsueh Mah's son who was taking my furniture and selling it. Her son was a cadre in her village, a Party member.

'I'll complain,' I said hotly.

Uncle Ting and Wanchun, who was there, looked uneasy.

'Not possible,' said Wanchun.

Uncle Ting said, 'We must ponder this, ponder this.'

'But why?'

'To accuse a Party member is serious business, very serious . . .'

But I went ahead, and Hsueh Mah's son was thrown out of the Party and punished. I said to Wanchun, 'The more scared you are, the more tyranny will grow. We must fight.'

Wanchun said, 'Big Sister, it is easier for you to fight than for me.'

Hsueh Mah dosed herself with a lot of medicines and forever wanted more money from me. She demanded a solemn promise that I would buy her a good wooden coffin and a new set of clothes, and that her coffined body would be sent back to her village, by train, for burial; she asked for the train ticket money in advance. 'I shall have it in my hand, and when I die, make sure that there is also some money for a horse cart to take the coffin from the railway station.' By the end she wanted a car, not a horse cart. Hsueh Mah was buried in common ground in Peking because the trains no longer took coffins to villages for burial. In 1963 she had placed her own picture, as large as my father's, by my father's picture, thus laying claim to having been Papa's wife. I took away Papa's picture, leaving Hsueh Mah alone on the wall.

During those days of April, I went to see some friends who lived near a village, and watched fields being made anew, wide and splendidly rectangular, and rows of people working together at planting, bowed over the furrows. Above them red flags shook in the wind with a noise like wings. Every day the newspapers would signal some achievement or new invention by a peasant or a worker. The people were mighty and invincible, an ocean of strength and wisdom. This was an immense attempt to mobilize one quarter of the earth's people to speed up the infrastructural work necessary, moving human energy, because it was in large supply, to modernize and industrialize China rapidly, and upon a sound agricultural basis. There must be an agricultural surplus before one could hope for enough funds for capital construction to proceed. The slogan of 'self-reliance' was heard everywhere. 'Pretty soon, perhaps we shall no longer need to rely on any aid,' said Wang

Wanchun. But he would not say any more. Instead, he told me about the national minorities. 'We don't know enough about their customs, and sometimes we have interfered with them.' The Miaos of Szechuan at the autumn festival would erect a pole with knives sticking out of it; and a young girl, singing, would climb the pole barefooted, her feet scaling the blades like climbing stairs. 'But she never cuts herself. And when she reaches the top, she begins to sing, and then the young Miao girls each choose a man and go into the forest with him for a night of love. But our cadres felt that this was immoral, and we sent army men "to maintain order". The Miaos were very discontented with this interference.'

Now this was changed. Much more attention was being paid to the national minority customs. 'Some of our people still believe that we the Hans are superior,' I said to Wanchun. 'But we are,' said he, surprised that I should doubt it.

A sparrow hunt started in Peking, part of a nationwide campaign to eliminate the four pests: flies, mosquitoes, rats and mice, and grain-eating birds. For three days the whole population turned out, banging gongs, beating drums, blowing whistles or just screaming; climbing on roofs and waving sticks, and blowing small trumpets to keep the sparrows flying. Exhausted, the sparrows fell down and died, and were carted away in great mounds of feathers and beaks and diminutive clawed feet. On the city wall's remaining parapets (the massive Ming Wall was being torn down to make way for new buildings and new roads), on the watchtowers of the gates, in the high pavilions of the Forbidden City, people clambered to dislodge sparrows. An energetic young girl put her foot through the roof tiles of Papa's house in her pursuit of a bird. In distraught small clouds the sparrows flew and fell and flew and fell. Europeans from the embassies and Western journalists joined in the hunt.

I wrote a piece about the sparrow hunt for the *New Yorker*, in which it was printed.* Roger Angell, the editor, wanted to

*'The Sparrow Shall Fall', *New Yorker*, October 10th, 1959.

cut out the end, but I did not let him do it. The piece as it stands displeased a good many people in China; but then I have always been sloppily sentimental about animals and birds.

The sparrow hunt was never repeated; for by the next year and for many years afterwards, owing to the dearth of birds, the trees of Peking would be assailed by insects. Caterpillars wrapped the foliage in great nets of silver strand, a lovely lethal sight, and when all the foliage was eaten up the trees died. I saw fields of cabbages with their leaves peppered with holes as worms gorged. 'We must distinguish between good and nefarious birds,' the cadres would now say. But it was hard to get away from the first effulgent clamour of 'Get rid of pests'. In the 1970s I would still find, in Szechuan, people catching sparrows as 'bad birds'.

I went to see old Mr Hua Nankuei, to thank him for having come to Papa's funeral ceremony at Papaoshan, although he walked with great difficulty. While we were talking, his son Simon came in, exuberant. He had been working, together with many of the students and teaching staff of Peking University, at the new reservoir which was being built near the Ming tombs. Simon looked fit. He was doing his year of labour re-education and would return to architecture by 1959. 'It is the happiest time of my life. The workers are simply splendid. They treat me as one of them, joke and talk with me.' Never had Simon felt so full of joy and hope, and to remind him that this was 'punishment' seemed otiose.

'I've been five days at the reservoir. We sleep in tents, we eat *wotou** three times a day. Nothing else. But it's splendid . . .' He had a friend who had done a stint in the countryside. 'He never wanted to come back to the city. The peasants chose the heaviest and the dirtiest work for themselves – they left easy tasks to him. 'You're not used to it, as we are.' They were grateful whenever my friend did anything. The peasant he boarded with the first night put up

---

**Wotou:* a coarse lumpy bread made of rye and millet.

a great barrier of blankets between himself and my friend on the *kang** they shared. "Why do you do this?" "You see . . . they . . . jump," the peasants replied guiltily. My friend put his arms around the peasant. What delicacy of heart! He wanted to keep his fleas to himself.'

A small wind went prowling through Peking the day I left, but it was almost May, and warm. Third and Fourth Brothers came to see me off; soon Fourth Brother would go to Manchuria, to a research institute there. 'At present we're busy with the heart campaign.'

The heart campaign symbolized an exchange of hearts between the Party and the intelligentsia: 'You give us your heart and we give you ours . . . our hearts are joined together in common endeavour.' It was meant as a pledge of the loyalty of the intellectuals to the Party, but also as a pledge that the Party would treat the intellectuals fairly, and trust them. There had been many meetings and much exhortation as each organization containing intellectuals overhauled itself for the coming Leap. Now parades with great hearts of satin or velvet carried in front of the processions signified a new and desirable harmony.

'Do you think it really helps to parade with a heart?' I asked Third Brother. 'Why not?' he replied. He was well, and happy in his work. Over a million office workers were going down to the countryside. Party and non-Party cadres. Third Brother was also going down for six weeks of labour. 'It will temper me,' said he, smiling confidently.

**Kang:* platform of stone or adobe which serves as the family bed in north China's peasant houses.

CHAPTER 8

That Other Life, Outside China

Back in Hong Kong, I inquired of Francis Pan about my American visa. Francis looked uneasy. Yes, the American Consulate had rung up, saying, 'The visa is ready for Miss Han to collect.' 'She's in Peking at the moment,' Francis had replied unguardedly. There was a pause and then the telephone voice had said, 'Oh, that changes everything, doesn't it?' 'I explained you had gone for your father's funeral,' said Francis, who felt he might have bungled things. Then a message came through that 'on second thoughts' my case had to be studied. Two months later, in Singapore, I was advised that I was not eligible for a visa, because I had joined a 'communist' organization, that is, the PAP, Lee Kuanyew's party, in Singapore! Yet this information, that I had filled up a membership card for the PAP, had been on my first application, which had been approved. The change of mind after I returned from Peking was blatant.

I could have fought the case. I nearly went to the American Consulate to say, 'Look, I only filled in a card to hear Harry Lee talk; and I'm told that he's so upset at the idea of my joining his party that he's said to his colleagues, "I don't want that woman around." It's all a joke, really.' But Americans at that time were impervious to such joking. I felt I would gain nothing by fighting the case. I might be compelled to make a public anti-China statement, and this I would not do. I had to accept that freedom of opinion had its limits everywhere, and also in America at that time.

From then on until 1977, I would not enter America except on a waiver, which meant applying to the State Department each time. And each time I got my waiver, until it became a farce. 'Oh, it's you again,' the Consulate officials in Hong Kong or Singapore would say wearily when I came in, all smiles, to tell them I *must* go to see my publisher, or I *must* go to fulfil my contract for lectures throughout the length and breadth of America . . . 'It takes us five hours to go through the files about you,' one very nice official would tell me with a half grin (full grins were out of the question for people needing waivers to enter the USA).

How mighty, how feared was America then! I had brought some silk back from China, and given it to a tailor in Hong Kong to make a dress, but he refused. 'This silk was made in China, Dr Han . . . I cannot work on it or the American Consulate will put me on the black list and I shall lose all my American customers . . .'

There was the matter of ducks' eggs. Since 1957, and for many years thereafter, each duck exported from Hong Kong to the markets of South East Asia was to be accompanied by a certificate of origin. This was a stamp upon its webbed foot, vetted by the American Consulate and certifying the duck was born in Hong Kong, from eggs laid in Hong Kong by parent ducks resident in Hong Kong. Certificates of origin were required for everything; furniture, silk, curios – they became an industry on their own. No antiques from China were to be purchased by Americans. No jade from China. An American friend of mine died of a heart attack because he had a magnificent jade collection, acquired before 1949. He intended to retire to California and sell his jade. But now he was ruined, for he could not take the jade with him, or sell it.

In these circumstances, to fight publicly would have inevitably strengthened the conviction that I was a communist. I preferred, therefore, to keep silent, to accept waivers, and to wait. Twenty years.

Meanwhile, I was selling the film rights of *The Mountain is Young* for a considerable sum of money to Paramount. *A Many-Splendoured Thing* had gone for a very small sum to Twentieth Century-Fox, and had proved an amazing success. It is still showing, a quarter of a century later, in many countries. Now I would ask a large figure for *The*

Mountain is Young and not worry whether a film was made or not. Francis reminded me of that occasion. ' "I'm going to take a walk and decide on the money," you said. When you came back, you stuck out for six figures and would not be moved.'

The negotiations dragged on, and Singapore's multi-millionaire film magnate, Loke Wantho, who had become my friend, took over, relaying my demands to Paramount. Loke Wantho had inherited a fortune from his very famous father, Loke Yew. He was capable and shrewd, and although English-educated, intelligent enough to know that his was not the enduring cultural pattern in Malaya. He had remained profoundly attached to his Chinese roots, and though extremely conservative and afraid of communism, he would talk and argue with me, and try to inform himself. Wantho owned the Cathay film organization in Singapore, which had purchased *A Many-Splendoured Thing* for distribution throughout South East Asia. He hoped that *The Mountain is Young* would be a similar success. I was not sanguine, but I did not care. 'Whatever happens, now I shall have a sum of money set by, and money buys freedom, undoubtedly.' Like Bernard Shaw and Saul Bellow, I think the labourer is worthy of his hire, and if I have done many things for no money, only for love, I have also bargained doggedly when no feelings have been involved. Until 1958 I had spent and given, given and spent. Now I would become more choosy, but I would still give, more or less judiciously. I would tailor my life not to possess material things in great abundance, for they are hindrances, fetters, bad habits, but to be able to go as free as possible. Even my three small houses in Johore Bahru were not a burden. The rent of two of them paid for the upkeep of all three, and the servants' wages. With Lao Chieh there as general manager, I could be away and all would be looked after: the dogs and the cats and the garden and the tenants; and Yungmei was now eighteen years old, and healthy.

When *The Mountain is Young* came out as a book it was declared 'hot stuff', the equivalent of today's porn. Some reviewers were sorry that it was not a replica of *A Many-Splendoured Thing*. But I could never repeat myself, and all my books would be different, one from the other. I had written *The Mountain is Young* with irony and laughter, to please myself; and literature, after all, should not be all heaving and smoulder and wrung-out soul. It should also be fun for the writer. But the world of literature then was not attuned to that mixture of mockery and malice, tinsel and gold, drabness and glory, poetry and banality; and yet that was what Nepal, what India were like: tragedy is farce and the ingredients of drama the commonest in laughter. I was cast in the mould of a lovelorn and tragic person, talking and living Lo-oh-ove, when it was precisely the contrary, and love for me was a rare episode in a busy existence. The misunderstanding went very far. An earnest young Englishwoman, the wife of some British officer or other, volunteered to help me type some of my work, but after a fortnight burst out, 'All we ever do is work, work, work. And I thought I'd have such a glorious time.'

Yet *The Mountain is Young* was a success, and continues to be reprinted. Many women readers wrote to me: they felt it solaced their frustration. 'You've described my husband exactly', was the burden of letters I received, and one middle-aged person stopped me on the street: 'Han Suyin, where did you meet my husband?' I goggled. 'I never met your husband.' 'But you've described him to a tee. It's just like him, even the way he makes love . . .'

Yungmei was now out of school, and idle, and rigorously conformist to the mores of her set. 'Everyone says you are a communist because you go to China so often'; 'Nobody likes your book on Malaya'; '*The Mountain is Young* is a dirty book . . .' She sought a father image, and had taken to sleeping with Pao's sword hanging over her bed. Not knowing what to do with the unwieldy sabre, I had transported it with our luggage everywhere, even in Johore Bahru. Perhaps I should now have told her she was adopted. But in China, talking it over with friends, everyone had seemed to think it was no trauma not to know. 'I only knew it when my mother died, and I loved her all the more for loving me so much that she could not bear to tell me she had not borne me,' one of my Chinese friends had said. And so I did not tell Yungmei, alleging to myself that she would be more hurt by knowing than not knowing.

Yungmei was growing very beautiful, and I did not grudge her the pleasure she took in swimming, going to parties and dancing. Unlike the intense, hardworking, revolt-filled students of Chinese schools whom I met in Nanyang University, the products of the English schools could spend a whole day doing absolutely nothing except reading comics, giggling and looking fondly at the pictures of American film stars. However, compared with today's youth, they were an angelic choir. No sex. They drank only tea or fruit juice. No drugs. In the tropics, where the nights are more vital and awake than the drowsy, heat-stunted days, they went out all night, and yet chaperoned each other, so that the most that could happen was a hand-in-hand look at the moon. The main danger was car accidents, for some of the boys, from twelve-car owning families, would drive with show-off speed; and I often lay awake fearing a crash, reassured when I heard at last the giggles and the soft Malayan singsong of goodnights from the garden below.

Yungmei now decided to study in London because so many of her friends were going there. I thought it was a good idea. She would not be out of her depth as she still had many childhood friends in England. In September of 1958 I took her to London, where I was expected for the launching of *The Mountain is Young* and a Foyle's lunch in my honour at the Dorchester Hotel.

In 1953 I had semi-adopted another girl, Hueiying, of the same age as Yungmei. Hueiying's mother had died, and at twelve she had been taken out of school by her father and made to cook and clean and look after five other children in the family. Her father sold pottery and was poor. I put Hueiying through school, paying the fees, and helping a little besides, and she did well, as also did her younger brother, who became an art designer of outstanding quality, won scholarships to England, and has his own design centre now in Kuala Lumpur. Hueiying would marry a very nice young man, who has since built a solid fortune in the Chinese medicine business throughout South East Asia. Other protégés of mine would also turn out successes, but the point was that Yungmei resented greatly my concern for other young people. I tried to explain to her that all the world's children, in a sense, are one's own. 'Why can't you be like other mothers?' she said; meaning: 'Why can't you concentrate on me, on me alone?' And this also stopped me. I though this jealousy of love part of that unconscious, deep-buried feeling of deprivation she must have suffered from, being unwanted, sold by her mother and sold not once but three times. No giving of love from me or anyone else would compensate entirely for this early absence of caring.

And then there was Ah Ping. Ah Ping was a waif adopted by Lao Chieh, and Lao Chieh, when she was angry with Ah Ping, would scream at her, 'I bought you and I'll sell you if you won't study properly.' She would also beat Ah Ping in the bad old Chinese way which maintains that it is wrong not to be strict with children. In Singapore society adopted girls were many, and were usually to be utilized, sooner or later, either as servants to the family or to be sold into prostitution. The defloration of a young virgin was the occasion for the 'mother' to regain her outlay, a large sum in return for her care of many years. I did not want Yungmei to think that this was going to happen to her; already she had mentioned to me one or two such cases.

All the time in London, this question beset me. Shall I tell her, shall I not? In the end I did not tell her, and that was wrong of me.

For in 1961 Yungmei, who was then studying in London, went to spend the Easter holiday with Joseph Hers and his family in Brussels. Joseph Hers had given me my scholarship to study in Belgium way back in 1935, when he headed a scholarship fund in China. He had returned to his native Belgium and married a very beautiful and vital woman, a sculptress and Greek. She took to Yungmei and surrounded her with much mothering and affection. Did this make Hers jealous? He was almost forty years older than his wife, and extremely tyrannical in his old age. He was also carrying on a very acerbic quarrel by letter with me. About China.

Hers insisted that China had failed. He sent me cuttings from various newspapers to prove this failure. He gloated over the sufferings that would come to the Chinese people. He wrote, 'Why on earth should China provoke India?', 'China has not one friend in the world today.' I wrote back, mordantly. Epistolary rage flourished. I said he was 'myopic . . . deliberately unobservant . . . thinking on such a small scale it made me laugh . . '

And then Hers told Yungmei that she was not my daughter, that she had been adopted. How did he know? I had not told him. Perhaps through missionary talk. The missionaries of Chengtu knew.

Yungmei took the knock. She did not write to me, and in fact she did not even say anything to me until six years later, when she had married and borne a child. What happened then? All I know is that she stopped studying. She then fell in love, but the outcome was not happy. However, as she said herself, 'I did not become a prostitute. I did not take drugs.' She not only survived; she recovered.

Of course there were difficult years between us; but never was there a complete break; always, somehow, we gravitated back towards each other. And there were good periods too. And now, I think, a great clearness has come in our relations, and they are good. I love her and I know she loves me, although at times she still reacts to the nightmares of her young days. But then, in this world, how many children have had far worse fates than hers? Going to China has helped her greatly to readjust, to understand, and to be enriched, not traumatized, by what has happened. For my Chinese friends all say to her, 'Oh, but there are so many like you . . .'

But I do not think I can forgive Hers, even dead, for what he did. It was the action of a soured old man, jealous and destructive. I think it is because he still hungered for the

China he had known, not the new China arising from the ashes of the past. For him there was no escape in the world except the world of China. He saw me go in and out, come closer to the heart of the change that was taking place. He then felt cast aside, unwanted. And that is why, I think, he did this to Yungmei.

That autumn of 1958 in London was the last time I would see Jonathan Cape alive. He threw a large party for me, and to it came Kossodo from Germany, Walter Minton of Putnam's, and Ragnar Svanstrom from Sweden. Walter Minton was a most impressive New Englander, and I was glad to see him in the flesh. I had liked his letters, and when I left Ted Weeks and Little, Brown, it was because I felt Ted and I had less and less to write to each other, despite Ted's effusiveness. I do not think it was his fault; perhaps we had started off with a misunderstanding, and it continued to grow.

A few English writers came to the party, including Peter and Ian Fleming, both published by Cape. Peter Fleming had been a friend of Ian's; they had bashed snakes in Burma together. The Flemings monopolized the fireplace and stood there, with their wives (I think) as for an official photograph, and behaving as if the party were in their honour. At some point the Flemings ceased speaking to anyone else (they ignored me throughout the party) and quarrelled with beautiful manners among themselves.

Jonathan was recovering badly from the palsy due to his stroke; his face remained affected and at meals he dribbled. 'I did call you Sunflower, didn't I?' he said to me. 'Yes you did, Jonathan.' 'That's right. Sunflower.' Walter Minton came to dinner in the most elegant white hand-woven socks and with a delightful unknown whose Jayne Mansfield exposure reduced Cape's Wren Howard to feverish small talk. 'Do you write?' she asked me. As for Ragnar, he was very sweet and very English, in the way only Swedes can be. He said 'Hear, hear', but louder than I had heard it in the House of Commons. Walter and I carried on a friendly quarrel over *The Mountain is Young*. He asserted that I must tone down the swarthy hero because in the United States people were sensitive to the colour problem. Firmly and uncompromisingly, therefore, he had made a change. In the American edition the hero was 'burnished' or 'suntanned'.

On to Paris with Yungmei, to see my French publishers. The latter gave a luncheon and invited Françoise Sagan, who came with her husband of that year, Guy Schoeller. Guy was an explorer, a marvellous horseman and for a while one of the editors at Stock, my publishers. I had wanted to meet Françoise Sagan because she was then at the height of her popularity and in Malaya the young like Yungmei saw in her a cult figure for themselves. Her cool, precise, rather new-precious way of dealing with emotion fitted the adolescent dialect which I had heard Yungmei use. But as usual when writers meet, there was little that we could talk about. Sagan talked about cars and speed: 'I like *vitesse*.' I did not speak of Asia, of China, India, Malaya, Nanyang University – all of it suddenly was too large, too clumsy, sweaty and human, and ridiculous as an ocean is ridiculous, through sheer enormity.

That early November in Paris was also the Algerian war November. There was a fetor about the city, something bewildered under the beauty and the archness, the rank smell of unleashed violence filled one's nostrils. I met a small, middle-aged, plump woman, badly dressed, who at first sight made one think of ironing boards and returning from market with heavy-laden baskets and the violaceous varicose legs of overworked women with children and a husband who has long stopped talking. But how deceptive this appearance! For the woman was all fire and spirit, and she became beautiful as the minutes went by, and it was Germaine Tillon, writer, ethnologist, member of the Resistance, deported to Ravensbruck in 1943.

Algerian workers' bodies were found hanging on trees in the Bois de Boulogne, and the Seine even carried a cadaver or two. Those who spoke against the war in Algeria were quite often regarded as traitors. General de Gaulle was back as leader of France, but no one at the time could predict what he would do about Algeria.

From Paris I went to Geneva, for a reunion with Lily Abegg of the *Neue Züricher Zeitung*. Lily had come to Malaya to stay with me; we liked each other and she defended me when people called me names. She had an excellent grasp of Asian politics.

Walking into the Chat Botté restaurant for dinner, Lily and I fell upon P. N. Sharma, my Indian photographer friend. 'How shrunk the world is getting! One day Peking, the next Delhi, and now Geneva!' Sharma was in Geneva to ring up Moscow. 'My fiancée is in Moscow.' He had fallen in love with a Russian girl on his last trip to Russia, some months previously; and had been trying to get her out of Russia to marry her. 'Panditji* himself wrote a letter for me to Khrushchev,' he said. The telephone call came through, and Sharma bounded away. He returned, transfigured, and opened his shirt and began to ripple his belly muscles up and down and sideways, to make us laugh, while the Swiss waiters remained stone-faced. Sharma left with me an alarm watch (not a clock, a watch) and sundry items, altogether a suitcase of things, which he had purchased for his fiancée. He wanted them taken to India but knew he would be searched by the redoubtable Indian customs and would have to pay heavy duty on the watch and other things. Would I take it all to Delhi for him on my way back to Malaya? I would.

I note that in 1958 I also visited Cambodia, took up yoga, opened painting exhibitions in Singapore, started collecting antiques for the museum in Kuala Lumpur, and became associated with the Malaysian Sociological Research Institute.

I had met Jean, a Eurasian lawyer whose mother was Vietnamese but who lived in Phnom Penh, during one of my sojourns in Hong Kong. He had written, inviting me to

*The Indian Prime Minister, Jawaharlal Nehru.

Cambodia to lecture to the Rotary Club, of which he was President. Over a five-day holiday weekend in Singapore, I flew to Phnom Penh.

Sun-drenched, drowsy and pleasant, Phnom Penh was a small town of 200,000 souls with languid, unhurried streets and small buildings, peopled mostly by Vietnamese and Chinese. The native Khmer people were not only a minority, but the labourers and rickshaw pullers. Even the marketing of meat and vegetables was in Vietnamese hands. The Hotel Royal and its swimming pool were the centre, navel of the French resident community in Phnom Penh. Cambodia's tranquil countryside appeared to me to have an abundance of land and to be sparsely peopled; one did not feel that the country was on the verge of a revolution. Poverty and exploitation are not so stark when there is lush greenness and water; and yet exploitation there certainly was, for the rice crops and the fish trade were controlled by aristocrat landlords, and rice milling by mill owners, who again were either Chinese or Vietnamese.

Everything in Cambodia seemed stamped by the personality of Prince Norodom Sihanouk. Within three days I was received by the Prince, and I liked him very much. My affection for him and his wife, Princess Monique, would grow with the years and with the tribulations that they suffered.

Sihanouk was talkative, ebullient, extremely intelligent and still very much a Khmer king. He loved his country with a single-minded, fierce passion which was very moving. He was immensely concerned about preserving Cambodia's independence; and was most touchy on the subject. That he also maintained a feudal order, a class of privileged nobles who exploited and oppressed the people, was sad but inevitable. For Sihanouk, in a country handicapped by a lack of doctors, of engineers, of technicians, and teachers, was prisoner of his class, of the aristocracy he belonged to. Personally, he was more enlightened and progressive than many another ruling head of state of Asia, and far more so than his neighbour, Ngo Dinh Diem, in South Vietnam. His personal charisma was very compelling. Sihanouk built schools and medical clinics and tried to improve the livelihood of the peasantry with canals for water and new houses. He tried to bring progress to Cambodia without a radical revolution. In his uncompromising neutrality, Sihanouk was regarded as perverse, erratic and dangerous by American State Department heads and officials. Among the British, his great friend was Malcolm MacDonald. Malcolm cultivated Sihanouk. 'He is of the utmost importance to us . . . alas we don't know it.'

At our first meeting Sihanouk talked of his worry about the expanding war in Vietnam. The United States was getting more and more involved; and the Prince felt that Cambodia might be caught in a pincer movement between South Vietnam and Thailand, both countries basking in enormous influxes of American money. Cambodia had repeatedly been conquered and vassalized by both the Thais and the Vietnamese; the walls of her Angkor monuments bore in stone stories of heroic battles against invaders. 'I want my country at peace, my people secure, not dragged into the hideousness of war,' he said, and there were tears in his eyes. And Sihanouk did achieve for seventeen years that major feat: of keeping Cambodia out of conflicts, while all around war and devastation flourished.

In 1955 Norodom Sihanouk had divested himself of his kingship to become premier and *samdech*, or chief of state, of his country. His rule was perforce personal, authoritarian, but he contrived to keep the bulk of his people contented. Although fiercely anti-communist, he went to China, fashioning a policy combining old tradition with new vision. He had been impressed with Chou Enlai's wisdom and performance at the Geneva Conference of 1954, which had liquidated the French empire of Indo-China. 'The Chinese understand national independence, as we do,' said the Prince.

Sihanouk had a long conversation with Mao Tsetung. Mao was an excellent historian where China was concerned but not so well-informed on the history of South East Asia, that turbulent, prolific region with its multitudinous ethnic groups. When Mao commented favourably on Ho Chih Minh, on the socialist system in Vietnam, Sihanouk, it is said, blew up. 'Do you know that the Vietnamese, socialist or not socialist, tried to overrun us in 1953?' Mao listened attentively while Sihanouk gave him a historical account of the relations between Cambodia and Vietnam, Cambodia and Thailand.

Sihanouk loved Chou Enlai. 'He is the most far-sighted statesman in the world, and he understands history.' Towards Mao Tsetung, Sihanouk was reverent, but a little baffled by the size and scope of Mao's thinking, that cosmic touch which sometimes induces vertigo.

At that time, America had a truly obsessional view of politics. Anyone who did not toe the line of satellitism in the name of 'freedom and democracy' – however arbitrary, contemptuous of human rights the heads of state cherished by Washington were in practice – was an enemy. Friendship with China was anathema. Sihanouk had to be brought down because he was too different. He was a friend of China; he was neutral; he would not be vassalized; he could not be bought.

Spasmodically, I did yoga. Whenever possible twice a week, with the yoga teacher, Mr Nayan, who lived in a small bungalow in Singapore.

Mr Nayan taught yoga free. He taught for love of people; he was fifty, but slim and youthful, small-boned, and he smelt sweet. A minor clerk in the government, he never thought of money and had no ambition. At the yoga classes we imbibed the peace he radiated. None of us ever inquired each other's names, or work. We just were; each one of us on his or her own mat, concentrating on the breathing, the positions, thinking of nothing else. And when I left, a surge of tranquil power and happiness would fill me, all tiredness gone. I often think of Mr Nayan; he seems to me immortal.

Suddenly, with independence, everyone in Malaya and

Singapore became interested in art. Local painters, hitherto unknown, appeared as if born by spontaneous generation. Exhibitions were held. And yet, when I had arrived in 1952, it was said that there could be no writers or painters in Malaya because the climate was against them. I had discovered Malayan Chinese literature; I would go on to discover Chinese painters, calligraphers, Malay painters, sculptors, ceramic artists . . . a generation of young artists afire with new endeavour.

And with this came, also very suddenly, an appreciation of antiques. People who had been breaking up their Ming plates to spike their wall tops against roving cats now brought them to the newly opened museum in Kuala Lumpur. The establishment of the museum was due to an Australian, Frank Sullivan, but now fully backed by the Prime Minister, Tunku Abdul Rahman.

Frank Sullivan had come to Malaya many years ago as a newsman, but he was now the Press Secretary for Tunku Abdul Rahman. Frank and I shared a fondness for Tunku (Frank was devoted to him) and now we shared the excitement over the painters and the museum.

This new enthusiasm for art went together with the beginning of a Malayan architecture. Architects like Kee Yeap, who had built my houses, were devising new styles for the houses of the wealthy. And whereas until then many a Chinese multi-millionaire holed up in an atap hut, even if he kept three cars outside it, his sons and daughters, university graduates, insisted on 'good taste' and Western comforts, bathroom, air-conditioner, refrigerator, and of course 'artistic' decorations on the walls. In the course of the next few years Singapore was to see many high-rise buildings, and Kuala Lumpur would prosper and adorn itself with some very stimulating architecture (part Arab, part everything else). English furniture, English styles, were out; everyone wanted to be Malayan; and batiks, once despised now became fashionable, as did paintings by local artists, some of whom used the batik techniques for their paintings.

In Nanyang University a splurge of amateur painting also

occurred. I duly opened exhibitions, attended showings, wrote forewords, signed books and stated that 'the artist is trying to express the new, surging identity of Malaya', whatever that meant. I bought pictures, more to help the eager executants (most of them young and some very poor) than for art's sake.

My endeavour to make known Malayan Chinese literature had borne some fruit, and Nanyang University students came to my clinic to hand me short stories and poems, to confide their dreams of writing major novels, and sometimes to borrow money. Most of them returned the money scrupulously, even when the situation was very trying for them.

A consciousness that there were such things as novels, novellas, short stories, plays and poetry emerged as a manifestation of national identity and a book of Malayan Chinese short stories, with a preface by myself, emerged.

But Singapore became more, not less, prohibitively reactionary after 1960. The springs of writing and creation withered. So many magazines especially from Nanyang University, would be accounted 'subversive'. Nanyang University produced a high-standard economics magazine (in Chinese); an English-language magazine (of varying quality, but a brave attempt), and a magazine in Malay (of good standard). All this was done by the students. The pampered English-language media Singapore University only produced a rather mediocre English-language magazine. And yet there was an excellent teaching staff, including the brilliant and energetic Professor of English Literature, my friend the poet D. J. Enright, and the novelist Patrick Anderson.

The English-educated were perceptive, intelligent. I would meet so many earnest young men and women among them; and one I remember best is the promising poet, Edwin Thumboo.* I had relieved his mother, a feckless and garrulous but attractive person, of a horrendous debt she

*Author of *Rib of Earth* and *Gods Can Die*, published by Heinemann Far East.

owed the egg-woman, who was a usurer. The egg-woman made small loans and sold trinkets to the housewives along the lanes where she peddled her eggs. She charged 'merely' 20 per cent per day interest, always pointing out it was so much less than the money-changing Sikhs who haunted Raffles' Place, waiting for penurious clerks outside the government buildings. They charged 50 per cent per day interest, nobly pointing out to their victims that in India it was customary to charge 100 per cent per day interest.

For an initial debt of fifty Singapore dollars, the total repayment due from Thumboo's mother was three thousand. Edwin struggled mightily to return the money; in this he was like so many of the Asian students that I would know. He had great compunction about owing anything to anyone.

Would that I could say the same about the only European student who came to my notice in those years! Pierre Ryckmans was Belgian, enamoured of Chinese culture, and had achieved the extraordinary feat of being admitted to Nanyang University, where he assiduously cultivated the more left-inclined students.

He had been to China in 1956 and now approached me, as he wanted to return to China and study there. I willingly wrote letters to China for him; but was not successful. Pierre then came to proffer a painting of his, a lion behind the bars of a cage. Not a work of art, but he wanted to indicate the spirit behind his slim, pale, scholarly exterior. I immediately, as a Chinese, made him a gift of five hundred dollars, which he graciously accepted.

Alas, perhaps naturally, Pierre Ryckmans repaid me as some other men whom I have helped have done. He has since become an eminent Sinologist, called Simon Leys. And he has written a highly fanciful account of meeting me, in 1972, to discuss the fate of some Chinese writers whom I knew, and whom he did not know.

I became involved with the Malaysian Sociological Research Institute in 1957 when a very infuriated Alex Josey came to me to complain about an American girl, Shirle Gordon. Besides being Lee Kuanyew's intimate friend, Alex Josey was also the South East Asia correspondent for *Eastern World*, a London based magazine run by a witty and mercurial Viennese called Hans Taussig.

I had met Hans in 1954 while I was in London waiting for Yungmei to recuperate from her lung operation. Hans and I got on very well; we exchanged many happy letters. Hans was always full of plans and *Eastern World* was a pioneer magazine, concentrating on news of Asia.

Eastern World was not prosperous; Hans asked me to help, which I did willingly, making loans of some few thousand pounds and in return acquiring a directorship and a say in the magazine. But my say was limited by the fact that I was in Singapore, too far away to attend board meetings in London.

One of the items on which we disagreed was the accrediting of correspondents to the magazine. Hans was generosity itself in distributing letters giving authority to people to write for *Eastern World*, since all its correspondents were unpaid volunteers. And now Hans, in a fit of good temper, had forgotten Alex Josey and given correspondent status to Shirle Gordon for South East Asia, India and the Middle East. Shirle Gordon had attended the independence celebrations in Kuala Lumpur in August 1957 as representative for *Eastern World* while Alex Josey, who for years had been *the* South East Asia correspondent for *Eastern World*, had been denied entrance. Understandably he was angry, and somehow or other thought it was my fault. I knew nothing of this switch, and Hans, questioned by letter, only said that 'we're all working for a good cause'.

Shirle Gordon was deemed eminently progressive; she had attended the Afro-Asian Writers' Conference in New Delhi in 1956. To this conference the Chinese had sent a prestigious posse of writers. The USSR had also sent eminent authors to this conference, and so had the Indian Communist Party. I, being merely a 'bourgeois' scribbler of near-pornography, had of course been ignored.

As a director of the board of *Eastern World* I wrote asking Miss Gordon to come to see me. A most striking, most beautiful, big-boned girl appeared; with an astounding, radiant ripe-wheat wave of gold hair hanging almost to the waist. The effect of such a mass of golden hair in the tropics, where everyone is dark-haired, cannot be gauged by Westerners. It even hit me right in the stomach, and as for what it did to the men . . . it drove them wild.

It was all a big mistake, said Shirle. She had been introduced by Clovis Maksoud of the Arab League, and also Arslan Humbaraci, a well-known Turkish-English correspondent, to Hans Taussig, and Hans had asked her to write for the magazine. I realized that susceptible Hans had once more been carried away by his endearing penchant for beautiful women; and who could resist that hair? Shirle told me she was an Arab scholar, she had sojourned for ten years or more in several Arab countries, Lebanon and Iraq and then Egypt, researching into Islamic culture for an American university. She was a sociologist and interested in the study of Malaysian society. Malaysian, not Malayan, she specified. The term, according to her, applied to a large area encompassing the Philippines, Indonesia, Malaya, and extending right across the Indian Ocean (which President Sukano of Indonesia always called the Indonesian Ocean) to Madagascar. All these lands, said Shirle, had similar ethnic groups and a fundamentally similar culture.

This theory of a 'greater Malaysia' had already been expounded, as I remembered reading in a magazine, by some American scholar named Pomeroy, resident in the Philippines. Pomeroy was reckoned a 'pro-communist', and there were floating rumours of a 'greater Malaysia' among left-wing circles in Indonesia too.

My curiosity was awakened. Shirle gave up being correspondent for *Eastern World* (but then so did Alex Josey), and settled instead to recruit adoring and willing men to help her establish the Malaysian Sociological Research Institute, and to run a newspaper called *The Seed*, with the motto 'Sow good seed into the sea, and an island will grow'.

Later a magazine, very handsome, called *Intisari*, a Malay word meaning essence, was to be published by the Institute.

The idea of the Institute appealed greatly to me. Its aim was to promote local research, to publish books describing and analysing conditions in 'Malaysia' by local scholars, for instance, on Islam and its impact on development in Malaya; on the many varied ethnic and cultural groups which here impinged upon each other; on the multitudinous aspects which made this mosaic of Malaya and Singapore so fascinating. There was indeed wide scope for sound scholarship and research; until then, beyond a very few British publications – not bad, but certainly colonial-oriented – there was nothing in the way of a serious team researching into the sociological problems of the area. And yet there were some excellent individuals such as Unku Aziz, the Malay economist who had taken up the cause of the Malay peasantry, and whose articles, books and speeches I followed with great attention, and Professor Fatimi, an Islamic scholar of renown.

Shirle was quickly surrounded by wealthy Arabs of Singapore's business community, and also by Malay religious teachers; for the core of the Institute's research was to be on Islam, and the relationship between Islam and the state, and Islam and the lives of the peoples of Malaysia. A grant from Prince Sadruddin, younger son of the Aga Khan, enabled the Institute to come into being.

I helped the Institute, both financially and in other ways. I had read the Chinese chronicles of the sea voyages of the fifteenth century that had brought fleets from China to Zanzibar, to trade porcelain and silk and incense for ivory and rhinoceros horn and ebony. I had read everything about Malacca and the visit of the Chinese Admiral Cheng Ho, a eunuch and a convert to Islam. I offered, on my next trip to China, to write a series of articles on Islam in China, and Shirle sounded enthusiastic. A programme for the publication of books was to be launched; also for a symposium of local writers.

Then I heard some rumours about Shirle's political

leanings, chiefly from her Arab friends. Nasser had expelled her from Egypt. Shirle maintained to me that it was because she was too progressive. As there was no coherence to the rumours, I decided that I would see how things worked out. Meanwhile, in order to facilitate the workings of the Institute I introduced Linda Chen to be a full-time translator there.

Linda Chen had been a student at the Chinese high school on Bukit Timah Road in Singapore, the one which had been twice assaulted by the police, and where many students and teachers had been arrested. Linda was among those arrested and detained by Special Branch in 1954, and again in 1956. Her husband had then come to me. Linda wanted to read my book on Malaya, . . . *And the Rain My Drink*, but Special Branch had refused. I wrote a nice letter to the Police Commissioner, requesting permission to visit Linda in detention and to give her my book, and permission was given with great good nature.

I drove to the detention camp for women (the women's jail), and there were the wardresses, Indian and Eurasian, middle-aged and young, all lined up in beautifully pressed khaki uniforms and with autograph books in hand. They were happy to see me, and the head wardress said, 'You've come to see Linda, our prize detainee. She's no trouble at all.' She called out to Linda, who was sunning herself in the courtyard, and I spoke to her through the grille. Linda was thin, bespectacled, and knew English, Malay and three Chinese dialects. She made one point forcibly during our first talk.

'I am a Malayan of Chinese descent. This is my country, and I have never worked for China or Chinese supremacy.'

'I believe you, Linda, and I know it, but you know how our Chinese origin is used against us, under any pretext.'

The police had tried to deport her to China, but it could not be done because she was born in Malaya of parents born in Malaya, and her Malay was perfect.

I would go to see her several times in jail; then she came out and worked for the Institute for about a year and a half. I

paid her salary, as I also paid for several other projects of the
Institute. I seldom saw Linda, chiefly because I had nothing
to say to her, partly because she was not allowed to cross the
Straits and come to Johore Bahru. We never really became
friends, although I did help her a little. Jail, I think, had
made her suspicious and bewildered. The events that took
place after 1960 were to increase her bewilderment. But I
think that she also avoided me because, in 1960, I began to
quarrel openly with the Malayan Communist Party on the
subject of Nanyang University.

Vincent's job in Nepal had ended in February 1958. The
road from Kathmandu across the foothills and the plains to
India was built. Vincent left the Indian army a few weeks
later. In 1958 he managed to come for the first time, for
about a week, to Singapore.

His coming was due to Leonard. Leonard was going that
summer to England, to take a course in adult education. He
had done well, and seemed headed to become the Director of
the Department for the whole of Singapore. However, in
1959, owing to the defeat of Lim Yewhock's government and
the victory of Harry Lee's PAP, Leonard would lose his job,
as the PAP now made a political appointment to the vacancy.
I had again asked for a divorce. But Leonard, I think, felt
that we might come together again. 'I'll never give you a
divorce. Tell that bastard I'll smash his face in if I see
him . . . Tell the coward to come here and I'll smash his jaw.'
Obviously Leonard was a bit irritable that day.

'Very well, I'll tell him.' I cabled Vincent: 'Come to
Singapore.' And Vincent came to Singapore. I told him that
Leonard wanted to smash his face in. 'I think the time has
come for a showdown.'

Loko Wantho loaned us his luxurious penthouse flat so
that we had total privacy. From the fifteenth floor of the
Cathay building, we saw all of Singapore, its lights and the
phosphorescent sea beyond the sequinned city. I drove
Vincent early the next morning to the Adult Education
Office and went as usual to my clinic. We were to meet for

lunch at the Cockpit Restaurant. 'If I have any jaw left,' said Vincent. The Cockpit was the breeding ground and hothouse for all Singapore gossip; I felt the time had come to flaunt my wonderful new man. That would keep everyone in Singapore busy for a while.

I was at the Cockpit early and Vincent came in, pretending to hold his jaw when he saw me. 'You know, Leonard is not a bad chap at all,' said he, grinning hugely. As if I had ever said the contrary!

Vincent and Leonard had arranged to go to dinner that night. Together. They came back very late to Wantho's flat, both slightly drunk, and hoarsely cheerful. I was, of course, extremely mortified. Oh, that complicity, that solidarity of men! 'You're angry because he didn't hit me aren't you?' said Vincent. The next day we three lunched together, at the Adelphi, a widely popular restaurant. My lawyer, Anthony Hills, was appalled. 'You're messing up any chances of a divorce.' But I trusted Leonard and luck.

We then thought up a plan, together with Anthony. Leonard was to go to London in July for his course. There he was to commit adultery (or pretend to) and furnish me with the evidence. Then, said Anthony, the divorce would take place before a court in London, and all silliness and publicity in Singapore or Malaya would be avoided.

'But I don't know any women in London,' protested Leonard. I then decided that I would ask Hans to help in respect of procuring an eligible partner for the misdemeanour to be committed.

Hans had told me one day that he had probably slept with a thousand women. Considering that since then the estimable writer Simenon has claimed a score of ten thousand, Hans was being moderate.

Hans replied with exuberant alacrity. The main difficulty, he wrote, after due consultation with Leonard, was to find a suitable companion. Leonard seemed disinclined to do anything to help. Hans had to find someone more or less respectable, not a streetwalker, as this would not impress an English court and would smack of collusion. Hans had 'just

what is needed . . . a virtuous lady in Manchester . . .'
Because Leonard showed continuing indolence in the
matter, Hans promised money to the Mancunian lady, and I
cabled him a hundred pounds for all incidentals.

In the course of time Leonard duly posted some hotel bills
to me. I handed them to Anthony. The case began in
London; not a word leaked into Singapore.

But alas, the lady had taken to Leonard, and refused to
recognize him. The case fell through. 'There's only one other
way. Leonard must divorce me,' I declared.

Anthony said this was highly dangerous. Leonard might
ask for a vast sum of money, and he might get it. But I
thought this would not happen. 'You don't understand
Leonard; he's an honourable man.'

For the time being, however, as I was extremely busy with
other matters, I decided not to press Leonard again. We
three would often lunch together, to the puzzlement of all
Singapore, and no bitterness or rancour, only good will and
amity, were left in our relations.

CHAPTER 9

The Leap in China: 1959–1960

In 1959 I began to teach in Nanyang University a three-month course entitled Contemporary Asian Literature. I taught at night, twice a week, for two hours. I was not paid, and at the end the Board, because some members were against my presence, declared that the course could not count towards graduation.

My intention was not only to open the minds of the students to what was happening elsewhere in Asia (colonialism had been only too successful in separating us from each other), but also to teach myself about other Asian countries. I wanted, besides, to have Malays admitted to Nanyang University and to make Malay one of the languages taught there.

But there was strong resentment, even among some progressive students, to admittance of Malays. The new set-up in independent Malaya privileged Malays so heavily that Nanyang University appeared to the Chinese students to be the last refuge for the Chinese-educated stream. Even if a Chinese student obtained the highest examination marks, he often was not granted admission to the new University at Kuala Lumpur, or to Singapore University; a Malay with lower marks would be given a place.

In 1959 the overseas Chinese situation exploded in Indonesia. Sukarno passed edicts to take all retail shops and all commerce out of Chinese hands. This led to pogroms, to racial strife, to the killing of many Chinese, but did not solve Indonesian economic problems; neither would it bring into being, suddenly, an Indonesian-manned web of trade and commerce. Consequently Indonesia would in the following years endure enormous inflation and countryside penury in consumer goods, which substantially eroded Sukarno's prestige and power. It is very risky to destroy one system of distribution and exchange and leave it to fate, heaven, chance suddenly to create the knowledge, the people and the capital, for another one.

This would not happen in Malaya, probably because of Prime Minister Tunku Abdul Rahman. It was due to his singular quality of tolerance (and a very shrewd sense of timing) that the extremists in his party,* who wanted to do the same thing as in Indonesia, were curbed.

In March 1959 I was asked by Ed Murrow to participate in his television programme, Small World. I was to discuss China together with Joseph Alsop and Robert Boothby.

Alsop was in America, I was in Hong Kong, Boothby in London. The hook-ups worked without a hitch and although I could not see his face, the heartening presence of Murrow filled the studio. I enjoyed the interview very much, especially as, it seems, I won the debate. This is what the *Reporter* had to say about it on April 2nd, 1959: 'As for the clobbering of Joseph Alsop by Han Suyin, that was history . . . The Asian writer caught the American columnist in statements about her China which were so sweeping in their assumptions and so dubious in their analogies that her indignation seemed amply justified. It was a great show.'

In 1974, reading Jo Alsop's columns and articles after he had (at last) visited China, I was glad to note that he seemed to have forgotten the gratuitous and startling assertions he was making in 1958. It takes courage (or amnesia) to contradict oneself so thoroughly.

Harry Sions, editor of *Holiday* magazine, had been delighted with my article, 'Peking Revisited', and now wanted one on Shanghai. He also discussed with me the possibility of a book on Mao. Inadvertently, after a public lecture of mine on China at Singapore University, the newspapers quite wrongly reported that I was going back to China to write a book on Mao Tsetung. I denied this, saying that I did not think I could even see Mao, but acknowledged

---

*UMNO: the United Malay National Organization.

that of course many people were tempted to write on a man of his stature. But the harm was done.

Apparently in China some middle cadre got hold of a garbled version of this and it was assumed that I had 'arrogantly' said I would interview Mao. And Chairman Mao was sacrosanct, to be mentioned only with the greatest reverence. But in that year of 1959, all was not well in China. There was irritability. Effluvia of this irritability seeped to me through Cousin Pengju in Hong Kong, who was bewildered by the refusal of visas, the tone of certain articles. Even if he worked for a Communist newspaper, Pengju and others like him in Hong Kong kept open their eyes and ears. They realized that the manner in which certain events were explained by China's propaganda organs was no explanation at all. An English friend of mine put it succinctly: 'China really needs peace, wants peace; the Chinese are honest, loyal and trustworthy, but the language that comes across makes them sound arrogant, boastful, conceited and bellicose.'

I had applied in March 1959, while in Hong Kong for the Ed Murrow television programme, for a visa to China, not only because I had in mind writing the article on Shanghai, but also because I had been invited to attend, in Canada, the Twenty-Eighth Couchiching Conference, organized by Toronto University and the Institute of Public Affairs of Canada. The letter of invitation from the President of the Canadian Institute, Murray Ross, was most cordial. The topic of the conference was to be 'Changing Asia' and I was expected to comment on China, on the Leap, the communes. Horrifying tales were circulating (à la Alsop) about the communes. Millions of people, it was said, had died in them; the communes were concentration camps where husbands and wives were segregated, and so on.

It was obvious that the Canadian government regarded the Couchiching Conference as an important platform for soundings about China. Since 1950, the government of Canada had tried to recognize China. In 1956 it had tried again, and now in 1959.

I was refused a visa for China. Why was I turned down? Because of this silly report that I was supposed to write a book on Mao and interview him. Yet my denial had been printed too. I again wrote, asking for a visa. Pengju encouraged me. Every time I wanted to write a letter to Peking, I had to use ways and means to get it delivered through Hong Kong, because of the censorship in Malaya. All this was rather nerve-fraying, and above all the growing feeling that perhaps, through the assessment of some cadre who put me down as 'unfriendly', I would never be allowed back to China.

Again I wrote, and cabled Kung Peng. No answer. The Couchiching Conference was taking place from August 8th to 16th; I suggested that I should visit China in July, as I had to be in Canada by August 6th and I needed some time to study and prepare my main speech, which was to be on social changes in China. I worried, worried. In March the Tibetan revolt had burst and the Dalai Lama had fled to India; the whole world was indignant at China's 'aggression', forgetting that Tibet was part of China. One of the best orchestrated propaganda campaigns occurred, at least five major Western countries co-operating, presswise, in this massive onslaught on China. And I would have to go to Canada without adequate preparation: without having seen the communes, which had only come to birth the previous summer; without being able to talk to Kung Peng in Peking about the events in Tibet.

I got a violent attack of psychosomatic colitis; and to cure myself flew to Calcutta. And there was Vincent, at the airport barrier, waiting. It was now June, and I had not seen him since the previous November. 'I am ill,' I said to him. 'I'll make you well,' he said. And just being with him cured me; my pain left me, and I fell asleep on his shoulder in the taxi taking us to the hotel. I slept twelve hours, my first good sleep in some weeks, and Vincent was there, by the bedside, when I woke up.

From Calcutta we took the train for Bhilai. Vincent was now working in a private concern belonging to Spitz, a very irascible Czech–Jew who had left Czechoslovakia for India when Hitler invaded his country. A small spare parts and equipment factory was being set up next to the Bhilai steel plant, which had been erected for the Indian government by the USSR, and there Vincent worked.

It was 130 degrees in the shade, the air like boiling glue; and I lay and sweated on a mat, sweating out the hours and my anxiety. And to Bhilai came a telegram fron Cousin Pengju announcing that a visa had been granted for August, or after October. Pengju wrote: 'Kung Peng was away and then she was ill; her office did not see the necessity for an immediate visa.' 'Peking is a bit isolated emotionally,' I wrote back to Pengju. 'It has no sense of urgency.' Here was the Dalai Lama, giving press conferences and interviews and speaking of the near-annihilation of his country. And there was the Couchiching Conference due in August in Canada ... I had no time now to go to China and then to Canada, and my intestinal troubles returned. I was angry, and wrote directly to Premier Chou Enlai, and after having made the necessary arrangements for the clinic – hiring another medical assistant – I flew off to Toronto.

The Conference was held in a series of bungalows built on the edge of Lake Couchiching. The motto of the conference was plain living and high thinking. High living and plain thinking would have been more agreeable. But, deliberately, the guests of the Conference lived in spartan conditions, and Murray Ross, looking like a boy scout, plunged into the cold lake water every morning.

The Conference was meant to represent all shades of opinion, and the Canadians had truly exerted themselves in that direction. But as one of them wryly said, 'We have got Big Brother watching us', meaning America. And the time picked could not have been less propitious. Never had I known public opinion more hostile to China than in 1959, because of the 'invasion' of Tibet, and the 'atrocities' of the communes. I pointed out that there had been no 'invasion' or 'aggression' in Tibet, since Tibet had been recognized even by Nehru as an integral part of China. But so many people were impervious to reasoning, almost hysterical in their verbal violence against China.

The unease and worry I felt about what was happening in China itself increased. Then I suddenly remembered someone I should not have forgotten. Robert Godet.

Robert Godet was a French explorer who had spent some months in the Tibetan monasteries in Kalimpong, on the Indian side of the Himalayas. The Indian army became suspicious of his movements and he was asked to leave; India was at the time coping with a Naga revolt in Assam and did not like Westerners travelling around these territories. Godet had come to Singapore in February 1958, and told me, 'There is going to be war between India and China.' He also told me that the Americans were parachuting weapons, in connivance with the Indians, to Tibetan guerrillas, and training Tibetan 'resistance' fighters in India and in the United States. 'Tell your Chinese friends the whole of Tibet will blow up,' said Godet. I paid no attention; a rupture between India and China appeared to me incredible at the time; yet already in 1958, letters, increasingly abrupt and irritable, were being exchanged between the foreign ministries of India and China. And now, in Couchiching, the hostility of the Indian delegate greatly disturbed me.

The Americans had a galaxy of talent, including Reischauer, United States Ambassador to Japan, an expert on Asia, a pleasant person with a Japanese wife. The recurrent thesis of many participants was the consolidation of the rest of Asia against China, that China must be kept 'under threat . . . until a change occurs in its system . . . that China must be "compelled" to behave in a civilized (?) way.' This 'pressure', to be exerted on behalf of democracy was the line of the US State Department, and the State Department was determined to win at Couchiching. But the Canadians did manage some opposition. The Americans were unable to get total condemnation of China, despite the help of the Indian representative. But the words 'invasion' and 'bellicose', 'aggressive madmen' and 'hideous massacres and atrocities' hovered like circling buzzards about Lake

Couchiching. And I could not shoot them all down.

While I was in Toronto, my sister Marianne began to ring me up, night after night, pouring out her pitiful frenzies, breathing her paranoid phantasms at me like liquor, all the way from Arizona. It gave me insomnia, and again bad bouts of stomach ache which now combined with rather severe haemorrhages to depress me. I flew back via London to India, stopping in New Delhi for a few more days with Vincent. And there I was again comforted and made whole. Despite the growing friction, my friend Natwar Singh, with whom I had had so many delightful rambles when he was a diplomat studying Chinese in Peking, came to see me. I also met the blind writer Ved Mehta of the *New Yorker*, who was travelling with Dom Moraes, son of the editor of the *Indian Express*. Dom Moraes lived in England and was about to receive the Hawthornden Prize for his poetry. Both of them had called upon the Dalai Lama and interviewed him; Dom described the Dalai's youth, his bewildered, naïve air, short-sighted eyes and striped socks. I knew the socks; they were the kind I had seen woven by the prisoners in the Peking model jail; they were being sold all over China. 'He's brought a lot of gold out of Tibet,' said my friend, the photographer P. N. Sharma, who was still waiting for his Russian girlfriend to be processed out of Moscow and to join him in India.

There was at this time an uproar in the Indian parliament over the news that the Chinese had built a road through the Aksai Chin region, now suddenly considered 'sacred soil of India', although Indian maps printed in Britain before 1950 had the region labelled 'undefined', and not included within India.

Felix Greene landed in Delhi. Felix had been Malcolm MacDonald's secretary, and I had first met him with Malcolm in 1956, when Felix was trying to get to China. He had, so far, not succeeded, although I had introduced him to Pengju. An idealistic, thoroughly sincere man, Felix was greatly agitated by what had happened in Tibet. Although he got the Chinese publications in London, he was unable to understand them, so badly did they present the Chinese view. Felix went to call on the Dalai Lama, and also went to see Krishna Menon, India's Defence Minister, whom I think he had known in England when Krishna was a member of the British Labour Party. Krishna, who lived on strong tea and made immensely long speeches (seven hours was nothing to him), played a magnificent melodramatic scene for Felix, holding his head in his hands, body bowed in agony, saying, 'Why, oh why are the Chinese doing this to us?' Felix was most impressed, although Vincent snorted gently, knowing his fellow-Indians and their genius for drama. So off Felix went to Burma, to see the Chinese Ambassador there. 'Read what we have published', he was told. Now he entreated me. 'Suyin, do tell them in Peking that they're not doing enough; the whole world is being turned against them.' 'I'll try.' I would also try (and succeed) in getting a visa for him; he would go to China in the summer of 1960.

I did not go to see the Dalai Lama (although I could easily have done so). I contented myself with listening to the Indian officials around me, and I realized how superior to the Chinese they were propaganda-wise. They had, of course, the advantage of writing directly in English, whereas all of the Chinese information was translated – and so badly translated.

I went back to Malaya. And then the border incidents between China and India, which had been multiplying, exploded into an armed clash, and there was an enormous outcry of 'betrayal' and 'invasion' by India and the rest of the world. China's 'expansionism' and 'aggression' were now blatant, according to every newspaper I saw.

I wrote two articles for the *Globe and Mail* of Canada, pointing out how the word 'aggression' was bandied about with little evidence to bolster it. My articles were necessarily limited, and certainly did not defend China. But they were meant to introduce some reason and common sense into the unmanageable hysteria which seemed to have seized so many intelligent people. And four days after writing them I left for China.

If in China in 1957 my doorstep had been 'cold' (which meant that I was officially ignored), it was Arctic Siberia now for me. From the moment I stepped down in Kuangchow it was obvious that I was in profound disfavour. The China Travel Service lady who took charge of me did not smile. She mentioned an interpreter, services to be paid by the day. Steady as a dripping tap, she aligned figures. I told her I did not need an interpreter. She said it was customary. I said I never had an interpreter . . .

No aeroplane ticket to Peking was available to me. I would have to go by train. There was no free compartment, only a top berth, with three men. All the hotels in Peking were booked; I must apply for a hotel when I got there.

At breakfast in the train the next morning I saw some Europeans, obviously 'fraternal delegates', eating three eggs and bacon with mounds of toast and marmalade. I asked for two eggs.

The restaurant waiter said, 'Oh, not for you, comrade, it's only for honoured guests from abroad.'

'I'm also from abroad.'

He chuckled. 'I thought you were a Uighur, from Sinkiang. One of us.'

He himself was a Hui, a Chinese Muslim. We became very friendly and he quietly slipped me one egg. Suddenly I felt no longer lonely. We chatted. 'There is a shortage of eggs this year; we keep them for honoured guests.'

In the train corridor stood two fraternal comrades from a communist party of a Western country, surrounded by a respectful cohort of Chinese officials.

'My, oh my, isn't it wonderful?' said one.

'Yes,' said the other, 'now in our country, that factory out there would stink, we'd have a terrible smell for miles around, but here, not a smell.'

'That's socialism in action,' said the other.

The suet of flattery oozed thick from their mouths; the six

Chinese who accompanied them (the more people in one's retinue, the higher one's rank) nodded and smiled happily. These were 'friendly' comrades. I recognized one of the two Anglo-Saxons. In fact, I had treated him for some eczematous eruption in Casualty in Hong Kong some years ago.

I nudged one of the Chinese on the rim of the gathering. 'I know this honoured guest. I'd like to greet him.'

The Chinese comrade looked me up and down. 'On what grounds do you wish to speak to the honoured guest?'

'On the ground that I was the doctor who treated his illness some years ago.'

The matter was relayed echelon by echelon, until it reached the top Party comrade who then deferentially told the honoured guest who deigned to look at me, and recognized me. He shook hands heartily, but with a shade of condescension. After all, I was only a bourgeois and I had no retinue, so I couldn't be important in China.

'You're here too, good, good. Nice to see you.'

Five years later, the same honoured guest would distinguish himself by his vituperations against China, and especially on the miserable state of the factories during the Leap.

Arrival in Peking; there was no place at the Hsinchiao Hotel. I had to go to a much smaller hotel. No room with bath, of course. No one to carry my luggage. I dropped a note to Kung Peng at the Foreign Ministry. Then waited. During those days of waiting I went out with Wang Wanchun, went to Papa's house, went to see Hualan. Wanchun took me out to a good restaurant, and we drank *maotai*, a very potent spirit from my province.

'Wanchun, there are queues and shortages in the shops.'

'We'll talk about it some other time.'

'How was Khrushchev's visit?' Khrushchev had arrived for October 1st, straight from meeting President Eisenhower at Camp David in September.

'We'll talk about it some other time,' said Wanchun.

From other friends, more loquacious, and from the

Western journalists at the Hsinchiao, my impression was confirmed. There was irascibility; tension. There were shortages. 'It's the Leap.' There were rumours also that 'something' had happened. A 'rift' with Russia was now openly discussed. The Western journalists at that time were all for Khrushchev. 'There he came, bouncing down from the plane like a rubber ball . . . he'd just made a big scoop . . . the Chinese stood like stone figures. Mao did not smile.'

I was received promptly, within four days, at the Foreign Ministry by Miss Chen. Miss Chen was Kung Peng's right hand, a quiet, hardworking girl, but our interview was at first unpleasant. It was obvious that I had done something wrong, unnerving, 'unfriendly'. Said Miss Chen: China was an *organized* country, there was a routine for visas and I had been given a visa. Why did I not come then? I was, by that time, quite ill, I told her. And afterwards it was too late. Miss Chen pointed out that the newspapers had referred to my writing about Chairman Mao. 'How can you believe every word you read in the outside newspapers? Do you believe what they write about you, and didn't you read my denial?' (So I was right in my guess. It was the reference to my possibly writing about Mao which had caused the refusal.) I mentioned Couchiching. 'We are not interested,' said Miss Chen. Neither were they interested in the Small World television show with Jo Alsop. 'Why are you people so arrogant?' I said abruptly. 'Why do you think you don't need people outside to put things straight?' Miss Chen, a very honest and shy person, opened her eyes wide with surprise. She had only done her duty as transmission belt for all the noes, and being a really nice girl, she immediately began, I think, to interrogate herself mutely. Had she, somehow, failed in courtesy? She looked at me, and did not reply. And suddenly the tone changed; she was no longer admonishing a child. We were talking. She took, even if unwillingly, the Small World tape which I gave her.

'Have a look at it. It will give you a better idea of what is being said about China abroad, and why Couchiching was necessary, even if you were not interested.'

'But what we publish—' began Miss Chen.

'It's no use, no use at all,' I said furiously, 'and anyway there is censorship in Malaya, and every time I want to read something I have to fly to Hong Kong.'

I grew to admire and really like Miss Chen, who had a thankless job; she was the person who had to 'admonish' and 'guide' newsmen who went wrong; because China never did censor messages or cables sent out. Simply, after a while, the Ministry issued warnings to newsmen considered not to be reporting properly. This duty fell upon Miss Chen.

Three more days, and I now saw Kung Peng, together with Miss Chen. Kung Peng had been very ill and she had also done a stint of labour in the countryside. And now I tried to give them an idea of the kind of emotion that was being propagated against China abroad. They were aware, but not entirely, not of its enormous impact: 'The work of a few reactionaries . . . the people are not fooled.' 'Oh yes they are.' But it is difficult to convey an atmosphere. 'We have stated correctly all the facts,' Kung Peng kept saying. 'But when people get emotional they ignore facts: and newspapers give them emotion, not facts.'

We talked for a long time, and all was well. I went back to the small hotel quite happily. My doorstep might be cold and I was lonely and not courted, but this did not mean I could not see my friends. The next day there was a room vacant at the Hsinchiao Hotel.

Hualan, who had been ill with a nervous breakdown, was very much better, although her organization still entreated her to rest, and sent her work to her home so that she might not tire herself. I asked her straightaway about Russia. After all, Hualan had been many years in Russia, and her mother was Polish. 'I think if we quarrel I shall feel the world has come to a stop.' But a few days later she said, 'Well, we must go on. Even friends quarrel.'

There was also a rumour of a crisis within the Party involving Peng Tehuai, the Minister of Defence. But this was countered by another rumour that Peng was doing a very hush job somewhere. However, the number of articles condemning 'right-opportunist ideas' among 'some cadres' pointed to some very furious inner debate.

I went to see Anna-Louise Strong. Anna-Louise, an American, was housed in a flat just below Rewi Alley, in the compound of what had once been the Italian Embassy and was now the Peace Council. In 1959 strains were already showing in the Peace Council and its solemn meetings, but neither Rewi nor anyone else would discuss this with me.

Anna-Louise had been in China in the 1920s; she had chronicled the early Revolution in some excellent books. She had known Ho Chih Minh then, and Borodin, and when the massacres of the Communists by Chiang Kaishek started she left China via the Gobi Desert in a car driven by Percy Chen, the ebullient, always happy, unbeatable-at-tennis son of the erstwhile Foreign Minister of China, Eugène Chen, who had been an overseas Chinese and Sun Yatsen's great friend.

Anna-Louise scarcely remembered this epic journey through China, although it was no mean feat to drive right through China when heads were rolling in every city, right through Central Asia and the Gobi Desert, and on through the steppes, across Siberia to Moscow . . . which is what Percy had done, bringing Anna-Louise to safety. 'It was unbearably hot,' was all Anna-Louise ever said to me about this Marco Polo-ish journey.

Anna-Louise stayed some years in Russia, but in the 1950s fell foul of Stalin and was denounced as a 'spy' and expelled. Immediately her own Party and many of her friends disowned her. 'No one asked my side of the story,' said Anna-Louise. She had been back in China in the 1940s during the war with Japan. She went to the Communist base at Yenan and was received by Mao Tsetung several times, notably in 1946, when she had a very famous interview with him, published as 'The atom bomb is a paper tiger'. And now she was back to live in China, since 1958 a guest of the government, and a most honoured one. Although seventy, she was incredibly active, pouring out articles and books, composing her 'Letter from China', which she sent to hundreds of Americans.

She loudly discounted all talk of a rift between China and Russia as absolute nonsense, and 'imperialist propaganda'. The old lady dreaded being left alone, and Rewi would say, 'Do go and chat with Anna-Louise', and all of us who could do so would drop in.

'I think people are very busy at the moment,' I said.

She asked me if I had heard about shortages.

'Yes, I have.'

'It's true then. But I had thought the harvests were terrific . . .'

I said, 'I've read Chou Enlai's report on China's 1959 economic plan. He mentions strains and problems and serious natural calamities.' In such a tremendous Leap Forward there were bound to be problems cropping up.

'When has anything new been easy or successful the first time? China is carving out a new road for mankind,' said Rewi Alley, who had come to join our talk.

The news of the poor harvest had by now solidified. It was 'quite bad', which meant rotten. There had been much drought in the north, floods in the south, and the cotton crop was affected. As for meat, it was becoming scarce. But one reason for its scarcity was that the peasants in the communes, in their delirious joy that 'communism has now come', had stuffed themselves with vast amounts of pork flesh, each peasant eating and carousing. 'Why save? The government will provide. This is communism.'

I visited the ten large public buildings erected in Peking to commemorate the tenth year of the People's Republic, 1959. Kung Peng told me she had worked on some of the marble tiles of the Great Hall of the People, polishing and polishing them, and 'Now I look at all that expanse of floor, and at the marble pillars, and I wonder which are the tiles I polished,' she said.

In railway sheds, in the courtyards of houses, in the basketball grounds of schools, I saw the relics of small brick furnaces; they had been used to make steel in the great steel drive of 1958. They were now partly ripped up, but black soot still encrusted their brick bases and a pipe or two lay forlorn athwart the ruin. It had been a truly fantastic endeavour: everyone had been making steel. 'There was soot all over the streets and all over the city; at night it was like a million fireflies. The masses now understood better the need for steel and for industrialization.' My friends said this but they also had reservations Each of them had made steel; but what was the point of making it in these small, primitive, hand-built stoves? 'But even mistakes are necessary . . . sometimes we learn more through making mistakes . . .'

'It's to wrest our people, by the only methods at our command, out of feudalism and into the modern era,' said Third Brother. He too had made steel, and 'it was hard to get the soot out of my hair . . . the city ran out of soap.'

Even the beautiful Madame Soong Chingling had made steel, setting an example. And millions of schoolchildren had made steel.

Looking at the ineffective small craters which littered the streets, I wondered. Were they, had they really been educative in their starkness? Well, perhaps. As I walked on and on, an immense warmth and protectiveness came upon me. 'It's fantastic, magnificent, appalling . . . and also perhaps idiotic . . . I don't know . . . no one else would have the courage to try this . . . you're trying to tell all of us that we must rely on ourselves, do everything the hard way because there is no other way, because we're going to be let down . . .' Thus I apostrophized my love, the faceless multi-millioned, whose courage and fortitude gripped my heart; and I both loved and of course feared, because its immensity would certainly swallow me. 'I'm with you, with you.' What could I do to speed up the process of maturation? I then had a brief, elusive vision of what it implied: one quarter of humanity, informed, intelligent, not submitting to fate and to the vagaries of tyrants . . . was this too much to expect? 'Teach me to feel things correctly,' I said to the small brick base with its derelict pipe. The Westerners in the Hsinchiao Hotel had not stopped laughing at the steel drive and I could not bear their laughter. 'It may be silly, but at least you're trying, trying to make the sun and the moon shine in a new heaven. Silly or not, I'm with you.'

'Our tenth year is not too lucky a one,' said Hualan, brewing coffee (a strangely flavoured one, an early crop from Hainan Island) in her living room. Tibet, Indonesia, India, and of course the unspoken, indigestible morsel, the trouble with the USSR. In Indonesia almost two million Chinese had been deprived of a living, and several hundred thousand were being repatriated to China in Chinese-chartered vessels. Yet many of those leaving had been born in Indonesia. Chen Yi had greatly exerted himself, with skill and patience, finally settling the matter of the Chinese in Indonesia, but of course it had been an added burden and expense on China when resources were strained by the Leap.

Hualan denied the rumour that major insults had been exchanged behind closed doors between Khrushchev, when he had come to Peking from seeing President Eisenhower, and his Chinese hosts. 'These are bad people who tell such things.' On the contrary, at the ballet evening Khrushchev and Mao had exchanged pleasantries about the beauty of the dancers, pleasantries which had left the translators round-eyed with shock.

I walked the streets and noted the first faint signs of tension, lassitude. People were thinner, they bustled less. Rations were being cut. There was a lot of cabbage being sold, but little else. The waiter in a restaurant reproved me for leaving some grains of rice at the bottom of my rice bowl.

I tried to get a haircut at the Peking Hotel, but was turned out. 'Comrade, this is only for honoured guests from outside.' I telephoned my family. Fourth Brother was in Manchuria, Third Brother was busy . . . I received a message, a certain Comrade Ku would see me; I was to go to his residence at five p.m. He seemed to be an important official, and would decide on a programme for me.

I duly arrived, around ten minutes to five; a woman servant opened the door. She seemed to recognize me when I murmured, 'Comrade Ku asked me to come', and showed me into a tiny study, where I sat. Next to the study were presumably Mr Ku's lodging quarters, for I could see another room with a narrow bed, a table and a chair. I sat and waited. And suddenly there was some commotion in the courtyard. I could hear the maid's voice: 'But she is waiting inside.'

Mr Ku erupted into the study. 'What are you doing in this room? You should never have come here.'

'Your servant put me here,' I said.

'It's a mistake,' he shouted. 'I have been waiting for you at the door.'

He ushered me across the courtyard into the living room, which was fairly large, with a big velvet-covered sofa and chairs. He was quite angry and our conversation was painful.

'I heard you want to go to Shanghai.'

'Yes, I do.'

'You must read our material on Shanghai. It is now a major industrial city. Can you do translations?'

'I don't think so . . . people usually translate me.'

'Translations are important. You should train yourself to translate.'

For a moment I thought he was offering me a job at the Foreign Language Press. He then began to explain 'policy'. 'We distinguish between enemies and friends. Facts are facts. We always rely on facts.'

'But there is also compromise,' I began.

'Never,' he shouted, 'we shall never compromise on principles.' He thought I was pleading for 'compromise' with Soviet Russia. 'We have the policies of Chairman Mao. We shall never compromise on these.'

The reason for my use of the word 'compromise' was because that very afternoon, at Hsinchiao Hotel, I had met some foreign diplomats and all of them had talked of Chinese 'intransigence'. 'The Chinese are behaving like arrogant mandarins now that Khrushchev wants to come to an understanding with the US.' The 'irascibility' of many officials in Peking was commented on. 'The Chinese seem to have a bad case of nerves,' said an Englishman. Other newsmen complained: 'We can't make contact with anyone . . . there's a sound barrier as well as an emotion barrier, no one gets through. The Great Leap has failed . . . and because of the border trouble with India, China hasn't got a friend in the world today . . . not even Russia. Some kind of compromise *must* be found to get out of the impasse.'

I had seized on the word 'compromise', used it with Mr Ku, and had greatly angered him. 'We shall never compromise on principles,' he repeated. 'You do not seem well-informed about our policies, you should read more, listen to our radio broadcasts.'

I forbore to tell him that radio or not, I could not *understand* what I read outside; only when I read the Chinese newspapers and was steeped in China's own atmosphere did it all begin to make excellent sense. It did not make sense to me abroad . . . But Mr Ku now looked at his watch, and we shook hands and I left. It had rained and the lane was narrow. I walked close to the wall, but a large black car went by and sloshed me with mud. Mr Ku, going to his next appointment. I became furious. I rang up Wanchun and told him about it. 'Old Ku is a good guy really, he is just a little stuck in his ways,' said Wanchun, who had now done eight months of manual labour and had got over his fear of denouncing Party cadres. He cheered me with funny stories, then told me soberly that there was a terrible drought in the north: 'That's why I think the winter will be bad.' A day later I was on my way to Shanghai.

All along the railway to Shanghai, I saw the impetus of the Leap Forward. Electric pylons bestriding the land, and the new shape of the fields, straight-edged; horizon-reaching rectangles where I remembered curvaceous small plots; a new geometry, defined by tree-lined canals. And new brick buildings with chimneys, obviously factories; and in every station enormous piles of machinery, steel rods, pumps, steel rails, awaiting transport to inland destinations. This impression of a frenetic upsurge in industrial building was confirmed during my ten days in Shanghai. Despite the errors of the Leap, the shortages owing to the agricultural disasters (which would become tragic in 1960–1), the Leap did achieve its main goal, which was accelerated industrial development.

All along the way I could see that the reports of 'natural calamities' were not exaggerations. Within the next two years, almost 70 per cent of the land, both in the north and the south, and even in Szechuan, would suffer from the vagaries of the weather. I crossed the Yellow River that October and missed it, as I had missed it on my way to Peking. For it was no more than a sand waste, with a narrow trough of water in its midst. And no one in the train said, 'We are now crossing the Yellow River.'

It was on this trip that I began to tell myself that I must study economics; try to relate what I read to what I saw. 'It is an obligation to acquire knowledge,' I repeated to myself. Only then would I be able to speak with coherence and authority. I would begin to teach myself, tracing first the history of the Industrial Revolution in the West, comparing the dislocations and the sufferings it had imposed upon Europe (for it was undoubtedly an agonizing process, causing enormous suffering to the people when it took place) and what was happening in China. And what had taken so long in Europe was now being telescoped into a few years, two or three decades, in China. Hence the hurry, the frenzy and the set-backs, the failures. Yet unless we in China hurried, we would fail.

And so to Shanghai; and immediately the sensation that here was a city at the heart of the Leap itself, an industrial city producing, producing. Not only because of the posters and the slogans and the exhortations: 'Walk on two legs', 'Self-reliance', but because of an air of excitement and well-being. The stores were full of manufactured goods and peasants walked and bought in the large department stores. Shanghai would not suffer as much as the other areas from the agricultural disasters which would be heaped upon the land for the next two years; both because its own countryside and communes would be relatively unharmed by natural calamities, and because it was working full blast on industrialization, its own industrial expansion and that of many sites inland. Already many thousands of able Shanghai workers were to be found scattered over wide areas of China; wherever a new industry was coming up, there one could find the thin, clever faces of Shanghai and hear the soft sibilant atonal Shanghai dialect, in Manchuria and in Szechuan, in Shensi and in Sinkiang. They spread technical knowledge, helping to train the millions of technicians required for the second Five Year Plan. The second Five Year Plan to end in 1962, was by definition to be over-fulfilled before time. Everywhere in the factories of Shanghai I heard of the plan having been over-fulfilled.

The most impressive thing about Shanghai was the new suburbs, forming satellite cities around it; there would be ten of them, each housing 300,000 to 500,000 people. Where there had been slums and fetid ponds were now parks, avenues with central flower beds, lined with buildings of new grey and red brick, four storeys high, flats for workers and their families, schools and hospitals and department stores.

Food shortages here were not apparent, nor was there that vague stir of unease which had begun in the north. But there were some itinerant pedlars on the streets selling crab claws and small dumplings, and the cadres turned a blind eye on this individual enterprise. For the pleasure of the ambience, I queued with others for the crab claws. None were left when my turn came. But the restaurants were full and well-stocked. And remembering the rationing in England, during the war, when many old people, alone, quietly and gently starved to death on rations, I thought that perhaps we too in China would see this, unless the next harvest was good. When it began to drizzle I was happy, for an autumn drizzle is excellent for the crops. And all around me people were saying, yes, there is rain, it is good for the crops, so that their main preoccupation, which was the harvest, would surface and their faces light up with quiet joy, and we all knew we were thinking the same way, were apprehensive in the same manner. In the communes round Shanghai different kinds of hardy and more productive rice were being tried, and the weather and its vagaries were discussed with great abandon. And flocks of sparrows went undisturbed, and films were shown praising 'useful' birds.

I visited at least a dozen factories, large and small. I saw a small one where pumps and other equipment were being made by old workers who had come out of retirement to help in the Great Leap. Everywhere this had happened; people coming to volunteer. By dint of energy and handcraft and patience these old men were producing some machinery; they chiselled and planed with small, inadequate hand tools. Their faces, lined and tired, were beautiful with quiet faith. Truly they believed that soon, soon, want would be over for ever, and plenty would come, freedom from hardship and penury . . . and they worked towards that new human freedom to come. 'We've been through the bad old times, we never want them again.' ABOLISH SUPERSTITION, UNFETTER THE MIND, shouted all the walls of the factories. DARE TO TEACH WATER TO CLIMB MOUNTAINS was carved on rock along roads we drove along. And everywhere in large characters was painted the motto of the Leap: TO DO THINGS FASTER, BETTER, MORE ECONOMICALLY BUT WITH GREATER RESULTS.

'Like ants,' said Comrade Liu, who took me around, 'gnawing a bone. We have to keep on gnawing at difficulties and obstacles, to make them disappear . . .'

Poetry came out from the people. Everywhere, in the city and in the communes. Poems of the Leap. And there were the women, now so visible, everywhere, working in the small factories in each lane; almost every small factory had a big story to tell. One grandmother led all the grandmothers in her street to start a small repair shop; now they were producing electric spare parts. 'We all want to do something to build up our country.'

The eradication of prostitution in Shanghai had taken

almost eight years, 'and we are still continuing with the movement,' said frail Miss Hu, who was in charge of the campaign. There had been altogether forty thousand registered prostitutes, and about the same number of unregistered, in the city of Shanghai before Liberation. 'There cannot truly be a women's liberation movement which does not also try to eradicate this most criminal and shameful blot upon womanhood,' said Miss Hu. Prostitution could only be eradicated through 'mass consciousness' of its evil. 'Some women, a very small percentage, like being prostitutes, or perhaps get used to it and see themselves as nothing else. Sometimes we talk to them all night, we do not let them go until we feel that an impression has been made.' Like water denting stone, the re-education programme went on and on, undiscouraged by temporary lapses. As for the pimps and the brothel keepers, 'They are the guilty ones. At first we talked to them, asking them to close the brothels voluntarily . . . we gave them six months in which to reform, then in November 1951 we issued our last warning. As you know, we have a system of graduated warnings. Many pimps and brothel keepers thought we were weak because we spoke softly,' said Miss Hu. They were being re-educated through labour; and some of them, the worst, were shot.

But reforming a prostitute also meant setting up a social system in which prostitution would be almost impossible, and this meant that both men and women must be conscious of the degradation of the human being that prostitution implies. It also involved moving the prostitutes away from Shanghai, where they were known; finding them work, getting them into a normal circuit of normal women, even getting them married. 'The prostitute is fundamentally frightened, frightened of everything.' More than 90 per cent of them were girls from the countryside lured to the big city of Shanghai by promise of good jobs and money in factories, and then sold into prostitution; or little girls, sold because of family want, in times of famine. 'Most of them cannot read or write. They are very emotional, getting angry, screaming, kicking, breaking things . . . but we never lose our tempers,

we never shout, we are patient, always, always we exhort.'
Miss Hu smiled like a small tired angel.

When the prostitutes begin to change mentally, they have
crises and nervous breakdowns. 'When people go from one
identity to another, they try to cling to what they think they
are . . . they feel they are losing themselves, when really all
they lose is a state of mind and a few habits.' (I know exactly
what Miss Hu is saying: have I not gone through this too?
Only two years ago the threat of a change of identity was
painful, unthinkable.) 'So we have to gauge when the
breaking point comes. It is when they appear most violent,
hostile, abusive, when outwardly it seems they will never
change. That is the death agony of the old self. Then there is
a period of semi-adaptation, a stuporous calm.' (Was I now in
a stuporous calm?)

'They become interested in new things, conscious of
having another function in society. They grope towards a
new being. But which one? How, where do they fit in? Can
they ever hope to be just like anyone else? There are vast
terrors in them still . . . most prostitutes have no sense of the
future. And now, suddenly, they have to think ahead. That is
when one has to be so cautious, so gentle, not to put them
off . . . We take them to parks, to enjoy flowers and birds
and trees, and to films, and to people who do not know what
they are and treat them like anyone else. We make them
participate in public campaigns such as that for planting
trees and flowers in the parks, or go to sewing and repair co-
operatives with other women who treat them as equals, who
think they are housewives . . .' The process at its shortest
took two years, sometimes five or six. 'But we have patience
and time, oh, plenty of time,' said Miss Hu. 'We never give
up, even if it takes ten years or more.' And never, said she,
must there be punishment or ostracism. 'They are victims,
they need care, affection . . .'

Linked to the eradication of prostitution was that of
venereal disease. Once again, it had to be done by the most
widespread propaganda, urging people to come to the clinics
for cure. 'No one is punished; on the contrary, people are

rewarded for coming up voluntarily.' Everyone suffering from venereal disease was treated free of charge, and then told to speak to others about it. This is what the Shanghai hospital doctors told me. As I knew already, the American doctor George Hatem – in Chinese Ma Haiteh – had been one of the chief medical experts in charge of this most successful drive.

Another clean-up was that of capitalists; and since Shanghai had been a great centre for business, it was appropriate that I should meet there efficient, handsome Mr Yung, who wore a Western suit and a very nice tie. He was now the manager of the factories he had once owned. He and his wife lived in their former house, a mansion with carpets, beautiful furniture and a large garden. The Cultural Revolution affected Mr Yung and his family, as it did every family in China. He had to leave the beautiful house he lived in and was reduced to a small worker's flat. But after two years of discomfort Mr Yung was given back his house. He is as neat and dapper today as when I saw him in that October of 1959. He is a member of the National People's Congress, a member of the People's Consultative Conference, a highly respected adviser on managerial matters, and represents one of the eight non-communist parties.

'It was difficult to adapt at first,' he said to me in October 1959, speaking of his first ten years under the communists. 'I wanted to resist, to burst out, sometimes to shout . . . but always I would talk it over with someone. I thought: who comes first, my people and my country, or me? When I remembered the humiliations we endured when we were weak and semi-colonized, there was no doubt in my mind. However I may dislike certain things, the Communist Party is, by and large, creating a strong, prosperous New China. No one will insult us again. And so my private resentments, which appeared large and important at first, became trivial. I grew into a feeling of oneness with others; sharing in everything, the good and the bad. I got peace of mind.'

That is what Mr Yung said twenty years ago, and having survived, he has proved his indestructibility.

One afternoon Comrade Liu came to say, 'You must now go back to Peking. Premier Chou Enlai wishes to see you.'

I was on the train that very evening; for with the small autumn rain soaking the land and fogging the fields, the aeroplane (which flew low and followed the markings of roads and railways) might not take off. I was in Peking by the end of the next day, and Comrade Ku was at the station, carrying a large fur coat. 'We were afraid you might be cold; you do not have enough clothes.' I was sorry that I had ever been angry with him. It was not his fault that his car had splashed mud on me. And I was such a maverick, not fitting into any pattern at all, no wonder I disconcerted Comrade Ku, and so many others.

Back at the Hsinchiao Hotel, I was told not to go out without leaving a message saying where I could be reached. The Premier was extremely busy, but would see me as soon as possible.

Kung Peng's friend Wu Chienta, a newsman who was also a student of foreign affairs, came to talk to me. I liked his company very much. He was a quiet, thoughtful young man with a steady intelligence; and we would entertain a lively correspondence in the course of the next twenty years. Wu was eminently reliable, had an astonishing memory and never misinterpreted any conversation or added any colour, weight or bias to anything I told him. In fact, he would correct me gently when I was inaccurate. We talked a great deal in the next few days, while I waited for Chou Enlai to be free, about foreign reactions to Chinese news coverage and information. 'It's most important to understand other people's psychological reactions,' said Wu. 'We don't have much opportunity to do so at present.'

The Hsinchiao Hotel was full of bad news about the harvests and the coming winter. 'There's going to be famine,' said one diplomat with a broad smile. I pored over the figures which had been published; the percentages. I could not understand them. I clung to Chou Enlai's casual words in his major report on the Chinese economy at the Leap; the *verified* figures, the *adjusted* plans . . . conceding that there had been inflated, unreliable reports, and that goals and targets had to be cut down for the future.

'Please, Hualan, tell me, how bad are things?'

'I don't think they are so bad, but there is certainly something wrong with the statistics.'

'I heard from the diplomats that the bureau of statistics had simply stopped working in 1958.'

'They did not have the techniques or the ability to cope with the reports which came up from below, and which appeared phantasmagorical to some of them.'

Thus a coal mine had reported mining in one day as many thousand tonnes of coal as it had mined in the previous year, and one man had had great praise lavished upon him because he boasted he could grow ten tonnes of wheat on a piece of land the size of a small room . . .

'People got carried away by their own enthusiasm,' said Hualan. 'They really believed that with three years of hard work they could magically transform the land. And many wonderful things have been done. But of course, temporarily, there was dislocation. No weighing machines in the new fields, and the fields were by then too large, so that no one really knew how much was produced. There were no bins to store the grain. The cadres just guessed at the harvest; much of it had not been harvested but left lying because the peasants had then been mobilized either into steel-making or into canal digging, and seventeen million people from the countryside had streamed into the new factories that were being built everywhere. In the south the banana trees were cut down in order to grow rice, and bananas were a staple crop producing ample income for many communes.

'We've also had an ultra-left wave,' said Hualan. Suddenly a rumour had spread: 'Communism is here.' And some communes had gone into an orgy of eating; killing pigs and ducks, and eating and eating. 'The government will give it back to you, this is communism.' Others had gone on a spree of buying, using all the funds they had been loaned by the government to purchase television sets, to erect cinemas. They had instituted free food, free clothes, free everything, including hair cuts. As a result, they had no reserves left.

And there had been a frenzy of work. 'Some cadres really had no common sense. They drove the work teams. Work, work, work.' A young man whom Hualan knew had worked around the clock, as a volunteer; and his heart had failed and he had died. 'Now we take death very seriously, as you know,' said Hualan. Within a week the most stringent orders had been given. Now everyone was guaranteed eight hours sleep.

There had been another anti-intellectual wave, when the peasants and the workers had been praised as 'the real heroes'. 'Of course they are heroic, but they don't know everything,' I said rashly. 'One must not pour cold water on the red hot fervour of the masses,' said Wanchun to me somewhat nervously. 'Does that mean no one can say: But it won't work?' He did not reply.

The engineers, the technical experts, the agricultural experts, knew that some of the claims made were sheer fantasy; they kept quiet. 'Because no rigorous scientific appraisal was made in time, there was no control over these massive projects . . . and the leaders were given all the wrong figures for many weeks.' But none of my friends would vouchsafe an explanation for this.

Hualan was having a small argument with her department because she wanted to change the sentence in an article: 'People who see this monument will faint and swoon with pleasure.' 'People who read this sentence,' said Hualan, 'will die of laughter.' I do not know whether she succeeded in changing it. I do know that several efforts of mine to change such confections ended always in dismal failure.

Again I would press Hualan about the USSR.

'I can only say that my Polish cousin has written a letter. She says Polish youth is now demoralized. And that in Russia people are getting away from socialism; they have been infected with the devil of "immediate enjoyment". They want good clothes, good things.' And the Russian collectives were not working well.

'Do you think the communes will work in China?'

'They're bound to work. It's a different system, and we have so many more poor peasants than Russia has. To our peasants the commune is an unbreakable iron bowl of rice.'

At the theatre, all round me, men and women were falling asleep in their seats. Tired and cold. 'We've all been told to rest more, and this winter, many offices will only operate half a day,' said Hualan. This state of affairs was to become more pronounced in 1960 when food became scarce. Hualan, her relatives, and many others voluntarily cut down their own rations of rice by one or two kilogrammes a month.

'There won't be any intellectuals to labour in the communes this winter,' said Wanchun. He had enjoyed his months in a commune. 'I learnt to lead a buffalo to water and to plant rice . . . when I came home, I realized how selfish I had been, letting my wife make up the fire, peel vegetables, cook, wash . . . now I help her. I feel ashamed that I had no eyes to see her labour.' He had also accompanied Chairman Mao, who indefatigably had gone into the provinces to find out what was really happening. 'You should have seen the Chairman, the concern on his face. He sat in the house of a very old woman, listening to her complaints, as if she were his mother.'

Third Brother came to see me. He told me that because of the food situation 'undesirables', that is, people with no occupation, were having to leave the city and be resettled in villages. The villages ate much better; they ate what they produced. It was the surplus that fed the cities. 'There isn't much surplus this year,' said Third Brother.

'Did anyone try to give warning in good time, when things went a bit out of control?' I asked my friend Yu, a biologist. He was studying insect pests and had been away for months in the rural areas, training peasants in recognizing and dealing with pests.

Yu smiled, turning his head away from me, letting the words float like gossamer upon the cold air, as if they did not belong to him. 'People who tried to warn about excessive zeal would again be called rightists . . . and you know that some cadres do not distinguish between bourgeois pessimism and sabotage . . .'

Perhaps that was the reason for this new campaign I had read about in the newspapers, about 'right opportunists' spreading defeatism . . .

This is what I thought at the time. I did not know that this new political campaign was due to the clash which had occurred in August 1959, at an important Party meeting when the Minister of Defence, Peng Tehuai, had written a 'letter of opinion' and circulated it, and spoken against the failings of the Leap. This was considered an attack upon the whole concept of the Great Leap Forward and the communes. But at the time no one in Peking told me anything about Peng Tehuai. It was a 'state secret'. It would be 1967 before what had occurred that August would be officially published.

Then Chou Enlai was free, and I was fetched to go to the Great Hall of the People. Kung Peng was there, and also some other officials, but I only saw Chou Enlai. He did not smile, and he looked a little tired, but he was as usual most courteous, though his brief look at me seemed to weigh me up to wonder whether I could . . . what? Twice in the next fifteen years he would again look at me with that appraising glance. Each time there had been a crisis which was state secret, known only to the leadership, whispered among the middle cadres. Perhaps Chou Enlai thought: What does she know?

Such interviews have an unspoken protocol. From the moment one passes the welcoming screen with its painting of a pine tree, placed across the entrance and cutting the room from view, every gesture and word, from preamble to introduction to core of the matter to conclusion, seems almost, at least in my memory, like a ballet, whose choreography is well understood by host and guest. I recall today what Chou Enlai said in those many hours that he so generously gave me. Hours of such moment and reaching import; talk which went from policy to human speculation; no secret revelations; no directives or commands. He never departed, even when angry, from an equable, courteous exchange of views; and his words seemed casual and effortless, and were all the more to be pondered. He never assumed that irksome stance of a 'teacher', yet Chou was teaching me all the time. 'Perhaps you will think again about this point', was all he would say when I looked blank. He always took a subject to pieces, dissecting with precision its several component parts and tackling them one by one. He was never vague, never did he ramble. His brilliance resided precisely in that what he said sounded so simple, and yet he would always grasp the intricate details in a discussion and reassemble them in another pattern so that what appeared to be one argument would suddenly become quite different. Never did he raise his voice or become angry, except once, at a Frenchman who proved both arrogant and stupid, and then Chou, who had been held down over four hours by the Frenchman, finally did show a little temper, in his curt goodbye.

And his adversaries, those who had come to overwhelm him with their ingenious arguments and sought to bully or to trap him, would find themselves, suddenly, with their most perfect contraptions of thought collapsing sand castles half melted by the tide, unrecognizable.

Chou started equably, as we drank our tea, about my father's death, expressing condolences and asking me whether all arrangements had been appropriate. He then went on to say that he was sorry there had been so much delay in granting me a visa that summer. Kung Peng was absent and the office had not acted swiftly. 'Oh no, Prime Minister, it was I, I was far too impatient,' I replied. For now I knew what a year of torment and catastrophe it had been for China. The harvest failures; the drought and the floods and the insect plagues; the abrupt cancellation in June, by the Russians, of agreements to help China in nuclear and scientific research; the Tibetan revolt in March and the border clashes with India through the summer and the autumn; and attacks (the launching of parachute troops) by

Chiang Kaishek from Taiwan – all this and more, which I would realize some months, some years later.

And all of it was upon the shoulders of Chou Enlai. Always, he would have to perform rescue operations; try to salvage, to patch up and to save; try to implement new policies and push China forward, forward in her development . . . I wanted to say, 'It is you, Prime Minister, who carries the burden of it all. And you have to work to set aright all that has gone wrong. And none of it has been your fault. You have kept your head, but others lost theirs, and now you have to be careful to give them face . . .' For Chou Enlai had said, 'We, the leadership, shall take full responsibility for what has gone amiss.' And always he would be the one to apologize, and he was apologizing to me for what was the fault of some clerk in the Department of Information.

Neither was it altogether the fault of the literal-minded middle cadres, however much they irritated me with their blockheaded fear of taking responsibility. Upon them had fallen an avalanche of directives, sometimes totally contradictory ones. They had had to interpret and implement them 'correctly' and they had been told not to 'pour cold water upon the red hot enthusiasm of the masses', and so they had duly whipped up fervour and enthusiasm, and they had excoriated as rightists anyone who enjoined caution; and all this was also responsible for some of the chaos that had ensued. For instance, the fact that the big steel-making campaign had coincided with harvest time so that millions of peasants had gone off to make steel, and millions of tonnes of grain had been left to rot on the fields.

'Last time we met,' said Chou Enlai, 'you had many questions. Have you any questions now?'

'Yes, Prime Minister. Why did you let the Dalai Lama go? You could have stopped him at any time.'

Of course, said Chou Enlai. By deploying troops of the Lhasa garrison and other garrisons along the roads, the Dalai Lama and his suite could have been stopped. It was known that there was a plot to get the Dalai Lama away to

India; in fact, a month or so before the event, an Indian newspaper had already announced such a possibility.* But any military action might have caused the Dalai Lama physical injury, and this would have seriously affected the Tibetan people. 'We gave him a chance to make up his mind.' The Dalai Lama was young. 'We have kept open his positions as Vice-Chairman of the National People's Congress, and as Chairman of the Committee for the Autonomy of Tibet. We have stated we believe he was ill-advised by his entourage.' The revolt had had only partial support from the population, and now there was peace and order in Lhasa.

We went on to the question of the border trouble with India, and to Nehru. Chou spoke in measured tones of map discrepancy, spreading map after map between us. All colonial privileges had come to an end with Liberation in 1949, and the British, who had 'manipulated' Tibet for a long time, had had to give up. Nehru had understood this in 1954, 'but now, somehow, he chooses not to understand it,' said Chou Enlai. Should I consult Nehru's own autobiography, published in England, I would find, in the last edition of 1956, that the map tracing in the book showed the border where the Chinese said it was, and not where the Indian government now claimed it to be. Was it possible that Nehru had not checked his own book and the map published inside it?

Chou Enlai was obviously puzzled by Nehru's character and his reactions. He assumed that Nehru would react in the way an Asian (meaning a Chinese) would react; and he debated whether Nehru himself was fully in control of what he was doing, or whether he was driven to it by the 'imperialists'. I think that the parliamentary flux and furore of the Indian Lok Sabha† had escaped Chou Enlai.

The whole trouble, said Chou, was that Asians knew too little about each other. Whereas the West had a pool of

---

*See *Lhasa, the Open City*.
†The Indian lower house of Parliament.

'China experts' and 'Indian experts', we had no such pool of experts in China. Despite geographical proximity, India and China had not had any direct contact during the many decades of colonial domination. This must be remedied, because India and China were the two great nations of Asia, twin pillars of Bandung, the hope of the Third World nations. Imperialism, said Chou Enlai (not calling it 'American' imperialism) wanted to provoke bad feeling between the two. 'But we are not frightened. We do not want war for a single day, but if we are attacked, we shall defend ourselves.'

Some people, said Chou Enlai, did not see clearly that 'imperialism does not change'. They put their hopes in what they called peace; in meetings which dangerously compromised socialism and the national independence of emergent nations. *Some* people even talked about a certain new spirit which would save the world . . . 'On this point, *some* people have illusions,' said Chou Enlai.

Nothing could have been clearer. Chou was referring to Khrushchev; to Khrushchev's Camp David meeting with Eisenhower; to Khrushchev's speech, praising the 'new spirit' of Camp David. Khrushchev was even then proclaiming that this was the start of an era of peace 'for the whole world'.

In 1959 Mao Tsetung and Chou Enlai saw in this new spirit yet another attempt at a division of power and world supremacy between the two super powers. And it was plain that China might be the victim of such a strategy.

But at the time I too believed in the Camp David spirit. I too, because I detested Stalin's excesses, had been enthused by Khrushchev's glib words about peace. I thought there would be an end, for ever, to atomic war threats . . . 'I too believe that this Camp David meeting is a good thing for the world, Prime Minister,' I said to Chou Enlai.

The silence that followed was one of total immobility. The secretary who took notes froze with pen in air. Mr Ku stared at me with horror in his eyes. Chou Enlai's face looked suddenly more tired, a creeping of small wrinkles which began around the eyes. But there was no anger in his voice when he said, 'We do not think so.' Peace was concrete, not an abstract proposition, and there was no evidence that there would be disarmament; on the contrary. Compromise must have its limits, but it did not mean selling out the peoples of the Third World. 'If it does, then it is not peace, only submission and servility. We must decide now whether all the peoples of the world have a right to their national liberation or whether they will be slaves for a thousand years . . . on this point we shall never compromise.'

Now I understood what the Western journalists had called 'Chinese intransigence'.

Chou Enlai had another engagement, and he saw me to my car, bowing formally, but without a smile, without that small repressed grin which lit up his face. Others climbed into the car with me, including Mr Ku. All were silent as we drove back to the hotel and I suddenly perceived with all my body's cells their tiredness, the strain under which they laboured. I said, 'I know what I'm going to do. I'm going to Delhi to see Nehru.'

I was back at the Hsinchiao, and one Western newsman had left an English newspaper for me; on the first page a large photograph of Nehru, a hunched and pacing man, the world a great weight on his shoulders. 'A sad and distraught man . . . saddened by China's treachery', was the caption. And it mentioned that it was his birthday. I sent a cable to Nehru for his birthday; this would prepare the ground for a meeting. And I left the next day for Hong Kong and for India.

CHAPTER 10

Jawaharlal Nehru: 1959–1964

I flew to Delhi on November 22nd, stopping only for two days in Malaya. Vincent was leaning on the airport barricade, watching me walk in the bright winter sun to the customs building. 'My life consists of hanging around airports, waiting for your plane to come in.'

Now I understood why Vincent had resigned. I realized the sacrifice that it had meant for a man who had been seventeen years an officer. He had done it for me. Even today I cannot quite understand why, why he gave up his career, because he did it so naturally, as if it was an easy thing to do. 'You've taken Nehru's blue-eyed boy away from him,' said an Indian diplomat to me. For Nehru had paid much attention to Vincent's road building, which was of strategic import. Vincent had built all the Himalayan highways in Kashmir, to secure the mountain bastions of India (ironically enough, also against a potential Chinese threat). He then had built the road from Nepal across the foothills to India, ensuring thus a semi-dependency for Nepal, the landlocked kingdom, upon Indian goodwill and Indian goods.

'Why the hell didn't you tell me that there was going to be trouble on the border?' I was furious now. He should have warned me. 'I *thought* there might be trouble,' he replied, 'and then someone would try to fix me because of you.' 'Fixing' people, getting them into difficulties with groundless accusations, is almost a habit, not only in India, but in all Asian countries. 'But you could have given me up,' I said, 'instead of giving up a seventeen-year career.' He might have become a brigadier, a full general; on retirement he might have become the director of a large company, with a big house and a motor car. All private businesses in India, and foreign businesses as well, always tried to recruit ex-army officers, the higher the better, as their top executives. The Indian army happens to be the best training ground for business management.

Vincent looked at me with his long-lashed eyes half-closed, and then he laughed. He laughed a long time, and the taxi driver turned round and also laughed. And I remain puzzled, and half angry, even now. Because anyone capable of such profligacy, of such extravagance, is for ever untamed, uncompelled, cannot be brought to any kind of servility. 'You don't understand my kind of love,' said Vincent cheerfully, as casually as noting the fact: 'Of course you have slanted eyes, you have Chinese eyes. And tiny eyelashes.' He accepts it. 'For you, it's China first, and that is your blessing and your curse. And after China, perhaps it's Yungmei. And after Yungmei, it's me. Perhaps. But for me, it's you.' That is how life is made and that is how Vincent takes it, and he sleeps soundly and is not tormented by love because he loves. And that is enough.

I too have a fixed pole star, magnet of my heart and brain. But it is not an easy thing, and perhaps it will be in the end unwholesome, an insanity to be scrutinized and categorized among the madnesses that besiege the mind. For how can one explain this obsession with an enormous mass called China, when I know so well that not one of the multi-millions will be either better or worse off, whatever I do or do not say?

'I am crazy, Vincent. Why do I do the things I do? Why did I decide to go to see Nehru?'

'Because that's the way you're made,' said Vincent.

So with strength in my voice and sureness of decision because of his arms around me, I told Vincent all that Chou Enlai had said. And how the idea of seeing Nehru was all my own. And Vincent said, 'I'll fix it,' and when we got to the Ashoka Hotel he rang up the Prime Minister's secretariat, and he got a very courteous secretary who said that he would relay the message and let us know, and then we sat waiting in the hotel room. And at that moment we were together half the world, the people of India and the people of China, knowing our future to be the same. 'Our people must never fight each other,' said Vincent. 'Some politicians in the West would like us to go to war with each other because then the whole of Asia would lapse into slavery again. And so it must not happen.' Of course when Vincent says 'the West' he does not mean only the United States and Europe; he includes Russia within the West, as I do; as so many Asians do. And that day in Delhi, we were not at all sure that, in the end, the USSR would not be more eager to see India and China confronting each other than America – however open and vigorous at the time American encouragement to Nehru to carry on challenging China appeared to be.

Two days later, in the evening, Nehru received me at Rashtrapathi Bhavan. The large living room was cool and silent; beautiful with soft glowing alabaster lamps and roseate carpets. All was lived with, ungarish, not the usual over-ornate Indian living room. Nehru came in, so young in the diffuse light, a spring in his step, in white with a rose in his buttonhole. 'How beautiful you look,' he exclaimed, and smiled, a truly fascinating smile.

Our conversation started well, on a note of personal affection, as I told him I was back from Peking; but it worsened perceptibly as it proceeded. Very slowly the smile disappeared from Nehru's face. He did not scowl, he merely turned to bronze. At no single moment during the next forty minutes did our words or minds meet, effect a link. Not for a second was there any real exchange. I blame myself for this. Each culture has its own particular climate which the culture-bearers engender as they proceed in the art of conversation, which is the highest of all arts, and the most perilous, since it is exchange of thought and feeling through the dangerous manipulation of words. When two culture-bearers confront each other, then what is said by one is heard quite differently by the other; and this happened now, I think. I should have greatly lengthened the preamble, taken my time, coquetted, continued the softening up, all the more since I knew how susceptible Nehru was in a very personal way. I should have said, 'Oh, dearest Panditji, Panditji, how

I have thought of you these days! My heart was in a turmoil because of you . . . I could not eat nor could I sleep . . .' I should have intuitively, unashamedly fawned, with unctuous, Asian wit (I tried, subsequently in letters, but it was too late and unconvincing). I should have taken days, not less than an hour over my plea, and tried to see him again and again.

Alas, I was back from China. Which means that I was my Chinese self uppermost, logical and reasonable and quiet and calm, but not appealing enough to emotion; only convinced that 'the superior man listens quietly, and weighs himself and the universe'. I had with me maps of the frontier, copies of the documents exchanged, including Chou Enlai's letter of November 7th to Nehru. The letter was courteous and clear, and a radical departure from the somewhat unhappy epistolary exchanges which had previously taken place. 'Your Excellency, Panditji, you know all these things better than I do. I shall only talk of my own preoccupation, the overall effect of a misunderstanding between the two greatest nations in Asia; and the dangers of such a situation.'

I agreed that the Chinese had been untactful, I even conceded the word 'arrogant', for it was true that some of the truculence of their written word gave an ill impression (oh, those translators, how I wished I could do something about Chinese translations!). But in *deed*, I said, the Chinese were never anything but modest, prudent and careful. They had shown clearly that they were ready to negotiate and to compromise. Peking's English was not as excellent as that used in Delhi, but the point was not who talked well, who used the better rhetoric, but the facts, the actual situation and its historical development. And was it not a strange coincidence that in 1959 such a wholesale avalanche of hostility towards China, from 'various quarters', should coincide with the unhappy border clash with India? I went on; I drew examples from history; drew a picture of 'both our struggling nations' and their need for the least amount of interference.

'It seems to me from what you say that the Chinese do want to talk,' said Nehru, as if making a discovery.

'Panditji, this is far more than just some border question left over by British colonialism. Only you can resolve it, for the sake of both our countries, for the sake of Asia.'

His face hardened imperceptibly here and I added quickly, 'I can see you have been hurt . . . have you been hurt?'

'Yes, I have been hurt,' said Nehru.

I returned to the hotel, and wrote down what had taken place, and also my assessment of Nehru's present mood. Nehru would not, or could not, change his stance and negotiate. Meanwhile, he was doing a saraband of remarkable political dexterity. The conclusion was that it suited him well not to negotiate the order at all. It was a matter of choice, and also, possibly of personal vanity. After all, the Chinese had published articles which lectured Nehru on his political deviations . . . and that had certainly not helped matters.

In the next months and years I would ponder over the roots of Nehru's decision. Obviously he had arrived at it gradually, reversing the stand he had taken in Bandung in April 1955, when he had gone out of his way to establish friendship with Chou Enlai and with China. When, and why, had he decided to change? I had been told by Malcolm in early 1957, when the slogan *'Hindi-Chini bhai bhai'** resounded everywhere still, that Nehru was unhappy with China. Something had happened. What precisely had happened in 1956 or 1957? All I could find out was that in 1956 Nehru had seemed to want to discuss the undemarcated border between the two countries with Chou Enlai, but that the Chinese were not ready for it; Chou Enlai had not been perceptive or alert enough at the time, and had pushed back the issue. Had the border problem been tackled then, and frontier delineation begun, the emotional fury unleashed in 1959 would not have happened. The Russian intention to utilize Sino-Indian border incidents in order to obtain

*'India-China friends for ever'.

leverage with the Indian government would not have worked. And had the border problem been settled before certain aspects of India's own developmental needs occurred to Nehru, history might have been somewhat different; at least for a couple of decades.

In December 1959, President Eisenhower came to Delhi. This meant a drastic change in American policy, which had been somewhat hostile towards India. Eisenhower praised 'this democratic country ... respected and revered ... throughout the councils of nations ...' Nehru said contentedly, 'Yes ... it's true that people look up to us.' He was gratified, and the image of 'democratic India' was to last a very long time.

And now there was a sudden multiplication of aid; whereas in the previous twelve years India had scarcely obtained 1·4 billion dollars in aid, now she obtained four billions in the next four years from the USA. Disapproval of India's 'neutralism' was over; her 'immorality' was as dead as Dulles. Nehru was the champion of Western values in Asia because of the border quarrel with 'Red' China. A special Help India lobby took shape in Washington, and functioned for many years. India needed immense funding for an industrial takeoff. And here, perhaps, is part of the answer to the puzzle of Nehru's change.

For Nehru was a master politician. He would not give up his great prestige with the other undeveloped nations of the Third World through too close an understanding with America. He preserved India's neutralist stance and became the Man of Peace, a role which he would play with superb aplomb at the first non-aligned conference in Belgrade in 1961.

Throughout those years, Nehru would exhibit pained bafflement at 'Chinese conduct' and 'treachery'. I cannot forbear to admire Nehru. What skill, what superb and ruthless use of the China bogey, to obtain from both the United States and the USSR the most massive aid ever extended to any country at peace!

Close on the heels of President Eisenhower came Nikita Khrushchev, in February 1960.

By that time I had cultivated the acquaintance of some Indian intellectuals near to the Indian Communist Party, all of whom professed themselves distraught by the India-China quarrel. Among these I shall only mention one, my dear friend Mulk Raj Anand, versatile, prolific, and a humanist as well as a world-renowned writer. Mulk actually came to Singapore to see me; he was most concerned about India-China relations and we made many plans to dampen the fury in India, which eschewed cogent and reasonable debate, and to explain Indian reactions to China.

When Khrushchev came to Delhi, Mulk was overjoyed and wrote to me, 'I think he has come to restore friendship betweem India and China.' Mulk felt this was essential; because the border dispute also placed the Indian Communist Party (though not a member, Mulk was a sympathizer) in a very invidious position.

However, my photographer friend P. N. Sharma was less trusting. 'Perhaps K. will do some good, perhaps not,' he wrote to me.

Of course Khrushchev did nothing to ease the border dispute. He pledged lavish aid to India and deplored China's 'stubbornness' and 'inability to accept the realities of today's world'. Within the next two years, twice as much aid went to India from the USSR as China had received; and Khrushchev's visit laid the foundation of the friendship and alliance, which continues today, between the USSR and India.

Nehru could afford now to show willingness to 'talk' with China. But 'negotiations' were refused. The opposition parties in parliament – notable among them the Swatantra Party – were vociferously against negotiations with China, which they considered to be a betrayal of India's cause; and an election was pending, and its results could be prejudiced by any inclination on the part of Nehru, suspected or real, to 'negotiate' with China.

Chou Enlai had not been inactive. In that year of 1960 he

had successfully obtained two boundary agreements where hitherto no frontier had been demarcated, one with Burma and one with Nepal. With Burma Chou Enlai had accepted the 1913 McMahon alignment, which had been set up by the British. This was a very big concession. For no Chinese government had ever before accepted the 1913 McMahon Line. Chou Enlai let drop hints that China might accept the McMahon Line, in the eastern sector of the China-India border, in return for the much smaller knob of the Aksai Chin in the western sector. It was through the Aksai Chin that the Chinese had built a road in early 1954, linking Tibet with Sinkiang. The Indians only realized that a road had been built in 1956, when the Chinese held a celebration at its completion.

Nehru's opposition clamoured: 'Not an inch of soil must be given up.' The only people who kept cool were the Indian army officers. 'Nobody really knows whom this piece of land belongs to,' said one Indian military man to me. After all, if there was fighting and dying to do, dying in frozen wastes no one has ever mapped out is not a particularly delightful prospect. Unfortunately Indian politicians did not need to be coolheaded; only vocal.

Chou Enlai came to Delhi for 'talks' in April 1960. He stayed several days, trying to talk with Nehru. And he found that it was like trying to cut water. 'I could not move Nehru at all. I think he had made up his mind,' said Chou Enlai to me some years later. 'As we were leaving for the airport,' (Chou was flying from Delhi to Kathmandu) 'Nehru talked to me at great length about the evil, reactionary upper caste, the Ranas of Nepal, telling me to beware of them,' said Chou Enlai with an amused smile. 'One newsman at the airport said to me, "Your Excellency, have you noticed something? India has just received a great deal of wheat, a gift from the USA." "Thank you for telling me," I replied, "then I understand fully the situation."'

I went on writing to Nehru, and he wrote back to me charming, affectionate, courteous replies. In none of them did he give anything away. I think he was amused, and perhaps a little scornful, of my obduracy and my idiocy. For it was, I confess, quite idiotic of me to think I could do anything to influence him. Nevertheless I persisted.

On my return from India to Malaya in December 1959 I had written a letter to the London *Times*, pointing out what Chou Enlai had mentioned about Nehru's own autobiography, which I had checked. The result, however, was merely some crushing correspondence from Peter Fleming, although he could not adequately explain why Nehru's own book showed on its map of India the borders where the Chinese said they were. Such, however, was the emotional pitch to which some Englishmen worked themselves that they managed to sound, and act, more irate than even the most hypersensitive Indian. Among those who succumbed to unchecked passion was, alas, my old friend Kingsley Martin of the prestigious *New Statesman*. I had flown back to Delhi in March 1960 for a few days with Vincent and in order to see Mulk Raj Anand, who had a 'plan' to approach Nehru and speak with him (nothing came of it), and there I found Kingsley and Dorothy Woodman. 'The Chinese have always been expansionist, it's in their blood,' roared Kingsley, staggering with pent-up rage.

'Our dear exalted friend [Nehru] is steadily moving to the right . . .' wrote Mulk, much distressed. He thought that All-India Radio might be interested in getting both of us talking about the border in a series of broadcasts. This scheme went the way of all our other schemes to air the border dispute in a sensible way.

'Nehru sees hundreds of people. He thrives on being all things to all men,' said Mulk to me after one more fruitless attempt. He was then invited to Moscow – for Mulk was also a Stalin Peace Prize winner for his books – and remained there several weeks. I think that he was given the USSR view, not only of the China-India border dispute, but, more importantly, of the Sino-Soviet dispute, which was now almost in the open. Under Moscow guidance the Indian Communist Party policy became to support Nehru 'at all costs'. 'Because,' as Mulk wrote to me, 'the position of the

Left is that all those who stand by the Prime Minister's basic policies have to push these policies and save him from himself, or rather from his so-called friends.' This meant that the Indian Communist Party would almost outdo the Swatantra Party in its anti-China stance.

Friendship with me became difficult for Mulk. But he courageously kept it up. By August 1960 he was in Europe, working for UNESCO and producing a most marvellous art magazine, *Marg*. He wrote to me that 'the mountains of bitterness and suspicion between India and China have now become higher even than the Himalayas . . .' This meant that our final scheme, which was to publish a book entitled *Across the Mountains*, containing our letters to each other about the India-China situation, was also to be given up.

Other Indian politicians, diplomats, also saw me; among them Jayaprakash Narayan. Unfortunately, Mr Narayan got a violent toothache within ten minutes of the start of our meeting.

I did not have so lethal an effect on army generals, friends of Vincent, with whom I continued to entertain the most courteous relations, despite the border dispute.

By 1961 I realized that there was no way in which the China-India border problem could be solved in the near future. Not only because Chou Enlai warned me of this, but because he had added, 'In the end we have to put our trust in the Indian people . . . in the people of the sub-continent.'

The use of the word sub-continent was very important. Chou Enlai was thoroughly acquainted with the Partition of India into India and Pakistan. And although Pakistan was most friendly with China, Chou Enlai, who thought in terms of history and people rather than of political procedures, also realized that one day India's influence might again – should the religious problem of an Islamic Pakistan and a Hindu India be resolved – extend over Pakistan. He therefore kept the options open. He told me, 'We do not want a morsellization, a fragmentation of India. India has fourteen main languages, and it is really a mosaic of peoples and cultures. We do not wish to see it fall into separate pieces, each piece manipulated against the others. That has been the history of India in the past; and that is why it fell a prey to colonialism.' In China, the homogeneity of the culture kept China together. Although the colonial powers had tried to divide China, it always came together again.

In 1962 it was P. N. Sharma who stuck his neck out. Although he, like Mulk Raj Anand, was connected with the Indian Communist Party – so many people in the Ministry of Foreign Affairs would be thus connected, both in Nehru's time and in the time of Indira Gandhi – yet he was bold enough to revolt against the remarkable structure of unfacts that was being erected in New Delhi and duly and faithfully transmitted, without being checked, by most of the Western correspondence placed there.

In April 1962 P. N. Sharma turned up in Hong Kong. I happened to be there, on my way to China. He had come especially to see me. Cousin Pengju and I saw P. N. Sharma together in my hotel room. Pengju was now running a Hong Kong monthly magazine called *Eastern Horizon*. It had published some of Sharma's photographs and wanted to publish some more. This gave Sharma an excuse for coming to Hong Kong.

P. N. told us that India was preparing for war, 'all along the whole border'; and that in the western sector of the border, in Kashmir and in Ladakh, facing the Aksai Chin, the Russians were now obligingly providing helicopters and other army equipment to the Indian army. Meanwhile, the CIA was just as obligingly providing means for dropping Tibetans trained in camps in the USA and sophisticated means of monitoring what was going on in China. (All this would be revealed as fact around 1974–5, when tempers and attitudes towards China had changed.)

P. N. Sharma also said that the Russian Ambassador in New Delhi had told a member of the Indian Foreign Affairs Ministry: 'Don't worry, we'll drop an atom bomb on Peking if they do anything.' At the time, Pengju and I could scarcely believe Sharma. But since then we have both realized that a tactic of Russian diplomacy is to make bombastic verbal pledges, which are not backed by the Kremlin but which overawe and influence the gullible in the Third World.

Sharma was unhappy. His Russian wife was proving 'extremely bourgeois'. She did not like Indian austerity. She did not like vegetarianism. (P. N. Sharma, being a high-caste Brahmin, was a strict vegetarian.) She wanted 'only to go out, to dance, to buy things'. Two years later, she would leave him and return to the USSR.

Pengju said, with Taoist wisdom, 'We must now go to lunch and eat well. One reflects better after digestion.' And so off we went to the best restaurant in Hong Kong, while P.N. continued to be agitated about what was being concocted in New Delhi. There were also, he said, receiving sets and detecting devices installed by the CIA 'somewhere in Kashmir', high up in the mountains. We managed to provide for him a totally vegetarian meal, even going to the extent of buying, on the way, a new set of crockery and implements, so that nothing he used would be contaminated by animal oil, and when P.N. said, in that enormously dramatic Indian way which I relish but do not share, 'I think there will be war', Pengju said sagely, 'War or no war, it is only the other face of peace. Now let us eat well, and toast our friendship.' He seemed totally unruffled by Sharma's revelations.

Pengju duly reported to his newspaper what P.N. had said. It elicited no surprise. 'We know there will have to be a show of force, sometime or other, do not worry,' was the message relayed to me. So I did not worry. I told P.N. not to worry. 'The Chinese are in full control of the situation. They are prepared. Do not worry.' I relayed the total message to P.N.: 'Sometimes it is necessary to do a *little fighting* to unblock people's minds.'

In July 1962 the Soviet Union began hostilities on the Chinese borders, in Sinkiang province. About 60,000 Kazakhs, of a national minority of Sinkiang, would be persuaded to flee to Soviet Russia.

I now think that this was the 'trigger', or signal for the Indians to proceed with what Nehru and his Defence Minister, Krishna Menon, had been preparing since 1961, and what was termed, in military language, a 'forward policy' on the border between India and China. The very fact that the Chinese did not seem to retaliate, had not even broadcast the Soviet incursions or their own losses, seemed to convince Nehru that the Chinese were pusillanimous, were frightened, and would not do or say anything if he pushed 'forward'.

I think he underestimated the Chinese. I think he did not listen to Sharma's warning, which was duly relayed to him: 'Be careful . . . the Chinese are prepared.' Neither did his entourage translate for him the fairly numerous newspaper articles of that summer, in which very plainly the Chinese warned that they were 'fully prepared'. Nehru preferred to trust his friends in the Kremlin and his advisers, of whom at the time a good few were members of the Indian Communist Party, subservient to Moscow.

From 1960 to 1962 India's Ministry of Defence, under Krishna Menon, had worked out the 'forward policy'. It was designed to probe, to push, to infiltrate, to annoy and to provoke. The decision was made because of the very difficult internal situation in China. The shortages, the drought, the aftermath of the Leap Forward and its errors. It was predicted by 'experts' in Hong Kong that China might now break up. And this was also the confident assessment (for the benefit of India) passed on by Moscow to New Delhi.

Nehru found himself confronted with reluctance, and even downright opposition, by his most tried and tested generals, who showed great hesitation towards the plans proposed by his Defence Minister. But then up came a General Kaul – no relation of my good friend Ambassador Tikki Kaul – and somehow he became in his turn Nehru's blue-eyed boy. In his interviews with Nehru he injected such jaunty confidence that the Prime Minister found any doubts he had swept away. A few highly placed commanders in the Indian army are on record as warning that they could not agree with Kaul's notions; that a large offensive, such as envisaged in the autumn of 1962, at a time when the passes were being blocked by snow, and with the unprepared state of the Indian battalions, was not only downright hazardous but a major onslaught on common sense. However, Nehru persisted, sustained by Krishna Menon, and on October 10th the final order was given, in Nehru's direct words: 'Drive the Chinese out'. The Indian army complied.

But of course, as was obvious, and known to everyone except perhaps to the Indians, the Chinese were prepared and waiting. After issuing the usual 'three solemn warnings' and imploring Nehru to 'withdraw from the brink of the precipice', the Chinese moved their border battalions on October 21st, eleven days after the Indian army took the offensive.

The Indian troops were not prepared for the winter. Many of them came from south India, and among them cases of frostbite, owing to inadequate clothing, would be numerous. They had not been supplied with adequate outfits for the high passes.

The Chinese came down the slopes and rolled the ill-clad Indian battalions right into the plains of India. And then the most surprising thing happened. The whole world, brainwashed by its press, forgot that eleven days previously Nehru had given the order to the Indian army to push forward, and saw only the spectacle of a Chinese army advancing like an avalanche into the plains of India. An enormous furore was created. This was once again proof of Chinese aggression. The cities of the plains even began to evacuate. The politicians who had been most raucous about 'not giving an inch of India's sacred soil' were of course the first to flee.

In November, twenty-five days after the beginning of the Chinese military reprisal, the Chinese government announced a total and unilateral military withdrawal to ten kilometres behind the McMahon Line, on the eastern sector; stated that all weapons and ammunition captured, and all prisoners, would be returned without any compensation demanded; gave the lists of the prisoners captured – who had been treated, mainly for frostbite but also for wounds, in

Chinese hospitals – and then sat down, waiting for Nehru to come to the negotiating table.

Many people in the world were puzzled; not least the newsmen and the agencies. How to explain what China had done? It did not fit into any known, recognized Western pattern of diplomacy . . . and therefore reasons had to be invented. With fertile fantasy, they were. But all of a sudden the current talk of China's 'bellicose, mad aggressivity' somehow rang false. However, no new words had been coined in the Western vocabulary to describe what China was doing. Hence one 'expert' even tried to invent a 'Russian ultimatum' to China, forgetting that the Moscow press was just as surprised as those in London, Washington and Paris.

Ordinary people, here and there, wrote to me. I think they began to recognize that there was a Chinese way of doing things, of thinking, of acting, which need not refer to what they were told in the newspapers, and that the fascination of China resided precisely in this different way of handling situations, people, facts. 'For clarity of thought, look towards China,' one person wrote to me. And another. 'Well done, China!' I have never received so many letters from all over the world, asking me to explain what China was doing, as I did then.

But perhaps the most important result was that in the Third World, among the emergent nations, suddenly Nehru's prestige had entirely crumbled, and China's stood higher than it had ever done.*

In China itself the explanation for the handling of the conflict was simple because it was historical, it had precedent, and it was treated in the grand manner which the Chinese affect.

For in China in October 1962 the major issue, the greater danger, was not the 'inconvenience' of Nehru's 'forward policy'. It was the Cuba affair of that same month, and the resulting Kennedy–Kruschchev shadow play of

*See Neville Maxwell, *India's China War* (Cape, 1970).

confrontation and collusion. Within the rivalry of the two super powers there always loomed, for China, the unwelcome spectre of an entente at the expense of China. This was not an imaginary threat; Stalin and Roosevelt had come very close at the Yalta talks to the division of China between the US and the USSR.

As for the Indian episode, it was quite secondary, needing brisk local dealing but no more. History in China is replete with border incursions from all sides. And this one had a precedent: it was, as Chou Enlai would say, a repetition of the episode 'Seven times capture and release Meng Hou'.

In the time of the Three Kingdoms in China, A.D. 220–80, a famous Chinese strategist named Chuke Liang was holding together the Kingdom of Shou, whose King, Liu Pei, had died, leaving an infant son.

Since my cousin Liu Pengju was a direct descendant of King Liu Pei, I had ample opportunity to talk about this episode with him, and he gave me an abundance of details, almost enough to write a book on its own about the characters involved.

The strategy of the military wizard Chuke Liang was to guard the Kingdom of Shou, which at the time extended from today's Szechuan down to today's frontier with Burma, against invasion from wayward tribal chieftains. These chieftains, mostly from the present-day Shan states of Burma, were often in league with other rival Chinese kingdoms, such as that of Wu, and received many gifts from Wu in order to attack Shou.

Such a tribal chieftain was Meng Hou, leader of the Yis; he had been recruited to become a constant marauder on the borders of the Kingdom of Shou. Chuke Liang personally led an armed expedition against Meng Hou. But since the aim of military action is not crude physical victory but a long-term peace, his tactics were to win over the whole tribe to allegiance, through their chieftain. Meng Hou must be captured alive and then released and challenged to a series of contests.

Every time Meng Hou was captured, he was released;

although he refused to swear allegiance, and each time insisted that he had lost the battle not through inferiority to Chuke Liang, but through fate, the weather or fewer men. Thus, seven times did battle occur; and seven times Chuke Liang released Meng Hou. The last time he let him go without a word, without even the usual admonition.

Then Meng Hou's heart was touched by the magnanimity of his foe; instead of walking away to rally his forces, his soul was changed and he swore friendship and eternal allegiance to Chuke Liang.

From A.D. 225 until today the Yis of south-west China have been included in the Chinese entity, as one of its fifty-odd national minorities. For 1,700 years the Yis and other tribal hosts of the border with Burma, have venerated Chuke Liang as a demigod. Cousin Pengju told me with much relish that when the Jesuits came to China and settled in Yunnan province (where all these encounters happened), they had been able to convert whole villages of Yis at a single stroke merely by telling them that Jesus Christ was the younger brother of Chuke Liang, and both of them sons of God.

Now, seventeen centuries later, Chou Enlai remembered the power of magnanimity and decided to treat Indian border incursions in the same way as the great strategist Chuke Liang had treated the border marauder Meng Hou.

None of this was reported in the Western press. But all the Chinese, whether in China, in Taiwan or in South East Asia, duly used the phrase, and overseas Chinese of all political blends would say to each other, 'Ah yes, seven times catch Meng Hou'. In Taiwan jubilation was apparent: even the head of the Taiwan intelligence in Hong Kong would approach me a year later with that phrase on his lips.

This was also a judgment passed upon Nehru. It meant that whatever he or his government envisaged to provoke China, China would retaliate with magnanimity. One day the Indian people would understand, 'Because,' said Chou Enlai, 'after all, they are Asians, as we are. They too are heirs to a long culture.' But I doubted that Nehru would understand or appreciate the comparison. Would the story of Meng Hou induce in him the proper humility? He would not relish being compared to a wayward tribal chieftain who had to be re-'educated' into Chinese civility, whose soul was likely to be touched by forbearance.

The military débâcle of 1962 was the beginning of Nehru's death. For his self-esteem was now dealt a mortal blow. Krishna Menon resigned. For a while all was, once again, emotional fury in India. Emergency regulations were passed suspending all laws. Anyone found commenting unfavourably on the defeat was likely to be arrested for spreading unwholesome rumours ... the small Chinese colony in Calcutta, most of them laundrymen and shoemakers and petty shopkeepers, had a gruesome time; a good many landed in concentration camps for some years.

'Astonishment almost blots out relief at the sudden Chinese decision,' wrote the magisterial London *Times*, commenting on the Chinese withdrawal. And slowly, among the experts, the realization that Nehru did not want to negotiate began to be seen as a weakness. For Nehru still refused to negotiate. 'This weakens India's case' was the comment of Malcolm MacDonald. Malcolm MacDonald had been transferred from India to Kenya because of the Mau Mau insurrection there. He was giving his usual splendid performance, making the unacceptable seem obvious and even desirable to both sides. 'Of course Chou Enlai showed very clearly that the Chinese were ready to accept the McMahon Line in exchange for that bit of the Aksai Chin, and Nehru knew it. The whole thing could have been solved with face for everyone. But our friend Jawaharlal did not want to negotiate ... it's a great pity.'

But the status quo on the border would remain undisturbed, 'with no more deliberate encroachments or provocative sallies from the Indian side'.*

In India the famous, secret and constantly leaked

*India's China War, op. cit.

Henderson-Brookes Report on what really happened in that October–November 1962 was being prepared.

General Henderson-Brookes was a fiercely moustached and delightful Anglo-Indian, almost the living portrait of Colonel Blimp, and I often met him in Calcutta as he was Vincent's good friend. The report that bears his name remains 'top secret', although Indian newsmen and others have been able to get segments of it, and so has the Western press. In it the Indian army blamed its Minister of Defence, Krishna Menon, and General Kaul, Nehru's choice, for the defeat. The army had warned that with winter coming the Indian troops were not in a condition to fight in the high passes.

'Those civilians screaming: Fight the Chinese! should be parachute-dropped out there,' said Henderson-Brookes jovially. 'They haven't a clue what it's like.' Both he and Vincent agreed that the Chinese would never have been able to carry out an invasion because the passes would have been snow-blocked behind them and they would have been left stranded. From the beginning only a very limited action was planned.

Because of emergency regulations, anyone with Chinese ancestry (father or grandfather Chinese) was not to be given a visa to India. This affected me directly. But Vincent's web of connections worked well; of course I obtained a visa. And I used it to go to see Nehru in 1963.

I would see him twice. Once from afar, at a party, where we merely exchanged greetings. But another time Nehru received me in the late afternoon for a talk.

It was again pleasantly cool in his air-conditioned room; a contrast to the broiling temperature outside. Nehru had wizened, shrunk, as do old people whose bones begin to shorten. His face was thinner, but he was extremely affable, in a stony way. This time he did not volunteer anything, letting me speak, letting me ask the questions. And I did not ask him any questions about the border. I knew that this was a buried crypt within him; so deeply buried that he would not even refer to it. So I did not refer to it either.

I had by then lived with the problem for some years.

We sat, Nehru and I, and had really nothing to say to each other. Nothing to say except: Well, here we are. And looking at him, old and tired, I felt old and tired too; as if we had been a warring couple, suddenly aware of the little time left to war or to love. So I talked of India. Not a word about China.

I told him that I was happy to see that India had made good progress. 'Yes,' he said, 'our peasants are quite comfortable now.' It was not so true, but I let it pass. By then I had become interested in India's Untouchables, another topic of long-term interest to me. But I knew that Nehru would say that the problem was being solved; whereas, as events have proved, it has not been solved at all, even now. I therefore avoided Untouchability. I was treating him carefully, like a sick person, a person who does not have a very long time to live. And indeed, he had only eight months more to live, though he and I did not know it as we faced each other with love and carefulness and kindness, and talked about India.

The expenditure of the Indian army had doubled. Aid was flowing in, abundantly, and from all sides. The myth of China's 'aggression' towards India was being ubiquitously sustained. Oh yes, said Nehru, life was more comfortable in India now for the common man. I avoided sudden jolts, and Nehru courteously responded in kind. He did not ask about Chou Enlai. I added a final sentence: 'Your Excellency, whatever may have happened, please be assured that Premier Chou Enlai's regard for you is entire.' 'Thank you. Please tell him I also regard him highly,' said Nehru.

Why, if there was nothing to say, did he receive me? Perhaps because, in a way, he needed contact of another kind.

In 1964 Nehru died. The Indian community in Malaya and Singapore held a ceremony and did me the honour of asking me to pronounce the funeral oration for Jawaharlal Nehru. I spoke only of Nehru's greatness, and how much I missed him personally. Which was true. I did miss him. I never reached him at all; in his presence all my emotions rang false, as did his to me. We evaded each other admirably, and this is also, perhaps, a kind of love.

CHAPTER 11

The Years of Want: 1960–1961

In the summer of 1960, my health broke down.

I had been to Cambodia in February, and begun a new book, *The Four Faces.* I continued to worry about the Sino-Indian border dispute. My clinic was very busy and my sister Marianne had been placed in a mental hospital. I had also quarrelled bitterly and long with the leftist Students' Union of Nanyang University; allegedly infiltrated by the Malayan Communist Party. The reason was that I had publicly approved of a speech made by Prime Minister Lee Kuanyew at Nanyang University, and this had angered the leftists. They published a very rude letter against me in the papers. For a while I was ostracized; then 108 students rallied to support me, and in the end I met the student representatives at my home, and there was a reconciliation. It enhanced my position as an independent, but now drew upon me the anger of the PAP government, which had begun to demand 'obsequious compliance', as the poet D. J. Enright, at the time teaching at the University of Singapore, would remark.

But worry over China was the main cause of my illness, because 1960 was a terrible year for China, and I knew it, sitting in my clinic and doctoring my patients in Singapore. I was often aroused at night by spasms of anxiety. I grew thin. The spectre of want in China stalked me. The reports in the Western newspapers were all of dire distress: of floods and drought and insect plagues and failure and disaster. Every time I opened a paper it contributed to my body's defeatism.

I haemorrhaged almost continuously. I developed a nasty skin eruption after being stung by an unknown insect. I went on working, driving myself. Soon I could not sit anywhere in safety; I might leave a great smear of blood on the seat. I had a curettage, but nothing was found. Then Vincent arrived. 'You need me to look after you. I'm going to look after you.'

Vincent abandoned his job with Spitz and Spitz was very angry. But Vincent was not helpless. Through an English friend, a delightful sturdy half-Scot named Workman, he had obtained an introduction which resulted swiftly in a job with Jardine Waugh, a branch of Jardine's in Singapore.

Throughout these years there had been the problem of Vincent's family. He never dreamed of letting them down. He would be able to provide for them as well as when he was in India.

The only snag was Lao Chieh. She had liked Leonard, who spoke perfect Cantonese. She strongly objected to Vincent, chiefly because of his colour. She would shout from the kitchen, 'A Kling devil! In this house! Who would have thought it possible!' Kling is a shortening of Kalinga, the ancient name of the Tamil kingdom, a word used throughout South East Asia for southern Indians.

Lao Chieh broke a number of my best plates and cups. She was so rude to Hamid, the Malay errand boy cum chauffeur, that he threatened to knife her. But my face was unmoved; my ears were deaf to shouts or crockery crashes, and the Siamese cats and the dogs climbed all over Vincent. The dogs now had someone they could wag tails at, bark at, who threw balls for them to catch . . . my prize Burmese, Titi, went berserk with adoration of Vincent. He would sit on the veranda watching the road, and when he saw Vincent's car he would leap, tear across the garden screaming raucously with excitement, to greet Vincent at the garden gate. Hamid was also happy. There was at last a man in the house, one of his swarthiness, who taught him to back the car. For despite the lessons I had paid for, he had never learned to back.

Lao Chieh calmed down. And then one Sunday Leonard came to lunch, amiable, unruffled. Lao Chieh now decided that she would accept the unexplainable.

'Now that you've come to stay with me, I'm leaving you to go to China,' I told Vincent. He had cured me almost, his nearness and that golden glow of happy warmth he exuded, and all the many mes jostling each other in ceaseless activity came to rest like a watchful sea, a healthy sea between two sides. 'You are my good earth,' I kept on repeating. 'Without you I go into bewilderment.'

But my spirit was not at rest; it would not be until I went to China. Vincent cured me so that I could go. With everything well in hand, in September I went back to China.

In the train from Hong Kong to the Chinese border a small Philippino who spoke in high-pitched singsong American talked to me unquenchably. He was a camera man and would take photographs of the Chinese travellers who came in and out of 'Red' China carrying unwieldy large packs on shoulder poles. 'I hear there's a terrible famine out there . . . I want to take photographs of these people coming out, they're eating just anything. No more rats left in China, they've all been eaten up.' In the train to Kuangchow some of the Westerners were craning their necks to catch glimpses of the 'famine' in China – or so they told me.

For me, this time was going home, a total feeling of return. No longer the seasick, topsy-turvy nausea, the mad roller-coaster careening. Growing in me was a fierce protectiveness for China. 'It's a failure, China has failed, the people are starving – rejoice, rejoice!' said the well-fed pink faces round me, and I hated them with savage fury.

I too craned, for I had to know. The trees were taller, green the fields which now lay in long rectangles with trim, straight borders. Never had there been such fields in China. The pattern of the countryside had changed. The hills bordering the faraway horizon were fuzzy with trees. Was there really a famine?

In Kuangchow the restaurants were full of foreigners and the food was lavish, for the bi-annual fair was on. I went to the fair before it was officially opened and was shown many new things, chiefly industrial machines, row upon row of them. From the window of my room at the Love the Masses Hotel I saw the grey, translucent Pearl River slide its flocks of junks and sampans; and I tramped the streets in a fine, small rain, and sat in a cinema to see a film on Nieh Erh, the musician of the old days in Yenan.

I visited Fo Shan, the town famous for ceramics. Fo Shan had won the national prize as the cleanest city in China that year. Its Ming dynasty temple, all its timbers so delicately dove-jointed that there was not a nail in the whole building, glowed with colour. I talked about Malaya with a poet and Miss Shen of the Friendship Association. We walked into shops. There were no apparent shortages, but then it was September, and because of the festival of October 1st there were always more consumer goods available at that time. The poet and I talked about Dostoevsky. He quoted Dostoevsky, that people are often irrational and do things against all sense and all reason and even their own benefit; this appeared preposterous to Miss Shen. 'Only imperialists are unreasonable,' she said.

On the train to Peking I shared a compartment with Comrade Li – very young and so pale that he looked exsanguinate, but he assured me that he was in perfect health – and a most exuberant and highly articulate Professor Chang. No cowed intellectual he. Long and loud and rumblingly he talked, scathingly he monologued. 'Too many administrative posts for intellectuals, too many meetings . . . not enough time for research . . . we've got to stick to research, expand it . . . we've got to have more time for academic pursuits.' He taught classical Chinese literature, and talked of the benefits and drawbacks to Chinese education should the Chinese language be romanized. It was an issue which we debated, my Chinese writer friends and I, almost every time we met. A topic inexhaustible, endless. In fact we are still debating it some twenty years later. Professor Chang did not want to give up the marvellous old classical language of China; 'yet China has to move into an industrial society: and language is a powerful brake upon invention unless it can become flexible, create new words and phrases'. He agreed with the simplification of the ideograms which was being achieved. 'Romanization versus simplification. I prefer the latter. Look at the Japanese. Ideograms haven't prevented their acquisition of science.'

Chang spoke enthusiastically of his investigations into

Ming and Sung literature; and also of the literatures of the national minorities. 'We emphasize Han literature too much, spare and bony and moralistic, as a model to be imitated; but I hold that we must fertilize it with other modes and moods, and the great beauty of other cultures accessible to us.' He shouted at dinner, 'Academic debate should not be turned into a political issue. This has been the trouble. Too many problems which are problems of research and scientific orientation are treated as political problems . . .' He thumped the table: 'I am not a communist; I do not believe in communism, but I love my country and I am willing to study Marxism; however, I maintain my own opinion . . .' Comrade Li read and slept, and never uttered a word. Only when we reached Peking would I discover that he had bone cancer and was being sent by his factory to the capital hospital for treatment.

'The Westerners say we have broken with our traditions. I tell you no government has ever paid so much attention to the total body of our heritage as this one,' said Professor Chang.

At each station we came down to do exercises; Comrade Li and I did some arm-waving, and bent at the waist and touched our toes; Professor Chang made a full exhibition of the art of shadow boxing, and did it very well. A team of athletes, girls about five foot eight inches and boys over six foot, who were in the next three compartments, also did exercises, and so did a team of Japanese businessmen. All the stations were beflowered; I plucked one small carnation, and then felt terribly guilty, pilfering public property. 'We're going to build many more railways,' shouted Professor Chang. 'We must. Have you seen the new bridge over the Yangtze River? You'll pass over it.' We did, and the loudspeaker on the train told us its length and size and how many tonnes of steel and concrete had gone into it, and we were of course impressed. We all manifested due reverence, and the lavatories were locked by the train attendant, a wonderfully chubby man with enormous dimples in his cheeks, who seemed to think that all life was laughter and who laughed all the time and washed the compartments and poured tea and entertained us indefatigably. 'Our new youth, they're magnificent,' bawled Professor Chang. 'It's adequate diet. Our children will be a head taller than we are.'

'How foolish you are to worry, to worry,' I thought. While the Professor slept, I looked at the beloved land through the window, and smiled to myself. 'How foolish you have been to worry so much.'

'Shortages, just shortages,' said Chang briskly when I broached the subject with him. Of course there were errors, and a lot of inexperience, and especially a lot of bombastic talk. 'But now everything will be taken in hand.' I would learn later that he was a member of one of the non-communist parties, and was going to Peking for important conferences. Once more the Chinese pendulum was swinging. The intelligentsia, rightist or not, was once again in demand for a needed economic readjustment. The next year, 1961, a New Hundred Flowers would be proclaimed...

As Chang siestaed, I read a letter from Felix Greene, who at last had obtained a visa to China. It had not been easy to get him there; Felix had asked me and Pengju to help. But it was only in 1959, after seeing Chou Enlai, and when Kung Peng and I had been discussing several ancillary matters, that I could do something. The reason for his not being admitted was because he had an enemy in the British Communist Party who had spoken ill of him as a 'capitalist'. 'Felix is a very good man; of course, he's not a communist, but he is truly concerned about the future of the world,' I managed to say, also pointing out his usefulness and enthusiasm.

On September 20th, 1960, he succeeded in taping a television interview with Premier Chou Enlai, the first one Chou had ever done, and this was a major scoop. 'The China visit . . . is the most significant thing that has ever happened to me,' wrote Felix. Felix had also met Edgar Snow in Peking. After much difficulty, Ed Snow finally had obtained US State Department permission to go to China. At the time, any American who went to 'Red' China was considered a traitor, and was very likely to have his or her passport removed. Ed was commissioned to write articles on China for *Look* magazine, and would also complete a thick and exhaustive book entitled *The Other Side of the River.**

Would we be able, Edgar Snow, Felix Greene, and myself, to establish better understanding between China and the Western world, so that China would no longer be considered a threatening, hostile planet on its own ? When would China be seen as she really was, neither Heaven nor Hell, but simply a very large country with an enormous number of hard-working, poor people, frighteningly poor, but indomitable in their determination to achieve prosperity and social justice and to get swiftly into the twentieth century? After all, this was not a new dream; already in 1911 Sun Yatsen had proclaimed it when China's first revolution had taken place. China must take 'her rightful place in the sun . . . equal among all the nations of the world.'

But there was the jargon. The exhortation, political and strenuous, sounding to Western ears a fanatic note. I understood the need to instil in the Chinese people conviction and faith, to exalt endeavour into significance and greatness, to strive to multiply effort, that human factor, by continuous preaching. After all, little else in the form of material benefit could be offered, at least for quite a time, to the Chinese masses. Only the emotional satisfaction of having surpassed themselves.

I had seen the almost mystic enthusiasm animating the people at the Great Leap Forward in the previous two years. What would I find in 1960? Had the exaltation been sustained? Was the British businessman right, when he told me, at lunch in Hong Kong on his return to China, that 'their bigotry has waned – reality has now hit them and the people are tired and bitter and disillusioned'? Or was Felix Greene right, who had come back with stars shining in his eyes and written, 'People are high-spirited and inspired . . .'?

---

*Edgar Snow, *The Other Side of the River* (Gollancz, 1963).

There was fine rain at 7.30 in the morning, when we reached Peking, and soon it became bitterly cold. Professor Chang was met reverently by a big car and Party cadres and whisked away. Just before leaving he said, 'One day China will be the most democratic country in the world, but it will take time; we do not have a democratic tradition and feudalism is still heavy upon our backs.'

Wang Wanchun was at the station to meet me, his face glowing with pleasure; we drove to the Hsinchiao Hotel, where he had breakfast with me and told me about the new rationing.

'The harvest has been bad. We have had many natural calamities; a bad drought in the north.' There were shortages. Wanchun produced his ration tickets for the toast he ate, and then I noticed that he was thinner because his collar was too large for him when he turned his head. 'I have enough because I am an intellectual,' said he. Rations differed according to work done. Steel workers got the most in bulk and grain, but intellectuals got more meat, sugar and fats. 'Brain work needs meat and fats,' said he.

Deliberately eating less was, however, absolutely apparent as soon as I went out of the hotel. It was a feature of all the meals I would have with writers, relatives and friends. We simply fell into a natural constriction of appetite, each one urging others to eat more while restraining the self, and all of us saying to each other, 'I'm already full. I've eaten so much.' When I dined with Westerners I was immediately and almost shockingly aware of this absence of self-withholding; absence of awareness about the preciousness of food.

In the evening, Lin Lin of the Friendship Association, who had written me such a nice letter in July, came to see me. He had always been thin; he now had no cheeks, and it was difficult to judge. Only when I saw him again in 1962 did I realize how gaunt he had become in 1960. An elegant man with a sense of humour; a lover of painting and calligraphy, I enjoyed his verve, the way he overcame his Fukkien accent, above all his activity. At a glance he could tell my mood, whether there was temporary chaos within me or whether I had solved a problem to my satisfaction. Have I such a readable face? He noticed that I had not enough warm clothes for the winter. 'It's going to be cold,' he warned. The morning's drizzle had become an icicle-bearing wind, and it was freezing hard. The next day the wind grew in strength; its winged cohorts of sand and ice came howling down upon the city, flayed its walls and turned the ground to iron.

Lin Lin arranged for me to meet the heads of Islam in China, scholars and mosque imams; and also to visit Buddhist temples and priests, in order to bring back some material for the Malayan Sociological Research Institute in Singapore. I spent many hours with Chinese Islamic scholars in Peking, in Kuangchow, in Sian. I visited the mosques everywhere; those which had not been closed. One-third of the East District of Peking was Muslim, with Muslim restaurants in almost every street.

It was in Sian, in the old and beautiful Ming mosque in Ox Street, that I found extensive documentation on Admiral Cheng Ho, the Islamic Chinese eunuch who had led seven great sea expeditions to South East Asia, to the African coasts and Zanzibar. There were stone stelae erected to him, one recording a voyage when he was accompanied by a Malay named Hassan. A storm arose and Hassan prayed to Allah, and the storm abated.

Islam's history in China is 1,300 years old. The 'pure and truthful' religion – for so the imperial edicts had proclaimed it to be – had come to China both by sea and by land: by sea, following the ships which the monsoon winds blew agreeably to Kuangchow. And from the minaret of the great mosque there, erected in the eighth century A.D., the merchants of Kuangchow watched for the return of the fleets. By land, it was brought by the Silk Road across the continent of Asia.

Prosperous Arab establishments had sprung up all along the south China coast; and Arab communities took Chinese names. Even today Arab blood can be discerned among the populations of coastal towns. Islam extended across north China in a large horizontal pale, from the confines of

Turkestan to the frontiers of Korea. In 1960 there were twelve million Muslims in China, grouped as a national minority, the Huis. When I protested that the Huis were actually Chinese, the imam of the Sian mosque pointed to the Jews, who were not a race but a religious group. To make the Huis, believers of Islam, a national minority gave them privileges, explained the imam. Throughout the years of want, the Han Chinese would be on short rations but there would be adequate feeding for the national minorities. And family planning, which was gradually being enforced upon the Han people – 93 per cent of China's total population – was not being enforced upon the fifty-odd national minorities.

I was amazed to find out that around six thousand pilgrims a year left China to go to Mecca, and much more so when I realized that a good many of them travelled via Hong Kong and Singapore. Oh, the marvellous and strange subtleties of Special Branch! I wondered whether they had an extra posse of plain-clothes policemen watching when the pilgrim ships carrying passengers from 'Red' China anchored in Singapore.

The Muslim Huis had their own special representatives at the National Assembly; they had their own Party cadres. Now they acceded to education, to universities; they had autonomous rights as to custom, religion, and to studying the Koran in Arabic script. There had only been thirty doctors among them in 1949; there were now 262. They had 129 university professors instead of the eleven there had been in 1949. All meat consumed by Muslims was killed by Muslim butchers. The Muslim Cultural Association had members who had studied in Cairo's El-Hazar University.

But of course there were changes; such as Ramadan, the month of fasting. It was not proscribed, but 'We absolve people from fasting who work in offices, schools and factories,' the ulama of the Great Mosque in Peking told me. There were 130,000 Huis in Peking, and 30,000 worked in factories.

Unlike Malaya, where four wives per man were still

permitted, here much effort was concentrated on trying to achieve monogamy. Whereas by 1958 monogamy became the rule among the Hans, in the Hui communities this would not occur until about 1965.

I wrote all this information down and prepared a report on it, and sent it to the Malayan Sociological Research Institute in Singapore.

Noticing my interest, Kung Peng gave me a series of volumes: the records of transactions and exchanges – cultural, commercial, diplomatic – between China and other countries of the world, starting in the Roman times before Christ. This provided an invaluable perspective. My self-appointed task (one for which I was naturally fitted, as Kung Peng obliquely let me know very often) was to convey views and news, the aroma, savour, atmosphere, reactions of the outer world to the great 'within' of China; and to convey the sensations of China to the outer world.

How thin were my friends becoming, how thin! And how rude to refer to their loss of weight! One had to say, 'You look very fit.' Though some of them, in the evening, returning from work, staggered with fatigue and empty stomachs, they would reply with a big smile, 'Yes, we are very fit. We have all the food we need.'

Wu Chienta looked the ghost of himself as he took me to lunch. He refused my invitations. He ate reticently, and would only say in his low agreeable voice that there were temporary difficulties owing to natural calamities; that there had been great advances in industry although there were 'shortcomings owing to inexperience', but these were 'not more than the equivalent of one finger in ten'. He had worked for almost a year in a commune, and was now an expert in balancing burdens (he could carry eighty kilogrammes) at both ends of the flexible bamboo shoulder pole. He always looked neat and well-scrubbed, but now he had eschewed hair oil and wore a crew cut. There was no hair oil to be had in Peking, except for foreigners, in the hotels and at the Friendship Store.

I bumped into Edgar Snow in the lift of the Hsinchiao Hotel. I spent the evening freezing in his room before the heat came on at ten p.m., while Ed unburdened himself, talking of his travels through China, and the major questions, and the minor ones, which occurred to him. I gave him an aspirin because he was beginning a cold. Everyone caught colds in Peking. Ed was now waiting for some final important interviews: one with Chairman Mao himself; another one (his second or third) with Premier Chou Enlai. Ed did appear a little puzzled – as Felix Greene had written to me – because he suffered from a surfeit of information; and because, unlike me, he took down every word, being a meticulous and painstaking man who did not rush to conclusions. He could not make up his mind about the shortages. There were shortages, avowedly, yet everywhere he went he also saw enormous progress. How bad, how significant, were the shortages and the shortcomings of the Great Leap Forward?

Ed told me how gruelling had been his quarrel with the US State Department. 'They treat anyone who wants to go to China as an incipient criminal.' The State Department did not think that Ed could be 'objective' about China, 'Which means that they don't think I'm going to write the things they want to hear.'

Another problem which bothered him a great deal was relations between China and Russia. How true were the reports of the Western press that these relations were getting worse? He was waiting to hear directly from Mao and Chou about them.

A reception was organized by the Foreign Ministry at the International Club; I think it was in honour of Ed Snow. There was a large spread of dishes, succulent in colour and taste. Kung Peng was there. She beamed at me. She was obviously much thinner. 'Come, I want to show you someone,' she said to me. And took me to a side table, where a tall gaunt man dressed in blue with a worker's cap on his head, which he removed in salute to everyone who came up to him, was cramming food into his mouth. I have never seen a man eat so fast or swallow such large mouthfuls making them disappear without chewing. He turned upon me heavily myopic glasses and removed his cap. His head was neatly shaved. It was Puyi, ex-Emperor of China.

Puyi had lost his throne when he was a mere infant, in 1911, at the first Chinese Revolution. He had been hauled out of private life and proclaimed 'Emperor of Manchuko' in 1931, when the Japanese invaded China and detached Manchuria's three provinces from her. He had been supplied with a Japanese wife and had become a puppet. In 1945 he had been abandoned by the Japanese in their precipitous retreat and captured by the Russians when they in turn invaded Manchuria.

Puyi was imprisoned in the USSR; he was then recuperated by the Chinese Communists, re-educated, living with workers and peasants, doing manual labour, receiving political indoctrination and stitching his own clothes. Now he was free. He would begin a new life, and that is why he had been invited to the reception. He was taking a course in botany at the university. Within another year, he had married again, a hospital nurse. He lived quietly, in a comfortable house. He would write his autobiography, which I purchased in 1963.

Kung Peng thought I might be interested in seeing him. I was. Ed was also led up to him and did exchange some words with him.* Back at the hotel, Ed said he was not attracted to Puyi. He had, after all, been a traitor. Some quislings in Europe had been executed at the end of the war; but in China Puyi was reintegrated in the new society, and would die of cancer in 1968.

In that winter of 1960, the gossip about divergences within the Communist Party became widespread. There was, so Peking 'small lane' rumour had it, a rift between Mao Tsetung and some other, unnamed Party leaders. This had to

*See *The Other Side of the River*, op. cit.

do with the Great Leap Forward, with the agricultural disasters which had occurred, and also with the expanding quarrel with the Soviet Union.

I did not know what really went on. The 'within' *Reference News*, which is circulated round about 50 million cadres and Westerners living and working in China, was inaccessible to mere visitors like myself. Peking is an outrageously gossipy city; an inventive city where people have fertile imaginations and love to create sensational stories. How could one believe all that was being said?

Information in Peking has three levels: the first level for 'fraternal comrades', who are shown secret Party documents and told things that are not told to the unbaptized, non-Party, not living in China people. Then there is the level of the overseas Chinese who visit their families, hear ordinary talk and are confronted with the problems which their relatives encounter. Overseas Chinese are also allowed to read the local provincial newspapers; whereas from 1960 onwards, I was not allowed to see them, even if they lay on the tables before me.

The third level is the level for visitors. Increasingly, and especially during the Cultural Revolution, it would become the level where heavy mendacity prevailed. From 1960 onwards, so much became 'secret' that the middle cadre, the interpreter who was in contact with visitors, was often in a quandary. What could he do, when he was supposed to inform 'honoured guests', but lie, lie and lie again, since he could not reveal anything of what went on? The habit of absurd secrecy started to assume fantastic proportions: even an academic discussion on a medical pursuit would come under a ban, as 'state secret'.

In conversation with Chinese officials, with Kung Peng, I would stress that all provincial radio stations in China were monitored by the American Consulate in Hong Kong; that a considerable number of local newspapers were almost daily smuggled out of China. 'The situation is that China's enemies know better what is going on in China than China's friends,' I would say again and again. But nothing could be done about it, such was the power of bureaucracy and its inertia. 'It is illegal for a friend of ours to know these things' was one of the prizewinning answers I received from an official. I thought then of all those eager, willing friends of China; for whom every word uttered by interpreters was the truth, the policy, the line, the very word of Mao himself. How many of them, in the years to come, would realize that they should have been, perhaps, a little more sceptical? And that even includes me, for I believed, by dint of hearing them, certain things which turned out later to be falsehoods.

But I was neither misled nor taken in that winter, nor for a good many subsequent years. My ear to the ground, my qualified criticisms, were not perturbing to Kung Peng. But they would be perturbing to others in the bureaucracy, and every year, therefore, I would have to do battle, not only outside China, but within China, in order to remain honest with myself.

As winter deepened and the days stretched a longer darkness, I saw the hunger grow, the queues at the food markets lengthen, the scarcity become more evident. I walked the streets; adopted the shuffle of those around me; a wordless eavesdropping when clothes obfuscated one's being: I had a wardrobe to look like an inhabitant. In the market, row upon row of small shops with nothing in them but a passive, seated salesman and empty shelves. No nails, no string, no shoes, no glasses, no . . . everywhere people with their heads well within their shoulders and scarcely lifting their feet went from store to store. No buttons, no needles, no thread, no kettles, no saucepans, no . . .

They stared at the bare shelves and went on to the next shop. Wearily and steadily.

But still it was not like Old China. And the difference was the Party cadres. They too shuffled, they too went hungry. They got thinner even more quickly than ordinary people did because they went on working; and so many of them, to give an example, had voluntarily cut their already scarce rations.

I got an idea of the scale of rations instituted that winter.

For the high intelligentsia, scientists, professors, researchers, writers and artists, more sugar, more fats and oils, more meat, an average of around 2,000 or more calories per day. 'The active brain needs a great deal more energy-giving food,' I was told again and again.

Less fat for the 'average intellectuals', the schoolteachers. This brought them to 1,800 calories or thereabouts.

For steelworkers and workers in heavy industries, thirty-five to forty catties (a cattie is half a kilogramme) of rice per month, but less fats, oils and sugar. They must have had an average of 2,500 calories per day.

For ordinary workers, round about thirty catties per month, depending on physical demand, and an average of 2,500 calories per day.

For students, possibly 2,000 calories per day; more protein than for the workers, but less carbohydrates. For lower office cadres and sedentary occupation workers, between twenty-six and thirty catties of grain per month; their calories worked out at 1,500 to 1,800 per day. Enough to live on. Not enough to keep them warm and active in the unheated houses and offices of that bitter winter.

The worst off, finally, were the city housewives, except when they were pregnant in a factory, in which case they got extra rations, equivalent to workers' rations. Otherwise, I realized, they would get 1,200 calories or less.

Of course each city, each region, each province differed in its allocation of rations. The north of China was possibly the worst off. There were some communes in north-west China where there would be no meat at all to eat throughout that winter and the next spring, only rough flour, maize mixed with rye and buckwheat, dumplings filled with seaweed, which were steamed. Seaweed, a great item of consumption in Japan, was at that time introduced in China and used as a filling; it proved important in sustaining the population until 1962.

North China was far too cold for winter vegetables except for cabbage. There were great mountains of cabbage to be seen everywhere along the streets of Peking; every lane had its cabbage hill. But sweet potatoes could not be had, nor was beancurd available, or beans of any kind.

However, in the kindergartens and nurseries in Peking and Shanghai, beancurd milk and peanuts were given to the children as extra food. The peanuts came from Szechuan; but in 1961 Szechuan would run out of peanuts.

Areas in south and west China did not at first suffer as badly as those in the north. In Szechuan, in 1960, there would be four vegetables a day available in all the communes; and milk for the sick and for the children in Chengtu. Then in 1961 Szechuan was badly hit by drought and by the fact that so much of the food it produced had been taken to feed other provinces.

I began to see in Peking and Sian and Taiyuan cases of beriberi on the street, in the queues waiting at the hospital gates. The swollen faces were obvious.

Before the Chinese New Year, which occurred at the end of January, the ration of pork and meat would go up; it had been reduced to about half a cattie per person per month; it would double for the two months of January and February. And there was also a small rise in poultry available, and in fish. But it was difficult to get people in the north to eat fish. They were not accustomed to it.

Every institution, factory, school and university department, as well as the ministries, would grow their own vegetables. In Peking and Sian and Lanchow and Taiyuan and Tientsin, hens and rabbits were bred indoors and quantities of edible vegetables would be grown in flower pots. Many of my friends would grow cabbages and tomatoes on their window sills or on shelves built near the windows.

The people swept up the falling leaves lining the roads in and out of the cities. The leaves made an infusion which was taken to prevent scurvy. The sweeping was a daily sight until there were no more leaves.

Resourcefully schools, factories, universities and administrative departments organized 'transport corps'. These teams went to the countryside communes to buy and bring back, sometimes on their backs, necessary food for the community. 'Some of these units are pretty smart; they have leased fields in the communes and entered directly into contracts with the communes to supply food and to raise pigs. Each unit has its own pigs,' Wanchun told me. This splendid ingenuity, ostensibly ignored, enabled the people to survive and to go on working. The bank in Chungking where Second Brother worked had a special 'transport team', and Second Brother became extremely adept at finding food.

'The Party keeps one eye open and one shut,' said Wang Wanchun, 'it knows what is going on, it ignores it.'

At first the villages ate better than the cities; peasants ate up the grain, the meat, everything that was available. But in some places requisition of grain and food left the peasants with almost nothing, and there were revolts. I saw evidence of such a one on the train going to Sian: about twenty people, some with chains on their feet. They were obviously peasants, and they were obviously being taken away as 'counter-revolutionaries'. These cases of arbitrariness would be denounced in 1961. A writer told me, 'Every small Party secretary at commune level can wield the power of a petty tyrant. It takes well-trained cadres, and disciplined ones, to resist corruption in times of hardship.'

In the communes I visited I was at times deluged with statistics proving how much more per *mu* of land was grown, all due to the Leap Forward, to close planting, to the water canals and reservoirs and wells. Of course these figures were correct for experimental plots; but I could not find full barns anywhere in 1960, although two years later a point was made of showing me the well-stored grain. The fundamental trouble was the hasty harvesting in 1958 and 1959, owing not only to the steel campaign in the first year of the Leap, but also to the drafting of so many millions for dam and canal building, and also of seventeen to twenty million peasants from the suburban communes to the cities and small towns to work in the thousands of new factories which had been erected.

More and more, as time went on, I heard about the 'communist wave' which had taken place in 1958. It had seized the land like a frenzy, had lasted about six months, and had done untold harm. With beating of drums, flag waving and dancing the peasants had celebrated the advent of communism. Money was abolished. Everything was free: clothes and haircuts, television sets were purchased with available funds and cinemas were built when electricity had not yet been installed. All private plots had been abolished; and privately owned trees felled as they were 'capitalist symbols'. Secondary occupations such as weaving and embroidery, basket making, making of noodles and curing of hams and of tobacco had all been abolished too. The slaughter of pigs was phenomenal. Eat, eat, eat. The state will provide. Then privately owned pigs and hens and ducks were collectivized, which meant that they were crammed together so that no one looked after them properly. How had this come about? Who had given the directives which led to this insanity? There were no directives, but a general permeation of overweening enthusiam, brooking no reason or caution of any kind. The losses were enormous. In 1960, they were being felt everywhere.

I saw pig cholera in the north, as I took the new railway which had been built from Sian to Chengtu, across the Tsingling Mountains. All along the roads, by the rail track, the peasants carried dying pigs, pigs that could no longer walk, to market, to be killed. Impassive, the other train passengers looked on. There were no eggs to be had anywhere. No meat in the restaurant dining car; I got a little tinned ham with cabbage.

'How did this come about, Hualan?' I sat with her and her sister, a painter. Her sister was back from the countryside. She and other teachers and the students of her academy of art had 'gone down' to teach the peasants in the communes. Peasants were now learning to write and to paint. Hualan thrived on difficulty; she was energetic and hopeful and had voluntarily cut down her grain ration from twenty-six catties a month to twenty-two, and then she would cut it to eighteen. She and her sister, as high-class intellectuals, got more sugar and fats and meat. 'That's enough for us, so long as we have coffee.' Coffee was very hard to get, but Hualan could obtain a supply from the shop for foreigners because of her Polish mother.

Hualan's sister the painter was not well; she had worked too hard in the countryside. She had bad haemorrhages. 'We were building a dam and we worked sometimes fourteen or sixteen hours a day.' One of the young, enthusiastic art students with her died of exhaustion; he had not wanted to stop working and he worked and worked, and suddenly he fell down dead.

'Everything was done too quickly, far too quickly,' Hualan and her sister told me. Now everyone was looking forward to readjustment. 'Premier Chou Enlai will do it. He will find a way to clean up the mess. He always does.' Everyone, it seemed, was looking towards Chou Enlai to salvage the situation.

'It will be better in the spring,' said Hualan.

All my friends stuck strips of newspaper around every window and door in their homes, for insulation against cold draughts. There was not going to be any coal that winter. 'We have to work with our coats on,' said my friend the writer, Yeh, and so he did, writing and sometimes blowing on his fingers when they became too cold to hold the pen.

Winter crept on. In the streets people walked very slowly, saving strength. They bicycled slowly. But there were no complaints. There were no beggars either. Everywhere in the small lanes shops sprang up for mending and cobbling and making do: for repairing kettles and pans and the soles of shoes, and garments that were getting threadbare, and for carding cotton for padded coats, and for blankets. In the market a tailor had found a new way of cutting clothes which economized on cloth. This was publicized and crowds came to watch and to learn. The ration of cotton that year would be very small: three metres per person. Only newborn babies would get a good deal, up to fifteen metres. And of course there was an allowance of clothes for funerals.*

I bought shoelaces in place of string. I used them to tie books I had bought and was sending to myself in Hong Kong. Shoelaces were suddenly plentiful, but they disappeared quickly. And there were no shoes, neither of leather (very expensive), nor of cloth.

Suddenly the market was invaded by African dates. They were all bought up in Peking within a day. But in Szechuan, where I went later, no one wanted them; because the consignment that reached Chengtu was full of worms.

Schools were closed part of the time to spare the strength of teachers and children. 'Everyone can take days off to sleep if they want to sleep.' No one exacted attendance. 'It is better to keep your strength and move as little as possible.' In the factories, too, the workers were on half time, to conserve their energy.

At the Hsinchiao Hotel and at the embassies to which I was invited, a polite game was going on. It was called 'counting the Chinese calories': estimating the calories the average Chinese man or woman consumed; evaluating how long the Chinese people could hold on with the rigorous diet they were on. 'It is quite impossible. They're getting less than 1,200 a day . . .'

I was stiff with fury. I wish I could say that true concern, real goodwill, was dominant. It was certainly there, among some individuals; some diplomats, some newsmen. But on the whole there was gloating and satisfaction that the Great Leap had 'come a cropper'. 'China's setbacks may make her less inflexible,' said a European ambassador. Among people from Third World countries there was surprise and genuine concern. 'I thought the Chinese knew how to run things . . . what's really happened?'

'We have enough, more than enough,' said my friends with thinning faces. Their smiles were pinched and a little haggard, but they carried on. Unfailingly courteous, they

*Every dead person is buried in a new set of clothes.

would invite me and ply me with food. To what incredible trouble had they gone to obtain this food; and perhaps, for this one meal, they had sacrificed a week's ration, or even the meat for a month . . . 'Please let me have the pleasure of inviting you,' I would say to them. The restaurants were open and foreigners could eat in them, although they were expensive. But my friends would fall silent for a space, and then smile and say, 'Oh, but it is so much more pleasant to eat at home.'

Pride, Chinese pride. Dignity. They would not even accept a meal from me. Especially because times were so hard, food so difficult to come by. How could I then reveal to foreigners who were not friends what my friends ate? Outside China there was a campaign humiliating China, launched in America. 'Feed thine enemy' was the slogan; and food was offered. 'We practise self-reliance, we have enough,' everyone said to me. And to deny this, at the time, would have been to insult them.

Hualan lost four kilos that winter; and almost everyone I knew lost far more. Yet it was I who caught one cold after another, whose nose streamed, who would come down with bronchitis in January, when the air and the earth rubbed each other raw and the wind clawed at my skin and tore it.

'We have enough, more than enough.' A Canadian doctor had sent me a small bar of soap to give to a Chinese doctor whom she had known. 'Our newspapers tell us there is no soap in China.' It was quite true that soap was extremely scarce, but the Chinese doctor handed me back the soap with a smile. So I had to post it back to Canada.

'The shortages are temporary . . . transient difficulties . . . soon with the spring harvest . . . natural calamities . . . but in the spring . . .' So everyone round me said.

There were no political meetings held anywhere that winter. People were too tired.

Around the shop for foreigners on Hatamen Street, at dusk, sometimes small groups of people collected to watch those going in and coming out laden with food parcels. They would watch quietly, then slowly shuffle away.

Suddenly everyone began to talk about fertilizers, and the need for them. Simon Hua told me that 'the Russians don't know much about chemical fertilizer factories'. There were meetings held by scientists, engineers, agronomists, and fertilizer factories were a-building in many places. Just as suddenly people were talking about alkalinity in soil. 'It's due to upsetting the water level by hasty water conservancy projects . . . one hundred million peasants have been building dams and reservoirs and there's a lot of improper building and inadequate drainage . . .' Simon's friend, a hydraulic engineer, had warned the cadres, but no one had paid heed.

I went to see Hsueh Mah; she now stayed in Papa's room. She had some coal. I brought her tins of food and she always asked for more. The Party cadre in charge of the street came in when I was with her. His face was swollen. Beriberi. 'I am ill, I am ill,' moaned Hsueh Mah. 'You are not well, your face is swollen,' I told the cadre, ignoring Hsueh Mah. I tried to give him a tin of ham but he refused politely. 'It is nothing. It comes from eating too much cabbage.'

One morning, through my hotel window, I watched an old woman with bound feet, a grandmother, come out on the street complaining that her hen had run away and very shortly several other old women, all with similarly bound feet, materialized on the street, out of the walls; they discussed with great civility the matter of the missing hen. 'Perhaps now she will come back,' said the first grandmother loudly, hobbling away cheerfully. I had no doubt that the street would look into the matter. Of course there must have been petty larceny. I think that after a certain point of hunger, inevitably, the social order does begin to be eroded.

However, the rationing was fairly well done and there was tight control so that prices did not go up; nevertheless, a small free market was allowed. 'One eye open, one eye shut,' said Wanchun. 'That's the wisdom of the Party. It allows certain things.' In fact, the Party was trying to stimulate free markets, and all private plots had been restored, and there would soon be another policy in agriculture, to undo the harm done by the 'communist wave'.

The hospitals were very busy caring for the sick, who were many. But the maternity hospital, which had been quite full in the previous year, was fairly empty. 'We do many abortions,' said the gynaecologist, a young woman, matter of factly. 'The women ask for it.' With food scarcity wombs were emptied speedily. There was also a great deal of both amenorrhoea and haemorrhage: amenorrhoea mostly among housewives and female workers. 'No periods since the cold set in. Nature's way of preserving the body.' 'But some people I know have haemorrhages,' I said. The gynaecologist laughed gently. 'Usually high-class intellectuals. Because they get more proteins and fats perhaps . . .'

How strange, I thought, woman's reaction to stress. There was I, well-fed in Malaya, suffering the same uterine troubles as women in Peking.

My overseas Chinese friend, Mr H, came to see me. He regularly returned to China, every two or three years. And now he was upset, for he had been back to his old village in Anhwei province to see his relatives. Things were not too good. Anhwei has always been a difficult province. And now it had no reserves; and a harsh winter, and the crazy, pushful cadres in Anhwei had liquidated the most gainful occupations of the peasants and left them only some rice and wheat, and then they had not been able to collect the harvest because of the steel campaign and the water conservancy projects . . .

Mr H had relations in the village. They now clung to him. Although they did not actually starve, they were very short of food, and panicky. 'You're so fat I'm going to eat and eat with you until I get as fat as you,' clamoured the head of the clan, who was Mr H's first cousin. He installed himself in Mr H's hotel for overseas Chinese and ate and ate at Mr H's expense. And Mr H, who from the age of twenty-four had been abroad in America, fed his cousin. 'It is the old, old fear of starvation which is coming up again; although the communes do provide subsistence,' said Mr H when he told me his story. 'But in Anhwei the peasants have reverted to old times. The people who die are the old and the babies. The old women are simply not given any food; and as for girl babies, I think that infanticide has come back . . .'

'The iron bowl. The communes are our unbreakable iron bowl.' So said the slogan, and it was also true. Never before had so many millions been provided for, even if they received only enough for survival. In the past landlords used to starve out fractious tenants by breaking their cooking utensils, which they could not replace because they were too poor even to buy a cooking pot. I thought back to England during the war years, the rationing, and the old people, the lonely, single individuals I had seen dying with sweet muteness of hunger . . . Here in China the strong did survive; the weak had a chance, but a lean one . . .

From 1960 onwards the communist government would buy grain abroad, in Canada, in Australia, for the cities, in order to allow the peasants to keep what they had.

I offered a waiter at the Hsinchiao Hotel a bar of chocolate. He refused a little angrily. 'I have enough to eat,' said he.

I lay in bed; the heat came on. I coughed and sneezed; it was always too hot at night in the hotel. But out there, in the web of lanes, dust and cold harried; in the darkness there would be deaths from pneumonia.

I took Wang Wanchun out to a restaurant. Not being a Party member, he was not averse to an occasional meal, and so we ate Peking duck, and it cost 23 *yuan*, four times as much as the previous year. The restaurants were, of course, prohibitively expensive, except those for the ordinary people, which retained the same prices but demanded ration coupons. The expensive restaurants did not ask for ration coupons.

I went to eat with my friends, Gladys Yang and her husband. They offered me a well-laid table. Gladys, as an Englishwoman, a foreigner, could get food from the foreign shops inaccessible to the Chinese. But her three children, who sat with us at the table, absolutely refused to eat the food spread out before them; they ate only half a bowl of rice and some cabbage. 'I am not hungry,' said the boy, scowling at his mother. Neither would the two girls eat what was before them.

'It's the schools,' said Gladys. 'The children have been told that this is a very bad year and that one must economize every mouthful of food, if possible.' And so she and I felt guilty, guilty, with all the food staring at us on the neat round plates and the children not eating, deliberately. And I think Gladys was sad, but she was also a little awed and proud that her children were able to understand, to participate, to show such self-control. 'I think that is what makes the strength of this country. It reacts, at times as one single body, a biological unity.' 'No one is going to moan and groan,' said her husband. 'We'll see it through, as we have so many bad times and good times in our long history. We'll see the bad times through.'

There were twelve Latin American delegations in Peking that October, including one led by Che Guevara, from Cuba. The Latin Americans at the Hsinchiao Hotel occupied large tables; their whole faces worked when they talked; and also their bodies. Their eyebrows went up and down. I had never seen so many handlebar moustaches, even in the officers' clubs of the Indian army, where such moustaches are carefully cultivated. A smooth-faced person must appear sinister, inhuman, in Latin America, I told Ed. 'I wonder that they are not disconcerted by the wrinkleless placidity of Chinese features.' 'What's the Spanish word for inscrutable?' asked Ed.

I went to see Third Brother and Sister-in-Law Jui at Peking University and, diffidently, to bring some tins of food. Third Brother was thinner, his neck scrawny. He had three children now, and a fourth was on the way. 'We have everything we need,' he said automatically as I handed over the ham and the honey and the dried walnuts and other eatables. A Canadian man named Fitzgerald had left behind him at the Hsinchiao Hotel some food and also some medicines; somehow or other they had fallen to me and I now brought them to Third Brother in case the children needed them.

Jui, who was still tremulous, easily upset, had been told by the Party woman in charge of welfare: 'Comrade, you must really find a way not to have another child. Four is enough.' Jui stuck to four children after that. She told me, 'I never wanted four, it just happened.'

Third Brother agreed that all classes at the University had been cut to spare the strength of students and teachers. The following spring it was envisaged to send 46 per cent of the city cadres down to the rural areas to help with the spring sowing and planting and to ensure a plentiful harvest. 'It's also a way to get the city fed at village level,' I said. Third Brother laughed his usual cheerful, noncommittal laugh.

I visited Simon Hua and his wife, Irène. They had extra rations since Irène was French and a foreign expert. Always, at home, throughout their almost three decades in China, they would eat French food, prepared by an old and faithful servant. Simon was no longer a 'rightist'. He had now been rehabilitated. And the house was warm and the food plentiful.

But Simon's father, Hua Nankuei, had died, and we talked about him for a long time, for he and my father had been inseparable friends. 'Both of them worked for China right up to the time they died,' said Simon. All these old engineers were forever afraid that something might go wrong with their beloved railways. Warlords and Japanese and new systems had come and gone, but all they cared for was to keep the railways running. 'They were indispensable, so they stayed on.'

'They were Chinese intellectuals, in love with China, in love with their people,' I said.

With the passing of Simon's father and the death of my father, only my Tibetan Uncle Liu remained of that batch of engineers trained in Belgium and France, who had humbly dreamed great dreams for China.

'China is the religion of every educated Chinese,' I

insisted. 'It was so for your father, for mine. It must be so for us too.'

'You are so Chinese in a way,' said Simon. 'All your reactions and your feelings . . . sometimes I feel that it is you who have never left China, and who live here, and that it is I, who came here in 1951, who is the foreigner.'

Where feeling was concerned, there was no doubt. Especially in that winter of 1960. Fiercely, wholeheartedly, I was defending China, even lying through my teeth (with a smile) to the diplomats and the newsmen who probed. Because only China was the heartbeat of my heart, the rise and fall of my blood, the substance of every cell of my body. I had not chosen this. It had chosen me. And all the more so when the wind howled like a wolf and winter fastened its iron will upon the land, and the whole world seemed to rise with glee to threaten China. Then, above all, I was Chinese.

It was Anna-Louise Strong who gave me the story about the Russians, which was only a wisp and a rumour until then.

In June 1960, both at the World Federation of the Trades Union Congress in Peking and at a meeting in Bucharest, there had been the most violent clashes between the Chinese and the Russians. In Bucharest Khrushchev had made a personal appearance, attacking Mao Tsetung as a dogmatist and a visionary. He had said, 'If the Chinese won't listen to us, there are ways and means of bringing them to heel.' He had called the Leap an exercise in waste and dogmatic extravagance.

Then in July, within a month, all Russian personnel, all experts and technicians, about twelve thousand of them, were abruptly withdrawn from China. In certain plants every blueprint and diagram was removed. Essential parts of machinery were also taken away. And no spare parts would be available. All construction work on many plants came to a standstill. Newly bought machinery was left to rust without shelter because the workers were inexperienced and there was no one to give orders; China did not have enough trained personnel to go round (and anyway, those who did give warning or say something cautionary were not listened to in those hectic days of the Leap Forward).

I went to the large Friendship Hostel, built a short distance out of the centre of Peking, in a park-like area. The hostel had housed several hundred Russian experts and their families. The buildings were imposing, Chinese style, with glazed green roof tiles, which must have cost an enormous amount. Inside the buildings were very large and beautiful flats with parquet floors, high ceilings, excellent furniture, bathrooms and the best plumbing in China. There were also two restaurants, one for Western food and one for Chinese food.

In that winter of 1960, the Friendship Hostel was sinister in its silent emptiness. Except for a few representatives of foreign communist parties who lived there, it was a ghostly, uninhabited city. The Canadian with whom I was going to lunch was a gloomily inarticulate man who spent the greater part of his time playing billiards. He had seen Edgar Snow, and Ed, fresh from major interviews, had implied to him – as to me – that the quarrel with the Russians would not become worse. 'I was worried sick. Ed's made my day,' said the Canadian. As many other communists from the West whom I would meet in Peking, he felt the earth would stop in its tracks if China and Russia fell out.

With us that day was a vivacious and garrulous woman, a foreign expert teaching in Peking. She was quite unable to utter a sentence without launching a couple of statistics. 'There's been a 29·4 per cent increase of wheat in the Ukraine in the last year . . . there are 41·2 per cent more sheep in Azerbaidjan . . .' She hugged and nursed and cradled and crooned statistics; they were her babies and she became upset if one questioned them. She and many others were easily irritated in those days of stress; and all of them were waiting, waiting to hear what was happening in Moscow.

For, ever since early November 1960, eighty-one communist parties of the world had been meeting in Moscow to thrash out differences; or rather, to argue, debate and come to a common declaration over the differences that had emerged between China and the USSR. There was no mention of anything material: of contracts, or economics, or joint ventures, or the demands from the Kremlin for immediate repayment . . . it was all on a very high plane of theoretical argument. Hours and days and weeks of debate; which would continue in the following years. Millions of words. And so many, so many were waiting, their souls suspended to what was going on in Moscow.

After lunch I wandered round the palatial Friendship Hostel. Nothing could be more helpless-making than the stolid look of these massive grey piles, with their bright glazed tile roofs in the sunswept dust of a Siberian wind, which swirled thick armfuls of fallen leaves (here they were not gathered) round and round the paved courtyards. And that bleary old-man look of the uncleaned windows behind which no one peeped or stirred. Desolation. Or so it seemed. 'Let us wait until the north wind has stopped. Then we shall see.'

Ed had had a long interview with Mao Tsetung on October 22nd; then he had talked again with Chou Enlai. After he left, I kept him and Felix acquainted with all modifications, because so many policies were changed in that winter of 1960-1. They both found my news somewhat disturbing, because I was telling them things that were diametrically the reverse of what they had been told. This was our first, but not our last, experience of how quickly things change in China.

For instance, the urban communes, which had been instituted in the cities in the first flush of the 'communist wave': all three of us were to see them; but I was to watch their disappearance. What remained was a web of small factories which have lasted until today: make-do and mend shops, embroidery shops, spare parts shops, electric bulb factories, cobbling shops, tailoring shops, established in every street, and chiefly operated by women; four million of them having been recruited for these auxiliary but indispensable services, which allowed more women to go into the factories for productive work.

In the rural communes, the mess halls, instituted in 1958 in the flush of 'everything must be collectivized since communism has now come', were already disappearing when I left. They would only serve people who did not live too far away. And the main complaint for everyone who ate in them was about quality. The stolid, realistic peasants pointed out that the food dispensed was absurdly bad; whereas the cook got fat. I was told the truth, that commune cooks were in many cases ex-landlords or rich peasants. Why so? Because somehow the job of cooking is regarded as a 'low' occupation. And this in a country famous for its cuisine! Can anyone explain to me this illogicality? But then, it was also true that ex-landlords and rich peasants were the only people available for such jobs, since poor and middle peasants were supposed to work the land.

Kung Peng invited me to dinner. We talked at great length, and frankly, of the 'shortcomings' of the Leap. This was, I think, because Premier Chou Enlai had said that the truth about the difficult agricultural situation must be told. Chen Yi too, in interviews with visitors, would blurt out how he had been carried away by a wave of euphoria in 1958. 'I believed a lot of the nonsense that I was told by some people,' he said. Kung Peng also told me, 'We trusted too much secondhand reports and grossly inflated figures . . . to tell the truth, the harvests were large, but they were guessed at.' There had been in some areas the determination to grow two crops where one had grown before; as a result, the peasants had harvested the first crop before it was ripe, and the grain had been unusable, but it had looked good to have so many sacks filled.

And then there were the producers of 'empty talk'. Some of them promised things that were totally impossible, but these were reported as if they had already been achieved, and then became hard fact – until they were exposed.

It was obviously painful for Kung Peng to go over the mistakes and the errors, the exuberance and the rashness; but this was only part of the story. She said not a word against the Russian sabotage, nor did she ascribe the evident industrial semi-collapse to anything but natural calamities and 'shortcomings in our way of doing things'. This, again, was due to Chou Enlai, who had said, 'It is up to us, the leadership, to take full responsibility for what has gone wrong.' Always, always, Chou Enlai would shoulder the total burden, when the mistakes were not of his doing; even when he, as well as Teng Hsiaoping, were warning, 'Stick to facts, and no boasting.' But what could this do when any sobering, waking up of people from the dream of immediate prosperity, was qualified as 'right-wing deviation' and 'pouring cold water on the people's fervour'?

'Kung Peng, I know all this,' I said, 'but I have full faith, full faith in the Chinese people. And I tell you that I also think that only with the system of the communes, only with the Communist Party, can China weather this period of disaster. I'm not saying this to please you, but I think that's how things are.'

I could compare with what happened in Old China: in times of famine and want, hoarders and millionaires making money out of the people's misery; prices shooting up; skeletons on the road, people eating mud . . . total social chaos. Here the centre held all things in place. And would hold.

A film was being shown in all the cinemas, and all over China. It was on Lenin during the great famine of the early years of the Soviet Revolution. It was not a very good film, but the point was obvious. The drawbacks, the shortfalls in food in China, were to be compared to that time in the USSR. At the same time, perhaps, it was a preparation for a new economic policy such as Lenin had carried out in those years.

The Chinese press was also full of articles on Lenin. But their aim was different. The articles were meant to point up the political correctness of the Chinese line. They were, I think, for the benefit of the great debate which was then going on in Moscow among the eighty-one communist parties and other affiliated parties of the world.

Lord Montgomery, hero of El Alamein, came to China on a private visit and was received by Mao Tsetung. Mao told Montgomery, 'We know something about fighting, about guerrilla war, about running villages. But we really do not know anything about economics. We shall have to learn it the hard way.' Montgomery predicted that China would prove a worthy friend and partner. He advocated making friends with China. He was politely ignored even in his own country.

I saw my first and only prostitute at dusk near the foreign bakery and cake shop in Hatamen Street. The cake shop had once been owned by a Greek family; and as a child I went there every Sunday with Mama, because on Sundays we were allowed a cake each. Later I gave private lessons in arithmetic to the daughter of the Greek cake shop owners and in return received a cup of chocolate and cakes to eat. Now the Greek owners had gone. The cake shop still functioned, however, and continues to do so today.

That evening I was bulkily clad, wore trousers; perhaps the would-be prostitute thought I was a man. She looked savagely at passers-by. She did not smile or speak. She wore a skirt and stockings and stretched one defiant, abrupt leg in front of me.

I told Rewi Alley about it that night, when I went to see him. 'Honey, there are bound to be such things in times of stress,' said he.

CHAPTER 12

Survival: 1960–1961

The railway from Peking via Sian and the north-west to Szechuan province had been built after Liberation; many new railways were undertaken, opening regions never accessible before. How glad Papa would have been to ride on them with me, I thought, as the locomotive puffed painfully up the mountain slopes and I watched a land so primitive that it was like being in another country. This was the area through which the Red Army had walked its way in the Long March. The locomotive engine often stopped for hours in the night, as if to catch breath.

It was extremely dry and cold on the north side of the Tsingling range separating the north-west from Szechuan, and most of the time I played cards with my fellow travellers. At each small railway station there were one or two food sellers, and everyone came down to buy, queuing in orderly fashion for rough loaves of coarse bread, and sometimes dumplings filled with seaweed.

Suddenly the land changed. The train gathered speed: it was now going downhill. The air was soft and moisture-laden. There was still poverty, but we were now in a moist green world, Szechuan, where the swallow does not depart all winter. And all of us sighed with relief as our necks eased out of our shoulders, and stiffness out of our bones. We repeated to each other how Szechuan was China's great treasure house, rice basket, and someone recited Li Po's poem: Oh how difficult are the roads to Szechuan!

We came to Chengtu without fanfare. There were bamboo groves on both sides of the road, and the thatched houses were rickety and moss-grown. The Szechuan cadres who greeted me were as thin as string. Although Szechuan was not a calamity area, and the crops that autumn had been fair, yet it was on strict rationing because it was supplying five provinces with rice. And by the spring of 1961 Szechuan would be hit by a most terrible drought, the worst for over a century, which lasted 180 days. The black, life-giving soil which squeaked with a myriad lives in every handful would become dead and caked in that puzzle pattern which is seen in parched fields when·all the water has been sucked out of the ground. But the real problem of Szechuan was that at the Leap close planting and other experiments and blanket application of directives ordered by ignorant cadres had brought the harvests right down, and there were no reserves.

Third Uncle and Third Aunt and their son, Sixth Brother, with his wife, and many cousins, gathered in Third Uncle's new house. It was almost like the old days, when the sun sparkled just before the New Year festival, and the Hall of the Ancestors was redolent with incense, while from the painted eaves hung parrots chained to pewter perches, squawking.

The government had moved Third Uncle because a school was to be erected on the site of his old house; and the new one was built according to his specification. 'The government is very kind to me now,' said Third Uncle contentedly. But, he added, I might have noticed, perhaps, some difficulties . . . which he knew were transient, of course . . . because certain people did not understand Szechuan or its agriculture . . . now we should hope that in the spring all would come right. He would not say more, and we did not discuss agriculture again. Everyone in the family was thinner, though not ill. There was enough for them to eat, but not enough to acquire that smooth padding of underskin fat which keeps one warm during the cold season.

'Come and eat with me at the restaurant of the People's Palace Guest House,' I said. 'We shall,' said Third Uncle, and rose immediately, dusting his grey wool gown, and swinging his arms to unstiffen them. 'Let us go.' He trusted me entirely to know that this was not sponging, and he would not pretend that he did not want a good meal. I ordered all the dishes I could think of, and Third Uncle gave no advice, although I doubted that the composition of the banquet was up to his standards. I was as nervous as the first time I had cooked a meal for him in Chungking, and thereafter was for ever without face as a housewife because, as the lid of the soup tureen was lifted there, on the top of the liquid, floated a big bluebottle . . . And Third Uncle, kindly, had said, 'It's only more meat in the soup,' and served himself, after spooning the fly out.

Third Uncle and Third Aunt and all my cousins ate with deliberate slowness, not hurrying. Good manners. At the end Third Aunt asked that all the food that was left be wrapped up, and she took it away with her, and the waiters nodded understandingly. But when I tried to have them to another meal, Third Uncle would not accept. 'Once is enough. It is too expensive,' said he. And this despite the fact that the Szechuan Party cadres who were taking me around urged him, saying, 'Your niece has come from so far on such a long journey . . . of course you must see more of each other . . .' Rationing in Szechuan was stricter than in Peking, and Third Uncle and Third Aunt could not give me a meal at their house.

Before I left Chengtu, Sixth Brother procured for me an enormous ten-kilo caulked basket of pickled beancurd; that wonderful red beancurd made in Pihsien, the small town where our Family has lived for three centuries or more. How had he obtained it? Nowhere had I seen beancurd that year. 'From a farmer I know . . .' The countryside ate up its own beancurd, and also ate up the noodles produced there. Sixth Brother had cycled twenty-five kilometres back and forth, after his work, to get the beancurd for me. It had such a wonderfully beancurdy tang that my room in the hotel was redolent with it; and outside in the corridor I would find groups of curious people, standing still, breathing in the beancurd smell; and that was because it was. in a woven basket daubed with clay, and then wrapped in oilskin, and the clay leaked slightly. The Family looked at the beancurd, and our mouths watered as we contemplated the paunchy container, but no one would share it with me. 'It's yours. It's yours.'

I walked about Chengtu, and of course I saw new factories, and was told about all the leaping advances, and duly recorded them, for much of it was real and true. The little cattle of Szechuan, shoed with grass shoes because of the eternal gooey black mud which ate into their hooves, did not look in bad shape. Small black pigs sauntered in the rutted mud lanes, and they did not have pig cholera – or so I hoped. There were hordes of young children about. 'There are too many children,' I said crisply. But the cadres smiled and said, 'But we have plenty.' Obviously they were not in agreement with the family planning policies I had heard about in Peking. 'Of course we *hope* each family won't have more than four children,' they said condescendingly. 'But it is difficult; we are still educating the masses.' The whole problem, it seemed to me, was that the propaganda for family planning was being done by one organization, the National Federation of Women, but that there was no co-ordination between them and the medical staff of hospitals and clinics. Only in the cities, and chiefly among the Party cadres, would there be family planning and also abortions; even then, the consent of the potential grandparents on both sides was first required. In the countryside, every baby born received a full adult ration of food from the very first day. And this militated against family planning. The quick-witted Szechuanese already had a jingle to sing that year: 'Oh, better produce a little meat ball than work for workpoints . . .' The meat ball means a baby.

Third Uncle continued to be active; this kept him cheerful. Inactivity made him morose and aged him. That winter he seemed to regain vital essence. He had kept his golden monkey fur, which covered his armchair and stopped arthritis. He filled many sheets with calligraphy, sitting at his beautiful Ming desk, which had been his father's and his grandfather's and even before that had served, and I coveted it greatly; but of course it disappeared at the Cultural Revolution.

Third Uncle talked in a leisurely but vague way of meetings which were being held; meetings of scholars, and intellectuals, convoked to put their heads together and readjust matters. 'It is not good to despise knowledge,' said he. He looked at all of us challengingly. 'Szechuan is still the treasure house of China,' he stated, with the pleasured assurance of a man well in his own country and his own skin. He asked me about Papa and about the funeral arrangements; he was glad there would be a stone with Papa's name engraved upon it, as well as his profession. 'Papa was never denounced as a rightist,' I asserted.

Third Uncle's prominent cheekbones stuck out a little more; his skin was smooth ivory over them, and he had small fits of silence; that was all that age and having less to eat imposed upon him. His vocabulary had both extended and shrunk; he searched within today's political phrases for convenient words which would not recall the past too much, yet at the same time convey a hint of the consolations of memory. The fact that his son, Sixth Brother, could never be moved out of Chengtu was great solace. For the government had a ruling that in every family, one grown-up son or daughter must remain with the old parents, to look after them, and therefore must be provided with a job in the same city.

I went to Chungking, and called on Third Sister and her husband. Third Sister was ill; she had not lost weight at all, but because she had heart trouble and high blood pressure she was an invalid and received extra food. Of course, when one had a weak heart one was dispensed from work, meetings and political sessions as well. 'She is very sensitive, very easily shocked,' said her husband, who was most concerned, and hovered round her chair (he had lost a great deal of weight).

Sixth Brother was the opposite of Third Sister. He actually enjoyed meetings and political debate: 'I like to argue.' He was happy with his job, which had to do with communications, telephones and cables throughout the whole province.

I gave Third Sister my basket of beancurd; it really leaked too much; I did not think I could take it all the way back to

Peking with me. She would share it with Second Brother,
who was in Chungking and who described to me how the
bank had organized teams of its employees to go to the
neighbouring communes and bring food back. 'But we have
not seen beancurd recently,' said he, and his mouth watered
as he looked at the basket. In the streets of Chungking the
shops were very bare. 'It's because the peasants from the
communes came into the city and bought up everything they
could lay hands on with the money which had been given to
set up the communes.' All of a sudden there were no more
socks or shoes or clothes, or satchels for schoolchildren or
exercise books or paper. Because there were now schools in
the communes and they needed paper and exercise
books . . .

I stood on the top terrace of the hippopotamic People's
Palace, the ornate balconies of which had been designed by
Third Sister, and I noted what I was to see in all the cities of
China: the new tall chimneys. Factory chimneys. All built
and waiting. But no smoke came out of them. And along the
banks of the Great River, and at the railway station and on
the streets and in courtyards, there would be piles, large and
small, of machine parts: tubes and shafts, and whole
machines too, and even dynamos without covers, and all this
was for the factories that had been built. But now the
factories were left, vacated, empty; some had no roofs or
doors or windows. I hoped that the pile of machinery would
be removed quickly, used elsewhere, would not rust . . . it
was such a waste, such a waste. But I would see the piles right
up to 1963, and then they had rusted.

Along all the streets were pedlars, squatting in front of
square pieces of cloth, selling screws for door jambs, and
tape, and small scissors, and a thousand other disparate and
wonder-making odds and ends; an empty bottle, a comb,
two rusty nails and sometimes a piece of embroidery. Before
them people squatted, choosing carefully, bargaining
slowly. 'We have some shortage of consumer goods, the
demand has been so great . . .' 'There's been too heavy an
investment in capital construction. Our light industry has

suffered somewhat . . .' 'Perhaps too many things have been attempted at once, too quickly . . .' Thus the cadres. But none of us would give birth to words that curse and alienate and bring on disaster by the power of invoking evil and calamity. We knew too well the power of words, the headlong precipitous thrust of words. For the strange alchemy whereby, with a casual and careless sentence, 'Communism is here', so much drama and want had come – was that not a lesson for us to be cautious? The only safe word, the one we all used, was 'readjustment'. And so at dinner we all agreed that the troubles were temporary and would be speedily over, and we beamed at each other and raised small thimble glasses of *maotai* wine, pledging our confidence in the future.

I went back to Peking, and the Foreign Minister, Chen Yi, received me. We talked pleasantly of many subjects, but not of the USSR. And this was because the conference in Moscow was still proceeding. Every day foreign diplomats anxiously scrutinized the Chinese newspapers (and their own) for hints of what was happening in Moscow among the eighty-one communist parties assembled there. The Chinese delegation was headed by Liu Shaochi, who in 1960 had become the Head of State; Mao had relinquished the chairmanship of the state, keeping the chairmanship of the Party. Rumour had it that Liu Shaochi favoured an accommodation or a compromise with the Russians, but that Teng Hsiaoping, the Secretary-General of the Chinese Communist Party, who was in Moscow with Liu, had upset the Russians with his bluntness . . .

Chen Yi talked about the massive aid programme to the Third World which China was launching. 'Whatever our sacrifices, we shall not give it up.' He said America was getting deeply involved in South East Asia, courting military adventure there in the name of 'containing Red China', and that this was dangerous for her. 'We want to untie knots, to smooth out difficulties . . . they wish to *make* difficulties. Yet we need peace, only peace . . .'

And then we talked about the internal situation. Yes, Chen Yi said, mistakes had been made. 'Look at me. I believed someone who told me: I can grow ten thousand catties of rice on twenty square metres of land . . .' There had been a breakdown in communication between the basic production level and the leadership. 'We did not really know what was happening below . . .' It was time, he said, to 'open up'.

Now this problem of 'opening up' rather than 'clamping down' was of course connected with the policy of the Hundred Flowers. 'There seems to be a tendency to fall for the loud mouths,' I said. 'Yes, there should be less big empty talk,' said Chen Yi. But how to get rid of the talkers and promote only the doers? Party members did not listen enough to the people; they behaved 'like tigers whose tails cannot be touched',* and they took revenge on anyone who criticized them.

'We must stop putting caps on people,† hanging political labels round their necks whenever they open their mouths and we don't like what they say . . . this is not helpful to our cause.' But the problem was there; and would recur, and assume fantastic proportions during the Cultural Revolution. Chen Yi himself was then called counter-revolutionary and brought before a kangaroo court to be grilled by young Red Guards.

Chen Yi then spoke of 'readjustment' and the need to enroll the efforts of the intellectuals 'to consolidate the gains of the Leap and eliminate the mistakes made'. This truly meant 'opening up', another Hundred Flowers; and in fact another Hundred Flowers would be launched, in early 1961, and both Chou Enlai and Chen Yi would be most active in promoting this new era of criticism and comparative freedom.‡ That meant another swing of the pendulum, that

---

*A saying by Mao Tsetung.
†Politically labelling them.
‡Chou Enlai's major speech of 1961 on democracy would only be officially published in 1979.

immense Chinese pendulum, going right-left, left-right, all through the history of the Revolution.

Kung Peng told me how Chen Yi had mislaid his ration book a few weeks previously and had been in dire distress for about a week; during which time he refused all privileges, including eating in a restaurant. His friends fed him until he could get a new ration book.

Chou Enlai also received me, later in December. He walked up and down, slowly, looking vaguely about the room. He was obviously under strain. But it was controlled strain. With him, passion and fury exteriorized as lambent ice. His voice shook a little when he was very tired or upset, but it was always cold, restrained and low. How thin he was! I noticed that his collar was too large for his neck now. He had not slept the night before, Kung Peng told me. Too much work. Nor the night before that. He slept about two hours a day, after lunch; and not always then. But there was a diamond-cutting elegance in his voice when he spoke of 'those who think they can bring us to our knees', who thought that because of China's difficulties she could be threatened and subdued.

Who was he talking about, America or Russia? He did not specify. In fact, throughout that year and the next no Chinese would openly accuse the Russians of anything. Chou Enlai said that America was like 'a man balancing an armful of eggs. He cannot move or he will lose them all'. This did not sound altogether threatening to China. Or again, that the US was like a man trying to catch ten fleas with ten fingers. This was actually citing Mao's jest: 'How difficult to put ten fingers on ten hopping fleas! The fleas hop at will, the fingers are bound to each other.' Obviously it was not, in Chou's mind, America that was the main 'threat' at this juncture.

Chou Enlai talked a long time of Lenin; of the hardships in the USSR during the 1920s. 'Nothing is ever acquired without pain . . . we shall overcome our present problems.' There was hardship, but there was no famine. 'You may go anywhere, you will meet problems and difficulties, but not the famines of the past . . . the Leap has already brought us results that people do not know about . . . those who think that China has failed, they will be surprised one day.'

As I watched his thin face with its beetling brows I thought, 'I am not going to give ammunition to those who rejoice when China is in dire straits.' Chou Enlai held China together with all the love and strength of his spirit and his body. And many they were, millions they were, who also, stoically, worked themselves to the bone, to death, and uncomplainingly gave up their lives for China . . . and would I insult them, their self-respect, their dignity? I thought, 'When the bad days are over and the sun shines there will be time enough to tell the world how a whole nation gritted its teeth and so many pinned a smile upon their faces; how they refused to be degraded with gifts and charity; how their insides ached with hunger, and their bodies were so cold, so cold in their icy small houses . . .'

Cold. All my friends were cold. Kung Peng did not light a fire; the heating only came on for two hours every night in the residential flats of the Foreign Ministry, just enough not to freeze entirely. When I went to my cousins', we all pretended not to notice the cold; but it was difficult to sit with one's legs and feet turning to ice.

And someone told me that Chou Enlai, too, did not light a fire, and in his office everyone was called upon to save coal and electricity. He sat in his overcoat and worked through the freezing night.

When I took my leave of Chou Enlai and returned to the hotel, I lay for a long time in bed with my head way down the side of the bed. I felt ashamed of myself, ashamed . . . but at that moment I too could have died if Chou Enlai had asked me to die. He was China's hope, and all depended on him.

The Chinese delegation of the Communist Party was now back from Moscow. It arrived at Peking airport, Liu Shaochi with a fur hat on his head and a coat with a fur collar. The Politburo turned out to greet him. But Mao Tsetung was not there; whereas he would be there a year later to greet Chou Enlai returning from Moscow, where he had bluntly told off Khrushchev.*

And that absence, that glacial non-presence of Mao filled the winter air until every breath we took seemed to be a shudder through the cheers and the jollity and the smiles of those who jostled each other there, who crowded to clap.

'Hualan, why do you think Mao Tsetung was not there?'

'I think the Chairman may be travelling; or in the south. Anyway, everyone else was there . . .'

Hualan would read the document brought back by the Chinese delegation, both in Russian and in Chinese; her organization would discuss it at meetings. It was of great length, and it was for study. But now because of the cold, 'we are enjoined to study it at home, we'll be more comfortable,' said Hualan. She and her sister poked fun at me as we sat companionably huddled in our coats, trying to pretend the stove was warm.

Hualan's brother came in. He was an engineer and worked on the aeroplanes at the airport. Most of them were Ilyushins, and quite old. There was an enormous dearth of spare parts and some aeroplanes were being cannibalized to keep the others running. Hualan's brother did not discuss his work. He was under great strain because he was a Eurasian and because the whole family had been in Soviet Russia for some years. But they were entirely Chinese in feeling, although they did not look Chinese.

We talked about the city cadres. Forty-six per cent of them were being sent to the countryside to help in the spring planting, which would take place right after Chinese New Year, in late January. 'If you went down to the countryside,' said Hualan, 'you would probably become the head of a brigade, or a model worker. Because you would not only fulfil quotas and beat norms, you would even crank up the shirkers.' Some of the cadres sent down to the countryside fell into an extraordinary passivity. They did not like manual

*See *Wind in the Tower*.

labour; they did not say it, they just took so much time bending down, making a hole in the ground, planting seed . . . and they kept on asking for discussion meetings because 'that means they can screw their backsides to a chair', and perhaps they would then be elected to some sedentary job in the team or brigade, something cultural or administrative. They kept on repeating, 'We must not be hasty.'

I replied that had I been back in China and a cadre – which of course I would have become – and been sent to the countryside, I would probably have been accused of trying to show off by working too hard; of being élitist, of sticking my neck out. I would be criticized for setting impossible norms. Hualan said, 'I was able to do three times as much planting as one large, fat man, an "administrator" cadre, was doing. And so of course it was resented.' We laughed heartily, knowing these reflexes of the bureaucracy. Had we not all known and survived them in Old China? Bureaucracy was negativism, procrastination, inefficiency, an affliction which preserved and continued. And it would take a lot more than even the Chinese Revolution to change bureaucracy. 'Bureaucrats flourish all over Europe,' I told Hualan. 'The trouble isn't too much socialism but far too little, as if socialism and bureaucracy were interchangeable words,' said Hualan's sister.

Based on the treatment meted out to some Eurasians who had worked in the communes and had been used as targets in criticism meetings simply because they were of 'mixed blood', I put up a protest to Kung Peng. 'This looking down on Eurasians comes from Old China; it is chauvinism. Something must be done about it.' But Kung Peng was tired that day (there were so many meetings to discuss the Moscow document) and she said somewhat crossly, 'That's the fault of the people who do not integrate.' But how can one integrate one's looks? How can one become anonymous and merge totally when one's nose and eyes and hair are different? However, the next day Kung Peng had thought it over, and when I saw Chou Enlai again, he would talk at length against Han chauvinism and condemn its manifestations. And he would help Eurasians in China, right up to his death.

Now that the Chinese delegation was back from Moscow, Anna-Louise Strong was radiant. She read the joint statement and could find no fault with it. She exuberated. 'All difficulties will be ironed out. We'll show the imperialists what socialist solidarity means.' And her hope was that of so many people, so many of good will, of high ideals, who believed in communism, in socialism! I certainly did not rejoice at the subsequent disenchantment; the trail of nervous breakdowns, of divorces and rejections, the agonizing dilemmas in front of so many communist party members of many nations, when the dispute, at last, became a total rupture in 1963–4. I was preserved from this internal turmoil simply because I was not a communist, and therefore had no faith or creed to resift. As long as something was good for the Chinese people, however illogical, however opposed to theory it appeared, I was for it. Not for ever, but only for the time that it did any good. For me there was no eternity in policies or in methods or in people. And in this simplicity I had ample space for all vagaries, seasonal and political. I did not erect great logical structures divorced from the solid, concrete, and changing realities of China. I told Anna-Louise all this; I also told Simon Hua.

'You do not have principles then,' said Simon.

'Only when principles work,' I replied.

And Anna-Louise: 'Well, my dear, I suppose you keep a cool head . . . maybe we need cool heads.' But she too was baffled by someone who did not profess great and majestic reasons to live and die for. 'And yet you are so concerned, you must believe.'

'I believe in the Chinese people.'

'That's not a class analysis,' replied Anna-Louise.

I called on Prince Norodom Sihanouk, who had arrived by train from Moscow via Siberia, for he hated aeroplanes. The

Western press had unleashed attacks on him, saying he visited the socialist countries 'too frequently'. Sihanouk, who was greatly concerned about the growing US-fomented war in Laos and Vietnam, had gone to Moscow to ask for the reopening of the Geneva Conference. 'The whole of Indo-China will go up in flames,' he said to me. All he wanted was to keep Cambodia neutral, out of the war.

The war in Laos was due to America. America was obsessed by the domino theory, had been caught in the trap of Indo-China since 1954, when Dulles saw every minor national liberation movement as a mighty enemy, communist-inspired.

A banquet was held in Peking for Prince Sihanouk, at the Great Hall of the People. I dressed up smartly, for Prince Sihanouk liked to have well-dressed people around him, and Sika, the Chinese wife of Charles Meyer, Sihanouk's private secretary, was covered in fabulous jewellery.

We assembled in the Great Hall of the People, trying to recognize the dignitaries, who kept to themselves in little knots. And then Liu Shaochi came in with Prince Sihanouk, and all the important people walking behind them. Liu had a great thick mop of beautiful white hair. I have never had any feeling for this man; yet I suppose he had his merits; how otherwise would he ascend so high? But he was impossibly colourless although handsome, with a tall spare figure and a good profile. I do not know why he radiated dullness; perhaps it was our fault, since inevitably we compared him to Mao. And only Chou Enlai was not dimmed by Mao's formidable aura.

Mao Tsetung was not at the reception.

Anna-Louise, clad in a fabulous imperial embroidered gown (she collected them and owned a remarkable collection before she died), observed wistfully, 'I was told Mao would be here; I looked forward to seeing him again.' Mao's absence made the whole reception hollow, as if it had not really happened. But with beautiful American non-diffidence and spontaneity Anna-Louise rushed into the vacuum, went up to Liu Shaochi and wrung his hand repeatedly. 'You've done a great job, a great job in Moscow,' said she.

Liu Shaochi smiled a glabrous, modest smile. He shook hands with Anna-Louise, shook hands with all those who went up to shake hands with him.

The reception's organized cheer ended. Everyone left according to protocol, in big black cars. I rode back with Charles Meyer and Sika. Charles was exultant. Sihanouk had already had talks with Chou Enlai and it looked as if there would be a successful meeting in Geneva the next spring to thrash out the matter of the war in Laos.

Wu Chienta came to my hotel room, bringing with him two copies of the Moscow declaration of the eighty-one parties, one in English and one in Chinese. I laid the texts on the second bed; and read and read every evening until my eyes gave out.

Lin Lin came in a week later and saw the texts on my bed and my bleary eyes. 'You really do work hard,' said he. 'I'm trying to educate myself,' I replied weakly. 'Because I don't want to be re-educated by others.' And Lin Lin laughed uproariously. Then Chienta came again, to ask me what I thought of the Moscow text. I kept him to lunch; but he insisted in handing out his grain coupon when he had a slice of bread. 'Most of the text seems to me all right but I don't understand the phrase "by parliamentary means". It contradicts the rest.' I thought that to envisage a revolution by parliamentary means in the Third World, which has not known any such process, was really quite extraordinary. 'It's very European, the text . . . it may work in Europe, perhaps.' 'Ah,' said Chienta beaming at me, 'your understanding has greatly improved.'

Only months later would I know that Mao Tsetung objected to the wording of the communiqué, and especially to that phrase. But at the time, and until 1963, this was not official. However, after Chienta had left me, I began to apprehend confusedly the possibility of a break between China and Russia. Unthinkable? Yes, it seemed unthinkable then.

Russia was so much more powerful than China. Even among the intelligentsia in China, covertly debating the same unthinkable possibility, one would come across people saying, 'How can we quarrel with the USSR? They have the atom bomb ... we shall be left without a friend in the world ...' It was, in fact, hard to get away from the notion that China needed a nuclear umbrella to shield her from what then appeared as a ferocious, war-bent enemy, the United States.

I did not know, at the time, that China was devoting many of her scarce resources to catching up in atomic energy. How else could she accede to dignity and respect among nations, save through her own exertions in acquiring nuclear equipment? 'Even if we go trouserless, we must have atomic knowhow,' said the ebullient Chen Yi to me.

Power. Of course the reality of power could not be avoided. How wonderlandish of intellectuals to ignore the power-wielding machine of which they are, after all, also a component, in an equilibrium of strength which made up the system in which they thought and spoke; a duplicity of the social body since they also carried dissent and fission within them.

A new drive, to 'walk on two legs', that is, to employ both more sophisticated machinery and the traditional implements, was on in China. 'You too can break mental fetters, can think scientifically,' was the message. In the end it was science, the scientific spirit, which liberated man from the kingdom of necessity and of want.

'This is what we believed when we were young,' a famous professor, Wu Wentsao said to me. Dr Wu was a very old friend, dating back to my Chungking days. His wife was the marvellous and renowned writer, Hsieh Pinhsin.

There would still be for a long time in China opposition to science, because it had come with the colonial powers; and the tendency to expunge everything 'foreign' would recur, disguised as revolutionary fervour. How could science become a homegrown product? A spontaneous function of the mind among the Chinese people? As we debated the process then, in 1960, it seemed to us that glorifying the names of the old Chinese inventors and making the people feel wise and creative might be a good beginning. 'During the Leap the masses were told that they could change heaven and earth,' said Dr Wu. But still 'foreign things' were identified politically with capitalism, and also with that small section of the intelligentsia which was both needed and suspect. 'The more science you learn from the West, the less revolutionary you become' was one of those unexplainable sayings which had sprung up during the Leap. And others were 'Rather be red than expert'; 'When one is revolutionary one does not need to study in a university'.

We were discovering these sayings with surprise; but we did not know that at the Cultural Revolution they would recur and be reinforced, until they became entirely identified with a so-called 'revolutionary line', which would cause great loss and suffering in China. Thus the claim, which I found in a newspaper of 1958, that a worker 'scientist' had proved Newton's law of gravity wrong. No evidence for this was given; it was simply published and spread all over China. Ten years later, during the Cultural Revolution, exactly the same claim, about the velocity of falling bodies, would reappear and be proclaimed as a 'discovery ... which breaks foreign models which have been used to restrict our thinking ...'

'Abolish superstition, unfetter the mind,' Mao Tsetung had said. 'Let foreign things serve China.' But this was turned into 'Abolish all rules and disciplines, and especially foreign ways of thinking which limit the mind.' And this would lead to machines being run at top speed and broken because all directives as to maintenance, method of running, were disregarded as foreign tricks to 'slow down' production.

'There's something wrong with the way we think,' said Hualan. 'It's feudal thinking,' I said. But that was no explanation. Her brother had been criticized because he had restricted the use of the aeroplane engines placed under his care. 'Only when we have more education shall we change . . . we have many people who are just barely literate . . . they want to know, but they don't know how to reason.'

'If we, the knowledge-bearers, give up this battle for science, then we shall have betrayed our people,' said Wu Wentsao to me.

Hualan was criticized in a meeting of her department for wearing skirts. 'It was the usual guy who finds fault with everyone,' she said. 'Comrades, if you wish me to go into trousers, I shall certainly leap into them with great pleasure, but will you please give me the necessary coupons to buy them? Unfortunately I only have skirts,' Hualan had replied. 'Everyone roared with laughter and it was all over,' said Hualan.

'Why not start a campaign of criticism against useless, idle, foolish, personal and non-political criticism?' I suggested to my writer friends. I nearly added, 'Do you think this would produce unemployment among certain Party committees?' 'I shall certainly criticize myself for uselessly criticizing myself,' replied one writer gravely. 'My performance is short of ideal, because things change so fast,' said another. Then someone told me about Pa Chin, the famous writer of *Family*, who had said that sometimes the campaigns to which writers were submitted made him think 'that we are all monkeys, made to jump through hoops'.

The great writer Lao Sheh was indefatigable in those years of stress. He produced and he produced, new plays and essays and a short novel and poems. He created twelve plays, arranged several Chinese opera scripts and wrote two novels between 1949 and 1962. And he also held eight official jobs. But now a new debate on literature was on, and the writers interrogated themselves. 'There is as yet no book which has truly described what has been done in China since Liberation,' said my old friend Yeh.

READJUSTMENT began.

Wu Chienta came to tell me about it. 'We shall be giving

all the policies to the people to carry out.' What this meant was that the Party cadres had been told, 'Hands off; give the people their heads.' Private plots restored; free markets; and encouragement for secondary occupations in rural areas. Above all, an enormous, wholesale campaign throughout all the rural areas, to 'speak bitterness', to complain of all that had gone wrong.

'How can one get the Chinese to grumble?' We had almost three thousand years of non-grumbling behind us. And how to train the people to protest; how to make this protest legal and admissible without having, immediately, the Party cadres screaming 'counter-revolutionary!' and inflicting punishment? The Chinese word *fan*, which means to revolt and oppose and protest, has always implied armed opposition since verbal opposition was always suppressed. This was the frightful undemocratic tradition which China had inherited and it showed all the signs of being passed on into the Party, except that Mao Tsetung and Chou Enlai strenuously, continuously, repeatedly, fought against it. 'Words must be listened to . . . Heaven won't fall, the earth won't stop turning,' Mao had said. But alas, the Party rank and file did not really understand what it meant to listen, to accept criticism and unpleasant opinions. 'How does one distinguish between valid criticism and malicious attack? Better stifle all protest.'

Perhaps in another generation some of these efforts at democracy would penetrate; but it all depends on how quickly China could achieve material security and a higher standard of living for her people. Democracy was inseparable from four factors: the industrial revolution, scientific thinking, some affluence, and universal education – and all four were the aims of Communist China, however awry things went.

I went to discuss this with the Yangs, and we argued about it for a long time. 'I hope that now there won't be any more thought-remoulding for the intelligentsia,' I said. 'It's been greatly softened down,' said Hsienyi. 'After all, our intelligentsia have had ten years of liberation and are adapting themselves . . .' Then Gladys would tell me how she had gone through the process. 'I was teaching in Nanking when Liberation came. I took part in the movement for thought-remoulding. It was extremely painful, but also fascinating. I wept, I broke down, I even became a little hysterical . . . but at the same time, we were all in it together and there was a sustaining togetherness. I watched myself become other, sprout another me, a personality which no longer suffered alienation. I did, in a way, become someone else, but not altogether; in the end I chose what adapted me and I remained myself. I co-operated in the process, even if, at times, I was co-operating in humiliating myself. Now I am able to see things in several ways at once.'

We discussed what I would have done; and Hsienyi said, 'You would have remained yourself in the end, but I think you would have pretended a lot.'

'There was deliberate sabotage,' said Hualan.

It was Christmas Day and Hualan was up and about, cooking a big duck for her mother. 'It is quite impossible that the ultra-left communist wave of 1958 was not due to sabotage,' she repeated.

Within this campaign for 'speaking bitterness' and for exposing all that had gone wrong during the Leap, most of the offences had been committed during that 'communist' period, including the militarization of some communes, which were run like barracks and in which some people had died from overwork and exposure to the weather.

Now the production team, which was the original 'natural' village, would be an autonomous unit doing its own accounting, planning its own crops and production. It would own its implements and organize its manpower so that there would no longer be any forcible drafting of manpower away from the village or taking away of needed handcarts and poles and tools and draft animals.

'No more boasting of over-fulfilling quotas is allowed.' Hualan said there had been a total breakdown in communication between what was happening and the top Party leadership. 'Don't boast, speak the truth' was the new slogan.

The Central Committee had issued a directive that before the Chinese New Year of 1961 everything must be put in order and all errors rectified, and all people unjustly accused must be rehabilitated. All private belongings confiscated in the rash of 'communism is here' must be returned.

'Less empty talk, more real work,' said Teng Hsiaoping. Hualan repeated all this with relish. 'But someone has committed sabotage,' she persisted.

'How?'

'There are two kinds of sabotage, my dear. One is to go slow, to drag one's feet; that's more visible and easily corrected. The other is to manifest hectic enthusiasm, to exaggerate, to prove ultra-left, to drive people at an inhuman pace. Chairman Mao has said that ultra-left is as bad as right. But this second form of sabotage is more dangerous than the first because it all sounds so revolutionary.'

'But who did it?'

'I don't know,' said Hualan. 'We are trying to find out.'

'But didn't Chairman Mao himself suffer from . . . a bit too much enthusiasm?'

Hualan bent over her duck. She was angry with me. 'The people love Chairman Mao, they love Premier Chou,' she replied. 'Chairman Mao never said that "communism was here".'

So, after the usual sifting and reappraisal, someone was going to be found guilty of sabotage during the Leap. I wondered who it would be. I went to Tientsin to meet the writer Yang Mo, a portly round-faced mother of four who had just written a book called *Song of Youth*.

'You are a friend, so we tell you our difficulties,' said Yang Mo, 'but our enemies would like us to fail.'

How European Tientsin still looked in some of its streets, notably the erstwhile British Concession. The hotel where I stayed – formerly a British-run hotel – was opposite Gordon Hall, the Gordon Hall of my childhood, where I had endured my school-leaving examinations. In my imagination it remained a massive, imposing fortress; how it had dwindled to some ridiculous copy of a large pub in Edinburgh! It was now a government office.

Here, too, there was no smoke from the factory chimneys. Yang Mo tried to explain but I said, 'Never mind. The factories are there; the machinery is not yet come; the workers have been recruited and are being paid by the state, but they have nothing to do. But there will be readjustment and all will be well.' Yang Mo touched my arm and smiled. I then asked abruptly about the writer Ting Ling, who had been condemned as a rightist. But Yang Mo did not know anything about her fellow-writer.

I left Peking in mid-January by train for Wuhan, to see the new bridge across the Yangtze River, to visit the factories, to see the Wuhan steel plant. The Wuhan steel plant was not working. Embers glowed in one of the furnaces. That was all. Why the stoppage? 'We have fulfilled our quota for the year,' said the engineer in charge. That of course was not true. But what else could I expect? That the Party committee in charge would tell me, 'Comrade, we've been left in the lurch. This plant was built by the Russians and it is not completed. And there are a lot of snags. And we do not have enough coal for stoking, there is a coal shortage, and not enough iron ore, and some of the machinery is not functioning as yet.' The workers seemed well-fed, but the Party committee in charge looked like a bunch of cadavers. The engineer wrung my hand and said quietly, 'Come back next year; by then, we shall have solved *all* our problems.'

The hotel in Wuhan was of course not heated; neither was there any hot water. I wore my fur coat to bed.

By now I had adapted myself. I walked downstairs and upstairs rather than use the lift, I washed in cold water, just one degree above zero, and I turned off all the electric lights I met. And this habit of thrift, frugality, which then began I could not lose. For years I would 'save electricity, save power' by walking up and down stairs, turning off lights . . . no more would I waste a single moment, a single thread, a single sheet of paper.

In Wuhan workers stayed at home to rest one day in two. Market stalls were organized in every street to spare the strain on housewives. The Wuhan Women's Federation did very good work. 'The small urban factory is most important in keeping up the standard of living,' said a splendid woman, forty years old, a beggar until she was twenty, now a Party member. She had organized the women in her street into several such factories. 'We repair kettles and saucepans. We make small earthenware stoves. We cobble shoes. We mend clothes and make children's clothes. We also manufacture spare parts for bicycles, for electric fixtures. We have started a rope factory.' The schools were closed; not because it was holiday time but because of the cold, to spare the children. Hibernation. 'Wait until the spring comes.'

I watched the huge stretch of the Yangtze, rolling its khaki water under the new bridge, and the beautiful parallelograms of the new fields on both banks. Within the next eighteen years two dozen bridges would span the great river, from its source down to the ocean.

To trust the Chinese people and the present government to make mistakes, to find them out and work out their own solutions; or to run to 'denounce' these failings and errors, the tyrannies and the flaws? Run to whom? To those in the West, sitting on their three hundred years of industrial revolution, with its carnage and exploitation and tyranny? To those who had indeed evolved democracy, but at the cost of how many bloody repressions? To those who had contributed to China's downfall and misery in the past and to China's present difficulties? They were so immensely concerned with freedom and liberties . . . but had we known these liberties when we were but their colonies? When China was a land of starving beggars, where was their beautiful indignation?

All I could do was trust. Trust the Chinese people.

In Hong Kong the press was at the railway station. 'I am

convinced that China will overcome her difficulties.' There is a photograph of me, looking almost like a missionary, saying this.

I was again reviled for not denouncing tyranny, for not speaking up for freedom. 'You've either been brainwashed or you've seen nothing,' said a very superior newsman to me.

Today I can still see the replete diplomats in Peking counting the calories of the average Chinese . . .

'China will solve her own problems . . . we lack nothing . . . we shall not beg.' I would not betray my people.

CHAPTER 13

The World Outside China: 1961–1962

The day after I reached Hong Kong I went to see Pierre Mardulyn, director of the Belgian bank. Pierre had been a friend of our family for many years. Mama used to go to the Belgian bank, taking me (I was eight years old then) to cash money which her father sent because Papa, though working, was not getting any pay . . . the warlords swallowed all the railway revenue.

'I want to send money to China, Pierre. How much cash is there in my account?' Pierre told me and I transferred it to the Bank of China in Hong Kong. Pierre said, 'Putting money in China at present is a dead loss.' Then his banker's instinct took over. 'On the other hand, it might pay off as a long-term gamble.'

The Bank of China director, Mr Huang, was frail and bespectacled and did not look surprised. 'There is of course a company for investments by overseas Chinese . . . we could transfer your money to it.'

My uselessness in China was now so obvious, so evident. For I had offered to stay, so involved had I become with the suffering and the dignity, the power of the people to absorb the suffering and to endure. But Kung Peng chided me. There was Vincent, she said. I had had the luck of finding a man who made me happy; it was not right to do things impetuously . . . There was really nothing I could do which was not already being done by other people. And so the only thing I could do was to send some money. Foreign exchange. US dollars. 'Bridges of understanding can be built, they must be built . . .' Chen Yi had said this. I could, perhaps, build a bridge. Between China and the rest of the world.

'I don't want this money, I want to give it to the Chinese government,' I said to Mr Huang. He smiled benignly. 'We have our policy. You will get 12 per cent per year interest, and after eight years the capital is returned to you. That is our policy.' I stressed I wanted neither capital nor interest. Mr Huang continued to smile and repeated that this was the policy. Twelve per cent, and of course no income tax since there is no income tax on individuals in China. After eight years, should the money remain in China, then the interest would come down to 2 or 3 per cent, as for ordinary Chinese currency in China.

I would not touch any of the money for many years; in fact not until 1972, when the Bank of China got in touch with me. 'You have a great deal of money with us . . . you must use it.'

Many thousands of overseas Chinese did what I did; put foreign exchange in China. Not with any intent to profit, but because at that time China needed foreign exchange. Several hundred millions of dollars must have thus gone into China in those bad years, 1960 to 1962. And a steady flood of parcels, food and clothing to help the families.

I flew back to Malaya. Many unsettled thoughts like feathered spring seeds flew in my brain. Because now, without any political indoctrination, or thought-remoulding, or compulsion, or persuasion, a transformation had taken place. Now it was in China that I felt at ease, secure, and it was when I crossed the border back into the world outside China that disquiet invaded me. Not a large disquiet; a nagging, small and constant one. It was a slight flapping around the heart, like the erratic wingbeat of a caged bird, a helplessness in the throat. Nothing that could be explained. How had this happened? Why had I changed?

Home. Vincent. I said to Vincent, 'I almost did not come back . . .' He replied, 'I thought you might not return.' Another me taking over, frogman swimming upwards from the sea floor. What had been important receded; what I had forgotten, concerns, worries, small pleasures and trivia, loomed larger now. Names which had lapsed from my memory in China returned to my tongue. And as I began once again to speak in English, my Chinese also went dormant. Anyone who manoeuvres in several languages has this experience; it takes a day or two, sometimes more, to go easily into the next medium.

In the next few weeks and months I was literally invaded by overseas Chinese, all of them anxious about one thing or another, all of them wanting something. They wanted to know whether parcels via Hong Kong could be received in China. No parcels could be sent to China from Malaya and Singapore. And there were men who had left their wives and children in China for many years, but now suddenly wanted them out. Could I get them out? Could I write a letter making sure that Old Mrs Su, someone's grandmother, aged eighty-five, was getting adequate hospital care? Could I . . . Someone else wanted to operate a ring for smuggling penicillin and vitamin B into China. Would I help, and make a lot of money?

The Secret Societies flexed their biceps and came in. A very nice man, whom I shall call Mr Liu, and who was 'protecting' the district where I practised, dropped into the clinic to have his smallpox vaccination and cholera shots before going to China. 'My brothers will look after me there,' said he. He went to China for three months, and came back. Would China ever get rid of her past when the past was waiting to pounce upon her future?

I wound up the clinic gradually, without haste. I had come to the end of my childhood longing. The medical me was being replaced by another me who fused medical diagnosis with social and historical perception. There were too many mes jostling, each one occupied with a single activity; I must merge them, and one or a few of them must be dismissed. It was impossible to continue doctoring all day, writing at night, and doing what I now wanted to do: document myself fully on China, the Chinese Revolution. There was simply not enough time in the day.

In that year of 1961 I began to be very uneasy about the Malayasian Sociological Research Institute.

The material I had brought back about the Islamic religion in China was not used. The policies of the Institute puzzled me. I would find its Secretary-General, who was Shirle Gordon, and who by the statutes of the Institute could never be fired or moved, – difficult. Shirle flung her beautiful blonde mane at me and hissed: So-and-so is a saboteur. No discussion was allowed; I was not called to general meetings; although my money remained welcome.

In 1962, a member of the Institute went, most mysteriously, on a trip to Moscow. By then, owing to my studies of Islam and my meetings with Arab scholars involved with the USSR, I was becoming suspicious. It seemed to me that research to illuminate the roles of the various peoples in South East Asia, that fantastic jumble of superposed and conflicting cultures and ethnic groups, was important, not pro-Russian or pro-Chinese propaganda.

Honest and truthful and sincere scholars of every kind were to be involved in the Institute; out of fascination for Shirle, or for the sake of knowledge, or Islam. In the 1970s the government in Kuala Lumpur would allegedly discover evidence that certain members of the Institute were colluding with a foreign embassy, engaging in intelligence activity. I do not know what became of Shirle Gordon, save that an item in a newspaper from Malaya reported that she had been expelled. I had left the Institute definitely by 1963.

I would also have a problem with the magazine in London, *Eastern World*, which I had subsidized. And for almost the same reasons: divergence of opinion as to how the magazine should be run. But I have always preserved a good memory of Hans Taussig and his capable and cheerful and competent assistant, Emma Leibovici. I wish, somehow, one could disentangle personal relationships from business and other decisions. But this seems difficult.

The struggle for power between the Prime Minister of Singapore, Harry Lee (Lee Kuanyew), and the left wing of his party (the PAP) became more acute in April 1961, when the PAP was defeated in a somewhat maverick by-election.

In that April the Prime Minister of Malaya, Tunku Abdul Rahman, proclaimed the intention of forming 'Malaysia'.

The switch from Malaya to Malaysia sounds simple. Actually it was not. Malaysia was devised by the British to get over the problem of a direct merging of Singapore and Malaya, in which the Malays would have been swamped by a Chinese majority. Erstwhile colonies, protectorates and other territories loosely connected within the British Empire's multiplicity of domination in South East Asia were to be federated to Malaya. This meant the territories of North Borneo, Sarawak and Brunei, totalling altogether about a million people. This inclusion would 'balance out' the racial equation, the Chinese majority, because, so it was stated, all the people in these territories were 'Malay'.

I do not know by what sleight of language, glibness of image, the British were able to convince the Malays of Malaya, at least for a while, though only for a while, that the Dayaks of North Borneo, who were animists and head hunters, and the Kadazans, who were Christians, and other various tribes, were all good Muslim Malays.

Only in tiny, oil-rich Brunei (Shell worked the oilfields) with the largest mosque in South East Asia, because of oil, and a Malay Sultan, were there 63,000 bona fide Malays out of a population of 80,000 . . . and in the end, the only territory to refuse to be included in the new Federation of Malaysia would be Brunei.

What no one talked about but everyone knew was that in order for Malaysia to be established a purge had to take place. And since the left wing of the PAP in Singapore now openly declared its opposition to Malaysia, of course they had to be purged. In August of 1961, this left wing would break away to form another party called the Socialist Front, or Barisan Socialis.

I watched the purge being prepared.

Firstly, there was a series of lurid articles in the *Straits Times* which beat any thriller in style, called 'The Open Conspiracy'. It purported to detail a plot by the Malayan Communist Party to take over Singapore. Secondly, Lee Kuanyew (he now refuted his English name of Harry) denounced the British, still the dominant influence in

Singapore. He said they were trying to force him to jail his own left wing. 'The British government has tried to manipulate the PAP ... into a position where the Communist Party will be attacked not by British Imperialism which is the supreme power in Singapore, but by us, the locally elected government, with its limited powers.' Thirdly, in Malaya itself the Emergency regulations, promulgated during British times and practised by the British Special Branch, were refurbished as an Internal Security Act. Preventive detention without trial, arbitrary arrest, and other efficient inventions were retained, and are used today.

Lee Kuanyew denounced the 'diabolical cynicism' of the British High Commissioner, Lord Selkirk. Lord Selkirk now courted the left wing of the PAP. Nothing was funnier to me than the sight of the left-wing leaders, among them, prominently, Lim Chingsiong, later the acknowledged leader of the new Barisan Socialis Party, and his aides, all reputed members or sympathizers of the Malayan Communist Party, all people who had been jailed at least once, if not twice, by the British Special Branch, sipping cocktails at receptions given by Lord and Lady Selkirk. The left-wing Barisan leaders came in open shirts while Lord and Lady Selkirk wore their most starchy get-ups. I could not help applauding, so excellently did Lord Selkirk perform.

A Chinese politician from Malaya came to see me. Citizenship laws for the Chinese were being tightened up; the Malays, confronted with merger between Singapore and Malaysia, wanted to make quite sure that they would remain a legal majority, even if not a real majority by head count. There was a lot of talk about birthrate. The Chinese birthrate was higher than the Malay birthrate – the Malays had so many more diseases, especially venereal, which engendered sterility – and the Chinese infant mortality rate was lower than the Malay.

This Chinese politician wanted to know what the Chinese government policy on the overseas Chinese would be. The overseas Chinese had not given up the hope that China would protect them. The Chiang Kaishek government, after all, had always claimed to 'protect' them. 'I am afraid there are going to be massacres and pogroms of the Chinese in the new-founded Malaysia,' said this politician.

I told him that the policy in Peking was: the overseas Chinese were to be encouraged to take the nationality of the country they lived in; to become good and loyal citizens; there could not be any dual nationality, nothing like what the British operated in their remaining colonies and what the Jews of Israel and the United States were able to enjoy.

'But we shall be second-class citizens, almost slaves, kept only because of the wealth we bring, for ever and ever,' objected this politician.

I could offer him nothing but cold comfort.

Had this discrimination in all fields profited the Malay population at large, the 'sons of the soil', I think one might have seen the end of this situation in not too long a time. But the establishment of privileged bureaucrats, achieved by reserving three out of four jobs in the administration to Malays; by lowering university standards for them; by not admitting to university brilliant Chinese students proficient in Malay and in English; and by establishing company directors and managers who are Malay in each company, thus creating entrepreneurs, does not really change the fact that 80 per cent of Malay rural families still live below what is called the 'acceptable' poverty level.

The newly formed party, the Barisan Socialis, with Lim Chingsiong as its head, was against merger and Malaysia. It declared that Singapore could live on its own. This was denounced as a 'communist plot', even though it has since become a reality and Singapore is held up as a shining example of prosperity.

Of course, it could only become prosperous when its radicals were curbed, since it had to enter the orbit of capitalism, however much the PAP would continue to call itself 'socialist'.

I sought out Lim Chingsiong for an interview. He was the idol of the Chinese middle-school and university students. He spoke three Chinese dialects, English and Malay, all of them fluently. He was handsome, with regular features, but I was surprised to note how unaggressive he was. In contrast to Lee Kuanyew's forceful, abrasive personality, Lim appeared hesitant, diffident, almost wistful. And above all, somewhat naïve.

Lim Chingsiong gave me a short biography of himself; but he was far more interested in talking about the Sino-Soviet dispute. 'I do not understand it,' said he. I offered to lend him whatever documentation I had, and duly brought him the clippings I had smuggled through. But the file would never be returned to me because Lim Chingsiong would go to jail shortly after, and all his belongings would be taken over by Special Branch; and I did not ask for my clippings to be returned.

The Students' Union of Nanyang University came out against Malaysia. In the summer of 1961 an attempt was made to break it up; and I was cited as supporting those who were breaking it. Of course I had to refute this, as it was not true. What was my intense surprise when my moderate refutation – which, however, had led to the Students' Union not collapsing – drew on my head the wrath not only of British officials like Lord Selkirk but also of influential British administrators like the Chancellor of Singapore University?

Meanwhile, Prime Minister Lee Kuanyew of Singapore had collided somewhat with the more conservative Malays of Malaysia. This was not at all his fault. It was due to his over-ebullient and enthusiastic friend, Alex Josey, who had proclaimed him 'The leader of the overseas Chinese – heir to five thousand years of Chinese civilization'. And Lee himself, in one of his more abrupt moods, was quoted in the press as remarking that the Malays themselves had 'come from China in the eleventh century', and that the 'sons of the soil' theory might as well apply to the Chinese.

This infuriated Malay extremists . . . a motion to jail Lee Kuanyew was even set afoot.

I went to see Prime Minister Tunku Abdul Rahman in April 1961, to confirm the matter of my giving scholarships both to Malay students to study Chinese at Nanyang University and to a Chinese to study Malay culture and literature. Tunku accepted the idea and the money,* and I would continue for five years providing for the one and only student – a Chinese – who elected to study Malay history, language and literature. No Malay student turned up.

I spoke with Tunku of the problem of the overseas Chinese; it was difficult for these hardy, industrious and thrifty people to understand the hostility towards them and the position they were in. 'But we built this country . . . it was jungle before we came . . . our work, our sweat, our lives have gone into this soil,' they would say, incredulous that they should be discriminated against.

Tunku agreed that they suffered from the relics of a colonial situation and that now they must adapt or would be 'neither fish nor fowl'. He let me understand that it was not possible *not* to discriminate against them, at least for a generation . . .

Malaysia would not adhere to the American edifice of SEATO, the South East Asia Treaty Organization, erected by Dulles in 1954 in order to counter the 'Red' threat in South East Asia. SEATO was aimed at China; but 'we Asians do not like SEATO, it bears a stigma,' said the wise Tunku. 'We shall ensure our own security . . . I've always said there cannot be two Chinas,' he added, showing his independence of mind. It meant that, in due course, Malaysia would recognize China.

Three days after seeing Tunku in Kuala Lumpur, I flew to Geneva to attend the conference on Laos, which had indeed convened. I received a letter from Cousin Pengju telling me that he would be there, and also Kung Peng, and Prince Sihanouk, and Malcolm MacDonald and Marshal Chen

*I began with a $12,000 scholarship.

Yi . . . would I come and join the party? It would be great fun. I did.

There was a muddled, muddy war in Laos, which had already lasted three years; the United States were involved in the usual tense, emotional manner which characterized them in the 1950s and 1960s. There were three Laotian princes, all related to each other, and each backed by one or other of the powers. They squabbled and denounced and intrigued and knotted and unknotted alliances; and all this was taken most seriously by the Washington experts, who saw the dread hand of 'Red' China everywhere.

However important the Laos question appeared to be at the time, I am afraid that I could not contrive to work up a passion for it; neither would I ever get clear all the ramifications of the tangled situation. The Laos war, it seemed to me, was but an episode, a boil in that rash of abscesses of war which would erupt, pus from a plagued body, throughout the Third World; wars by proxy between the two superpowers, the US and the USSR. But Sihanouk of Cambodia was perturbed, and had reason to be. For with war in Vietnam and war in Laos, when would war come to his beloved country, Cambodia, wedged between the two?

I never understood why Laos, with its two million people, was, in the eyes of America, so important, needed such a torrent of corruptive aid, and weapons, and why so much hysteria was involved in the process. As to my keeping track of Boum Oum, Souvanna Phouma, Quim Pholsema (whom Malcolm nicknamed quinine for short), Nai Champassak, Phoumi Nosavan, Vong Vichit, and others – it was more than I could do.

I lunched with Malcolm, who was staying at the Beau Rivage Hotel; I called several times on Prince Sihanouk, and listened to his exposés; and of course I went to see Marshal Chen Yi and had hours of relaxed, cheerful talk which romped from the colour of Lake Leman, to Rousseau's island in Switzerland, to the knots of war to be untied in Laos and Vietnam. Pengju did his newspaper work, but also prepared a whimsical delight for himself: interviews, not of political personages, but of residents in Switzerland such as Charlie Chaplin, Graham Greene, and Brigitte Bardot . . . he also wanted to interview Françoise Sagan, going to Paris for the purpose, but she was not available.

Sihanouk had rented a magnificent villa; and the Chinese too had rented quite a large estate. 'The conference will last a long time,' was the prediction. 'Why are there so many Chinese in the delegation?' one journalist asked Pengju. 'Because there are a lot of people in China,' Pengju replied. 'The Americans want to isolate us, but we're very much here,' said Chen Yi at dinner. Despite all protocol, it was obvious that the Laos conference was also the opportunity for discreet, unofficial meetings, casual soundings. Ambassador Wang Pingnan, one of the best and ablest of Chinese diplomats, a man Chou Enlai trusted greatly, was also there. He was Ambassador to Poland, and in charge of the intermittent talks at ambassadorial level between the US and China. These talks had begun, at Chou Enlai's suggestion, in 1955, and though given no publicity, were of major significance.

Every delegation was stuffed with important people. The American one, led by Averell Harriman; Ambassador Parsons, once holding the Laos post, was now Assistant Secretary of State, and perhaps that is why Laos loomed so large in the United States' preoccupations.

A remarkable arrangement whereby Harriman and Chen Yi could shake hands, and even, possibly, exchange a few remarks, was worked out. It was at a party thrown by a neutral country, and timing was so perfect that as Chen Yi hovered courteously in the entrance to the main hall, taking leave of his host, Harriman arrived and could shake hands with Chen Yi. This was History. Dulles in 1954 had refused to shake hands with Chou Enlai.

Of the tortuous course, the eddies and ripples and whirlpools; the treacherous undercurrents of the conference, I can say little; for I had no role in it, merely hovered on its outskirts. The only manifestation of my presence was an article called 'Swans on Lake Leman: personal portraits of

Chen Yi, Malcolm MacDonald and Prince Sihanouk at the Geneva Conference'. It was printed in *L'Express* of Paris.

There was a large garden party for the delegations. The weather was superb, Swiss-postcard bright, and I was sitting, I think with the French, when I noticed that the Western delegates mixed quite freely; but that no one came near the Chinese table. So I walked up to them and sat down with them. Chen Yi was there, and his wife Chang Tsien, a beautiful woman with a lovely smile. I could see, out of the corner of my eye, two Englishmen stare in my direction with great ire. Why were they so angry? But as the garden party began to move towards its end I saw Malcolm edging nearer. 'Malcolm, I want to introduce to you my dear friend Kung Peng.' Malcolm, as usual, was superb. He smiled with great charm, and shook hands and said, 'But of course, I've heard so much about you from Suyin.' And then he was chatting with Chen Yi and Chang Tsien. I shall never know whether or not Malcolm's proximity at that moment was a dexterous calculation of steps. A few days later Malcolm charmed Chen Yi at a dinner given by the latter; he stood on his head and then turned somersaults (Malcolm used to turn somersaults right down the street in Singapore). I told Malcolm how much we missed him; his successors in South East Asia were uniformly dour, celluloid-collared and impossible to talk to.

Malcolm went to China in 1962, at the end of the Laos conference. When he returned to Hong Kong he gave an enthusiastic press conference, praising China. 'The Chinese are quite right and they are doing things which have never been done before by any other people on earth,' he said to me. 'If only I could get it into the heads of the Americans that China is not a danger to them, that the Chinese want peace above all, the whole world would be changed . . .'

But within England, and from the Labour government, Malcolm would encounter frowning hostility. Because so many members of Britain's Labour government had a sentimental attachment to the USSR. Some of Malcolm's projected articles, due to be written for large circulated newspapers, never appeared.

On my return to Singapore from Geneva I was bodily searched at the airport. This meant that Special Branch – or someone – had decided to make life uncomfortable for me.

I have always suffered from the mountain of mail which awaits me, everywhere, when I return from a trip. This time it was from my sister Marianne. She had to be looked after. Tiza and Mama had come to stay with her, then moved out and Tiza had found a job; and then they would not open the door when Marianne rang the bell and thumped on the wood. 'Yet I know they are there, I can see the curtains move,' wrote Marianne to me. 'She disturbs Mama's sleep,' wrote Tiza. No one lied. Everyone said what they really believed, and upon this grew the great tree of Marianne's mental breakdown. In 1960 Tiza had written to say that Marianne had been committed to a mental hospital; Tiza had signed the papers committing her. I started corresponding with Marianne's doctors; and now, in 1961, she was discharged and came to Malaya: I had asked her to come.

She was much better; but convinced that her husband had been poisoned; that she had cancer. As the days went by her strangeness increased. She now refused to take the pills she had been provided with. 'They' had changed the colour of the pills behind her back, she explained. Vincent, accustomed to a wider panorama of erratic behaviour through his Indian culture, could see nothing wrong with her.

Menina Mesquita, who had helped me type my manuscripts ever since 1954, came to Malaya. She had brought her typewriter, and expected me to work as she had always seen me work. But she found me strangely disassembled. I was emptied and empty; I waffled. My book on Cambodia, *The Four Faces*, was ended. I was now toying with a film script set in Cambodia. A French producer, M. Coureau, wanted to shoot a picture there. I was half-hearted about the script. Menina's buoyancy also depressed me. Unconsciously, I was already abandoning South East Asia; but this underground germination of my books on China was not perceptible. I also filed and refiled my father's papers, and letters, and poetry . . .

As a result of this in-between state, I would write a book called *Winter Love*, which was about a lesbian affair in England. It would be published in America and also in England as a novella, part of a volume entitled *Two Loves*; the other part, also a novella, being based on the film script I wrote for the film in Cambodia, entitled *Cast But One Shadow*.

Menina hated *Winter Love*. My French publisher was puzzled, and thought it an early novella written in my younger days, reminiscent of some adolescent effusions, like Colette. It was not so. *Winter Love* was based on some of the emotional links I had seen forged while I was in England during the war, when there were so few men about and it seemed absolutely normal that women should go two by two. But my main reason for writing it had to do with reviews of *The Mountain is Young*. Its critics had complained that I had always dozens of characters and was unable to handle a taut, tense situation with only two or three persons. I thought: Let me try. And the result was *Winter Love*.

I would go again to Cambodia, accompanying the film crew shooting *Cast But One Shadow* in the ruins of Angkor. The whole enterprise was directed by a small, Spanish-looking Frenchman, full of fire, fun and talent, named Marzelle. The film was made, and shown in Singapore. Tunku Abdul Rahman came to the première and politely said, 'A very nice film.' It was disastrous; infected with slowness, turgid. The languor of Cambodia had crept into all of us, the jungle and the leprous magnificence of Angkor were timeless . . . so was the picture.

I thereupon wrote the novella *Cast But One Shadow* in three weeks. It was very different from the film.

I had immensely enjoyed galloping around Cambodia with Prince Sihanouk, whose physical energy was

astounding. '*Comment vous sentez-vous aujourd'hui, Madame?*'
he would inquire, his face showing · great concern.
'*Monseigneur, je suis claquée.*' It delighted Sihanouk to know
that I could not stand the pace of his excursions. After a
whole day of travel, interviews, speech making, inspections,
we danced all night until six in the morning, when regretfully
Sihanouk, who had danced, sung several songs of his own
composition, played the clarinet, conducted the orchestra,
announced we would have two hours' rest . . . before going
off to the beach for a swim, followed by a banquet and
dancing, and then off by jeep to open some hospital or
school or to consecrate a canal, or to do some digging on the
projected railroad from Sihanoukville Port to Phnom
Penh . . . After a week of following Sihanouk around, one
was really *claquée*. 'I kill all my ministers,' said Sihanouk,
thoroughly happy.

It was a great comfort to me when Algernon, of Special
Branch, told me he had been assigned to make a report on
me and my subversive ideas. I had once been shown (by a
friend) an item embedded in my police files: 'Subject was
seen to have tea in the company of three students at the
Orchard Road Tea Shop. Subject then went to Cold Storage
and purchased a quarter pound of cheese and two tins of
pears in syrup. Subject then drove home without stopping.'
How baffling the cheese, the pears, became. What had been
my intentions in purchasing them? ·

With Algernon, my files would become at least more
intellectualized. For he was intelligent, and with pebble
glasses, he never tired of telling all and sundry his own story:
the story of his having been a Communist Party member,
and then having opted out of the Party. This had given
him compassion, a dimension of understanding of the
compulsions in Asia and among Asian intellectuals, which
others lacked.

Algernon had joined the Party because of his father's
death.

His father had been interned with the British in the same

camp by the Japanese during the war, because he looked so white. And in camp there had been no colour-bar at all, of course, so that Algernon's father forgot that he was a Eurasian. Then the war ended, the British returned, and in the renovated office where his father worked as chief clerk appeared suddenly two toilets, one for Europeans only, the other for 'natives', lower down the same corridor.

Algernon's father, having forgotten he was a Eurasian, went into the European toilet. He was hauled up by the boss, a young man fresh from England, in front of all the staff. 'Don't let me catch you doing it again,' said the boss. Algernon's father went home, lay on the bed with his head to the wall, and was dead two days later.

Joining the Party was easy then; many youths, even from English-speaking schools, were doing so. And young people from wealthy families as well. For over four years Algernon went on believing. He became a courier for the Party and then, one day, arriving in a certain foreign country, he found that a purge had occurred, and the people he had to meet had all been shot. He returned to Malaya to find the top echelon of the Malayan Communist Party in confusion. Their head, Loi Teck, had absconded to Hong Kong with thirty million dollars, the sum total of the Party's subscriptions.

Algernon left the Party, and now he strove to make Special Branch change their methods, which had been somewhat brutal, and reason with suspects. 'The funny thing is that I'm convinced one day we'll all find a middle of the road way to co-exist,' he said. And again: 'Leaving the Party was worse than anything . . . I had terrible withdrawal symptoms . . . nausea, nervous breakdown . . . I found it hard to put together all the bits of myself.'

But he had done so. I found him a valuable human being.

Leonard was now in the book publishing world, and did well. Despite Anthony's groans of distress, I obtained a divorce, with me as the guilty party, and all it cost me was fifty pounds.

Distressed students regularly poured in upon me. All kinds of distress: jail, no money, no job. One student with nasopharyngeal cancer, to go to England for treatment. A student from Nanyang University questioned by Special Branch: he could no longer walk. For days he had been held in the vertical position with a beam between his legs and a weight upon his back; the sciatic nerves of both legs were injured. Others had been made to sit on blocks of ice for hours during the Emergency. Repressive measures and torture are never new. They seem to be passed on as precious heirlooms, handed down the centuries, and from one country to another.

In February 1962 I went to Cairo to attend the Second Afro-Asian Writers' Conference taking place there. I was curious to know what an Afro-Asian conference was like, and certainly I wanted to meet Asian writers, for my course on contemporary Asian literature at Nanyang University.

I flew to Delhi and there changed to an aeroplane for Cairo, which left around midnight. And who should I see at the airport but Mulk Raj Anand, surrounded by roughly 150 friends. Mulk was being garlanded; wreaths of champak and jasmine wrapped in cellophane were being placed around his neck; only his eyes and the top of his head protruded above the garlands. Mulk's friends alternatively sung hymns of praise to him or shouted slogans. Someone dived into the crowd holding a tray with a cup of coffee on it for Mulk. 'Mulk, Mulk,' I cried, but I was too far away. I wrestled my way to the departure door and caught up with Mulk, who greeted me with effusive disquiet. 'I've got to talk to you about some very important things, Suyin. We shall sit together,' said he.

During the rest of the night, in the aeroplane, Mulk talked to me. 'Suyin, the most important thing in the world is *peace*. We must have peace *at all costs*, otherwise the world will see a nuclear catastrophe. We shall all be dead unless there is *peace*. Think of Hiroshima; there will be ten thousand Hiroshimas. Think of the devastation! Humanity will cease to exist. Our Chinese comrades unfortunately don't see it that way. They're playing with fire. Now you can do an enormous amount of good at the conference. You can stand up for peace and the whole world will be grateful to you for it.'

On and on went Mulk, radiating honesty and horror, earnestness and supplication. He was extremely worried. 'The Americans are ready to destroy the whole world if they are challenged.' I protested. 'No, Mulk. As far as I know, the Americans on the contrary are preparing for brush-fire wars, for small wars erupting here and there, for what they call "counter-insurgency".'

What Mulk was really saying – but he did not know it himself – was that the Third World must *not* have liberation struggles; must not fight for independence, because any small, local conflict might bring about an atomic holocaust . . . and this of course was utter nonsense, as has been amply proved since.

On arrival in Cairo, Mulk was wreathed and greeted by a small posse of people, including two Chinese delegates, and I by no one. For of course the Chinese had no idea that I was coming as an observer (I had arranged this directly with Youssef El-Sebai, the secretary, and the Egyptian government). The Chinese shook hands cordially with me, but were perplexed. What did I represent? Why had I come? And why with Mulk? 'Comrade Mao Tun is leading our delegation,' they said to me. 'I'll be so glad to see His Excellency the Minister of Culture, Mao Tun,' I replied. 'I shall ring him up tomorrow.'

Thomas Cook's of Singapore had reserved a room for me in a small hotel in Cairo. It was indeed small; but outside my door, in the corridor, lounged a huge six-foot-two Egyptian, Hamid. He slept there. He would stop everyone from coming to see me. I was at first puzzled, but later realized that he was anxious to guarantee my morality since I was a single, unaccompanied woman. I grew quite fond of Hamid in 1962; but when in 1965 Vincent came with me to Cairo, and we booked in at the same hotel (it had a certain ambience), the situation became acute as Hamid burst in throughout the night, every hour or so, to make sure that we were not sleeping together. We moved to the Semiramis.

In the afternoon of my first day in Cairo, I went to Mulk's grandiose hotel (the delegates to the Afro-Asian Writers' Conference were lavishly lodged and fed). Mulk was in the lobby, conversing with a Chinese. I came closer, the man turned his head . . . it was my dear, dear friend, Old Yeh!

'It's worth coming to Cairo just to see you again,' I said happily. We sat companionably while Mulk went on explaining with great force his point of view – which at the time was the Russian view – to Yeh. Since the whole of the Writers' Conference was a political gimmick, part of the struggle between the Russians and the Chinese on the ideological plane, there were from the start any number of people like Mulk going round putting their point of view to other writers, for all resolutions would finally be voted upon.

In the end all the writers, poets, artists, novelists, assembled (and some of them were great names) would be caught in the theoretical argument, which was also a power struggle. I do not blame them for 'wasting their time', as I am sure some Western writers would have said. For these writers in Cairo had consciences; and they knew that the future of the world did depend on this struggle.

For whereas Russia argued that there must be 'peace' and therefore that all countries must keep quiet and not indulge in 'national liberation struggles' which would simply end in a nuclear war, the Chinese argued that this was not so, that local liberation struggles would go on, and they would not lead to nuclear war. The Russians drew a dreadful picture of American imperialism stopping at nothing to exterminate mankind. Only the USSR could stop American ferocity . . . by what means it must be left to the Kremlin to decide, and therefore it was important to follow Russia's leadership.

Not so, said the Chinese. What the Russians and their satellites were proposing was blind obedience, 'the peace of slaves'. It was removing the sovereignty of the independent nations to decide for themselves whether they would or would not engage in a struggle for their own liberation. It was admitting that 'only two superpowers can make the rain fall or the sun shine' upon the world.

An Arab writer came to fetch Mulk, and Yeh and I walked out into the soft, balmy cooking-scented night. For it was Ramadan, the Muslim fasting month. Egypt fasted all day but ate enormously after sunset and before dawn. The night was uproarious with all the shops open and blazing fires to roast meat, and people laughed and strolled and children played.

I called on Mao Tun, whom I had met in Peking in 1956, and who looked very well. In the delegation was the Vice-Minister of Culture, Hsia Yen, a thin and wiry man bursting with nervous energy and talent and intelligence; also two poets I knew, and the frail, diminutive, brilliant writer, Hsieh Pinhsin, Heart of Ice. Pinhsin was sixteen years older than I, but looked beautiful and young. She had started writing in the early 1920s when she was still a student. She used a pseudonym, and in her literature class no one knew – and one day the professor arrived with her first book in his hand, which had been widely acclaimed, and started to teach from it the very class in which she sat as a student! Her English was mellifluous and perfect, for after Chinese university she had been to Wellesley. I had read Heart of Ice when I was a student at Yenching University; two generations, and now three generations of Chinese women read her love stories . . .

Mao Tun wanted to know why I had come with Mulk. 'We happened to be on the same plane,' I said, and he looked relieved. 'I am not going to talk at all,' I added. 'But even if you do not talk, people will ascribe to you notions and opinions,' said Yeh.

The Cairo meeting was to last four days; and I do not recall a single speech in its entirety. Only long-drawn and somewhat dreary hours and plaudits or folded arms as delegates succeeded each other on the rostrum. The serried ranks of writers – I still have a photograph of them. How many countries were there? I think nineteen or so. Japanese and Indians, Chinese and Turks and Ceylonese, and Arab countries, and the Indonesians and some African countries, and the Russians in various delegations according to their several republics. The most outstanding person, where looks were concerned, was Kenneth Kaunda of Zambia, not yet head of state. He was magnificent, sweeping by in pure white robes. The one who caused the greatest uproar was Nazim Hikmet, the Turkish writer, a leonine-looking man who strode in a great fanfare of handclaps to do battle against Mao Tun: 'The tiger of American imperialism is not a paper tiger,' he roared. 'It has atomic teeth!' Mao Tun shook his head and smiled.

Algerians, Egyptians, other delegations tried to steer a middle course; taking neither one side of the argument nor the other. Malek Haddad, the Algerian poet, recited French poetry; came to drink coffee with me and talk of the Algerian war, which was coming to an end; the Evian Accords would be broached that month. The Japanese took notes and made few speeches, and invited me to Japan, where I would go that autumn.

The meeting itself merely consecrated the rift between China and Russia; from then onwards, at every conference, symposium, meeting, the battle would rage; and so many writers would be involved, some of them for years, in these skirmishes and alarums and excursions.

The embassies of various countries threw gargantuan dinners; after sundown everyone was extremely hungry. The men would crowd round the tables, and the food would disappear . . . another batch of food would come up . . . the men would crowd again. We, the women, could neither push nor shove and consequently never reached the table at all except towards the end of the reception, when a lot of the men were picking their teeth and exhaling small burps of fulfilment.

'I don't see what good all these speeches do,' I said to Yeh and Pinhsin at the end of the conference. 'Oh, my dear, that's the way the struggle has to be conducted,' said Pinhsin, while Yeh merely smiled. Pinhsin spent a great deal of her time with the Japanese writers, many of whom she knew personally, since she and her husband* had been teaching in Japan before returning to China in 1951.

On the last day, I think, Mulk came to me. It was the crucial day for a final communiqué to be issued. 'You're not going to talk, Suyin?' 'No, Mulk.' A shadow crossed his face but he smiled, kissed my cheek gently, and went. I wanted to tell Mulk that the core of the longwinded arguments, of that strenuous and somewhat futile battle of wits and phrases, was really *power*. Nothing but power, which creates, of course, its own reality. But Mulk was innocent, and full of idealism, and so I did not tell him.

I explored Cairo, loving the tall-wheeled carts, so high-perched with their diminutive pulling donkeys or their majestic camels and their load of silent, black-clad women. I discovered Egypt's darker people, the Nubians, and their great beauty. For while the 'upper classes' were short, fairly white-skinned Levantines, the lower classes, the servants like my chaperone Hamid, and the market vegetable sellers and the carters, and the women who swung great loads and bales, all were like the Egyptians of old, the people of the ancient pharaonic cities sculptured in stone; and they had skins of burnished gold. How handsome, with their long, slim legs and that extraordinary acute angle between corner of eye, nostril and earlobe they were! I could never stop watching them walk, as long-legged birds walk, picking up their toes. They were all profile as they lifted their faces to the sun.

I went down the Nile to Luxor, taking the night train, and cursing Cook's all the way for its discomfort. In Luxor the hotel was splendidly English – with mostly German tourists. Afternoon tea was served by the handsome 'real' Egyptians (as I now called them to myself) in white gloves. I hired a guide (Cook's recommendation) and experienced the disadvantages of being a single woman touring ancient monuments. The guide, a young man, evidently thought that

---

*The eminent Dr Wu Wentsao. See pp. 394–6.

his services would include bed, since, he said, he had satisfied a few American and English women who had come to Luxor. And he produced letters to confirm it. I indicated that I was not interested and he did not insist, but came to see me off with a large bunch of yellow daisies and zinnias.

A farewell reception was given in Cairo by President Nasser for all the delegations. We massed into an immense hall with journalists and sundry diplomats. The marble floor was so highly polished that it not only glared but sent people spilling if they walked too fast. We stood and we stood. Not a chair in sight. We stood for two, three hours . . . Nasser talked. And went on talking. I looked at him. He was a walking, moving, talking picture of himself; a picture one saw in every house, every shop, every cinema, every school, in every taxi, smiling that sun-burst smile, with radiantly white teeth, well-spaced. He had those teeth; and they were white. And he was tall, taller than the average, well-put-together and well-dressed. A clever man; a hardworking man. He appeared not to notice that after the first ninety minutes a woman had fallen to the floor and had had to be removed; in another thirty minutes two more slid to the horizontal. Heart of Ice and I stood; she untired, straight and slight and unbreakable, me clutching at her, my shoes off, hopping from one collapsing arch to the other.

I also called upon the eminent Dr Khalid, the Head of El-Hazar University, and therefore the Pope of Islam, or its equivalent. He had a face whose chin and nose aspired to meet, and a most beautiful voice. It was important for an Islamic leader to have a fine voice; to chant from the minarets the daily prayer; to thunder and to expostulate and to inflame the roaring multitudes . . .

'Allah will bless your work,' said he in melodious Arabic, with the sound of sunset prayer in it. A Copt journalist friend, who went with me everywhere, translated. I asked Dr Khalid about family planning. What was Islam's attitude to limitation of births, and birth control? There was nothing against it in the Koran, replied Dr Khalid, provided the laws of marriage were kept, the sanctity of the family . . . he went on and on; it was a most beautiful speech, and my Copt friend translated, and I am still unclear as to what Islam really thinks of family planning.

Hassanein Heikal, the very able editor of the newspaper *Al Haram*, Egypt's *New York Times*, and Nasser's confidant and friend, invited me to lunch. Heikal would not pronounce as to Nasser's intentions, save to stress Egypt's important role among the non-aligned countries of the world. My Copt friend was more informative. 'For Nasser, it's the Soviet Union and America. He has to play between those two; only those two can really help. China . . . not for thirty years . . . China is poor, and she is not powerful . . . maybe in thirty years . . .'

The Pakistan Guild of Writers had invited me to visit Pakistan, and from Cairo I flew to Karachi. The Guild was lavish in its hospitality. From the moment I stepped down from the aeroplane in Karachi I was entertained most royally, with a warmth, a prodigality, a joy which has remained with me.

At the airport was a small and happy crowd of writers, H. Mottaher Husain and Jamiluddin Ali and also two women, Mumtaz Shirin and Mussarrat Temuri. Temuri was to be my companion on all the trips I made through Pakistan; and a most amusing, stalwart and lovable travelling partner she proved.

I duly toured monuments and museums and gardens and hospitals and universities and schools, duly went to dinners and receptions, and to private houses to meet writers and artists. The museums in Pakistan were prodigiously interesting, but handicapped by lack of money. Thus in Peshawar there were some extraordinary pieces in the museum – invaluable relics of early Graeco-Indian art that had been excavated in British times. But now the museum was only allotted twelve thousand rupees a year and archaeological diggings could not continue for lack of funds. The curator, enthusiastic, knowledgeable, was very thin. He looked starved. What can one do with only twelve thousand rupees a year on which to run such an immense and wonderful museum?

Neither was the Guild of Writers precisely affluent. Many writers worked very hard for what could be considered a pittance. Since the Guild was government-supported, it was obvious that dissenting writers would not be particularly helped; but was it not like this all over resurgent Asia? Except for Japan, and to a certain extent India, and until an affluent readership, picking and buying its own books, could make the writer financially independent . . . I wondered whether in China, one day, when everyone would be able to read, the Federation of Writers would not be faced with a vast demand for 'more books, different books, better books'.* Readership was a function of literacy. Now in Pakistan there were five languages. Urdu was the main and official language, and I was very pleased with my visit to the compilers of the great Urdu dictionary. They had been working on it for some years, and it would soon be done. In Cairo I had discussed with writers the fact that the ordinary language that people spoke and classical Arabic, in which literature was written, were now wide apart. 'We have to keep on inventing a new written language, a new vocabulary,' said the writers. I told them that the same adaptation had been made in China in the 1920s.

Purdah still prevailed in Pakistan. In Lahore University each classroom was neatly divided in two by a large curtain; boys one side, girls the other. And yet in the beautiful hanging gardens and among the fountains, boys and girls, women and men, walked about, and some were veiled and some were not.

I would be invited to dinner by an official; would go into the house and be received by several women (the hostess and her friends or sisters, all bejewelled and made up). And when the men were announced, the women would disappear into inner rooms, and I would be left alone with the men. The further north I went, the more purdah. In one household in

*This is happening now.

Peshawar, that of a writer, the women were behind hermetically shuttered windows on the first floor. One could only guess at their being there. I could sense them as my eyes travelled over the blind wood of the shutters. They must have peered down at me, at my naked face sitting in the main room below with men. My host the writer had three wives. He told me that he had a hard time because he had to rent shelf space at the local all-purpose shop in order to be able to sell his books. He had found his books covered with dust. 'You only pay me to keep your books, not to clean them,' the shopkeeper had retorted.

Jamila came to see me. Beautiful and young, she had twelve 24-carat gold bracelets studded with rubies coiled like red-eyed snakes upon her arms. She had written a best-seller, which had won a prize. 'But I used a man's name, otherwise no one would have published me.' Then it was found out that the writer was a woman. The prize had evaporated and she was blamed for doing such an unwomanly thing. Her husband, a landlord, was kind to her. 'All he wants is a son.' He let her do what she liked 'in the house, but I am not allowed to leave the house; coming to see you he allowed because you are well-loved everywhere ... Look, these are my chains,' she said, lifting her gold-laden arms. Jamila had been married to breed, not to write; her in-laws were always around her; she produced a son who died at birth.

Temuri and I went by car up the Khyber Pass, and on the road met a small posse of fierce-looking horsemen all slung about with rifles and ammunition. 'Oh,' said Temuri a little nervously, 'I'm afraid they mean to rape us.' We had non-veiled faces, and the Khyber horsemen were not used to this and therefore had dared approach the car. But the driver talked to the men and I think he told them that the government would not like it if they raped us. Temuri and I gazed fixedly into space, unmoving as statues. The horsemen rode away, and after that Temuri, much shaken, told me about her family.

'My family lived in Lucknow, in India, but when Partition came and British India was split into India and Pakistan, my family decided to come to Pakistan.' Temuri was already in Karachi then. 'But there was madness upon the land; people went crazy, Hindus and Muslims killed each other for weeks ... two million people, perhaps more, died at Partition.' There were Hindu killer bands on all the roads to Pakistan. They stopped the carts and cars and trains and killed all the Muslims that they found.

'When the train with my family in it pulled into Karachi station I was waiting there, but the train carried only corpses ... there was a dreadful smell ... and fifty-five of the fifty-six members of my family on the train were dead; only my niece, six years old, was alive because she had buried herself under the bodies ...'

And so we talked of Partition, and looked down at the bleak grey-brown slopes of the bare Khyber Pass, and thought of so many of the massacres of history; history so abundant, so revelling in blood, everywhere, in every corner of the earth, and here at this grey duct between the cliffs too. We drove across the Pass and found a village. All the rooftops were flat, since there was little rain. We both needed to pee but there was no convenience except one of the rooftops; they were layered with clean sand. There we urinated, the whole village in the street staring at us and blinking against the sun to catch a view.

Up to the Kingdom of Swat, ensconced among the mountains between Pakistan and Afghanistan, and oh, the road, the locking cliffs and the ecstasy of stark and void, sudden realization that all life is exiguous, a narrow condemned valley. Swat was a narrow corridor hewn out of rock, and along the rockface of the cliffs were carvings of uncommonly Greek-looking buddhas. The inhabitants of Swat had the same noses coming straight down from the forehead as the Greeks, for Alexander of Macedon had been here; and Swat was a relic of the great ancient Graeco-Indian kingdoms. Prince Aurangzeb of Swat received me at dinner. He was tall and fair; he, his wife and his brother were all three patrician handsome. We had a very lively and somewhat heated dispute about China, but in 1966

Aurangzeb would write to me: 'I have changed my mind and joined your ranks about China.'

From West Pakistan I flew to Dacca in East Pakistan (now Bangladesh), and how depressing it was! Whereas I had found West Pakistan lively and sinewy and vital, and had enjoyed uproarious conversational tussles, here was furtive and clammy depression, a hothouse stillness. Physically a totally different people: Bengalis with enormous charcoal velvet eyes and pointed faces; fine bones, not burly. And Dacca was not prosperous. Therein lay the bitterness which surfaced among the writers. For the only link between East and West Pakistan was religion, Islam. It was frequently mentioned, but was it enough? The writers said, 'We are treated as second-rate citizens.' (Like the Chinese in Malaya, I thought.) East Pakistan grew the jute, and jute supplied so much of the money needed for the divided country (all the breadth of India between them – who had invented this absurdity? The British). 'We receive nothing in return for what we give. The money goes out, nothing is put back, we are drained of wealth.' And indeed the country looked to me unkempt, the standard of living much lower than in Peshawar, Lahore and Karachi.

I was entertained by a couple of famous writers (famous in the Bengali language) one evening. For me they had burnt incense and set little lights throughout their house; and I felt ashamed and uncomfortable, for they had worked so painstakingly, as if, because I had such access to the Western world, I was superior . . . yet how I longed to tell them it was a fluke, hazard, circumstance . . . a love and a death; I longed to tell them: 'Actually, I am a cadaver-eater; my fame rests upon a corpse.' But would they understand such self-clarity? 'You must learn to be a little brutal with barbarians,' said I. 'I would not have had such material success without some brutality, both received and given. You must accept the existence of brutality.' They were shocked; for they strove so hard to be meek and likeable, to live up to an ideal of goodness (but how precarious it was). I told them that babies came into life kicking and bawling, and sometimes one must kick and bawl one's way through, but trying to kick only the strong, not the weak. I do not think they understood.

Could I make these Asian writers confident when they were so penurious, so dependent on the government to subsidize them, when their reading public was so restricted? 'It will all change,' I said. But I could not promise that Western writers would care for fellow-authors in Dacca, or Peshawar, or even in China; I could not promise that women writers in London would think of Jamilia raising her gold-heavy arms. How few, how very few of them would ever be translated for readers in the West . . .

On the way back from Dacca, I stopped over in Madras, for Vincent had a week's leave from Jardine Waugh in Singapore. Vincent and I spent four days in Colombo, at the Galle Face Hotel. We had a room perched on the rockface; and just below was the ocean, and its colour and sound and presence filled the room; the beat and roar of its power made love to us all night. We were always damp with spray, and the insane sea wind rushed in through all the open windows.

When we returned to Malaya, I prepared to go back to China. I left in mid-June, via Hong Kong, and there I was to see Pengju once again. We never knew it would be the last time. In that July, a telegram came to me while I was in Peking. Pengju had been invited on the inaugural flight of some Arab airline; the aeroplane had gone into a mountain, and all aboard had been killed. I miss him terribly, even today.

CHAPTER 14

China – 1962–1964: Resurgence

Never was China twice the same; untiring as the ocean, there was always tumult and conflict beneath her outer placidity. Whenever I have the illusion of a tranquil China, I know it is the imprisoning eye of another storm.

In that summer of 1962 China was resurgent. The hunger and the want of the three bad years, 1959 to 1961, were going and in the air was promise of a good autumn harvest despite renewed accounts of droughts and floods and insect plagues. But now the words 'natural calamities' were automatic, on all lips; the merest cloud in the sky would be interpreted as a hailstorm . . . 'We're a bit allergic to the weather because we've had such a bad time with it,' Yang Hsienyi, who had now put on weight, said to me. As so many people were putting on weight, eating more, eating audibly, visibly. 'The Old Man in Heaven has been unkind to us for three long years,' said the cadres, peering cautiously towards the sky. 'We still have many problems.'

Kuangchow burst with energy. New whitewash on the walls of the houses, new paint. And by the side of the usual human labour – men pulling carts, men carrying loads; and how long this would still go on, how long – there were new blue and white buses, new trucks and lorries. 'Diesel oil buses and trolley buses,' pointed out Comrade Chen, the poet, cryptic face hinting at a major change. The major change was that oil had been discovered during the Leap; in a region where the Russians had said there could be no oil. And the trolley buses showed that China could now make reactors and heavy water, which was a technological advance. 'Since the great Leap we have made our own trucks.' New wide avenues cut a swathe through the city; new flats were coming up 'for workers of the industrial complex'. There was a new sports stadium and a new park. 'We are beautifying the city.' And bicycles: a steady stream of bicycles, not only in the city but also in the countryside. 'We began to supply bicycles to the countryside communes last year. We make them ourselves.'

There were new areas with houses built by and for the overseas Chinese who had returned from Indonesia: neat tarred roads, and the houses looking exactly like the middle-class bungalows of Singapore; with electric light, running water, refrigerators. 'They must have what they are used to.' Between 1959 and 1961 almost a million overseas Chinese had returned and been resettled. They had started pineapple, rubber and coffee plantations in south China. 'We try to integrate them, but they have different habits . . .' The overseas Chinese indeed looked different; when they walked in the streets, with money in their pockets and jaunty suits and permed hair and make-up they were visible, too visible in the pastel subduedness of China's cities. There were special shops for them where they would buy tins of better cigarettes, and jade carvings, and clothes. How difficult for the government not to privilege them. 'It provokes subjective reactions if they feel deprived,' said the comrade from the Overseas Chinese Department. But at the Cultural Revolution in 1966 the overseas Chinese would pay dearly for these privileges.

I dallied in the south because the provinces are so much more creative and interesting than official, stiff Peking, where the ghosts of past emperors still reside, and the bureaucrats congregate. I needed to find my family origins for my book, *The Crippled Tree*. And the root was here, in this province, among the Hakkas of Meihsien district.

Comrade Chen was also a Hakka, and he gave me a book of his poems and an old novel, *Flowers in a Mirror*, which dated back to 1783. Together we went to Egret Island to see the dainty, snow-plumed birds in their sanctuary, and then by boat to the lychee fruit plantations. The heavy lychee clusters pulled the boughs of the squat, strong trees to the waiting mirror of the water; our boat glided among the branches. At one time during the Leap, said Comrade Chen, there had been 'precipitancy', and some ultra-leftists had advocated doing away with the lychee trees. Others had wanted to swell the figures of harvest for lychee fruit, and gathered it unripe. 'We have now corrected these errors . . . the people gave us their opinion on these harmful things . . . we must listen more to the people.' I remembered my previous visit, when I had been told that meetings were held everywhere to assess errors, to have the people 'speak up their bitterness'. Obviously this had been done. But I also remembered that, at the time, there was a search for the culprits of the 'ultra-left' communist wave which had hit the Leap in 1958. Had the culprits been found? Now there was total silence on that point . . .

'When shall we truly obtain deliverance from the kingdom of necessity?' Thus Comrade Chen, quoting Mao Tsetung, but not telling me that it was Mao.

There were rumours that in January of 1962, five months previously, Mao had made a most important speech to seven thousand of the prominent Party leaders, to intellectuals, provincial Party secretaries, on democracy. He had stressed the need for it; without it, there could be no real socialism, and no material progress either. But the speech was not made public, nor would it be 'official' or printed until the autumn of 1978, sixteen years later.

There are pages and pages in my notebooks of those years about the new projects, new canals, new improved rice breeds, new experiments – everywhere this spurt of strength, and everywhere too the demand for knowledge. Not a sickly world of listless shuffling; a strong clamour, and a thousand, a million demands. How would they be fulfilled?

A peasant woman in a flowered blouse perched on the back of a sturdy bicycle (the bicycles for rural communes were heavier than for city denizens), a child strapped to her back in the colourful embroidered carry-baby; another one between her and her husband riding the machine, and the eldest child in front, legs dangling over the handlebars . . . A new food-canning factory, weaving factory, plastics factory, chemical fertilizer factory . . . much talk about chemical fertilizers. 'Our peasants do not like chemicals. They say they burn the soil. But we must modernize agriculture, mechanize agriculture.'

I went to see Meihsien, a typical Hakka district. Not far from it Hua Hsien, forty-eight kilometres from Kuangchow, the birthplace of the leader of the great Taiping peasant rebellion, a man named Hung Hsiuchuan. There had been so many peasant revolts in China, through the centuries. At least a major one per century, three thousand minor ones in the last two millennia. It was through peasant revolts that dynasties were changed and the imperial throne conquered.

I told Comrade Chen, since he too was a Hakka, how my family originally went to Szechuan from the district of Meihsien; because Szechuan had been laid waste and depopulated in forty years of war, in the seventeenth century, when the Manchus conquered China. And the Hakkas, always land hungry, always relegated to the worst land and to hilly slopes because they were really refugees, nomads,* hunted down from north China by the great invasions between the ninth and the twelfth centuries, had heard of available land in Szechuan and settled there. And that is how we were now identified with Szechuan, but also proud of our Hakka origin.

My grandmother was a Hung, from the same clan and village as the leader of the Taiping rebellion. When I went to see the house of Hung, the Taiping King of the Heavenly Kingdom, I discovered that over 90 per cent of the people in his village were still named Hung. But this is not strange. All Chinese villages are clan villages, even today. Always around 70 to 90 per cent of the village families have the same family name, and so village girls are always betrothed to boys from other villages because the Chinese have a horror of incest. Two people bearing the same family name, in the past, were not allowed to wed. Yet in all of China, because of the antiquity of its clan names, there are only 186 family names among the 900 million Chinese.

---

*The word Hakka means 'the guest people', indicating their refugee status.

Peasant revolts . . . the present communist revolution had also sprung from massive peasant uprisings. What else, in a country of over 400 million peasants, and only 2 to 3 million workers by 1949? But Mao Tsetung, himself a peasant, had gone beyond the usual pattern; he had utilized this great strength of the peasantry for a modern type of revolution. He was attempting to leap a stage in history; to go directly from feudalism – with very little capitalism superimposed upon it – into socialism. Theoretically it could not be done . . . could it be done? It must be done. There was no other way if China wanted to catch up with the developed world by the year A.D. 2000. And so the Leap . . . a phenomenal attempt to hurry, to catapult China into her own future. Was it crazy? Was it a failure?

For the next four years, until the Cultural Revolution began in 1966, I would travel my fill, going everywhere I could possibly go; far south and north and to Szechuan and Yunnan, to see the new and the old, the traditional and the revolutionary side by side; travel in and out of time and within China's time, which is her continuum of being. All that happened in the past was still so accessible, still argued about and discussed as if it were just familiar yesterday. China's Revolution of today was thus not a break, not a rejection, it was an integral part of China's many becomings, of her eternity. The Revolution would go through many metamorphoses, as an insect does, larva and caterpillar and butterfly, and yet is always the essential insect.

Through eight provinces and many major cities in 1962 and 1963, through communes and scattered villages, going by train and sometimes by car, deep away from towns, nowhere was there any sign of famine or of beriberi or even of gross malnutrition, as there had been in 1960–1. I wrote to Edgar Snow and to Felix Greene:

Everywhere the streets are full of vegetables and fruit in small mountains; pears and peaches and apples and raisins and four kinds of melon and ten different kinds of vegetables, including tomatoes and carrots, parsley and onions. In Sian, in Taiyuan, in the cities of the north . . . in Peking too, except that in Peking much of the fruit seems to have been plucked too early. I am told it is to avoid the hailstorms in August.

All this produce was unbelievably cheap: four *fen* for a kilo of melon, three *fen* for a kilo of carrots, five *fen* for a kilo of onions, one or two *fen* for a bagful of spinach.* In Yunnan province sugar was off the ration. There were great mounds of cakes and sweets and almonds and peanuts, and such a surplus of pears that half the crop had to be given to the pigs to eat; because there was not enough transport to send it to markets outside the producing areas. In Szechuan delicious oranges littered the streets of Chengtu; a pound of sugar was given free to anyone who would buy a pint of milk. In the Leap new milch-cow farms had been established, but such was the rooted prejudice and horror for milk ('It smells bad, it tastes bad, it gives stomach ache, it's only good for very sick people'), that even with the gift, few people would take milk.

The oil ration in the provinces of the Yangtze Valley was twice that in Peking, and the meat ration in Wuhan was three times that in Peking. Everywhere people were eating, eating. A perceptible fattening process was on. And visible in all the streets of the cities, except in Peking, pedlars and small shops, free markets; very few queues.

In the courtyards of houses in north China, rabbit hutches under the eaves. But the price of rabbit meat had taken a steep fall. Where it had been a *yuan* or two for a month-old rabbit a year previously, it was now twenty *fen*. There were many delicious ways of preparing rabbit, and I often travelled with comrades carrying, in the plastic bags made in the new plastics factories (difficult to get a plastic bag, everyone wanted one!), rabbit steeped in soya sauce and ginger and then gently roasted.

---

*100 *fen* = 1 *yuan*. In the 1960s 1 *yuan* was equivalent to half a US dollar.

Seaweed growing, which had been started in 1959, was not given up; seaweed continued to be used, mixed with maize, to make unleavened bread; and for animal fodder. But people were gradually abandoning it. By 1964 no one would use seaweed for food any more.

In that spring, according to doctors I saw in various hospitals, there had been an increase in mortality among young infants after measles. Otherwise no main epidemics had occurred. As for tuberculosis, I checked up again on the figures I had acquired on the previous visit to the sanatorium in Tientsin, but could come to no conclusion.

Cotton was still extremely short. Still only an average of two metres per person per year; except of course for new born babies (10 metres) and also funeral clothes. Everyone, including the middle cadres, wore patched clothes, worn clothes. Cloth shoes were difficult to get, but now there were factories making plastic sandals for summer and cloth shoes with plastic soles for the rest of the year. No one liked them; it would be quite a hard process to teach the Chinese to wear synthetic materials; they loved cotton so much, it was so comfortable. 'But in the end we must expand synthetics, we cannot go on planting enough cotton for everyone,' said an official in the cotton industry. That year the first nylon shirts were produced. They were called 'thoroughly cool'. Everyone promptly called them 'thoroughly stifling'.

Patching, contriving, retrieving clothing became a profession, an art. Patching factories manned by housewives were found in every small lane. In Chungking some pedlars were selling tanned and softened skins of rats, which were used for patches and for the uppers of shoes. The rats of Chungking had been notorious in the past; large, heavy creatures, they attacked cats and ate them up. They had been decimated in repeated 'get rid of pests' campaigns since 1949. They were said to have disappeared; but clever rat catchers still found them, and now they became useful at last.

The teahouses and restaurants which had been closed during the 'ultra-left' phase of the Leap were opened again.

In Kuangchow they were pretty, adorned with flower pots; in Chengtu the teahouses in the park were full of people, and in Peking too there were teahouses and small restaurants. But it was still difficult to get chickens' eggs because the demand for hens was still very high. Every family owned at least one hen, if not more; hens were kept on balconies, in bedrooms, in coops suspended from windows . . . A doctor friend of mine had an upstairs neighbour whose eight hens were conducted by him or by his wife, every morning, down five flights of stairs to the communal garden, there to pick and scratch. My medical friend was irritated because the clucking woke him and the excreta which were left upon the stairs were not cleared up. 'People are very ingenious when given their heads,' said he. On this gallinaceous enterprise the Party kept 'one eye open, one eye shut', allowing it because it was necessary; but by 1964, when it was no longer necessary to keep hens at home because eggs had come back on the market, the Health Ministry started a small 'health' campaign, and hens on balconies and in flats were not allowed. However, since there was no law against it, people went on keeping them for quite a long time.

There were also, here and there, faint reminders of the fact that not so welcome things were returning, in the wake of the relaxation which now existed. Thus in 1963 it was obvious to me that large clan houses, which had belonged to wealthy landlord families, were being repaired and repainted in some areas. There was also the fact that despite the commune system some villages were being worked to the benefit of one person only. Was this a return of landlordsim? Or was there a new class of landlords? In some communes the private plots flourished but communal fields of grain looked neglected. In others one could see along the road groups of peasants going off to work on house building or hiring themselves out for day work in city suburban factories because in that way they made a little more money. Grain planting, self-reliance in grain, was the official government policy; but peasants made more money from secondary crops, rape oil, tobacco, ginseng, pigs and chickens and ducks, and hiring manpower out to the cities.

Yet there was progress. I sat in a village where electric light had come at the Leap and the wonder of it had not ceased; the wonder of light at night, making it possible for people to look at each other in the new small sun of the single bulb hanging from the centre of a room. The schoolmaster said proudly, 'Now we can have night schools for the peasants.' There were many villages which had thus the gift of light bestowed upon them. And with electric power came flour mills; so that the so-common sight of the past of a woman or a mule, or sometimes both, milling flour between two stones, pushing and pulling, disappeared totally in China.

It was hot in Peking; 39 to 40 degrees Centigrade (over 100 degrees Fahrenheit), and there had been in 1961 the worst drought ever seen, both in the north and also in Szechuan province.

'We are concentrating on producing water pumps,' said the engineers. In whatever city I was I would climb to the top floor of the tallest building and watch. I watched the tall chimneys of the factories. I watched for smoke, for that lazy elongated cloud, grey or black or yellow, which indicated industrial activity. As one watches a new born baby for breath. Because that would mean industry had picked up; and there were machines and men working producing what was needful . . . and no sight ever made me more glad than that of new electric pylons bestriding the fields to make the wheels turn, to feed the lathes.

'We are brimming with confidence,' said Wu Chienta, toughened by yet another spell in a commune, where 'there was enough to eat'. The peasants were now encouraged to store grain for themselves, whereas during the early part of the Leap this had been discouraged as 'capitalist enterprise'. Mao Tsetung himself had said that 'too much was requisitioned' from the peasantry then. 'It spoilt the relations between the Party and the masses,' said Chienta, soberly.

There was a faint, stray rumour in Peking that Mao criticized himself for 'rashness' and having had too much trust in inflated reports from below during the early part of the Leap.

Wanchun has learnt to lead water buffaloes to pasture, to reckon time by the burning of an incense stick. He has stopped asking me to bring him English cigarettes. He now smokes the ordinary Peony brand. 'When I saw the work that went into growing tobacco . . .' Three years ago, when he had seen me clean my hotel room (it was a windy day and within half an hour everything was filmed over with Peking's inexorable dust), he had cried, 'How can a high-class intellectual like you do such menial work?'

The slogan is: Consolidation, readjustment, filling in and elevation; which means to garner and salvage what lessons the Leap has taught (good ones and bad ones) and to improve the quality of production.

A new poem by Mao is also being quoted: 'On perilous high peaks dwells beauty in her infinite variety.' 'Of course we must reach for the sky,' says Hualan. She too brims with tough assurance. 'No one is going to help us, to lift us up; we shall have to do it all ourselves.'

Round Taiyuan, capital of Shansi province, the commune fields are green, though further south, in Honan, they appear parched. This is because there are pumps, pumping underground water. The city is cool at dusk and there are many bicycles. The people do not look hungry; and the women wear flowered blouses.

The Confucian temple in Sian is a museum. Round the 1,095 stelae of stone, carved through the centuries, a forest of historical records, schoolchildren are gathered, listening intently to the guides. Everything is pink at sunset, the beautiful houses with their carved brick ornaments and eaves and their roofs with everted tiles convex to the sun. All the Buddhist monuments are well-preserved. 'Many delegations from Buddhist countries come here to worship,' say the cadres. Here in Sian, as in so many other Chinese cities, I see women with incense sticks bunched in their hands, praying in the temples and sanctuaries of the past.

'We allow religion, though of course we do not approve,' say the cadres tolerantly. Professor Wu, historian, curator of the museum, is with me while I visit the old temples and the new factories.

In the streets of Sian are many pedlars, selling ribbons and summer hats, ladles and kettles and pots and wooden combs and nails . . . private enterprise again; 'We allow these small things.' There are also free markets in the countryside with an abundance of food: 'We allow these small things.' By now I know the formula: the Party keeps one eye open one eye shut. I wonder whether both eyes will open and once more there will be an ultra-left wave, sweeping away these relics of private enterprise. Or can they be allowed and integrated in a socialist system?

I go to see a project, the tapping of subsurface water, twenty-five kilometrès from Sian. It is obvious that this is the work of engineers and geologists, of intellectuals; but the cadres there insist that everything was done by the peasantry. They quote proudly from Mao: 'The people, only the people, are the locomotive of history . . .' As if the intelligentsia were not also the people.

But this shows that the problem has not yet been solved: the fusion of the intellectual and his acceptance by the majority of workers and peasants. Although since 1961 the intelligentsia has been back and is honoured again instead of being humiliated, and there have been many rehabilitations of 'rightists', there is also, there will be for a long time, resentment of intellectuals. 'Class struggle', it is called. And it is quite true that some of the intellectuals are quite insufferable, and that it is only too easy for an élite to form once more, another mandarin class.

Back to Szechuan again. Here the slogan is: Produce pigs. The target is: a pig for every person in Szechuan.

Pigs are my favourite topic, my favourite animal, the mainstay of China's fields, the reliable standard of rural prosperity. I see the pigs change their anatomy . . . there are now far fewer of the small black Chinese pigs with lordosis of the spine. Most of them are mixed breeds, for large male pigs have been imported from England. The pig is bigger, the spine is straight . . . 'But our peasants complain that the foreign-mixed pig is not so good to eat,' say the cadres. I look at these Eurasian pigs and I feel sympathy.

Here, as everywhere else in China, the pigs have been collectivized and decollectivized twice since 1956, and the result has been bad. They have been badly fed and badly looked after, and everyone now says it. In 1960 I was told in one place: 'Out of 170 pigs in 1957 in our village, only twenty-eight were left in 1959.' The team which achieved the worst records had only four pigs left out of two hundred. But the masses can never be blamed for anything. The Party has to blame itself, to take responsibility for anything that goes wrong: for its own obscurantism and authoritarianism and the wrong methods and policies it applies so literally, and indiscriminately always. Anything that goes right, however, is due to the 'correct leadership' of the Party.

'Last year we only had leaves and some wild grass to feed our pigs . . . the drought was terrible in Szechuan. Even the bamboo split on its stem.' This is what the peasants say. They add, 'Now we have learnt . . .'

'Learnt what?'

'To walk on two legs.'

'What does it mean?'

'It means that the pigs are partly collectivized and partly private.'

The big boar, the sows, are the common property of the production team (which is the village), but the piglets are sold to individual members to look after and to fatten. 'Then we buy back the grown pig when he has reached 220 catties and is ready for the market. The commune member is given meat coupons equivalent to one quarter the pig's weight, and a sum of money, and is also paid for the manure he contributed from the pig. Then he buys more piglets.' This judicious mixture seems to work.

Such excursions in rural areas cannot provide anyone with a total picture; they have to be supplemented with numerous tales by those of my friends who have lived and done their manual labour with the peasantry. Such a one is Danny, who is an overseas Chinese from Canada, and was two years in a commune. 'The peasants just watched me at first. They are so quick to perceive if one is disgusted by them; they are humble and they go away, but one can never be friendly . . . to become real friends, one must adopt them as they are, dirt and all.' He was a tremendous success because he got up early on his first morning to sweep the courtyard. 'Then they would tell me, slowly, their stories. About the cadres. They knew very well who were the good ones and who the bad ones.' Danny had seen both kinds during his two years. 'It's my impression that most of them are good, but then they are mostly the older type . . . some of the young ones are pretty brutal, and they behave like landlords. They force the peasants to work for them, cut wood and draw water, and build them their new houses . . .'

Once again I am in Chengtu; and I bring tinned food, a Yunnan ham, clothes and extra ration coupons to my Family. The extra coupons are issued by the Bank of China in proportion to the interest paid on my capital; they empower my Family to shop at the overseas store in Chengtu. Of course I also have to provide some money, because the goods in that store are more expensive than in the usual shops for the Chinese population.

There are many ration coupons: 'You won't be able to use them all, not in ten years,' says the official who unwinds the long chain of tickets for grain, meat, oil and cotton. 'We shall use them soberly, only as we need something,' says Third Uncle matter of factly.

'I am in good health,' announces Third Uncle, but he walks painfully, with a cane; he has lost the lithe, soft step he had. And now he is worried by the idea of his own death. What worries him is the disposition of his body after death. He feels that a coffin made of the best lanmu wood should be his; lanmu keeps the body from the putrefaction of after-life. He talks a little about a coffin; but no one, not even me, ventures to say: I shall buy you a coffin. Because, somehow, we feel that this might draw upon the Family the attention of ill-wishers who would say, 'See these unrepentant bourgeois . . . still wasting money on extravagant coffins.'

Our premonition turns out to be right. For during the Cultural Revolution, a friend of mine living in Hong Kong came to me in great agitation. Her mother lived in Shanghai, and of course had provided for herself an excellent coffin, which she kept in her bedroom. But the young Red Guards had criticized her for being so old-fashioned, and had removed the coffin . . . 'Can you find a way to get the coffin back to her? She cannot sleep well without having it by her bed,' said my friend to me.

I understand Third Uncle's worry, but still I keep silent. Sometimes I feel that I know what is prudent and what is careless better than the Family . . . He and Third Aunt, and all the Family, have survived pretty well until now, and I intend that this should go on. In 1962 all the Family eats well, and now with the extra rations they will even have a little more.

Nostalgia; retracing my footsteps, checking on old places I knew . . . with my younger cousins I go up to the Taoist temple among the Tsing Cheng mountains. These are the offshoots of the great staircase ranges which climb up and up to the Himalayan plateaus. I know the Taoist temple: I went there with Pao, my husband, in 1940.

At the time we were carried in bamboo chairs up the mountain, Pao and I. Men carried the chairs: skeletal men in rags, and at every halt they wanted a little money, to smoke opium. And Pao reviled and scolded them for doing so. But they gazed at him with hard faces and glazed eyes. Who was he, so well-nourished, to tell them not to smoke a few opium dregs to take away the pain of hunger, the pain of pitiless labour in their bones? Only with opium could they carry us up to the top . . .

And so when we arrived at the beautiful temple Pao was in a bad temper, and after a long lecture on virtue, and how it was lack of virtue that had brought China to her miserable estate, he beat me in the bedroom. And I remember also that there were many bedbugs; all through the night I caught them, and killed them . . .

But now there was no opium, not anywhere; everywhere I looked at the people carefully; looking for the yellow faces, the parchment skin, but I saw only young round faces, good bodies. The monastery was just as it had been but it had now become a production team. The monks grew vegetables and made their own incense. Around the temple grew gingko, maidenhair trees, one of them almost 1,700 years old, and a small fountain cascaded deliberately down rocks, pouring music as it went from trough to trough of stone.

All that region was famous; here was the great Ming River, tributary of the Yangtze, which had been divided by the engineer Li Ping over two thousand years ago; instead of being an angry turbulent stream rushing through the Szechuan plain, it had become a million rivulets, irrigating 400,000 hectares of rice fields; and this made Szechuan the richest land in all China. But now more work had to be done on the river; 800,000 hectares could be irrigated.

Szechuan opera is more fun, less stilted, nearer to folk art than Peking opera. The lyrics are far less official. Szechuan opera allows the singers to ad lib; and so, right in the middle of the most tragic scenes, there is a quip, and laughter, and comedy interrupts the tears. It is this mixture of ribald farce and classic tragedy that disconcerts the purists of the Peking opera. Then there is the chorus, singing from behind a screen, singing the unspoken thoughts of the actors on stage. It gives depth to the opera, and tension. And all Szechuan opera, somehow or other, contrives to make fun of bureaucrats, mandarins, authority. This is what has prevented it from having a more official appeal. Peking opera is far more 'establishment'.

I call on the opera actors and singers. They have returned from three months of manual labour, practising 'togetherness, new inspiration, creative fusion'; which means that they have lived, worked, eaten with the peasants, that this has led them to write new scripts and to revise some of their notions of opera, and finally that they have also compiled a new repertoire, based on stories and legends (which are innumerable) among the people. 'It is most enriching,' they say.

There are forty open and one hundred closed gestures in Szechuan opera. In the old courtyard of the temple which serves as the opera school, the actors and singers demonstrate their skill. There is much less 'warlike expression' in Szechuan opera than in Peking opera; themes about love, flirting and especially poking fun at bureaucrats and evil officials are in every repertoire. There are twenty-six walking gestures and most of them depict the human passions, love and evil, and they are satire, not acrobatics. Szechuan opera is over ten centuries old. 'It has no connection with Peking opera, which was Mongol influenced,' the chief star, who has been on stage since he was eight and is now thirty-two, tells me.

Before Liberation all provincial opera, just like Peking opera, was badly remunerated. Most artists were poverty stricken, save for one or two renowned singers. But now all of them are paid salaries, are given houses; and there is an institute of research into Szechuan opera, and four hundred students to train. The institute sends teams all over Szechuan for likely scripts and folk tales and old operas (many are now resurrected). It has accumulated 1,470 old scripts, and is studying them. The institute also sends teams to all the schools, to recruit new students from the children.

The artists show me the fan gestures and the walking gestures and how they combine; how the edge of a scholar's dress can be made to undulate slightly to indicate hurry, distress or love. 'The eyes are the most important feature,' says the famous woman singer, Chen Shoufang, one of the greatest and best-loved of Szechuan artists. 'There are eighteen eye expressions.' She demonstrates. 'In Peking opera the forehead of the woman actor is painted narrow and low; in Szechuan the forehead is painted large and noble, and the body is held much straighter.' The institute is printing books and textbooks, and photographing gestures, and the way faces are painted; there is a whole street devoted to embroidering the clothes that the actors and singers wear. 'We must train for posterity, to elevate and to enrich.'

Of all provincial operas, Szechuan opera was to suffer most from the wrath and fury of Chiang Ching, Madame Mao, who would allow only one kind of opera, the one she sanctioned.

But in 1962 and 1963, all is hope and advance in that domain. And of course, because the physical output of the singers is high, they have large rations of meat and oil. 'But our steel workers in Szechuan get more than in Peking; the ration here is forty or even forty-five catties of grain a month per man.' During the bad years, they tell me, 'our playing and singing did a lot to sustain morale'.

And what about mechanization of agriculture in Szechuan? There is much talk about it in 1963 and 1964. We walk through fields that are still garden patches, handmade and asymmetrical; and they will not change for a very long time; because to change their conformation will require altering the whole of the immense web of water canalicules through the plain. Each field is bordered by a neat hem of water; making bigger fields means blocking off these capillary vessels which irrigate the plain and turn it into one enormous liver. It means digging new and larger canals. Can this be done? And when mechanization comes, what will happen to all the redundant people in this prolific land?

Problems. Problems. But everyone tells me that the production team manages its own land, animals, tools and manpower, and its own workpoints, and is responsible for what it sells to the state. Now the private plot *cannot* be removed, they tell me (the fury of the 1958 'communist phase' is gone).

But mechanization will upset this pattern, which is stable but still a feudal, small producers' pattern, perhaps even more than any 'communist wave' . . .

Chou Enlai's 'readjustment' is working.

In July 1961 Foreign Minister Chen Yi has made a most

important speech, talking of the need to use intellectuals intelligently. He has made it to the graduates of the institutes and schools of higher learning in Peking. He says that 'intellectuals must primarily re-educate themselves . . . coercion and compulsion will not work.' He says that 'class origin' must not be the main criterion by which to judge anyone. 'People can only be judged by their own behaviour, not by their association with a brother, father, mother, sister.' A bad tendency has grown up now in the Party to judge everyone by three generations of ancestors; and whatever his own merits, however zealous, politically conscious, enthusiastic, hardworking, he will *not* be trusted or usefully employed if his 'class origin' is bad. Nonsense, says Chen Yi.

He says also that 'Red and expert' does not mean that one can be judged solely on glib politicalese. Politics alone do not compensate for lack of knowledge; empty slogans 'are like the Buddhist prayers . . . they don't achieve anything'. Expertise and knowledge are precious and valuable; and they must be cared for. 'Even if politically the intellectuals still have lingering bourgeois ideas and habits', they can be useful and must be used properly and taken care of.

All those once labelled 'rightists' and since rehabilitated should not be compelled, every time there is a campaign, to criticize themselves again and again, or hold themselves isolated from others, says Chen Yi.

Chou Enlai has made a speech deploring the lack of democracy, saying people are afraid to act, speak, think . . . yet Mao had enjoined them to do so.* And Mao has made a major speech, in January 1962, which I cannot lay my hands on (not until 1978!), saying it is necessary and indispensable for China's progress to develop democracy, to safeguard legality, to create 'a vigorous and lively political situation in which there is both centralism and democracy, both discipline and freedom, both unity of will and personal ease of mind . . .'

---

*This all-important speech addressed to the intelligentsia in 1961 would only be made public in 1979.

I am happy; especially as I hear that once again work on a legal code is being undertaken; that the framing of laws, interrupted during the Leap, is starting again.

Chungking is bustling with life. The fungoid-like sheds clinging to the steep cliffs above the river have gone. New brick settlements, uniformly dull but neat and with water and electric light, replace them. Chungking is now a large industrial city, with 4½ million people.

I visit the Seven Star Cliff Commune, 76,000 people in 18,000 families. Of these 76,000, 36,000 are children under sixteen, in thirteen primary schools and one middle school and one technical school. Nineteen thousand of the 36,000 children are under seven years old.

The labour force of the commune is 12,000; 80 per cent women. That is because the men work in factories adjacent to the commune and don't count as commune labour force; while the women work on the land.

There are 214 nurseries; mess halls have been kept because they are practical and necessary. There are twenty-six small factory repair shops and flour mills; beancurd and noodles and vegetable pickles are made and sold to the city. There are night schools for the illiterate women. 'The women came out to work in 1958 . . . for the first three months not one of them even asked for a salary.' 'We started making ball-bearings by hand during the Leap,' say the women. 'We also made light bulbs . . . the day the lights came on everyone beat drums and cymbals and danced.'

It is August and very hot, 42 degrees Centigrade by day and by night. But everywhere people move, work; at night they drag their beds outside and sleep in the streets for coolness. 'Once upon a time there was malaria here, but all the mosquitoes are gone, and there is no longer malaria in Chungking.'

I go down the Yangtze Gorges from Chungking to Wuhan. The dreaded rocks in mid-stream have been blasted; the channel, though narrow, now allows steamboats. 'You are the first foreigner for years to take this trip,' says the captain of the small, old boat which takes me. (The larger boat will soon be ready. In fact Prince Sihanouk will inaugurate it in 1964, going down the Yangtze Gorges with Chou Enlai, sketching and singing all the way.)

I am given a tiny bunk ensconced just above the boilers – and it is August, and I boil gently. But I am almost all day on the bridge, to look up at the 1,000-metre-high sheer walls between which the Great River has carved its fortuitous channel, and to hear the mighty song the wind plays high above my head, among the crests. At night the boat anchors, and then it is very still, there is no breeze, and we suffocate in silence.

All along the river are landmarks of history; battles and kingdoms wrested and won. Here the ancestor of my dead cousin Pengju, King Liu Pei, and his genius strategist Chuke Liang, fought back and forth for the kingdom of Szechuan.

At Wanhsien in the evening, about twenty men are defecating on the slope, and our boat anchors in full sight of them. They defecate and fan themselves and exchange jokes. Downstream a junk is still being pulled up by a string of men, and I think of my mother in 1913, her boat being pulled up, up, up the great river, through these very gorges, for weeks and weeks . . . and at the time the river was dangerous, full of treacherous rocks and whirlpools and the junks often broke up.

I visit the Wuhan steel works and they are going full blast. 'We have surmounted our difficulties,' says the same engineer whom I met in 1961. 'We even have a new, totally Chinese-designed blast furnace.' The words 'self reliance' hang heavy and proud in the resurrected city.

In Yunnan province are new factories, an industrial complex: in the capital city, Kunming, new roads. The Stillwell Road, built under the command of the well-remembered American General Stillwell during the Second World War, which linked up with the Burma Road, is well-kept.

On Saturday evenings a dance is held at the place where I

am staying, which is the former palace of a former warlord of Yunnan. It is a dance for the cadres, and of course I cannot join in; I have been advised to rest as I 'look tired'. Meekly I withdraw, but later stroll down the terrace and peer through the lighted windows with their thin veiling. The cadres dance sedately, a foxtrot, a waltz; the tunes are very old-fashioned, they make me think of Victor Sylvester's orchestra during the Second World War.

In the communes of Kiangsu province I visit the silkworm farms; white and russet and yellow, the silkworms spread their cocoons in large flat baskets: three qualities of silk. 'Owing to inexperience and natural calamities', a hard time was had by the silkworms during the three bad years; and the mulberry trees too were afflicted. But now all is well and recovering. In the large sheds, kept at even warmth, the women come and go, the girls with deft hands and silent feet.

To Nanchang in Hunan province, to see the new industries, but also to see the hotel room where Chou Enlai in July 1927 planned the capture of the city; defied the orders of Stalin to 'give up weapons'. August 1st was the day of Nanchang's capture, and it remains Red Army Day, in commemoration of that historic event. Here are heroic oil paintings of Chou Enlai surrounded by famous generals. But in some of the photographs of those heroic years, one man is effaced, erased, blotted out.

That man is Peng Tehuai, former Minister of Defence, former Long Marcher. A prestigious man, a man well-loved by the soldiers, a simple and a very straightforward man, but not always, perhaps, very polite or wary.

What has happened to Peng Tehuai? No one talks about him. No one will answer me if I ask. Even Ed Snow does not know.

It is now Marshal Lin Piao who is in command of the Red Army. We all know it. But we also know that Peng Tehuai has not been denounced. Several times in the history of the Chinese Party, leaders who took 'the wrong line' have been castigated, openly denounced. Peng Tehuai has not been openly condemned. This means he has a hope of returning.

I go to Chingkangshan, the first Red base founded by Mao Tsetung in 1927. Here Mao came with seven hundred men after the terrible massacres by Chiang Kaishek in 1927. It is an eagle eyrie in the wild mountains. All the villages, tiny and very poor, are Hakka. The Hakkas knew the pathways up these mountains and down to the plains, and Mao Tsetung relied on them as guides and porters. Chingkangshan is a most important place in New China, for here the Revolution was born again.

At the time of my travels, before the Cultural Revolution of 1966, there were very few tourists and travellers, and nothing had been done to 'prettify' the holy places of the Revolution. In Chingkangshan there was no large hotel; neither was there in Yenan, only a guest house, with no running water and the latrines outside. Now the Confucian temple in Kuangchow, which housed the peasant training school where Mao taught, has become a huge and bleak modern palace, and the caves of Yenan have all been painted and cemented, outside and in. And there is a large hotel in Chingkangshan.

I went all over the crannied hamlets perched along the crests. Just below this mountain eyrie was a small plain, the end of a valley. Here it was that the fiery Szechuan military commander, Chu Teh, led his ragged remnants of Communist battalions to unite with the mountain guerrillas of Mao Tsetung. And without this fusion, perhaps the Revolution would not have happened; fragmented, divided, those forces would have become terrorist bands of men running for their lives, and hunted everywhere . . .

We stood to look at the monument, a plain one, commemorating this event. Chu Teh was a great hero, a most courageous man. During the Long March he accomplished great feats, unknown until after his death in 1976.

But Chu Teh, like so many other Long Marchers, was to be attacked, vilified, during the Cultural Revolution. Millions of Red Guards then went on long treks to the sacred places of the Chinese Revolution. Many went to

Chingkangshan. But from 1966 to 1971 Chu Teh had become a non-person in Chingkangshan. A very large oil painting showing Mao Tsetung meeting Lin Piao, no one else, had taken the place of the former painting showing Chu Teh with Mao; and the monument had been removed (it was to be replaced when Lin Piao died in 1971). Millions of young Red Guards, ignorant of history, were told that it was Lin Piao who had operated this union with Mao, and that Chu Teh was only a vile, counter-revolutionary saboteur.

Back to Peking. Browsing in bookstores; seeing new and old plays. The New Hundred Flowers has taken on. The intelligentsia is very visible and audible. Some of the cadres are wearing most expensive suits . . .

There are new plays conveying political lessons. One called *Comrade, You've Taken the Wrong Road* is obviously a warning to the USSR. But by 1963 there are also plays showing bribery and corruption among the Party cadres (young, naïve workers and Party cadres seduced, of course, by landlords who bestow their beautiful daughters upon them so as to infiltrate the Party). All plays point up political lessons, but some are well done. And there are also plays with no political lessons at all, which are just great fun.

Chou Enlai is busy encouraging the arts, music, the dance (as well as managing all China). He seems to have Mao's approval and trust. In October 1961, when he returned from having outfaced Khrushchev at the Twenty-Second Congress in Moscow, Mao Tsetung was at the airport to welcome him, carrying a large bunch of lilies of the valley. This meant that Chou was a stalwart fighter against 'revisionism'.

'Chou Enlai is more and more popular,' says Hualan. A saying goes round in Peking: 'What is it that Chou Enlai does not do? Three things: he does not sleep, does not look after himself, and does not stop working.'

Kung Peng takes me to see a comedy called *The Pressgang*. It is hilarious, based on the forcible recruiting of soldiers, such as I had seen myself, in old Kuomintang days. It eschews tragedy, everything ends well. 'We should write many more comedies,' says Kung Peng. 'People want to laugh . . . we're much too serious.'

But in 1966, *The Pressgang* is dubbed 'counter-revolutionary' and a poisonous weed'. So are many other plays and operas which I have enjoyed in those years.

'And I took you to it,' said Kung Peng when she saw me in 1966. She had been under fire and criticized all day. She had not eaten all day. But she smiled at me, and was kind.

'I did not see any harm in *The Pressgang*,' I said.

'Neither did I.' We did not say any more; she for my sake, and I for hers.

In 1962 it was obvious that the Communist Party was being subjected to another 'rectification'. 'Some . . . have become steeped in bureaucracy, exhibit feelings of insolence and self-satisfaction, forget realities . . . estrange themselves from the masses,' wrote the *People's Daily*.

'It's no fun being a Party member in China . . . constant rectifications and shake-ups,' said Simon Hua. 'Too much hard work, too little pay, and there's a new generation of youngsters who don't want to become Party members unless it means a cushy job in the cities.'

And then again, rumours, small-lane gossip, this time about Mao. 'Even the sun has black spots . . . we must not be frightened of mentioning defects and errors in the Party.' The sentence floated around Peking. Mao Tsetung was identified with the sun because of the song: 'The East is Red'.

> The east is red, the sun has risen
> In China is born Mao Tsetung . . .

Is someone criticizing Mao?

'We need more students, highly trained students, better students.' This from the Peking University educationalists. There is talk of two levels of education, of a ministry of higher and one of lower education. The higher education one will take in charge specialized 'teaching points', which are really special schools and research institutes of very high grade, with all the best facilities. This is élitism of a kind, of course. And not everyone agrees to these schemes.

My dearest friend and former boss, Professor Hou Paochang of the Pathology Department of Hong Kong University, with whom I chopped up so many livers, is now back in China. For good. Hou has come back to teach at the Higher Medical Institute. Medical studies have been cut down to five years; some people even advocated three years as sufficient (and during the Cultural Revolution in Manchuria some hospitals would turn out two-year graduates!). But at the Institute there are eight years of study; to form a solid nucleus of top-grade medical scientists and researchers.

Hou gave me a wonderful dinner; for which he borrowed the cook of a friend of his, General Fu Tsoyi. Fu Tsoyi was Chiang Kaishek's general; a pragmatic man, he saw who was winning and in 1948 relinquished Peking to the Communists, with much charm and little fighting. Since then he has held any number of posts in Communist China, and led a Ministry of Water Conservancy.

Fu Tsoyi's cook is one of the best in China, and a delegate at the National Assembly. He kindly comes to cook dinner; Fu Tsoyi sends his ministerial car to fetch him and to bring him back. I have never eaten such a dinner, never in my whole life.

Hou tells me that modernization must be pushed ahead. 'It is nonsense to debase intelligence in the name of socialism,' he says.

I tell Kung Peng I am going to write about China. 'I have waited six years. Other people rush to pen a book after one visit.' And in the end, no book can really convey anything but one's own experience, assumptions, judgments . . . I shall not try to do more.

'Whatever you know, you can only project one-tenth of it, like the tip of an iceberg,' says Kung Peng's husband, Chiao Kuanhua.

We talk about history. I ask: why is there no history of the Chinese Communist Party, of the Revolution, of recent history in China? A book did appear in 1959, but it has now been withdrawn. Through the years until 1978, again and again, I would complain: why no book on history? How can you teach the young what has happened without a history book?

But when history is a movable thing, when people have to be deleted (and reinserted), it is very difficult to make a definitive book, especially for teaching purposes. And in China above all, where the written word carries so much weight, where people who fall into disgrace have their photographs effaced from magazines, their names expunged from books . . . I complain in 1962 and 1963 about this, to Hualan and also to Kung Peng. 'It was a Russian habit . . . I don't think we should copy the Russians in this instance.' But I have not had a reply, not even today. And the habit of expunging, deleting, effacing, has been maintained.*

In June 1962 the Chinese press reported on preparations by Chiang Kaishek to invade the coastal areas of China – with the assent of the USA. Parachute drops, agents going into China, surprise attacks, the capture of documents by raids on coastal districts had occurred since 1949.

Chiang Kaishek's proclamation brought out in the rural areas of the coastal provinces ex-landlords and rich peasants. I am always astonished at the number of landlords and rich peasants who remain, and are seemingly very active. As soon as they heard that Chiang Kaishek might return, the landlords came to the peasant associations: 'Ha, now you will have to give us back our lands. I have kept all the records of what you owe me. Every penny must be paid back. We shall now settle accounts.' Landlord-formed bands of hooligans seized villages, passing themselves off as Party members. They pillaged grain stores. 'Sometimes they

*It seems, however, that now it will be given up (author's note of 1980).

pretend to be the militia. They have weapons parachuted from Taiwan,' said the cadres.

No one seemed exceptionally worried in 1962. But the trouble festered.

Marshal Chen Yi gave me lunch, to thank me for having written him up in an article for the Paris *L'Express*. Chen Yi's cook was not as excellent as Fu Tsoyi's, but the Marshal did not have the heart to admonish him, and stoically endured tasteless meals.

We talked of Montesquieu and Voltaire, Machiavelli and Churchill, and Rousseau of course; Chen Yi had gone especially on pilgrimage to Rousseau's tomb while in Switzerland. Then he talked about the situation. The harvest was short by several million tonnes (about five million) said he; so 'We shall buy again from Canada and Australia, as we have done since 1960 . . . we need to replenish our reserves; we also need to make up our stock of good seed. Of course, now the population has increased, we need 200 million tonnes a year; we are aiming to double it, and then we shall have a large surplus.' But whatever the difficulties, still things were better than in Old China. 'Everyone nowadays is employed. In my family there were thirty people and only my father worked for all of them . . . some went into pawnshops to become apprentices, working for nothing but food for three years. My father was a clerk at twelve dollars a month in the salt gabelle. Today any little girl in a department store gets thirty *yuan* . . . our young people do not know the hard times we've had . . .'

Fish seemed to interest Chen Yi. He reminded me how in Szechuan a coloured wooden fish was placed on the table to close a meal; to symbolize plenty, but to take the place of unobtainable fish as well. In north China millions had never eaten fish in their lives. And breeding, preserving, cooking and even eating fish, all these steps required education, persuasion. In a village in Kansu province a child had choked on a fish bone. 'That village will never touch fish again, not for a hundred years,' said Chen Yi. To educate people into one food habit and out of another required almost a political campaign. 'Changing food habits changes the economy of a country,' said Chen Yi.

Chou Enlai was not in a good mood. He frowned; he was tired. There were many long drawn out debates and conferences that summer, and the foreign diplomats had noticed an unusual number of 'higher-ups' gathered at the seaside resort of Peitaiho. Obviously a major Party meeting was on. Dean Rusk had announced in Washington that the policy of the United States was 'containment of China'. China was *the* enemy.

Chou talked about South East Asia. It was obvious that he was anxious about the war in Vietnam, which was expanding. He gave me a broad hint not to go too 'left' in Malaya and Singapore; because 'there will not be socialism there for a considerable length of time'. Malaysia, said Chou, was a British, not an American invention. It was not, for China, a preoccupation. The British and the Americans were not in agreement on South East Asian policy. Therefore it was not a priority in his scheme of things. Chou also referred to the successful conclusion of the overseas Chinese problem in Indonesia. Indonesia was now a very good friend of China's. She would not enter into a 'containment belt' project against China.

I told him that I would be going to Japan, and to Indonesia, in the autumn. He nodded briefly, very preoccupied.

I would see him again, on happier occasions, when we talked of history, of many things. I had never seen him as exhausted as that summer of 1962. He must have had many things on his mind.

I met Nien again. I was eating by myself in the Hsinchiao Hotel on the sixth floor – the European floor, for there I could have small snacks – when she came in.

Nien was exquisitely dressed, in some sort of pale beige silk, with a touch of gold at the neck, and high-heeled shoes, also beige, on her feet. Her hair was carefully waved, and her face a perfection of make-up (even in Chungking, during the war years, she had worn the most marvellous make-up). I could not at first believe it was Nien, because I had seen all my other friends from Yenching University, and we all – including myself – kept scrubbed faces without make-up, and short clean hair without adornment, and wore very simple, faded clothes. I looked much like them in those years, not though deliberate concealment, but because it was so much more pleasant to merge. I was stopped on the streets, or even in the hotel, by people asking me the way or for information.

Nien was with an English couple, business people, obviously opulent, representatives of an oil company.

It was some years since our last meeting, in Chungking during the war.* She had been there with her husband, Cheng Kanghsi. At the time he was an important member of Chiang Kaishek's Foreign Ministry. He had even been sent, with Pao, on a mission to India during the war to negotiate having Chinese troops trained in India, under Stillwell.

'Oh, it's you,' said Nien. She was surprised, as I was; her eyes travelled over my clothes, my striped Chinese socks (shades of the Dalai Lama), my soft cotton Chinese shoes, my baggy Chinese trousers, my open-collared, comfortable, shabby shirt; all Peking made. And of course my face. No make-up. But then I seldom wore make-up.

'Nien, what are you doing here? Where do you come from?'

'I live here,' said she. 'I live in Shanghai. I've come up to Peking to see my friends.' She introduced the business couple.

I was even more astonished. I nearly said, 'But if you live here, how come you dress the way you do? I thought you had just arrived from Paris or London . . .'

We all sat together. Nien saw me staring at her clothes, and she smiled that dainty, tiptoe smile of hers which I had

*See *Birdless Summer*, 1939–42.

found so arrogant when we were together at the university. 'To look at us, of course one would think you were living here and I was living abroad . . . you look exactly like . . . an interpreter.'

'All writers are chameleons, Nien. I like it when people come up to me and say: Comrade, can you direct me to Goldfish Street? And I can.'

Nien had been a brilliant student at Yenching University. And she had copiously snubbed me. Repeatedly and thoroughly. Something which now I fully understood, of course. Her husband, Cheng Kanghsi, was from a wealthy family, and a graduate of the prestigious Tsinghua University. And he had become a high official under Chiang Kaishek.

Pao had told me that Kanghsi had made some nasty allusions to my lack of virginity in front of Pao and other members of the mission while they were in India. This was the greatest shame that any man in China could ever endure. It was horrible. Pao should have returned to kill me immediately, to wash his honour clean . . . But since Pao was a fabulator, and since I am a person who likes to make friends out of enemies because it is a better revenge, I did nothing. However, on the street in Chungking one afternoon, Nien and Kanghsi cut me dead; but then so many people pushed me down because I was a Eurasian . . . how many insults of all kinds I absorbed, digested, converted into cynical strength throughout the years . . .

Two months after cutting me dead, Kanghsi and Nien had invited us to dinner. Pao and they talked of schemes and projects. Kanghsi needed Pao because Pao had just been picked as aide-de-camp to Chiang Kaishek; and Kanghsi was ambitious. No one talked to me at all. I just ate, drank tea, and sat waiting for the time to go, an illiterate peasant wife, ignored in a corner.

Kanghsi had become an ambassador under Chiang Kaishek. But when Liberation came in 1949, of course he 'saw the light' and gave up Chiang, and stayed on in Shanghai, and was classified, with his wife Nien, as a patriotic national-capitalist. He established connections with Shell Oil; and had not only possibly been instrumental in the Dutch recognizing China, but was also the Shell representative in China. And China, of course, needed oil, for oil had not then been discovered in abundance in China, not before the Leap of 1958–9.

Then Kanghsi had died of kidney cancer, and Nien took his place with Shell, and carried on as their representative, and brought up their only daughter, and lived comfortably in Shanghai. According to friends of hers whom I met later, she had a fabulously beautiful house, full of antiques and exquisite porcelain, and at least eight servants: in Shanghai, in communist China! She also had bank accounts in Switzerland and in London. Her shoes and clothes she bought in London and Paris, on her frequent trips abroad.

Nien was not alone in having such privileges, a life in China completely out of touch with the people of China. There were, after all, 90,000 or so national-capitalists in Shanghai, who continued to live in great luxury, on 3 to 5 per cent tax free interest paid on bonds, which were compensation for the factories and properties that had been nationalized by the government. All of them had servants, imported cars, refrigerators and television sets; and they had bred a new generation of golden youths, who went to university.

Can one wonder, then, at the resentment of the sons of workers and peasants, who had slogged and endured and died for the Revolution, at these small enclaves from the past, maintained by the government? Yet they *had* to be maintained. They too were necessary for China's grand scheme for the future.

The son of one of these national-capitalists, for instance, did nothing at all except breed goldfish. Others made friends with the offspring of high officials in the Party, and so rottenness came in . . . One national-capitalist I met had the rents of twenty-two houses and blocks of flats to spend; another had an income of two million *yuan* (one million US dollars) a year. Tax free. All of it.

Nien said, 'The Party understands. They will not ask more of me than I can give. I cannot be anything but what I am. Meanwhile I am pretty useful. I am the agent between the Chinese Ministry of Trade and a foreign concern . . .' She held a lifeline in her hands, at the time. Until oil was discovered in China.

Nien gave me her address and telephone number in Shanghai. 'Do come to see me when next you come by,' said she. And rose, graceful on her high heels. Italian shoes.

But although I was briefly in Shanghai in the next few years, I did not go to see her. And now I feel guilty about it. Because when the Cultural Revolution came in 1966, then of course Nien was a target. Such an obvious one! Of course the Red Guards who were under the control of Mao's wife and her acolytes surged into Nien's house. Of course they smashed everything.

Nien went through a kangaroo court of youngsters. And these youngsters included her own daughter, who was a Red Guard, who participated in the condemnation of her mother . . . Nien was sentenced to work manually, cleaning an office. This was not a very harsh thing, on the whole: my friend Kung Peng, who was a high Party official, had to do the same during the Cultural Revolution; and her husband, Chiao Kuanhua, was treated worse. But because Nien had never endured any hardship, had never had her image of herself smashed in the cauldron of revolution, she could not bear it. I think her daughter's condemnation of her was the last straw. She committed suicide.

So many of my friends, my whole family, were similarly scourged: Third Brother, Sixth Brother, Third Uncle and Third Aunt. But they endured.

I still feel that I should have made the effort to see Nien; to talk to her, although she might have shattered me again with her assurance.

CHAPTER 15

Departure from Malaya: 1962–1964

When I returned from China to Singapore I was again body-searched, and my clothes and luggage jumbled mercilessly. 'Orders, Doctor, *lah*,' said the customs men regretfully; friendly in their deliberate harassment.

In that year and the next my two novellas, *Cast But One Shadow*, and *Winter Love*, were published, as well as stories in the *New Yorker* and articles in several magazines. Outwardly I continued to busy myself as usual; in my mind I was preparing to write my series of books on China describing the story of my Family and what had happened to them before and after the Chinese Revolution; intermingled with my own life story.

In late September 1962, I went to a Quaker-organized conference for diplomats, held in a resort called Puntjak Pas, in the mountains near Bogor, Java. The convener was Russell-Johnston, a tall, frail-looking New Englander.

At Puntjak Pas many diplomats congregated, including Poles and Czechs, and the Russian Ambassador. India was also represented, by a likeable person named Ghosh. Mr Ghosh and I were at cross purposes; he talked a great deal about China's 'traditional expansionism' and 'aggression', and was supported – none too well – by the British delegate. The American representative, a remarkable young man named Levine, was uncommonly non-hostile about China. He said to me one day, when we happened to be alone, 'I do hope that China's experiment does succeed, otherwise America and Russia may be at each other's throats on the plains of China.' Which put the geopolitics of our planet into a new perspective for me.

Puntjak Pas was high in the mountains and the rain cascaded coldly down the abundant foliage of the park in which our bungalows were erected. There were many speeches. I tried hard not to be aggressive to the USSR; I thought the Russian delegate amiable and handsome.

After the conference I stayed with my Indonesian friend, Lasmijah Hardy, in Djakarta. Lasmijah's house was pretty, with a garden like a small trim jungle and a well for sweet water in its middle. She had almost a thousand sarongs, some hand-painted and very valuable. Two women sat all day unrolling and then rolling them up again; they were stacked row upon row on shelves, like scrolls.

There was hunger and want in the villages of Java. Djakarta was full of soldiers. The military seemed to occupy every institution I visited. Even the hospital and the university seemed to be run by the military. There was a total erosion of all public utilities; the post office, the telephones, the buses . . . inflation was ugly and continuous and would become quite colossal.

In the villages, any manufactured object was of a price beyond the reach of most of the people. There was the usual subsistence economy: rice and bananas, and some vegetables. In the city, food was extremely expensive. The cashier of a bank only came once a month to her office, because her monthly salary only enabled her to pay one bus fare to and from her house to work.

Lasmijah, as other wealthy Indonesian women, gave asylum to many of her relatives, who of course cooked and washed and cleaned and rolled the sarongs. 'They come from my village,' Lasmijah would say. President Sukarno made many speeches; he would exhort his people to 'eat rats' if they had no other meat. The military and the wealthy seemed to have everything, including enormous new cars. They deplored the economic depression which was due, they said, to the influence of the Indonesian Communist Party, and Sukarno's kindness to them. Actually the catastrophic economic situation was the result of a number of causes, not the least being corruption; and the ousting of many small producers and merchants from the countryside (because they were overseas Chinese) had disrupted a whole level of production and commercial transactions. Now the army controlled almost every commodity: paper, rubber, sugar, medicines. Under the label of 'nationalization' it took over enterprises. Army generals (and navy and air force commanders too) shared the profits, and nothing went back to the people.

I met Subandrio, the Foreign Minister. He had just returned from a tour of Malaya and Singapore, and was very agitated about Malaysia. He felt that it was a threat to the structure of Indonesia, and especially he seemed afraid that Sumatra, so large and so unpeopled (only seventeen million at the time), might fall a prey to 'neo-colonial' Malaysia. 'We are very greatly helped by the Soviet Union,' said Subandrio. The USSR supplied the equipment of the Indonesian army, navy and air force.

I could not say to him that Premier Chou Enlai had appeared to think that Malaysia, despite its reprehensible beginnings, was a better bargain than a very large confederation under one or the other of the superpowers. And it was, of course, useless to repeat to Subandrio the remark of my friend Rewi Alley, in Peking, who had said, 'How curious that the USSR should help the Indonesian army, which is notoriously hostile to the Indonesian Communist Party.'

Subandrio seemed to believe that Lee Kuanyew was a true 'socialist'. At the time the word was one to pink the cheek of the anaemic, to brighten the eyes of all of us virgin children of Asia . . . Since then, how often have we been raped with that word?

I did not tell Subandrio that I thought merger would not take place between Singapore and Malaya. At seven or eight in the morning when interviews are held, before the heat makes one drowsy, I am not at my most articulate.

The next day, also at seven in the morning, I saw Sukarno. Breakfast with Sukarno was almost obligatory in Djakarta for every VIP. I waited in the large living room; on the walls hung many large and bafflingly bad oil paintings of women (all very properly dressed). Sukarno came in. He was arrayed in a heavy cloth uniform (air force I think). He had a major fear of draughts, could not bear air conditioning, and so no fan could ever be turned on in his presence. I have seen him raise his collar, shiver and glare at a whirring fan. He had a *songkok* upon his head and he kept it on because it enhanced his looks and hid his baldness. He was a vital man, exuding lustrous vitality, and he now saw me, pulled in his stomach and straightened his *songkok* and advanced jauntily, carrying a short stick like a British army officer.

We sat and talked; about Malaysia. 'You know the British and the Americans want to take Sumatra and Borneo from Indonesia, leaving Java with its sixty-two million people to stew,' said he. He did not care who ran Malaysia, but he was worried about its ultimate use as a confederation against Indonesia.

One was here in the presence of another kind of politics; Malay-Indonesian politics, in which there is always the possibility of *mushawaira*, consultation, entente, in the midst of much sound and fury and mutual imprecation. And this is what would happen. Within another eighteen months, Subandrio and Tunku Abdul Rahman would meet in Manila, and make up; and Tunku would even launch the idea of MAPHILINDO, a confederation of all the Malay races in Malaysia, the Philippines and Indonesia. But this would remain a stillborn idea because in such a troika of course it would be huge Indonesia which would dominate. Finally, some years later, the ASEAN, or Association of South East Asian Nations, would be promoted, and it would try to keep away from superpower military alliances and entanglements.

I walked on the streets of Djakarta. A depressing city; and such beautiful people . . .

I saw tanks on the street. There was a police parade. The police, in tanks, rolled down the street. I watched, unbelieving. Why tanks?

I had met in Cairo, in February 1962, the Indonesian writers' delegation. I met the writers again. Of course a good many were communists or sympathizers. But the Indonesian Communist Party was supposed to be respectable: there were communist ministers in the government, including Aidit, the head of the Party. Everyone said the Party was immensely strong; the strongest in Asia after the Chinese Party: it had three million members.

I went to the seaside for a day with some of the Indonesian writers. It was a day surfeit with beauty and light; the sea was brittle sapphire, there was a wonderful small wind, and the fishermen sailed in, swinging their curved boats, a ballet on the glistening water. The silver fish came spilling out of the nets; we stood on the pale beach bargaining for the fish, and ate those we chose, grilled with chilli and citronella and fresh coconut and unripe mango. 'Oh, what a succulent country you have, a mouth-watering country,' I said. 'You must take great care of your country. It is a paradise.'

But the writers talked of the economic problems. There were too many people in Java and too few in Sumatra and the many other islands; Indonesia was large and communications between the several thousand islands were bad. Sukarno has started a programme of population transfer, which was called 'transmigration'.

'Have you seen the police tanks? I smell danger,' I said. But the writers laughed. 'The Party has three million members, we are well prepared . . . and President Sukarno is good to us. We need not fear anything.'

The villages glowed ochre and emerald, laughing women and children stood under coconut palms and waved at us as we drove by. There was misery and want, but with the sun and the spiced air it did not appear loathsome. Yet some of the writers were so poor that they could not afford the paper on which to write their novels, or even a lengthy article . . .

I went to see Aidit, the head of the Indonesian Communist Party. He was a small man, with a round head, large soft brown eyes, and a very gentle manner. He was with Lukman and Njoto, the two vice-chairmen of the Party. I thanked Aidit for granting me an interview; he had some weeks previously given an interview to Alex Josey. I wanted to verify a few statements that Josey had made. Aidit replied with great candour. He thought Alex Josey was a 'true socialist', he said.

'Have you seen the tanks on the streets?' I asked. 'Who supplies tanks to the police?'

'They are American tanks,' said Njoto. 'But the USSR supplies the army; we have many friends among the military.'

'I'm sorry, but it just does not smell right to me. Don't you feel there may be a military coup?'

'Oh,' said Aidit, 'we are well prepared.' The communist militia in the villages numbered almost a million men, said he.

But it did not seem to me that the militia was well-weaponed; perhaps they had old rifles, and possibly bamboo spears, as had been used against the Japanese during the war.

'But we have the people with us,' said Aidit simply, as a crushing argument.

Aidit had led a life of great courage and self-sacrifice; he had much experience in insurrection. How could I say: I think you're going to be massacred, just as Chiang Kaishek massacred the Communists in China in 1927?

And why should I think so?

That winter, dropping into Peking briefly, I could not help telling Kung Peng that I was worried about Aidit. But I could not tell her why. And as usual when she did not wish to discuss something with me, she merely said, 'Comrade Aidit is a good comrade.' After all, he was the head of a three-million-strong party . . .

I decided I would forget my foolish premonitions; I was overcautious, owing to my warlord experiences in childhood.

And yet, so many times, when I do what my mind tells me to do and my belly tells me is wrong, I end up wrong. When I take time to listen to that buried restlessness without a voice which lies in entrails, not heart, I am fairly often right.

On September 30th, 1965 there was a coup in Indonesia. No

one even today knows exactly what took place to precipitate the blood bath. It seems that the army had planned a coup against the PKI* which the Communists attempted to forestall by a coup of their own, entirely botched, under a certain army colonel who was a Communist.

The massacres that followed were truly horrible. 'The river was bright red with blood; and the bodies floated like dead fish,' some escapees, refugees in Holland would later tell me. The estimated number of killed varies from 300,000 to 600,000. No one will ever know.

I would meet a Party member, one writer, who had escaped. I asked him about Aidit, and Njoto, and Lukman. 'All dead,' he said simply. In the first days of October, 'Comrade Aidit was like a man lost, he did not know what to do . . . that is why our losses were so heavy.'

But in those years before the coup, the 'left' indeed looked strong in Indonesia, especially at a big reception which I attended at Sukarno's palace. Sukarno came in, in army uniform, surrounded by his ministers; among them Aidit and Njoto. The press, the diplomats attended. Sukarno made a speech announcing 'confrontation' with Malaysia, which meant a cutting-off of trade. But the trade was chiefly smuggling through Singapore, so that did not amount to much of a threat for Malaysia. However, paradoxically, while the left-wing newspapers praised confrontation (*konfrontasi* in Indonesian), its existence allowed the military to remain in a position of dominance, with the key economic sectors in their hands; under the slogans of discipline and 'preparation against imperialism and neo-colonialism'.

Twice again before the coup of 1965 put an end to his prestigious career, I was to meet Sukarno, once in Cairo, and once in Cambodia. We never clicked. I never felt for him that immediacy and rapport which I felt with Chou Enlai, and Chen Yi, and Sihanouk, and Tunku Abdul Rahman – all so

*Indonesian Communist Party.

dissimilar persons, but persons I could talk to. With
Sukarno, perhaps because of his over-abundant masculinity
(and his awareness of it), I was always at a loss. A little as
with Nehru; except that Nehru radiated self-satisfied
intellect rather than conscious sexuality.

In Cairo Sukarno was too busy with a belly-dancer to pay
much attention to the conversations he was having with
Chou Enlai and Nasser: he baffled the earnest Chinese
thoroughly. In Cambodia he was accompanied by a very
beautiful American girl, so that even Prince Sihanouk
became – despite his suave and impeccable courtesy – a little
confused. How could Aidit ever have placed so much trust in
the hands of this great, magnetic, popular, but rather erratic
Sukarno?

In the summer of 1965 I received through the Indonesian
Consulate in Hong Kong an invitation from Sukarno to
come and live in Indonesia . . . a house was being given to
me . . . I declined politely.

And then came the coup of that September. Friends of
mine died. Others are exiles. Still others are in jail, perhaps
for the rest of their lives.

Back from Indonesia and on to Japan; invited by the
Japanese Foreign Ministry for a fortnight's tour.

It was then October 1962, a month of crises. The Cuba
crisis, the Sino-Indian border war . . . I left Singapore for
Tokyo on October 10th, the day Nehru ordered the Indian
army to 'throw the Chinese out'.

As I landed in Tokyo, the Foreign Ministry representative
met me. Mrs Oiwa was a lady diminutive and prim, but of
delicate beauty; a widow. She would accompany me
everywhere. Everything had been thought out, arranged; I
was handed my programme. Everything was minuted, and
when the programme said Mrs Oiwa would call at 8.15, she
called at 8.15. At 8.25 we would, arrive at the museum
(factory, ministry, hospital), and at 8.25 and ten seconds
I would descend from the car and be greeted by the
director (manager, chief surgeon). At 8.34, after a talk,

we would start the visit . . . and so on, for two weeks.

It was most restful to be time-programmed, especially after Indonesia, where I had had gruelling experiences with the vagaries of my friends' idea of time. In fact, so exasperated had I become that I had said, 'You cannot make a revolution if you don't have a notion of time. Great battles have been lost because battalions arrived late.'

I knew very little of Japan until my visit, except that we had been at war, and there had been untold suffering in China because of that war; and even now it was difficult to make many Chinese, both in China and overseas, accept the idea of friendship with Japan. But I was, I confess, captivated, charmed, and remain reverent towards the enormous capacity of the Japanese always to learn – always on the alert to better themselves.

The variety and excellence of what I saw, the iron discipline of the conversations (led at a gallop), all fell into a hypnotic rhythm for me. I was a particle of some large, overall plan, and since I was tired, I let myself go. I had two hours with the writer Kawabata, who was to become a Nobel Prize winner; and here Japanese efficiency broke down, because we could not find his house in Tokyo, where houses are not properly numbered and one wanders round a *ku*, or district, asking for the person one seeks.

A weekend in a Japanese inn. Introduction to its pleasures, including a dip in the very hot pool. In the morning I saw the hotel maid wash the pebbles of the garden pond, rubbing them clean and putting them back into the clear sparkling water, one by one . . .

Visits to magnificent factories; shipyards and steel-making plants; a transistor factory: rows of young girls, all programmed; little red lights twinkling when one of them temporarily left her seat, away from the slowly rolling rubber ribbon in front of her. The girls were paid so much, they lived in dormitories, and at the age of twenty-three they left to get married because after that their eyes were no longer sharp and accurate. The savings on their salaries were programmed to meet the required dowry for an eligible bride . . .

The enormous sense of belonging of every Japanese . . . a vast invisible mesh which seemed to hold all together, utilized to create 'company spirit'. The Honda spirit, the Toyota spirit . . . the company morning hymn; feudal loyalty metamorphosed, transformed into a technological bond . . . Japan was for me a revelation of how 'the past can be made to serve the present', a phrase which Mao Tsetung had used frequently. It was also an example of 'making things foreign serve Japan'. And Mao wanted China to do the same. But could it be done? Sun Yatsen's phrase, when he visited Japan in 1923, stuck in my mind: 'Japan and China . . . have a common destiny.' And had not China's first reform movements been stimulated by the example of Japan's Meiji reform?

Two things preoccupied many of the Japanese I met. The first was the Nobel Prize for Literature. Invariably I would be asked (an interval of ten seconds was left in conversations for this question) 'Do you think that Japan will win the Nobel Prize?' Of course, it was an oblique way of finding out if I read Japanese authors.

The second preoccupation was baseball. Two of my interviews had to be postponed because of important baseball matches. Everywhere on the streets, on the pavements, in front of the shops, one could see Japanese men making the gestures of wielding a bat and hitting a ball.

I had many pleasant meetings with writers, including some I had met in Cairo, among them the President of the Pen Club, Yoko Matsuoka, who arranged a party for me. But the party coincided with the Cuba crisis, and among the invited writers were some who felt the world was coming to an end. One of them discussed seriously with me his intention to die that very night. 'Perhaps tomorrow there will be nuclear war,' said he. He did not want to be a victim of nuclear war . . . he had seen Hiroshima.

I strongly dissuaded him. 'Nothing will happen. The Cuba

crisis is a "confrontation" [shades of Sukarno!] and there's something artificial about it . . .' 'Artificial!' exclaimed the writer with great indignation. 'It's a tragedy! A tragedy involving the whole world!'

I apologized for not being able to take it seriously. 'I just lack a sense of tragedy, even in my own personal life.'

The writer promised to wait. And of course he is still alive. So is the world.

Suicide was a national fascination, though waning. I went to see a Japanese film. The scene of *sepuku* (disembowelling) was so realistic that I fainted (it was also extremely hot and overcrowded in the small cinema). 'Oh,' said Mrs Oiwa, bending over me as I came to, 'you have a soft heart.'

'I thought it was . . . so cruel to give the young boy a wooden dagger to disembowel with, Mrs Oiwa . . . he had to try so many times . . .'

(The process, filmed in detail, included the victim biting off his own tongue to stop himself from screaming.)

'Yes,' said dear Mrs Oiwa, shaking her head, 'so cruel to give him a *wooden* dagger. He should have been given a good sharp dagger, that would have been *so* kind.'

In the large stores on the Ginza, gentle, porcelain-faced girls stood white-gloved at the foot of the escalators, saluting and thanking everyone who went up or down; eight hours a day. I learnt about the special sex equipment provided for lonely women and widows; artificial objects they could use themselves. So practical. Abortions so calmly accepted and performed; no guilt feeling about them. 'You are really a very wonderful people, Mrs Oiwa,' I said.

The Foreign Ministry gave me a banquet at a renowned geisha house; the geishas plied me with drink; we talked politics, which meant, of course, China. The Japanese view was then very much modelled on the American view: the domino theory in South East Asia. The Ministry officials felt that China was in the process of inner disruption. I said that countries like China are so huge and unmanageable, and yet have such a spring and bounce to them, such power of survival, that they cannot be crammed into any economic or political framework; but then I was no political expert.

On October 23rd, while I was still in Tokyo, Vincent rang up from Singapore. He was calling about the Sino-Indian border; for on the previous day the Chinese had started to push back the Indian troops and were coming down the passes into the plains. Vincent was worried because he could be recalled for military duty. I rushed to book the next aeroplane; cut my visit short by a day, and returned to Singapore.

The next few weeks were fairly tense for both of us. And then in November came relief, with China's unilateral withdrawal. Vincent and I hugged each other so tight, as if we would never let go. 'I told you not to worry,' said Vincent. But he had been very worried. But now there would not be war, not between India and China. And that meant that Asia had a chance to grow and to prosper.

In December 1962, Vincent and I met the representatives of the Chinese press of Singapore and Malaya, and members of the Nanyang University Graduates' Union. We were expected to give them a talk on the India-China border conflict.

I spoke moderately. For I would not, in any way, stress the Chinese case in such a way as to offend the Indian community of Singapore and Malaya. Racial hostility, communalism, riots and bloodshed are easily stirred up.

Vincent spoke after me. He, too, did not argue the rights or wrongs of the case. He said that border conflicts occurred between many countries thoughout the world; they must not be exaggerated; and he felt sure that all would be settled peacefully through negotiation, one day. Meanwhile the Chinese and the Indian people would continue to be friends, as they had been for two thousand years.

Yet at the time, deep hysteria prevailed in India. Calcutta's 14,000-strong Chinese community was raided – laundrymen, tailors, shoemakers and shopkeepers were assaulted, their goods confiscated; many were interned and lost all their belongings. Emergency regulations, which allow the suspension of human rights and of all normal law procedures, were applied; they gave the police in India unlimited power. The Chinese in Calcutta were Indian citizens, with Indian passports. They spoke Bengali or Hindi, and English; most of them were born in India, had never set foot in China . . . they were condemned by their faces alone.

As for the Indian people, the Indian government had decreed that it was 'treason' to 'spread rumours' or 'doubt' about the official explanation of 'savage Chinese aggression'. The all-obliterating *unfact* acted very thoroughly.

At the time, in the United States, a general called Maxwell Taylor was making a report to Congress, telling the facts; but this report was not made public.

'Such is democracy,' I said to Vincent. The limits of freedom to tell the truth, in both worlds, were never more apparent to me than in 1962.

Vincent's courageous and modest action in speaking so wisely, to appease inflamed emotions, was to be utilized against him shortly thereafter.

In 1962 a referendum asking the people of Singapore to vote on 'merger and Malaysia' was set up. The English weekly, *The Economist*, called it 'calculated dishonesty'.

And so it was. For although the main issue was merger, whether the people of Singapore wanted or not to join in Malaysia, this was not a part of the referendum at all. The people were asked to vote only for the *terms* under which they would join Malaysia, and three choices were offered to them:

A. To join Malaysia with the Singapore government retaining its autonomy in labour and in education.
B. To join Malaysia on the same terms as Penang, Malacca or any other state of Malaya.
C. To join Malaysia on the same terms as would apply to North Borneo, Sarawak and Brunei. (The only hitch about C was that these terms had not yet been defined

when the referendum took place, which meant that C
did not exist, and so only the choice between A and B
remained.)

What palpable fear over the referendum in Singapore!
Dread and terror; an underground campaign of threats. 'We
have been told to tell the children in our schools to tell their
parents to vote A.' Schoolteachers I knew said this to me.
'Although polling is supposed to be secret, every ticket is
marked, and so the police will know who votes what.'
Another rumour, but people are so easily scared . . . It was
hinted that vote B would lead to 300,000 Singaporeans
losing their citizenship and becoming stateless . . . the
inevitability of voting for A became very clear.

The opposition party, Barisan Socialis, called on the
people to cast blank 'protest' votes at the dishonesty of the
referendum. But the PAP government let it be known that
any blank vote would count as a B vote. Of course A won.

The anti-merger explosion occurred, of all places, in
Brunei, the oil-rich little sultanate which was supposed to
join Malaysia; which had 84,000 people of whom 63,000
were Malays . . . almost the only Malays in the three
territories, meant to 'balance out' the Chinese.

The Azahari rebellion, for such was its name, was led by a
thin bespectacled Malay, Azahari, whom one saw
occasionally hanging around political meetings in Singapore.
He was a bookseller by trade, and an important man in the
running of the People's Party (Party Rakyat) in Brunei. It
was, of course, vaguely 'socialist' in orientation.

Azahari was an opponent of the fusion proposed. But
then, so was Brunei's Sultan (although this was an
unsayable, unpublishable fact). On December 8th, Party
Rakyat started an insurrection, led by what was called the
North Borneo National Army. In Sarawak too a rebellion
against the merger began. Strangely, Azahari himself was
eight hundred miles away, in Manila, when the insurrection
started.

British battalions, Gurkhas, and the Queen's Own

Highlanders, were flown into Brunei. The 'rebellion' was held to be a 'communist plot'. It was of course crushed. The role of the Sultan of Brunei (whose support for Azahari was obvious) remained unstated. The role of the 'protective power', the United Kingdom, was very clear: to restore law and order through military action. It took several months to 'mop up' the so-called rebellion, which was a genuinely popular uprising, with 80 per cent of Brunei's male population between eighteen and forty taking part.

The Special Branch launched a crackdown (what else?). In Malaya, fifty persons were arrested for conspiracy. In Singapore, the Barisan Socialis came out openly on the side of the rebels. The head of the Barisan Socialis, Lim Chingsiong, and other leaders were arrested in February 1963. Linda Chen, the girl to whom I had given a job at the Malaysian Sociological Research Institute, was re-arrested.

And then came the turn of Nanyang University. A police raid, at night: 117 students rounded up. All university publications banned. Nanyang University out of bounds to everyone except persons with special permits from the police.

In the course of 1963, I would help some students, not communists, but people implicated in writing for banned magazines, to make quiet exits from the green gulag of Singapore.

But I never went near Nanyang University again.

I went to Brunei in February 1963 to find out what had happened. Journalists returning from there spoke of savage pursuit of the rebels with dogs; of the Dayak head hunters of neighbouring Sarawak being mobilized to perform some large-scale massacres. Even English publications found the role of the British army 'distasteful' and the methods employed 'gruesome'.

Brunei's small capital looked like a spectral town, because most of its stilt-perched houses were shuttered, their doors closed. The rest of the town seemed to consist of one very large new mosque, the British Resident's mansion, the

Sultan's palace, and the Yacht Club – the snob club of Brunei.

'I wish Azahari had succeeded,' a prominent British 'government servant' said to me. We were at the Yacht Club and not alone. Nervously, I looked around. One went to jail in Singapore for expressing such sentiments.

'We knew Azahari. He ran the only decent bookshop in town . . . he only wanted to keep Brunei out of Malaysia,' continued this seasoned official. 'And so does the Sultan, who's now sitting on the fence . . .'

Six months later people were still being processed in Brunei for their share in the rebellion.

'Half the male population of Kampong Ayer is under detention . . . that's why the women and children stay locked up in their houses,' said the Englishman as he got up and left.

In Sarawak, next door to Brunei, the police patrolled the streets; they were police from Singapore.

The Chinese businessmen were rapturous about Lee Kuanyew. 'Wait until he starts running Malaysia. There'll be no trouble with the workers then.'

In North Borneo, Donald Stephens, later to become Prime Minister of the territory when it joined Malaysia, had lunch with me. He was then editor of the leading newspaper and the chief of the Kadazan, the natives of North Borneo. 'I am being cajoled and pressured and threatened and bribed to get into Malaysia,' he said. 'Azahari was not a bum and a liar, as Alex Josey calls him. He just wanted Brunei to remain independent. And it will, you will see.' He was right. Brunei stayed out of Malaysia.

'We're scared of Singapore,' continued Stephens. 'Lee Kuanyew has sixty thousand unemployed Chinese, and we don't want them flooding us out here.' He did not wish for interference from Malaya either. 'We, the Kadazans, the Muruts, the Dayaks of North Borneo, we're only 450,000 people. We're not Malays. We are not Muslim. And now there are imams and Muslim preachers all over the place, trying to convert us.' He wondered aloud where Tunku had got the idea that these inclusions would 'balance out' the potential Chinese majority. 'If Tunku ever finds out how he's been fooled, he'll push Singapore out,' he prophesied. And again he was right.

In May of 1963, Vincent and I took our first holiday together in Europe. Vincent's contract with Jardine Waugh had expired, but he had signed a new one. The company wanted him to go to Sweden in order to study some new machinery to be sold in South East Asia. So off we went together, to Sweden, and then on holiday to Austria, to England and to France.

In England Vincent felt at home from the very first day; something which was never true about me. Because, although he had never been to England before (in fact he had not left India until he had come to Singapore for me), he had been so thoroughly impregnated by English manners and moods and ways of doing things that he found everything natural and uncomplicated.

On the return journey, Vincent remained for another fortnight with his family in India, while I, after calling on Nehru, returned to Singapore.

It was now August, and I was expecting Vincent back that very day, by the aeroplane from Calcutta; he was due back at work the following day. Another three hours and I would start driving across the Causeway, to Singapore airport, to meet him. The telephone rang. It was Vincent calling from Calcutta, and sounding puzzled. 'I am not allowed on any aeroplane to Singapore . . . the airline company has just notified me. I am not allowed to land in Singapore. No reason given. Just orders.'

'But why?'

'No reason has been given.'

'Try flying to Kuala Lumpur,' I said.

'I've tried. But that's also impossible. Orders from Singapore.'

Although that August the two carriers were still separate (Malaysia would be established in September), the police and the governments of Singapore and of Malaya had agreed on 'joint action' in control of travel and entry.

'Don't panic, I'll think of a way.'

I rang up Vincent's boss, Charles Letts. Charles was a solid, reliable man, and he liked Vincent. But he would never, of course, cross Authority. Not in an arbitrary state like Singapore. He said contritely, 'Well, if Vincent can't get back, I'm afraid his contract with us falls through.' Which meant that, automatically, Vincent had lost his job.

Lao Chieh came in to say, 'Someone is looking for you.' From the way she said it, I knew she was worried.

In the garden was a small car, and emerging from it was a Singapore trade unionist of the PAP whom I knew rather well. Let us call him K. Why had K come to see me? He had never called before. He walked up the stairs to the veranda. 'What a nice house,' said he.

By this time my insides were beginning to pain me very much. Someone was trying to hurt Vincent, but it was only to get at me. 'The bloody cowards. They don't *dare* to attack me, so they do this to Vincent.' I became slowly very angry, and as K sat down, I faced him with my anger.

'You haven't come to talk about my house, or Malaya,' I said. 'Why have you come?'

'I was just passing by,' said K.

'What a coincidence,' I said. 'The very day, half an hour after I get the news that Vincent has been banned from landing in Singapore.'

K raised his eyebrows, pretending surprised ignorance. But of course, that was precisely the reason why he had come.

It was so obvious. Someone wanted me to knuckle down, to pray for mercy, to let Vincent return. As the poet, D. J. Enright had said, 'They'll only accept obsequiousness . . .'

'There's been no banishment order. There's no reason given. You know Vincent has never been involved in any politics. Why pick on him? Why not pick on me? Because it's me you people want to hurt, don't you?'

'I don't know what you are talking about,' said K.

'Oh, you know. Anyway it's illegal; I'll sue.'

K smiled. 'According to the Internal Security Act, the government can prevent anyone from landing, and no reasons need to be given. None at all.' So of course he knew. And he had come to offer a deal. 'Perhaps if you went to talk to some people . . .'

'I won't. But you could talk to Rajaratnam.* He's your friend.'

'I don't think he had anything to do with it,' said K, giving up pretending.

He told me Special Branch didn't like some of my activities. But I knew that it was not Special Branch which had chosen this singular method. This was personal vindictiveness. I was registered in Malaya; could not be touched by the Singapore government; Vincent was only registered in Singapore, at his place of work, and could be affected by a local dictum.

'I'm going to fight this, you'd better tell your bosses,' I said to K. 'I'll fight it.'

K smiled and his canines protruded a bit. 'You cannot. There's nothing in writing,' he said.

I telephoned David Marshall, my lawyer friend, the ex-Prime Minister of Singapore. He sized up the situation and said, 'Well, it is true that under our set-up there is little you can do.'

I went to see my film magnate millionaire friend, Loke Wantho. 'Wantho, only Tunku can help. Please, will you talk to him?' And Wantho said he would. 'You're asking me to stick my neck out, but I'll do it for you.'

While Wantho acted, I waited. I went to parties, more than usual, showing myself everywhere. Everyone knew what had happened; no one said anything. Everyone expected me to leave. I did not. I lost weight very rapidly, however, but apart from that even managed to go to see my dear Malay friend, Che Katijah, a member of the ultra-

*Now Foreign Minister of Singapore.

conservative Pan-Malayan Islamic Party. She represented the Malay rural people, which is why I liked her. I continued to take down from Che Katijah bits of her own life story, which I found quite fascinating, and they were published as a series of articles in the magazine *Eastern Horizon* which Cousin Pengju had started in Hong Kong.*

But already the buzzards circled. One 'businessman', whose brother was in Special Branch, burst in upon me one afternoon.

'You're selling your houses, Doctor?'

'I'm not selling.'

'But you're going away.'

'I'm not going away.'

He looked at me, a little surprised. Then decided I was bluffing. 'I have good price for you,' he announced loudly. Then he tapped a wall, threw a derogatory look at the garden, and mentioned a ridiculous sum.

'Go away. I'm not selling. I'm not leaving Malaya.'

Lao Chieh was valiant. She went to the market as usual. She did not leave me (so many people would have been frightened, would have abandoned me).

I went to Kuala Lumpur to see the Indian High Commissioner: Vincent was an Indian citizen and the case should be taken up by the Indian authorities. But he was supercilious. 'I am not responsible if the Colonel has done something against the government . . .'

'He has done nothing against the government, and you know it.' Where was the evidence? What was he accused of? The Indian High Commissioner kept silent.

Meanwhile, I had asked Vincent to fly to Hong Kong. And to wait there. With the emergency regulations in India, I could not easily obtain a visa to India (because of my Chinese origin). In Hong Kong he was safe and I could come to see him.

I now learned that there was indeed a charge against

*The life of Che Katijah binte Sidek, published under the title 'Arjasni' by *Eastern Horizon* magazine, Hong Kong.

Vincent. He was said to have declared, in his speech of 1962 to the Nanyang University Graduates' Union, that 'India is wrong and China is right'. He had *not* said anything of the kind. But this had been reported, apparently to the New Delhi government.

However, it was not the Indian government who had refused to allow Vincent to land in Singapore, or detained him in India. It was the Singapore authorities, who had nothing to do with the Sino-Indian conflict! In fact, when Vincent's father, who was a Senator, and the President of the ultra-conservative Swatantra Party, demanded a probe into the allegations, he was told that this was a 'semi-official' report, but 'it is not even in writing; only a verbal message'.

Presented with this impalpable accusation, the Indian government of course took no action at all. On the Singapore side, two lawyers told me that nothing could be done because the authorities they approached simply denied knowing anything about Vincent or his case. He had become a non-person! 'There's nothing in the files.'

After six weeks Tunku did find a temporary way out. He could not grant Vincent permanent residence in Malaya, but Vincent would be allowed multiple entries, at any time, each entry not to exceed three weeks. That was the best that could be done. 'Tunku is very fond of you,' said Loke Wantho, 'though certain members of his cabinet are not.'

Frank Sullivan, Tunku's personal secretary, was at Kuala Lumpur airport with me when Vincent landed from Hong Kong, for Christmas.

Vincent was back. Cheerful as usual, his hair curled as usual; radiating a natural happiness. Lao Chieh had a smile creasing all of her smooth face. The cats – who had been off their food, as I had – picked up; and suddenly the house was full of joy again.

'What shall we do now?' said Vincent. He had, of course, lost his job; and it would be difficult to get another one in Malaya or Singapore after what had happened. Police or government opprobrium was a black mark against being employed.

'We'll move to Hong Kong,' I said. 'Anyway, I cannot write about China with half my files in London and the other half in Hong Kong, and the censorship here.'

But we had to move slowly, without undue haste. I retained a suite in a new hotel being built in Hong Kong, the President. This suite was to be our home for the next four to five years.

We began to pack and send our things to Hong Kong. Meanwhile, there were the usual Chinese New Year parties, and we attended the one given by Loke Wantho; which was a way of showing ourselves to all of Singapore. Rajaratnam was of course there. 'I had nothing to do with Vincent's banning,' said he precipitately to me. I believed him. Rajaratnam is not a mean person.

We rented all three of my houses (I would sell them later), gave Lao Chieh a large sum of retirement money, and continued to visit Malaya two or three times a year, for three weeks at a time. In 1965 Tunku wrote to me, and I was offered permanent residence in Malaya, which was a wonderfully kind and trusting thing to do. But by then I felt that, to write about China, I could not profitably live in Malaya, so I had to decline very regretfully.

And in 1965, suddenly, Singapore was thrown out of the Federation of Malaysia, by the will, primarily, of Tunku Abdul Rahman. Singapore became a separate, independent state, and a most thriving one. And I wrote an article demanding why people in the past had been jailed and had suffered harassment, precisely for wanting an independent Singapore, when this was now accomplished and everyone seemed to think that it was all for the best. But no one paid heed, nor were the prisoners released.

Leaving Malaya and Singapore meant also losing sight, partly, of so many lives which had come into mine; and which had brought me so much of value. So many, so many now to be filed away. I shall only write about Lim Chingsiong, because when I meet again those students of Nanyang University whom I was able to rescue from jail (all of them happily employed in other countries now) we always, somehow, talk about Lim Chingsiong.

'Others can give up, but not Lim Chingsiong.' So often this was said in the years of his incarceration as, one by one, the detainees recanted and were freed. Linda Chen gave up, and went to England. The years passed. The prisons of Singapore and Malaya are not particularly nice places. The use of torture is not banned. Worst of all are the isolation cells; some of metal, and under the Equator sun metal does become very hot. The unfortunate prisoner is alone sometimes for weeks inside the metal cage.

The government of Lee Kuanyew prefers not to have too many people in jail for political opposition. Each prisoner is offered 'recantation'; and the promise not to indulge in politics again gives them the right to leave for England. Lim Chingsiong took eight years to give up. He was then allowed to go to England.

But his brain has gone. Some say it is because of what he suffered in jail in Singapore.

In 1977, walking down a certain street in London with a Chinese friend, I saw Lim Chingsiong. The street has many Chinese shops selling vegetables, spices, beancurd, fruit, soy sauce and tins from Hong Kong and from China. My friend nudged me: 'Look, that man, that is Lim Chingsiong.'

Setting up the stalls for the fresh vegetables, helping to cart the garbage: a handyman in a vegetable shop in London. He was fatter. Or rather, he was no longer what he was because everything had gone out of him. The meaning of flabbiness came as I looked at his face. Lim Chingsiong.

'Sometimes people come and jeer at him, and all he does is to hold his head in his hands,' said my friend. 'We think that he is still afraid of being hit on the head. He was often hit on the head when he was in jail.'

But I remember Lim Chingsiong when he was handsome, a little indecisive, but with a certain shine about him, perhaps a little too much candour. I prefer to remember him that way.

CHAPTER 16

Towards the Cultural Revolution: 1964–1965

Living in Hong Kong had many advantages. We occupied two suites at the President Hotel, and I had no household cares. Vincent found it difficult to get a job (he was forty-seven). He went to India to do temporary consultant engineering work while I was in China, but he would always drop everything to return to Hong Kong when I was back. And for this total gift of his life there are no words which would not mutilate the perfection. In China I did not need him; and he knew it. But outside China I did. He blessed my heart with laughter. 'You keep me young. Without you I could not work.' He would smile that slightly quizzical smile, knowing he was feeding my absences from him, accepting to seek me beyond mere waiting: so we would live successfully for twenty-three years.

The years 1964–5 were years almost of abundance in China; people robust, well-fleshed; in the cities new buses – blue and white in Kuangchow, red in Peking – and hosts of bicycles; in the shops and markets, so many consumer goods, although not as great a variety as in 1957. A certain chic returning to women's clothes; hairdressers busy giving perms. Silk and brocade in the better stores, crowds jostling to buy. And the restaurants full, everywhere; but especially full of middle-ranking and fairly high-ranking officials. Ordinary people eat at home when food is plentiful; only when there is penury do they eat in restaurants.

Even the toys of my childhood were making a return after their disappearance in 1958. Glossy, gaudy paper windmills, painted lanterns and kites, and little tigers of soft cloth; and many new toys: dolls and trains and aeroplanes and boats, mechanical toys for a new generation of Chinese children oriented towards science, technical knowledge. My nephew wants a train.

The adolescents are tall, a head taller than their parents at thirteen or fourteen. 'It's the food,' says Jui. My nieces have beautiful straight legs. The children run and laugh and play and sing, in groups, always in large groups, like starlings. In the spring and summer, from all the offices people erupt, young and middle-aged, coming out twice a day to do the regulation twenty minutes' exercises to keep fit. In the numerous parks – the old and the new parks – under the trees there are games of Chinese chess, acrobats train, and old men do shadow boxing to keep their joints supple. Flower shops have reopened; they are crowded with people buying jasmine and camellias in pots.

The Hong Kong newspapers and magazines comment on China's remarkable recovery. 'The industrial increase has been considerable . . .' Some conjecture that there will be another Leap Forward. But China still buys foreign wheat every year. Chen Yi tells me that this is in order to keep Western markets open to Chinese goods, to promote more active trade, and to replenish stocks in China.

There is renewed aestheticism; scholars browse in the old bookshops; old painting scrolls are highly prized; the art of calligraphy is back; there are many exhibitions: of stamps, of photographs, of woodcuts, of paintings, of carved jades, of embroidery. The romantic novel, *The Dream of the Red Chamber*, is reprinted and I do not know how many millions of copies it has sold. In a China with so many millions of new readers, in the villages, in the factories, any book will have a first printing of at least half a million copies.

Relaxation. Couples in love dawdle in the Summer Palace or boat among the lotus of the Peihai Park. Many questions are asked of me: about the West. Is it true that Western women have washing machines? That one presses a button and a meal comes out of the oven, all cooked?

I wrote an article for the *Daily Mirror* noting this new concern for material comforts.

Agricultural mechanization. I fly over the loess region of

north China, that one million square kilometres of gulch and gully, the product of erosion, of centuries of deforestation. I note among the yellow ocean of silt large, flat, verdant plains. State farms. They are mechanized. But elsewhere there is little mechanization: in several provinces I am shown footpowered threshers and some rice-planting machines (the latter do not function – they will never function properly).

Never have there been more symposia and reunions of scientists, engineers and medical men. Intellectuals show liveliness and vigour; there is argument and debate. Among the writers, too, there is a new spirit – almost defiance. Some writers have been talking about humanism, about the creative impulse and its needs . . .

Never have there been so many Western businessmen in China. For the rupture with the Soviet Union is complete by the summer of 1964. Throughout a whole year and a month the ideological dispute has raged: brilliant and vituperative editorials have appeared; millions of words, a veritable avalanche of denunciation. 'We shall never trust them again . . . they sold us shoddy old machines . . . then they withheld the spare parts, to bring us to our knees.' Never again. China is repaying the aid the USSR gave between 1953 and 1960. By 1965 all debts are cleared. Now, obviously, China is turning to the West for the industrial machines and the technology she needs. De Gaulle has recognized China. French businessmen are here to sell prefabricated houses. Simon Hua, the architect, is enchanted. 'We need to do a lot of rehousing.' Japanese businessmen swarm in many cities. Armed with notebooks and cameras, they interrogate hotel and restaurant waiters. 'What do you eat in the morning? What does it cost? What did you pay for your bicycle? How much cloth do you get a year?' British businessmen are holding an industrial exhibition, and hundreds of thousands of workers and technicians and engineers will come to it. Canadians are also here, and others. There is a West German businessman, and he speaks excellent Chinese, at the hotel.

In the Hsinchiao Hotel an old waiter from before Liberation is teaching the young. 'Muffins for tea,' he says.

There are muffins. He shows the young waiters how to pour coffee for the guests.

'There is a change of policy . . . an opening to the West . . . people are relaxed. It is quite wonderful,' says Freddy Dahlmann, a Belgian businessman who has been my friend for many years and now heads Belgium's first trade delegation to Peking.

But within this sunny, peaceful, pleasant and impressive landscape there lurk intermittent, elusive hints of bad weather. From time to time one hears a small rumble, as of distant thunder. In the tranquil stillness a small seismic shock, as in my Peking childhood, when an earthquake would suddenly move our house and the lamp would sway, only to settle into immobility again.

In the early summer of 1964, the perturbation sensed still appears to me – because I want to be happy, I do not wish to go through the throes of worry again – merely a verbal campaign, something like those health drives which take place yearly, when prizes are given to the cleanest cities. But I cannot avoid being troubled by certain things. To begin with, the very obvious: the large, top-heavy and somewhat arrogant bureaucracy; the privileges now openly flaunted by some officials. They have suits of the finest cloth, superbly cut. They eat in the best restaurants, and black official cars chauffeured by large, burly drivers carry their wives and children to the shops, to school, to the parks. And then, a perceptible number of privileged youngsters, belonging to the families of high officials, hold parties and dress as the young in Hong Kong, and look like a new wealthy class. In fact, that year the words 'very Kong' come into the vocabulary of the young, to indicate this Hong Kong style.

Wang Wanchun comes to lunch with me, and talks about 'the four cleans'.

'What is that?'

'It's part of the socialist education movement which began last year . . .'

The socialist education movement, described as a 'deep-reaching, soul-searching' political campaign, is designed to alter attitudes and behaviour and conduct from bourgeois and capitalist modes. 'The relations between the Party and the people in some rural areas have not been too good . . . it's designed to purify the Party.' Is this another rectification?

After the Leap, the Party allowed private production and black markets for a while; and then some Party cadres (the word some is so indefinite, but it is constantly used and always with a hasty additional clause: of course, extremely few in number) became corrupt profiteers and exploiters, as in the old feudal way. Then Chairman Mao issued 'Ten Points' for an overhaul of the rural areas – 'To check this general loosening of conduct, the squandering, the corruption,' said Wanchun. Mao called for a clean-up: the clean-up of granaries, of commune accounts, of the methods of giving workpoints, of commune property as distinct from private. He urged the cadres to participate in collective labour. Apparently public granaries occasionally became the 'private property' of Party cadres in the commune; accounts, and money coming in, were used for private purchases, and some cadres allotted themselves a very large number of workpoints for 'administrative work' – from five to ten times the average.

'Please may I read the Ten Points?' I asked a middle cadre.

'Sorry. Secret document. Not for outsiders.'

'But I can get them in Hong Kong, I expect . . . they are available there . . .'

'Our friends *do not* read information stolen from China.'

It would be the same in January 1965, when I asked to see the Twenty-Three Points, also on the socialist education movement, and issued by Chairman Mao. The Twenty-Three Points are considered by some scholars the first tentative blueprint for the Cultural Revolution. I agree, for the preamble says: 'The key point . . . is to rectify those people in positions of authority in the Party who take the capitalist road . . .' The Cultural Revolution grew out of the socialist education movement, and the twenty-three-point document bridged the two campaigns. There was always reticence in the cities about the socialist education movement. There it was known as 'the four cleans', meaning anti-corruption, bribery, bureaucracy and arrogance among Party cadres.

Perhaps too much pushiness on my part led to my temporary 'demotion'. A good few receptions given to 'friends' and visitors passed me by. Neither would I be allowed to interview people I asked to see.

'But X. [a French writer on his first visit] has been invited . . . he has had an interview.'

'Yes, but he is *very* famous,' is the retort.

Another reply I get is: 'Our leaders are too busy.' I take this as a 'rectification' of my by now notorious 'bad temper'. A middle cadre prefers a docile, even-tempered, unquestioning honoured guest, to be led about.

Anyway, neither Premier Chou Enlai nor Marshal Chen Yi refused to see me, and to me they were the people who mattered most. I was once vouchsafed an explanation for the 'lesson' I was getting. 'You are friendly towards our workers and peasants, but sometimes with our Party cadres you are quite rude.' 'I don't like meaningless lectures,' I replied; which did not help my case ('refractoriness'). Soon, however, I left for the provinces. And in the provinces no one had demoted me. In Szechuan I learnt a great deal about the socialist education movement.

At Tayee, some eighty kilometres from Chengtu, rose the palace once owned by the great landlord, Liu Wentsai. A medieval tyrant, he died during the Land Reform of 1951–2. His mansion was a museum of atrocities. The gruesome tortures he practised upon his serfs were represented by figures in clay, fashioned by local sculptors from the art academy in Chungking: ragged and stunted peasants, defenceless under the whips of the landlord's servants, their children wrested from them to be sold by the truculent mercenaries of Lord Liu; dungeons and jails, the cages into which the peasants were thrust, too small for a man to stand; the pool of water in which feet rotted . . . all this, of course, was Old China. The sculptures were vividly realistic.

At the same time, another exhibition was held in the

palace, on the socialist education movement. 'We don't usually show this to people from abroad,' said the Szechuan cadre taking me around. 'The four cleans started in this district last year. We checked up on corruption, theft, exploitation . . . some cadres (very few, of course) were using grain from the stores to sell on the black market; they forced the peasants to build new houses for them, free of charge; they did not pay for their food . . .' There were four 'uncleans' among the Party cadres, 'class status, political history, ideology and work style. Bad elements, counter-revolutionaries, landlords, have in some places taken over Party organizations; have even killed good cadres . . . all this has to be cleaned up.' The campaign would take a year in the district of Tayee.

If the Soviet Union had gone wrong, it was because Party degeneration had set in, unchecked. 'Stalin's methods were not the correct ones. The struggle is very sharp,' the cadre added, meaning that physical incidents, and bloody ones, occurred.

Twelve rooms housed the exhibition of the socialist education movement: walls were covered with pictures, drawn and painted, showing cases of embezzlement, corruption, bribery, theft, and even murder. 'We have uncovered 274 serious cases in the district. Schoolchildren are brought here, to see that making a revolution is not easy; that, even in our socialism, class struggle continues . . .'

One case showed how a peasant, a low-level Party member, having protested at the extortions of the cadre in charge of his village, was beaten to death by order of the latter.

'When the clean-up is satisfactory, the commune members are happy, the peasants feel elated, and production goes up. The masses are not vindictive; they readily forgive cadres who clean themselves with self-criticism.'

In December 1964 Chou Enlai said, 'The overthrown landlords . . . remain powerful . . . new bourgeois elements . . . new exploiters . . . are being generated in the Party, in government organs, in cultural and educational sectors . . .

Revisionism as in the Soviet Union is the first step towards becoming another imperialism. China must not change colour; must not lose its revolution . . . the revolution must continue . . .'

The great problem is youth, the 'successors to the Revolution'. As summer proceeds, everyone talks about the younger generation, about training revolutionary successors. The papers are full of the subject. 'What is the next generation like? We don't know.' There have been cases of hooliganism in Peking, at night, in the streets . . . something inconceivable in 1956.

Whereas at one time Kung Peng seemed absolutely sure that my difficulties with Yungmei stemmed from our being in a capitalist society, now she listens carefully as I talk of the generation gap, of the difficulty of transmitting experience, of continuing a tradition, a revolution, a culture, a spirit and a way of life. 'Only through the word . . . but the word must be convincing, bolstered by action . . .'

'We don't know our youth. They haven't been tried out,' she replies. Youth is everywhere, clean-limbed, healthy, uproariously joyful, candid-eyed, unsubdued, because now it is no longer done to beat and ill-treat children as in the past; because now the young dare to discuss with their parents, to argue against them, a thing they never did before; something which, in Vincent's Indian family, is still not done: his sons, aged twenty-five and twenty-eight, do not dare contradict him when he speaks. India is as patriarchal as Old China was. But now the father's rule is weakened in China. What will the father's role be in another twenty years?

The young whirr on their new bicycles; they fill the buses; great streams of children (healthy, healthy!) come out of the schools at midday, and every lane is crammed with babies, and on the great sunny Square of Heavenly Peace long queues of kindergarten toddlers in brightly coloured clothes, holding each other's neat apron strings, wait to view the monument to the Heroes of the Revolution, which bears an inscription by Chou Enlai.

'They have never eaten bitterness . . . never known hunger or pain . . . they do not know what the past was like, just one generation ago. They do not understand the long and dolorous Calvary, to the security of today . . . they think that everything is *owed* them: education and health and a job and security and care . . . everything. They are cocooned; they do not know what it really is like to fight in an enemy world, for dignity, for equality . . .'

Chen Yi had already said to me in 1963, 'All that the young want is a bicycle and a transistor radio, a fountain pen in their pocket and a good life in the cities.'

The Communist Youth League, through its Chairman, Hu Yaopang, has voiced its concern: 'Brought up under conditions of peace and stability . . . the young are lulled into a false sense of security . . . they look for a life of ease . . .'

There is a campaign on, to write history as lived by the people; the history of the peasantry who slaved for so many emperors of China; to educate young people who do not know history. Chou Enlai has asked people like the celebrated actors, Mei Lanfang and Chou Hsinfang, to write their own autobiographies, to tell the next generation how penurious, how precarious, was the life of an opera star in the past. He wants the young people to have a wide understanding of what Old China was like.

There is an undiscussed problem. Every year, many millions of young people are coming on the labour market. 'Our industry is not developing swiftly enough to use them.' Chen Yi, always startling in frankness, has said this soberly to me. If not industry, the only other gateway to employment is agriculture . . . and so the trek to the communes of young, educated people who can read and write, going to the backward villages where amenities are lacking. But how else to lift up the villages and their inhabitants?

In 1964 this is going on all over China. The young leave for faraway provinces, alien lands to them, so strong are provincialism and feudal family ties. They go, and will labour as peasants, but they are also to become bookkeepers, tractor drivers, village school teachers, agro-technicians, health workers, veterinarians. In 1965 the barefoot doctors, young para-medical personnel, aged between seventeen and twenty-five, begin to serve the rural areas in primary health care. A million of them by 1974.

These educated young are counted upon to build and maintain small fertilizer plants, small methane gas plants, small electrical plants for flour mills, and improved agricultural tools workshops – all this lower level industrialization is the great need of Asian rural society. The communes will then become agro-industrial complexes with more processing of agricultural produce: canning factories, mushroom factories, seedling care, chicken, duck and pig raising – so much can be done to make life for the peasant prosperous and to achieve a high, diversified production.

The alternative is to have cities crammed full of half-baked 'educated youths'; unemployed mouths to feed. I cannot see any other way in which China can cope with the problem of the many millions of youths apart from a very strong family planning programme and this *'hsia fang'*, sending them down to the villages of rural China.

Old Yeh's two sons are studying: they are mentally prepared for manual labour. They hope to return from the communes in two or three years, and to enter a university. 'It is not demeaning to become a worker or a peasant,' says Old Yeh pleasantly, mildly, perhaps a little sad at the thought that his sons may not be high-class intellectuals as he is, but placing the common weal before his own wishes. So many of my friends face similar problems for their children; because there is not enough place in the universities, and there is an immense, overwhelming tide of workers' and peasants' children coming up, coming up, also going to the universities. 'We need two hundred more universities within the next ten years,' says Simon Hua to me. He has three children.

In education there is a campaign against 'revisionist' teaching. Much of Chinese education since 1949 has been on the Soviet pattern. Until 1958, it was the correct political stance to scorn the 'capitalist' pattern. But the Leap put an end to that. Since 1961 and the Sino-Soviet rift, Third Brother can freely say that sciences are just as advanced, if not more so, in the Western world as in the Soviet Union. Fortunately many professors have gone on staunchly teaching their best, without falling into the aberrations of the Stalin era in Russia. Of course some of them were dubbed rightists in 1957, but now, in 1964, there is a strong demand to rehabilitate rightists.

Never have I seen the intelligentsia more academically free in its pursuits than in early 1964 (though by the end of the year unease is plain to see). Institutes of higher learning have been created. Fundamental research is back. It was very seriously interfered with: in 1956 Chou Enlai restored it, but again, during the Leap, it was derided as 'useless'. 'What is the use of looking at the wings of a fly?' said an article of the time, criticizing studies in genetics.

In the factories I witness a great struggle: in some the managers have regained a power of decision; they have restored a rigorous framework of rules; the workers are paid according to efficiency; there are bonuses for better work done; political meetings are pared to the bone. But in others it is not so.

Unquestionably, an anti-intelligentsia wave looms below the surface. The Western businessmen in Peking are joyful, thinking of much business to come, of an accelerated industrial pace for China. The Cultural Revolution will catch all of them, all of us, unawares. Already there are warnings. Youth 'must not become infected with the bad habits of some bourgeois intellectuals', warns an article. The anti-intellectual wave calls for battle against Soviet 'revisionism'. I watch as a most terrifying misconception is built up: any expression of aesthetics, material ease, culture, intellect, is in danger of being labelled 'revisionist'. To collect old books, to like flowers, to sing, is revisionist. To want a good education is becoming revisionist. 'Progress and material ease are not revisionist . . . they are the goals of the Revolution and of socialism . . .' I say feebly. But I am only a bourgeois. China's pendulum is swinging. It always overswings.

This anti-revisionist war takes on so many aspects that it involves every domain of action and thought; none as eclectic as the contest around the phrases: 'one divides into two' and 'two can combine into one'.

I am confronted with these postulates at a dinner party with writers, a most delightful and witty banquet, to which came even the famous Chou Yang, whom we all privately called, at the time, the Emperor of Literature, because he was in charge of the ideological correctness of literary creation. We drank a great deal and in the amiable banter Wan, the literary critic, asked me smilingly what I thought of the sentence 'Two can combine into one'.

I had seen articles condemning this phrase. But the hermeticism of intra-Party struggle escaped me – as it escaped the majority of the Chinese. I knew, though, that many crises in the Party were first presented as highly philosophical debates or couched in historical terms relating to situations in some previous century (B.C. or A.D.). It takes weeks, even months, to arrive at the final dénouement, to know who is being aimed at, and by whom, and what it is all about.

'It reminds me of Taoism,' I said. 'At the Beginning was the Unique; then one divides into two, two becomes multitude . . . but perhaps I'm remembering it all wrong.' Wan gave me a nice smile, almost as if to say, 'You've passed the test.' Only two weeks later, reading articles and documents, would I realize the divisive heretical significance of the phrase 'two can combine into one'.

'One divides into two.' Mao had said it; it was the Chinese formulation of dialectics, which recognizes that all phenomena, situations, events, persons, things, in the world, are dual, made up of separate, contradictory units or segments which 'struggle' against each other, and that this action/reaction state is the cause of all change processes. Nature knows not immobility. Its only constancy is the constancy of change; and also of reversal, for in the struggle one or other of the 'contradictions' ultimately wins, and a new being, situation, event, thing, is created with a new set of contradictory units or segments . . . and so on *in aeternum*. This is dialectics, 'one divides into two', and dialectical thinking lies at the core of scientific thinking.

The phrase 'two combines into one', however, opened another realm of speculation, that opposites are not concrete, but symbolic; that the Unique, the One, has two aspects, but remains the only reality; that the very nature of things compels a seeking for reunion and fusion of apparent opposites.

This syllogistic view appeared, at the time, a plea to side with the Soviet Union in the fraternity of a 'socialist camp', monolithic and indivisible. Not surprisingly, it was fiercely denounced as 'revisionist'. But the 'one divides into two' dialectics implied that class struggle, contradictions in society, and therefore turmoil, was incessant, even within socialism; and in 1964 this posed an enormous problem. Should there be 'politics in command of everything', which meant that the very basis of all action would be class struggle? And should the class struggle in China be sharpened to bring about swifter change (for theory held that 'revolution stimulates production'), or should attempts at class conciliation, at concentrating on productivity, be made, in order to accelerate progress? The technologists, the managerial layers, and some of the Party leaders, held that China needed internal peace, a diminution of political emphasis, an end to the 'mass campaigns', which might educate the multitudes but which disrupted production, a dampening of class struggles, which always ended in the intellectuals getting mauled, pushed around, browbeaten. But this 'technological view' also meant *more* centralization, directives from above; less decision making processes in the hands of the common people and above all, élitism.

Which was the right way for China, taking into account its history, its feudal past, its present handicaps? The Leap had been one attempt to solve by crash methods the problems of progress. What other experiments would be tried?

Peking's small-lane rumour that year was that rehabilitations of 'rightests' were proceeding. In fact, I was to see two of the main 'rightists' of 1957 sitting, much at ease, attending a theatrical performance, surrounded by their families and by an aura of respect.

By 1964 it was well known (although never mentioned openly) that Peng Tehuai had been called a 'rightist opportunist' because he had greatly criticized the Leap and the communes. He had lost his post as Defence Minister, but not his Party membership or his freedom. Lin Piao, who abroad was reputed to be a military strategist because of his prowess during the anti-Japanese war, was now Defence Minister. In China Lin Piao was simply known to have Mao's trust.

So many plans, projects, schemes, which I first heard of in those two years of 1964 and 1965 are the ones which are being taken up now, in 1978 and 1979. Among the dozen or so schemes I call to mind is the development of hydroelectric power in Tibet and Szechuan. Some 70 per cent of China's hydro-electric power sources lie in Tibet and Kweichow, Szechuan and Yunnan provinces, along the upper reaches of the Yangtze and Brahmaputra rivers. In 1964 there were meetings and technical articles and discussions about building a major dam in the Yangtze's upper reaches; the industrialization of the area, which is immensely rich in minerals of all kinds, depended on this energy grid. Another scheme, whereby the surplus water of the voluminous Yangtze River would be directed northwards into the drought-afflicted areas of the Yellow River basin, was also first mooted in 1964.

In education, the invisible struggle was pursued through articles of dissimilar content and orientation closely following each other in the press. Thus the plan to erect 'special' schools for the specially talented (189 of them are being erected today) was lauded in one article, and in another it was castigated as deflecting youth from integration with the masses, the workers, the peasants, the soldiers. The Ministry of Education was to be split into two in 1965: one department for higher education, for an élite of researchers and top specialists in all fields, and one for lower education, to run the part-labour, part-study schools which had first been created during the Great Leap Forward of 1958. The latter were to be set up in rural areas. They ploughed their own fields, reared pigs, planted their own vegetables. Expenses were drastically cut, but the teachers sent to them were of inferior quality. Then, there were in 1964 some 120 million children aged from seven to twelve in primary school. How could China afford universal education? How could she, while dispensing literacy to all, train an élite corps of scientists in order to reach, very rapidly, international standards in all scientific and technological sectors? Yet Mao Tsetung had set this as the target for China: by the year 2000 to reach the highest levels in technology and science existing in the world. How could this be achieved?

As the summer of 1964 slipped into autumn I became disquieted by what was happening among the writers. There had been a renewal of creativity and debate on writing since 1961 and the Second Hundred Flowers; but now again broadside attacks on literary men who sapped the Party spirit in literature were occurring. A debate about the portrayal of 'middle characters', that is, people neither heroic prototypes nor villains, ended in the criticism of its proponent, a writer named Shao. 'Comrade Chou Yang never makes an ideological mistake,' I was told. Apparently Chou Yang had expounded the correct attitude. 'He understands Mao Tsetung Thought in literature thoroughly.' But Chou Yang's criticism of other writers in 1964 lacked the severity he had displayed in 1957 against Hu Feng, Ting Ling and other non-conformists. And he himself would be attacked and reviled, in an extreme manner, and for ten years, from 1966.

There was controversy about certain films, books and plays which had been published or performed. In June 1964 a reform of the Peking opera was proclaimed. Peking opera must reflect present day scenes and aspirations, the workers, soldiers, peasants, wrote the *People's Daily*; an end to feudal themes, stories of princes and scholars and beautiful ladies. Yet in 1964 there had been new and popular operas of the old type, but incorporating some modern ideas, such as *The Yang Family Women Warriors*. Its theme was the equality of women. There were successful revivals of *The White-Haired Girl*, an opera first performed in Yenan in the 1940s. There were also one or two 'new type' operas, and I was one of the first to see *Spark Among the Reeds*, which I liked very much. 'We do need new stories, new themes, new plays and new operas,' I said to Kung Peng. 'Of course I love the old plays and dramas, and they should continue, but we should have both.'

At the time, *Spark Among the Reeds* had nothing to do with Chiang Ching, Mao's wife. Her name was not mentioned in connection with the script, the music or anything to do with the opera. Neither was *The Red Regiment of Women*, later to become one of her favourite shows, connected with her. It had first been shown in 1962,* and had won a prize then. Only after 1966 would these new operas be ascribed to Chiang Ching. Undoubtedly, however, in 1964 she did emerge from retirement, and was given a position in the Ministry of Culture, and immediately attempted to take over one of the opera groups in Peking.

In 1965 quotations from a speech she had made, asserting that 'All opera heroes . . . must be positive figures', appeared. This meant that no vacillation, doubt, no ordinary human emotion, could be allowed the 'hero' or the 'heroine' of the new operas. Only 'positive characters', in literature as well, were recognized. 'Middle characters' were anathema.

Attacks began against a film I had greatly liked, called *Early Spring in February*. It was based on a love story written by a young communist who had died in 1931, Jou Shih. The script and the film had received the ardent support of Hsia

*As a film.

Yen, himself an able and prolific playwright (he managed to write fifteen plays within the short space of two years), who was Vice-Minister of Culture, and whom I had met in Cairo in 1962. Another film, which Hsia Yen had scripted, *Lin's Family Shop*, based on a story by no less a person than Mao Tun, the Minister of Culture, was also being attacked. Yet, to see these and other remarkable films, there were queues of young people a kilometre long in front of the cinemas.

'This is a moving, beautifully done film,' I said of *Early Spring in February* to Hsing Chiang, my companion. Kung Peng had specially asked her friend, Hsing Chiang, who had been her schoolmate in Shanghai and who spoke Spanish as well as English, to look after me. Hsing Chiang was to prove, through the difficult years of the Cultural Revolution, reliable, staunch, patient, loyal; trying hard to help me avoid the worst mistakes caused by my hasty temper. Now she looked at me quietly and said, 'Not everyone holds the same opinion about this film.' It was soon denounced as a poisonous weed; and by 1965 both Mao Tun and Hsia Yen were being criticized, and became invisible . . . I would not see Hsia Yen again until 1978.

Mao Tsetung Thought. Everyone is enjoined to study the four volumes of his *Selected Works*; to understand Mao Tsetung Thought, which helps scientists in their science, writers to write, and economists to plan . . . Gradually the emphasis becomes more and more adulatory.

I have been looking for a history of the Communist Party in China; the one which appeared in 1959* has been withdrawn: 'Certain events were incorrect.' There is no book on recent history in China. There will be no history book available for many years. 'The correct assessment of events,' I am told, delays such a book. Only when 'we have absolutely fixed every person and event in history' will a history book be written. 'How Confucianist!' I exclaim. The Chinese Revolution, like the Russian Revolution, rubs out

*By Ho Kanchih; in this book there is little mention of Lin Piao.

the faces and names of those who were heroes for a while and later assessed as traitors or deviationists. 'Correct appraisal' will therefore take a very long time.

'In fact,' says a certain Comrade Ku, who is jovial, and much more talkative than most, 'one never knows whether a communist is a good communist and a good comrade until he is dead.'

I say, 'History goes on being reassessed again and again.' No one pays attention.

This lack of historical knowledge will cost dear; it will be a major cause for the destructiveness of the adolescent (and ignorant) Red Guards during the Cultural Revolution. For they do *not* know what happened, and are gullible, and easily cheated.

Anna-Louise Strong and I are asked whether we would like to try our hand at translating Chairman Mao's poems. 'They are untranslatable,' says Anna-Louise firmly. I try, but give up in three days. I have, however, translated my favourite Sung dynasty poetess, Li Tsingchao, and the translations are printed under a pseudonym in *Chinese Literature*. This will lead to a suspicion that I have tried to infuse unsuspecting readers with 'feudal and bourgeois' ideas . . . but Hsing Chiang saves me by telling everyone that I translated these poems 'a very long time ago', when I was less enlightened.

There is the army. Its presence. A constant and growing eulogy of the army. Under Lin Piao, the army is undergoing a great ideological reform; and the whole country is enjoined to model itself on the PLA. In 1965, officers' uniforms are abolished. Marshals and generals dress as privates do (but there are differences – officers wear leather shoes).

The army is everywhere; in every institution and factory, and especially in the schools. Not generals or officers, but simple, green-clad, plimsolled soldiers, candid and courteous, polite and earnest and hardworking. They are there to learn, to be trained, so they say: there is no army takeover, simply their presence, to enhance enthusiasm, as they preach

Mao Tsetung Thought. They willingly do the dirty work; clean floors and sweep courtyards with great cheerfulness. For this is Mao Tsetung Thought, *to serve the people*; everywhere abnegation, modesty. Children's books are full of an array of army heroes, who give their lives in self-sacrifice to save others . . . Schoolchildren spend a portion of their summer holidays in sports camps, where they also do military drill. The photographs fill the West with horror: children with guns! Yet China is threatened in 1965, 'contained' and constrained and hemmed in; she is apparently without a friend (although the delegations to Peking swell in size, and Mao says, 'We have friends all over the world'). In 1965 the threat from America appears to grow more menacing; and articles appear in American papers about war with China. McNamara clarions: 'China is *the* enemy'. The war in Vietnam is expanding swiftly – perhaps that is why·the army is already in situ everywhere.

I lay sleepless, interrogating the ceiling. By now I had read and reread Mao; all that was available of him. Through the decades he had striven to build a Communist Party which would constantly rejuvenate itself, purify itself, through 'rectification' movements, criticism and self-criticism, not punishing dissent by physical extermination, but allowing it within limits. 'The minority is often right,' Mao had said. He had been in the minority for some years of his Party life. He had suffered greatly from the Stalinist-like purges and methods of former Party leaders. He realized that orderly dissent was necessary, was essential for the Party to function, because there was a fundamental contradiction to solve.

In a socialist state, with a single party in absolute power, it is within that party that the seeds of degeneration, corruption, of a return to the past are to be found, nowhere else. But if a revolution is to be kept going, and this means maintaining enthusiasm and devotion, sacrifice, then the system must allow the people to denounce corruption and squandering among Party members. It must, in fact, train 'rebels' to revolt against Party cadres who betray and misuse the ethic of socialism. But how could this be done, when any criticism of a Party cadre was handled as counter-revolutionary, as an attack on the whole Party? Mao met this problem head-on in many of his speeches. Again and again he tried to differentiate between 'attacks against the Party' and 'denunciation of individual wrong-doing'. The whole point of the Hundred Flowers was the fact that limited dissent must be encouraged. And now the socialist education movement was bolstering, reinforcing, strengthening grassroots organizations of ordinary poor peasants so that they would have more say in the communes and be less bullied by Party cadres. But would it work?

At present, the material ingredients which make a revolution were absent from the Chinese scene. There had been peace for many years; food, though not abundant, was sufficient; there was security for the vast majority of the people. But there was undoubtedly deliquescence within the Party; the fighting guerrillas of the pre-Liberation days were getting old. Since 1949 there had been a large intake of untried, unseasoned and possibly opportunistic members: seventeen million members by 1964, four times more than in 1950. The Party was swamped by people with no experience of the Revolution in its fighting years. How could the untrained young, not knowing Party history, not toughened by bitter experience, distinguish between what was true socialism and what was not within a Party dedicated to bringing about socialism.

I did not dare ask this question aloud. I was sure that the middle cadres would resent it, because their shuttered minds were not ready for such speculation. Only Chou Enlai, Chen Yi and Kung Peng would understand. 'If and when I see Chou Enlai, I shall hint towards it . . . He must have this problem much on his mind.' Had he not said that there was 'degeneration' in some Party organizations?

Lenin had said that politics was 'concentrated economics'. Finally it was a problem of economics; *how* to achieve, in the shortest possible time, material prosperity. In 1960 Mao had already said to Lord Montgomery: 'We know about fighting, we know a bit about running villages . . . but we don't know anything about building a new socialist economy . . . we'll have to learn the hard way . . .'

Mao had written, 'Let us hope that the price we shall have to pay for learning how to build socialism will not be as heavy as the one we have to pay to win the Revolution . . .'

The price to pay was to be the Cultural Revolution.

In 1965, two fundamentally opposed concepts confronted each other in China. The first was that the superstructure of ideas, behaviour, consciousness, the relations governing economic production and productivity, could not change before the material environment, the productive forces, had changed. This *almost* conceded that only the introduction of industrialization, of forcible and accelerated technology, would change man, that man can only become other through change in environment, not through volition, will.

The other concept was that consciousness, awareness of the problems and a change in the relations of production, could be achieved before the material basis was changed, and indeed acted to propel material change forward. In other words, first change the whole apparatus of thinking, and this would produce material change; just as Galileo, Newton, Einstein changed the world by seeing the universe in a different way . . .

But in both arguments the instrument whereby policies were implemented was declared to be the Communist Party. 'Our cadres should have a high political consciousness,' my friend Chienta said to me in all seriousness. But what did he mean? Can one be highly aware when one's knowledge of reality is restricted?

A British diplomat, seeing the eagerness for knowledge, the developing scientific institutes, said to me, 'In ten or twenty years, if China continues as she does today, she will have a large pool of literate, scientifically minded, studious people, ready for a real breakthrough in technology and in science . . .'

'Seek truth from facts'; 'Less talk, more work' – small, haphazard phrases coming from seasoned scientists. But to a Chinese-attuned ear they have a political backing.

I read somewhere that 'the young do not want to join the Party . . . it's too exacting . . . the pay is very low . . .' The average age of the Party cadre at grassroots level, in 1965, is forty.

Philosophers I talk with say, 'There must be a campaign to obliterate the gap between theory and practice.' Which means: Less empty talk. Economists say, 'We have to use our heads . . . even the highest ones can make mistakes . . .' Which means perhaps Mao? They also say, 'Since the Leap our productivity has not gone up; even on state farms there is too much of the sickle and the spade.' Which means the whole point of agricultural mechanization has suffered a defeat. Mechanization requires investment, capital accumulation. How can it be brought about quickly? Meanwhile, there are the millions of young, every year, coming up on the labour market, coming up . . . Family planning is mooted strongly that year, and I go to Yunnan and Szechuan to find out how it is performed.

'We have 250 per cent more women attending our clinic this year than last year,' says the doctor in charge in Kunming, capital of Yunnan province.

'And how many did you have last year?'

'Ten.'

So that means thirty-five women this year, out of nineteen million inhabitants.

I go to my favourite Peihai Park to drink tea under the willows. At the next table three soldiers sit, and one reads aloud the poems of Mao Tsetung. One of his eyes is of a lighter colour than the other. He is twenty, a poor peasant's son; he learnt to read in the mass literacy drive carried out during the Great Leap Forward of 1958. 'Fifty million people like me gained sight then,' says he, meaning they learnt to read. 'I want to be a writer. I want to write poetry.' He spends all his pay on books. He asks me whether I can help him to get a translation of Rousseau, and 'some poetry of the French Revolution . . . it was a great revolution, like our own . . . I want to read about it, and about the Paris Commune. I want to know the poets of those magnificent years.'

Third Uncle is sleek and well in 1964. He has a new house and in the sitting room are some pieces of good furniture, and of course his tea cupboard. In Chengtu the Spring Flower Festival has been restored; everyone has gone to it. The Taoist temple has reopened. Round it all the markets flourish. I visit the temple, to pay respects to the venerable anarchist, agnostic Lao Tze, riding his black buffalo in search of Verity, Reality . . .

On October 15th, Hsing Chiang says to me quietly, 'Khrushchev has fallen.' She has just heard it on the radio.

The next day China explodes her first atom bomb.

Joy. Third Uncle is happy. My cousins are happy. A Mongol second cousin of mine by marriage, who has a wonderful voice, sings extracts from *Boris Godunov*, and the windows vibrate, the glass quivers. He indeed has a marvellous voice; but he will be in jail for three years at the Cultural Revolution, wrongfully accused . . . I would only know of it in 1977.

China has destroyed the blackmail of atomic supremacy. Khrushchev has been shown up. 'I am proud to be an Asian,' says Tunku Abdul Rahman of Malaysia, voicing what every Asian, irrespective of politics, feels over China's bomb. All of us feel that Chairman Mao was right. This explosion, somehow, justifies many things for us (even, perhaps, the unjustifiable). 'Now our spine has straightened, we walk tall,' says anti-communist Francis Pan to me in Hong Kong.

Before my departure in 1964, Kung Peng gives me a wonderful farewell dinner; I meet many people from the Ministry of Foreign Affairs, among them the remarkable scholar and diplomat, Wang Pingnan, whom I know already from the Laos Conference of 1961. Ambassador to Poland, he carries on with patience the long negotiations with the Americans in Warsaw, keeping hold of the tenuous

Ariadne's thread through the labyrinth of hostility and hatred. There are also at the dinner Huang Hua, young and fiery, going to be ambassador in Cairo; and so many others.

The dinner is so delightful, so civilized, that I feel quite ridiculous with qualms and questions. I feel cocooned, safe . . . China is a Great Mother, a wise one . . . the people will find their way. I am reassured and when my body leaves China, my heart remains, as usual; this is a condition of my being now. I know that I serve best outside. 'China will need knowledge, science from abroad . . . a different viewpoint . . .' This has been conveyed to me, as to others. Cultural cross-fertilization is essential for China's future. Chou Enlai believes in cross-fertilization. After all, the glorious Tang were so magnificent because they opened wide the doors of China . . . and their emperors were part Uighur, and Uighurs are the ancestors of the Turks – 'That is why the first Tang emperors were called Big Noses,' says Rewi Alley, who knows everything about China, to me.

My first lecture tour to the United States began in January 1965. During the next fourteen years, lecturing on China would become an adventitious part of my activities. I would travel a great deal: all over Europe, to America and to Canada, to Mexico and to Australia, to Japan, to Africa and to India. I would lecture in the most unlikely places, to the most conservative audiences: to the Paris Military Academy several times, to the Indian Military College in New Delhi, to assemblies of priests and to the disciples of Gandhi in Gujarat. I would appear on television many times in America, attend symposia and seminars on China, travelling through the United States on four major and two minor lecture tours.

On this initial tour of 1965, my first stop was Honolulu, with a *lei* welcome with hula dancers. There was a happy reunion with some of my old dormitory mates from Yenching University, where we had all been students together from 1933 to 1935. They sang 'Love is a Many-Splendoured Thing' at me, and I tried to look surprised and delighted. My lecture there was not a success; Honolulu was too far from everything that happened, too remote from the Vietnam war, a thousand light years away from Asia and her problems. Its obvious beauty was exasperating because it just wallowed in it.

I was introduced to the social distinction between one-digit and two-digit millionaires. At an imposing dinner, the statuesque twenty-four-year-old wife of a seventy-year-old two-digit millionaire burst into howls and sobs in the middle of the steak course.

We flew to San Francisco. The power, the greatness, the technological might of America captured us. I had come prepared to despise a little, to resent certainly; but I forgot all about this as Vincent's enchantment seized me. For Vincent, the engineer, the revelation was America's man-made beauty. The elevated highways flinging themselves horizonwards, the bridge crossing the sea at San Francisco, the skyscrapers, the dams, the airports; all that spelt human power, the potential of conquest of the universe. 'They'll walk the stars,' said he. For me, it was America's natural beauty, its space and immensity, but also an anxious emptiness. How empty, truly empty, America seemed to my eyes, accustomed to the crowds of Asia.

We toured a great deal of America by car, driving ourselves, stopping anywhere, discovering its tiny townlets and its enormous cities. I lectured to the Mormons in Salt Lake City, at the Synagogue in Los Angeles, and at countless women's organizations and clubs, and today I regret not a minute of the time spent. It was necessary, and it was also for me a time of learning.

We stayed with Felix Greene at Palo Alto; Felix was busy lecturing up and down America, against the Vietnam war. I too would pronounce on this war; and I said how pernicious it would be for America. But who would listen then? 'The computers have told us that if you hit an Asian hard enough he gives in' was one of the memorable sayings of 1965; 'Our bombing will shorten the war . . .' from a merciful old lady. At times it was slightly unpleasant; but on the whole I was agreeably astonished by the politeness, the courtesy, the splendid self-control of my audiences; for what I said was at times very unpalatable and blistering – and Americans were emotional then about their role in promoting democracy in Asia. Cold logic is never taken willingly; it is too much like unsweetened medicine.

In Georgia, Alabama and Tennessee, Vincent's colour caused a problem. I did not see the glossy chocolate satin of his skin as anything but beautiful; understandably, not everyone had the same reaction. At a certain Junior League the well-bred sponsors fell back one step, then took a firm grip on their nether limbs and came forward to shake hands. Having ascertained that Vincent was Indian and not Afro-American, they were totally charming. In a restaurant, a pall of silence settled upon the noisy men at the bar as we walked in. We waited twenty minutes before a waitress came up. 'Where you folk from?' 'India.' The audible sigh of relief! In yet another small town we were denounced by the foul-mouthed local tycoon; but at night three Afro-Americans, waiters, came to our room to wring our hands. Six years later, by 1971, there was already a noticeable change. And these incidents were compensated by the general kindness, the real goodness, which we found everywhere.

All the time we were reading in the newspapers about muggings and killings and rape and violence; yet all seemed so calm, so tranquil. Vincent paid no heed until we reached Los Angeles and we went for a stroll after dinner. It was only 9.30 at night but suddenly Vincent stopped: 'Do you realize that we are the only people *walking* on this main street?' We were; and behind us, a police car was trailing us . . . We turned back to the hotel.

The waste of America. Too much food on every plate – I was totally unable to consume so much food. Garbage, things thrown away, mountains of useless motor cars . . . the waste. And gradually, a bleak and inward energy drain: for everywhere, after a while, we were assaulted by sameness. A conformism numbing in its unspoken, absolute authority. The people were so dissimilar in bone structure and hair colouring and eyes; but they all strove so hard to be like each other, and so earnestly did they diversify their garments to conform to the idea of being individual. The same coffee in all the cafeterias, hotels, and restaurants, dispensed by interchangeable waitresses. Identical air hostesses, all making the same mistake in English as they announced a takeoff: 'We shall be departing *momentarily*.' The same glazed eyes and tightened jaws of men sitting in cars, driving to the cities at dawn in one immense commuting flow. The same lack of books and bookshops; and me hunting hopelessly for books on drugstore shelves, behind the sanitary toilet articles.

But also: the splendid Greyhound buses, webbing America; with their marvellous, tranquil drivers. The slums of the big cities; silent nightmares all alike, suddenly erupting into shrieks and running. The entire absence of chic at every and any level among the women. American compunction, self-interrogation, hankering for righteousness and a lost paradise.

Television with Mr Gerald Ford was a delightful experience. A sincere man, easy to talk to, and modest; he did not pretend to know anything about Asia, and was surprised to hear that the Vietnamese were not Chinese. A meeting with Ambassador Goldberg, on the eve of a March 1965 meeting in Moscow designed to drum China out of the 'socialist camp': 'What will China do now?' 'She doesn't give a damn.' A meeting with Senator Fulbright, highly recommended to me by Felix Greene. I found him insubstantial; striving hard to be all things to all visitors. A good man, withal.

My most intelligent audience was at the Naval Officers' World Affairs Seminar at Bremerton. I left with the distinct impression that not all among the naval officers agreed with the Vietnam war, or Kennedy's advisers; that in fact they saw the geopolitical map of the world far more clearly than the White House pundits of that time – the Bundys and that bright, brittle, sophisticated crowd from the Eastern seaboard universities.

Astonishing to my Asian-conditioned experience was the genuine fairness and the comparative accuracy of the American press. My way of looking at truth was wary; as something extremely prone to slip away, to twist out of the grasp. Lao Tze's search for verity had proved both arduous and wayward, and in the end, possibly, he did not know whether he was not dreaming of himself searching for verity. Americans were mightily in love with truth. But it of course also escaped them; and when I tried to communicate my surprise and gratification at discovering fragments of veracity adhering to a rock of lies, they were nonplussed. But even the small town newspapers reported, scrupulously and fairly, what I said. Fabulous.

Yungmei had married an American. In November 1964 I had received a letter from her telling me that she was marrying Sidney. 'Sidney who?' I cabled back. But had no answer. Fortunately she had given me an address in New York, and we discovered Sidney Glazier, film producer, and Yungmei's husband. I thought, looking at him, that she had chosen the right man for her season of uncertainty; but of course it would not last. Sidney was impulsive, enthusiastic, protective, captivated by Yungmei's apparent frailty (actually she is Chinese-tough). However, because of Sidney and his American openness and his Jewish articulate boldness with words, it was possible for Yungmei to emerge from the murk of reticence about her adoption and to discuss it openly at last.

People marry through need; divorce also through need, often vicariously, because they have not resolved their own lack of purpose. In Yungmei's case, I think the only good thing I did was to try to keep relations with her, her child, and Sidney as normal and amicable as possible. I saw no reason to do ugly, vulgar things to another human being. And Sidney was to prove the most generous of ex-husbands, and the best of fathers.

For Yungmei now would have a child, Karen. And Karen is so very much like me in some ways that it is almost unbelievable. But I do not know whether she has had enough obstacles, difficulties, worries, in her growing up to make her strive for anything . . . only through fighting does one really grow into something. I have a fear that she may have been over-protected, too much 'thought for', too occupied with many things. And has no time or loneliness left to think with, to really grow into giving as well as taking.

In April we left America for Europe. Our eyes were not accustomed to large roaming; and kept hitting houses and crossroads. All the streets were too short and the cars diminutive. England was toyland.

In London I inaugurated, along with at least ten other people, including Vanessa Redgrave, the Society for Anglo-Chinese Understanding (SACU). I was invited to talk at the Oxford Union on the subject of the Vietnam war, my opponent being Patrick Gordon Walker. The President of the Oxford Union that year was Tariq Ali, a young Pakistani of Trotskyite views and wealthy landlord background. The debate was lively. I lost by eleven votes to Gordon Walker. 'Well, we've won,' said he. 'Not on the battlefield,' I replied with asperity.

In June I flew to Tanzania while Vincent went to see his family in India. My Egyptian friends, Mustafa and Leila El-Issawi, had invited me to Dar Es Salaam, where Mustafa was the UAR Ambassador. I had known them in Singapore, and we had become good friends. Mustafa told me that 'someone in the Singapore government' had warned Nasser that I was Jewish. 'But we have our own intelligence and we know it is not true,' said Mustafa. I told him that the Kuomintang had first spread that rumour, and the Special Branch in Singapore had merely picked it up and placed it in my dossier.

Tanzania was sisal plantations, mostly run by Greeks, and a dust bowl beginning in its centre owing to overcutting of the forests; and the most magnificent landscapes, mountains and rivers I had seen so far. Zanzibar island, just off the coast, exhibited relics of the Chinese expeditions of the Ming dynasty. I called on the Chinese Ambassador, who told me about the projected railway to be built by China between Tanzania and Zambia. I called on the American Ambassador, and he introduced me to one of the leaders of the Angola resistance, fighting against Portugal, and his American wife.

On to Kenya, where Malcolm was now High Commissioner. Jomo Kenyatta brandished a fly whisk and was amiably tipsy from early morning on. I wanted to ask him about the custom of clitoridectomy, which I considered horrendous, especially when it was, as in Sudan, pharaonic, that is, practised with ablation of all the external genitalia. But Jomo Kenyatta was in favour of clitoridectomy. And only in 1979 would the subject of women thus mutilated be taken up in a major way. Thirty million women, for whom love-making is deliberately made agony.

I went to the flamingo lake to see a hundred thousand pink flamingoes take wing from the bronze water, transforming the world into a whirl of pink feather.

My cousin, Armand Denis, lived in Kenya, and I went to see him. Armand was one of the world's first ecologists; he had fought since childhood against the massacre of animals. 'I only shoot with a camera,' said he. He and his American wife, Michaela, had made many films for the BBC. In 1962 he had come to Malaya, and deplored Asia's swift change. 'It's plastic, jazz and politics.' He became infuriated by the conditions at the zoo in Johore Bahru, where we found a black panther with a badly mutilated paw (caught in a trap). In our passion for our fellow beasts Armand and I were much alike. Armand had once taken a cheetah to a cinema in Paris. Unfortunately some dogs appeared on the screen, and the cheetah went berserk with excitement.

Armand's house in Nairobi was upon the crest of a hill; it dominated a sea-like plain through which Masai tribes travelled, their dust cloud floating in silence. The Masai were dying out; they stalked in a great muteness; perched like long-legged storks in contemplation of the empty days ahead.

I was going from Nairobi to Algiers, where an Afro-Asian meeting of heads of state of the Third World was to be held. President Sukarno had called it the meeting of the 'emergent nations'. Chou Enlai, who had made a successful tour of fourteen African countries in 1963–4, deploying great diplomatic skill, was also going to attend. It was meant to be the successor of the epochal Bandung meeting of 1955.

One afternoon Malcolm said to me, 'The Algiers meeting is off.' It had fallen apart because Ben Bella had been deposed and Houari Boumedienne had taken his place in Algeria. Some of the Kenyan ministers seemed to think it a great blow; others criticized China because Chou Enlai insisted that this was an internal Algerian affair which should not influence the venue. However, the meeting was postponed, and finally it was not held at all.

So I went back to Cairo instead, where Vincent now joined me. Kung Peng arrived from Algiers; she was staying at the Chinese Embassy, and we went to see her. Kung Peng was happy to meet Vincent, and said she hoped he would come to China. But Vincent's Indian passport was not valid for China. The Indian government would not allow its citizens to go there.

Kung Peng and I talked politics, policies and methods; I felt that China was far too candid about the Third World. 'I agree that at times we think people have read the documents we send to them . . . but they haven't,' said she. I said that China gave great lashings of aid to the Third World, 'and perhaps it's a bit too much'. The discovery of the lack of seriousness, the fecklessness, of many 'heads of state' was a shock to Kung Peng. She told me that the Indian delegation had lobbied on behalf of the Soviet Union attending the Algiers conference, insisting that it was an Asian country and should be included among Afro-Asian states.

With Vincent I went to see the Palestinian refugee camps at Gaza. The train sailed through the swelling desert and the heat felled us. Gaza, by the sea, was bleak and torrid; from it rose the smell of misery, the nauseous and heart-wrenching odour of hopelessness. We were walked by the Egyptian guides through the camps, squeezed through alleyways between overcrowded shacks, stopping to listen to endless, woeful tales. 'Now you must write a *book* about all you have heard today,' said the guide impressively. I felt utterly miserable because I knew I could not write anything about this accumulation of pain, this monstrous debasement.

The Commander-in-Chief of the United Nations forces quartered for peacekeeping purposes by the Gaza strip was a jerky, punctilious Indian officer, immensely bored. He blamed Nasser for everything. 'Egypt should take in all the refugees . . . they're the same race,' said he. I pointed out the fallacy of what he said, but he would not listen. The immense horror of the suffering multitudes he looked after, that perpetual lament which rose from all four quarters of Gaza, infuriated him. He longed for leave.

From Cairo back to Malaya, to Kuala Lumpur, to see Frank Sullivan and Tunku Abdul Rahman. Tunku received me amiably, and we had coffee. He made mild fun of Lee Kuanyew. It was obvious that now, having got rid of Singapore, he felt considerably better. We stayed at the British High Commission with Anthony and Dorothea Head; Dorothea was painting my portrait. We discussed the failed merger between Singapore and Malaya. Arrests continued in Singapore. The multi-millionaire Tan Laksai, who had founded Nanyang University, had been deprived of his citizenship. Somehow I felt that the British were not unhappy with the new arrangement. Perhaps they had planned it all along.

In September I received a message from Kung Peng. Would I come up to Peking for a few days? I went.

Autumn was heart-stopping in its beauty that year; long golden shadows lay across the Western Hills; the sky was high and flawless and the air gentle; Kung Peng and I took walks in the hills and watched the magpies flit through the ancestral silver pines. I roamed the bookshops; Kung Peng gave me Lin Piao's pamphlet, *Long Live the Victory of the*

People's War, and it was obvious that this was a document which was at the time required reading for all Party cadres, and also for the people; because the title on the cover was in red. I procured for myself, however, two more pamphlets: one was by Lo Juiching, at the time Vice-Chairman of the National Defence Council and Chief of Staff of the Army. The other was by the very popular and prestigious Marshal Ho Lung, whose exploits had almost become a legend. Both were Long Marchers; seasoned and greatly admired Party members. But the titles of the pamphlets were respectively in blue and in green; which meant that they were not as official as Lin Piao's. I read all three together. Of course there were differences in viewpoint as to the role and function of the PLA in all of them; but at the time it did not strike me that they heralded the shaking changes to follow, nor that both Lo Juiching and Ho Lung were to be, so soon, so mercilessly attacked.

For in that autumn the rupture in the Party between Mao Tsetung and Liu Shaochi was coming to a head; but no one among the middle cadres (as I verified through the years) was aware of it. 'We knew there was a big debate, but *never* thought it would be Liu Shaochi ... why, right up until spring 1966 his book was recommended study for us, along with Chairman Mao's books ...'

Neither were they aware that both Ho Lung and Lo Juiching would be in dire trouble very shortly; and a good part of the trouble would be due to the pamphlets expressing their opinions, which were not Lin Piao's opinions.

While waiting for Premier Chou Enlai to see me – for obviously this is why Kung Peng had asked me to come – I had a long interview with the prominent economist, Yung Lungkwei. He was a Director of the Economics Department of the State Planning Commission; a very striking man, most clear-minded. I wrote up a part of what he told me for an article in the Hong Kong *Far Eastern Economic Review*. And I derived a strong impression of both the fundamental solidity of the system which had been laid out, and also of its errors and omissions and weaknesses. With all debts cleared, said Yung, China was poised for a material takeoff; of course it was also necessary to overhaul and streamline her industrial framework (because most of the machines had been procured from Russia, and now they would come from the West, I thought). 'We want what is most advanced . . . as Chairman Mao says, we don't want to crawl behind others . . .' Yung also refuted the idea of having a wealthy, advanced urban and luxurious China sitting on top of a feudal, backward, exploited rural China. 'We are not going the way of India,' said he.

Then I saw Chou Enlai. It was the seventh time. The interview was again, as in 1956, in his own apartment, in the Chungnanhai. Kung Peng came with me. The small patch of garden in front of his apartment was a blaze of dahlias, for his wife, Teng Yingchao, loved flowers. She had cultivated roses in the hard terrain of Yenan during the war; and in later years she would come to see me with an armful of her home-grown peonies.

There was still the same old sofa; the books, the saggy and worn armchairs; the curtain separating bedroom from living room. Under a chair, discreetly, a pair of well-worn slippers . . . Chou Enlai had hastily changed into shoes for my coming.

I wish I could reproduce what we talked about. But then, are words themselves so important? I might misconstrue or be misconstrued, were I to report his words exactly. He changed my bone marrow. He was, truly, not only my teacher, but my guide for life.

And this is where mere words betray, discolour, do not reflect the intensity of silence, the apprehension of a spirit waiting in muteness, receiving in muteness so much more than banal words.

What did he talk about? Everything, and nothing. Of Vietnam: the possibilities of escalation, the probabilities or not of involving China in conflict with America. I felt Chou did not think this likely, but: 'We are fully prepared and they know it. We are even prepared to be attacked from four sides at once . . . India, Japan, the USSR, and the United

States . . . we have planned for all contingencies.' He said, 'If we are invaded or attacked, the war will have no boundaries . . . but until then we shall not indulge in any provocation . . .'

And then, more important to him, and also to me, for in the end all external policy was conditioned, shaped, by internal affairs, we talked of the situation in China. Looking back now, with hindsight, with so much more wisdom and knowledge than in those early, groping years of mine, it seems to me that what Chou Enlai was trying to do was to. warn me. Warn me of the impending turmoil. Warn me to keep calm and cool-headed. To go on thinking on my own.

For in that September Mao Tsetung was in Shanghai, and riding towards the break with Liu Shaochi. And Chou Enlai knew what it would mean; though he did not know, at the time, what shape the rupture would take. And so he talked about China's achievements; of the necessity of social change inherent to economic change; and of the Long March, which had been China's 'from the kingdom of misery to today's sufficiency . . .' But so much remained to be done. Another and a longer march . . .

Chou Enlai knew that I had now embarked on lecture tours in America. We discussed America, not at length, but pithily enough. I had, I said, the feeling that the Vietnam war would still be long. He felt that 'one day, as in Korea, the American people will have had enough of it, and there will be a débâcle . . .' Now I realize that Chou Enlai, in that autumn of 1965, was aware that a crisis would take place in America's foreign policy.

But 1965 was an unpropitious year for cool reason in America. With McNamara clamouring that China was *the* enemy, with McGeorge Bundy refusing to shake my hand because I was a 'Red', with even Margaret Mead refusing to talk to me because I was a 'communist' – how could I do anything? Nevertheless, through all possible means and all possible people, Chou hoped to project China as she really was: Edgar Snow had again come to China in 1964, and had had an interview with Mao. It was becoming increasingly hard to keep China out of the United Nations, Chou remarked. In that year of 1965 China would obtain exactly half the votes in favour of admitting her.

Now, more than ever, I was a Chou Enlai addict. I would try my best to follow his thinking. But a statesman confronted with the immensity of China, the enormous weight of her poverty, the hostility of a world in arms against her, and the multitudinous complexity of her internal problems, perforce had to adopt a sinuous line, a course not always clearly charted. Chou had to use everything and everyone, including his friends; he had to be ruthless, devious, charming, flexible, impassive, glib, unsparing to himself and to all he knew in the pursuit of a single goal: China, China's future, the happiness of the Chinese people.

I did not always understand this. But I would see him keep China going under the most desperate circumstances. I would see him appreciating the rarity and worth of talent and trying to shield it. Never would he intrude himself, his own person, his likes or dislikes, his own interest in survival, in all this. I have never known anyone so brave, so single-minded. And all my life I will be a follower of Chou Enlai.

When I left Peking, Wang Wanchun came to see me off. 'Write to me,' said he happily.

This was the last time I would see Wanchun. For in 1966, the next year, when I sought him out, I was not allowed to see him. He was 'busy'. Wanchun died during the Cultural Revolution, in that hot and ugly summer of 1967, and I feel burdened and harrowed because he had written to me in the spring, 'You must write to me, write to me'. And like a fool, I did. I should *not* have listened to him. I feel that my letter helped to end his life, because precisely in that spring and summer, posters were put up against me in Shanghai, accusing me of being 'an American agent'. Wanchun was probably accused of 'passing information to outsiders' and 'having illicit relations with a foreigner'. I was also linked with Pearl Buck; both of us accused of writing malicious things against China (and me pornography).

But, many years later, when I was told of his death, I was told that it was because 'he did not trust in the future . . . he was accused of adultery[!] and he could not stand it . . . he threw himself out of a window'.

Threw or was thrown? During the McCarthy period in America people also 'threw' themselves out of windows. But I do not see Wanchun leaping into the street, because he had such a sense of humour. And now I shall never know.

Outstanding fiction in paperback from Grafton Books

Muriel Spark

The Abbess of Crewe	£1.95 ☐
The Only Problem	£2.50 ☐
Territorial Rights	£1.25 ☐
Not To Disturb	£1.25 ☐
Loitering with Intent	£1.25 ☐
Bang-Bang You're Dead	£1.25 ☐
The Hothouse by the East River	£1.25 ☐
Going up to Sotheby's	£1.25 ☐
The Takeover	£1.95 ☐

Toni Morrison

Song of Solomon	£2.50 ☐
The Bluest Eye	£2.50 ☐
Sula	£2.50 ☐
Tar Baby	£1.95 ☐

Erica Jong

Parachutes and Kisses	£2.95 ☐
Fear of Flying	£2.95 ☐
How to Save Your Own Life	£2.50 ☐
Fanny	£2.95 ☐
Selected Poems II	£1.25 ☐
At the Edge of the Body	£1.25 ☐

Anita Brookner

Family and Friends	£2.50 ☐
A Start in Life	£2.50 ☐
Providence	£2.50 ☐
Look at Me	£2.50 ☐
Hotel du Lac	£2.50 ☐

To order direct from the publisher just tick the titles you want and fill in the order form.

A selection of titles by Han Suyin available in paperback from Grafton Books

China: Autobiography, History

The Crippled Tree	£2.95	☐
A Mortal Flower	£3.95	☐
Birdless Summer	£2.95	☐
My House Has Two Doors	£3.95	☐
Phoenix Harvest	£2.95	☐

Novels

A Many-Splendoured Thing	£2.95	☐
Destination Chungking	£2.95	☐
. . . And the Rain My Drink	£2.95	☐
The Mountain is Young	£3.95	☐
Cast But One Shadow and Winter Love	£2.95	☐
The Four Faces	£2.95	☐

Non-Fiction

The Morning Deluge (Volume 1): Mao Tsetung and the Chinese Revolution 1893–1935	£1.75	☐
The Morning Deluge (Volume 2): Mao Tsetung and the Chinese Revolution 1935–1953	£1.75	☐
Wind in the Tower: Mao Tsetung and the Chinese Revolution 1949–1976	£1.75	☐

To order direct from the publisher just tick the titles you want and fill in the order form.

All these books are available at your local bookshop or newsagent, or can be ordered direct from the publisher.

To order direct from the publishers just tick the titles you want and fill in the form below.

Name _____

Address _____

_____